THE POLITICS OF PES
IN ECCLESIASTES

Society of Biblical Literature

Number 12

THE POLITICS OF PESSIMISM IN ECCLESIASTES
A Social-Science Perspective

Volume Editor
Victor H. Matthews

THE POLITICS OF PESSIMISM IN ECCLESIASTES

A Social-Science Perspective

by

Mark R. Sneed

Society of Biblical Literature
Atlanta

THE POLITICS OF PESSIMISM IN ECCLESIASTES
A Social-Science Perspective

Library of Congress Cataloging-in-Publication Data
Sneed, Mark R.
    The politics of pessimism in Ecclesiastes : a social-science perspective / by Mark Ronnie Sneed.
      p. cm. — (Society of Biblical Literature ancient Israel and its literature ; v. 12)
    Includes bibliographical references and index.
    ISBN 978-1-58983-610-5 (paper binding : alk. paper) — ISBN 978-1-58983-635-8 (electronic format)
    1. Bible. O.T. Ecclesiastes—Criticism, interpretation, etc. 2. Bible. O.T. Ecclesiastes—Social scientific criticism. 3. Sociology, Biblical. 4. Pessimism. I. Title.
BS1475.52.S64 2011
223'.8067—dc23

                                                          2011049877

19 18 17 16 15 14 13 12   5 4 3 2 1
Printed on acid-free, recycled paper conforming to
ANSI/NISO Z39.48-1992 (R1997) and ISO 9706:1994
standards for paper permanence.

To
Herbert B. Huffmon
Teacher, Counselor, Advocate, Mentor, and Friend

Contents

Acknowledgments xi

Abbreviations xiii

Introduction 1
  The Book's Skepticism 4
  The Book's Pessimism 7

1. Qohelet's Heterodox Character:
   Non–Social-Science Approaches 13
   Ideational Approaches 13
   Non-Ideational Explanations for Qohelet's Heterodoxy 20

2. Explaining Qohelet's Heterodox Character:
   Social-Science Approaches 55
   Marxian Approaches 55
   Postcolonial Approaches 66
   Durkheimian Approaches 69
   Grand Theories 76
   Anthropological Approach 81
   Conclusion 82

3. Qohelet's Sociohistorical Context 85
   Brief History of the Ptolemaic Kingdom (Third Century B.C.E.) 85
   Ptolemaic Administration 88
   Ptolemaic Taxation 91
   General Benefits of Ptolemaic Governance of Judah 98
   Social Stratification in Ptolemaic Jerusalem 102
   The Degree of Hellenization in Ptolemaic Judah 120
   Conclusion 123

4. Qohelet and His Audience's Social Location 125
   Possible Allusions to the Milieu in Qohelet 127
   Hellenistic Influence in Qohelet 131

Qohelet: Aristocrat or Middle Class? 131
Qohelet's Scribal Audience 143
Qohelet and the Scribal Status Group 144
Qohelet as Intellectual 150
Conclusion 154

5. Synchronic (Literary) Analysis
   of the Book of Qohelet 155
   The Meaning of הֶבֶל in the Hebrew Bible 155
   The Meaning of הֶבֶל in Qohelet 157
   God as Primary Orientation for Qohelet and His Audience 164
   God and Humanity: The Great Divide 165
   Qohelet—No Modern Existentialist! 168
   Qohelet's Rhetoric 170
   Conclusion 174

6. Qohelet, the Problem of Evil, and Cognitive Dissonance 177
   Theodicy Strategies in the Hebrew Bible 180
   Qohelet's Theodicy Strategies 184
   The Assets and Liabilities of Redefining God's Standard
   of Judgment 187
   The Social Location of Theodicy 190
   Qohelet's Non-Salvific Religious Perspective 194
   Qohelet's Mitigation of Cognitive Dissonance 197
   Conclusion 202

7. Qohelet's Irrational Response to the (Over-)Rationalization
   of Traditional Wisdom 203
   The Struggle between the Rational and the Irrational 204
   The Process of Rationalization 207
   The Rationalization of Religion 210
   Rationalization and Consistency 214
   Irrational (or Non-Rational) Reaction 216
   Weber and the Rationalization of Yahwism 217
   Rationalization in the Wisdom Tradition 219
   The Feasibility of the Doctrine of Retribution 222
   Qohelet's Irrational Response to the Over-Rationalization
   of the Wisdom Tradition 224
   Conclusion 228

8. The Positive Power of Qohelet's Pessimism 231
   Generic Pessimism. 234
   Lowering Expectations in Qohelet. 240
   Conclusion 252

9. The Sociology of the Book of Qohelet's Canonicity. 255
   The Degree of Qohelet's Heterodoxy 255
   Qohelet's Canonization as a Misperception. 266
   Conclusion 276

Conclusion 279

Bibliography 283

Index of Ancient Sources 319

Index of Modern Authors 326

Index of Subjects 337

Acknowledgments

This work is a heavily revised dissertation completed back in 1990 at Drew University. First and foremost, thanks go to Victor Matthews of Southwest Missouri State University, editor for this volume of the series Ancient Israel and Its Literature. I often refer to him as "Mr. Bibliography" to my friends because of his vast encyclopedic knowledge of secondary literature relating to the ancient Near East and the social sciences. His bibliographic websites are famous, and his breadth in this area enabled me to update the dissertation with speed. He was also helpful with my often colloquial style of writing. This book is much stronger because of Victor.

Thanks are also due to the library staff at Lubbock Christian University and in particular Holly Matthews, the interlibrary loan facilitator. Without the library's help, I could not have written this book. Their dedication and hard work enabled me to receive numerous publications in a convenient and timely manner. I am grateful also to my Dean and Provost, who lightened my committee responsibility for the 2010–11 school year.

Also, thanks are due to three colleagues here at LCU: Stacy Patty, Michael Martin, and Jeff Cary. My conversations with them about my book ideas were inspiring and clarifying. In addition, my conversations with Derek McNamara, former colleague and my best friend, have been helpful as well.

Finally, I express my gratitude to my wife, Arlene, who has put up with so many inconveniences on account of this book, remaining patient and supportive throughout the process, and to my son Zachary, who has made life more interesting and enjoyable during this period.

Abbreviations

AB	Anchor Bible
ABD	*The Anchor Bible Dictionary*. Edited by David Noel Freedman. 6 vols. New York: Doubleday, 1992.
ABR	*Australian Biblical Review*
ACEBT	*Amsterdamse Cahiers voor Exegese en bijbelse Theologie*
AEL	Lichtheim, Miriam. *Ancient Egyptian Literature: A Book of Readings*. 3 vols. Berkeley: University of California Press, 1971–80.
AGJU	Arbeiten zur Geschichte des antiken Judentums und des Urchristentums
ANET	*Ancient Near Eastern Texts Relating to the Old Testament*. Edited by James B. Pritchard. 3rd. ed. Princeton: Princeton University Press, 1969.
ArBib	The Aramaic Bible
ASSR	*Archive de sciences sociales des religions*
AUSS	*Andrews University Seminary Studies*
BA	*Biblical Archaeologist*
BAIAS	*Bulletin of the Anglo-Israel Archeological Society*
BASOR	*Bulletin of the American Schools of Oriental Research*
BDB	Brown, Francis, S. R. Driver, and Charles A. Briggs. *A Hebrew and English Lexicon of the Old Testament*. Oxford: Clarendon, 1907.
BETL	Bibliotheca ephemeridum theologicarum lovaniensium
Bib	*Biblica*
BibInt	*Biblical Interpretation*
BJS	Brown Judaic Studies
BKAT	Biblischer Kommentar, Altes Testament.
BN	*Biblische Notizen*
BRev	*Bible Review*
BT	*The Bible Translator*
BZ	*Biblische Zeitschrift*
BZAW	Beihefte zur Zeitschrift für die alttestamentliche Wissenschaft
CBQ	*Catholic Biblical Quarterly*

CBQMS	Catholic Biblical Quarterly Monograph Series
CC	Continental Commentaries
CHJ	*The Cambridge History of Judaism*. Edited by W. D. Davies and Louis Finkelstein. Cambridge: Cambridge University Press, 1984-.
CJAS	Christianity and Judaism in Antiquity
CPJ	*Corpus papyrorum judaicarum*. Edited by Victor Tcherikover. 3 vols. Cambridge, Mass.: Harvard University Press, 1957–64.
CRINT	Compendia rerum iudaicarum ad Novum Testamentum
EdF	Erträge der Forschung
ER	*The Encyclopedia of Religion*. Edited by M. Eliade. 16 vols. New York: Macmillan, 1987.
EvQ	*Evangelical Quarterly*
ExpTim	*Expository Times*
Hor	*Horizons*
HS	*Hebrew Studies*
HTR	*Harvard Theological Review*
HUCA	*Hebrew Union College Annual*
IB	*The Interpreter's Bible*. Edited by G. A. Buttrick et al. 12 vols. New York: Abingdon-Cokesbury, 1951–57.
IBC	Interpretation: A Bible Commentary for Teaching and Preaching
IBT	Interpreting Biblical Texts
ICC	International Critical Commentary
Int	*Interpretation*
IRT	Issues in Religion and Theology
JAAR	*Journal of the American Academy of Religion*
JAOS	*Journal of the American Oriental Society*
JETS	*Journal of the Evangelical Theological Society*
JBL	*Journal of Biblical Literature*
JJS	*Journal of Jewish Studies*
JNES	*Journal of Near Eastern Studies*
JNSL	*Journal of Northwest Semitic Languages*
JQR	*Jewish Quarterly Review*
JRE	*Journal of Religious Ethics*
JSJ	*Journal for the Study of Judaism in the Persian, Hellenistic, and Roman Period*
JSJSup	Journal for the Study of Judaism Supplements
JSOT	*Journal for the Study of the Old Testament*
JSOTSup	Journal for the Study of the Old Testament: Supplement Series
JSS	*Journal of Semitic Studies*
JTSA	*Journal of Theology for Southern Africa*

KAT	Kommentar zum Alten Testament
LAE	*The Literature of Ancient Egypt: An Anthology of Stories, Instructions, Stelae, Autobiographies, and Poetry.* Edited by William Kelly Simpson. New Haven: Yale University Press, 1972.
LCL	Loeb Classical Library
LSJ	Liddell, H. G., R. Scott, H. S. Jones, *A Greek-English Lexicon.* 9th ed. with revised supplement. Oxford: Clarendon, 1996.
MDOG	Mitteilungen der Deutschen Orient-Gesellschaft
NCB	New Century Bible
NICOT	New International Commentary on the Old Testament
NIB	*The New Interpreter's Bible*
NTS	*New Testament Studies*
Numen	*Numen: International Review for the History of Religions*
OBT	Overtures to Biblical Theology
OLA	Orientalia lovaniensia analecta
OTE	*Old Testament Essays*
OTG	Old Testament Guides
OTL	Old Testament Library
OTWSA	Ou-Testamentiese Werkgemeenskap, South Africa
PSB	*Princeton Seminary Bulletin*
RB	*Revue biblique*
RBL	*Review of Biblical Literature*
RHPR	*Revue d'histoire et de philosophie religieuses*
ResQ	*Restoration Quarterly*
RTP	*Revue de théologie et de philosophie*
SBL	Society of Biblical Literature
SBLDS	Society of Biblical Literature Dissertation Series
Semeiast	Semeia Studies
SJLA	Studies in Judaism in Late Antiquity
SJOT	*Scandinavian Journal of the Old Testament*
SJT	*Scottish Journal of Theology*
SOTSMS	Society for Old Testament Studies Monograph Series
Sound	*Soundings*
SUNT	Studien zur Umwelt des Neuen Testaments
TBT	*The Bible Today*
TDOT	*Theological Dictionary of the Old Testament.* Edited by G. J. Botterweck and H. Ringgren. Translated by J. T. Willis, G. W. Bromiley, and D. E. Green. 8 vols. Grand Rapids: Eerdmans, 1974-.
THAT	*Theologisches Handwörterbuch zum Alten Testament.* Edited by E. Jenni, with assistance from C. Westermann. 2 vols. Munich: Kaiser, 1971-76.

TLOT	*Theological Lexicon of the Old Testament.* Edited by E. Jenni, with assistance from C. Westermann. Translated by M. E. Biddle. 3 vols. Peabody, Mass.: Hendrickson, 1997.
TOTC	Tyndale Old Testament Commentaries
TQ	*Theologische Quartalschrift*
TZ	*Theologische Zeitschrift*
UF	*Ugarit-Forschungen*
VS	*Verbum Salutis*
VT	*Vetus Testamentum*
VTSup	Supplements to Vetus Testamentum
WBC	Word Biblical Commentary
WHJP	World History of the Jewish People
ZAW	*Zeitschrift für die alttestamentliche Wissenschaft*
ZRGG	*Zeitschrift für Religions- und Geistesgeschichte*
ZTK	*Zeitschrift für Theologie und Kirche*

Introduction

Biblical scholars must face reality. In terms of the canon, Qohelet is the "odd book in" as James Crenshaw describes.[1] The book is easily the strangest in the Bible.[2] It can aptly be described as a "frightening guest . . . in the canon."[3] Gerhard von Rad refers to "the farthest frontier of Jahwism where Ecclesiastes pitched his camp."[4] Similarly, C. L. Seow describes the book as being on "the margins of the canon."[5] Qohelet's conception of God is especially troubling for most readers, past and present. Is Qohelet's deity the God of Abraham, Isaac, and Jacob? Qohelet never uses the appellation יהוה for God. Qohelet counsels caution: "Guard your steps when you go to the house of God; to draw near to listen is better than the sacrifice offered by fools. . . . Never be rash with your mouth, nor let your heart be quick to utter a word before God, for god is in heaven, and you upon earth; therefore let your words be few" (5:1–2).[6] While this counsel mimics the prophets (1 Sam 15:22; Mic 6:6–8; Hos 6:6), what is missing is an intimate relationship with Yahweh. Job makes a similar statement about the transcendence of God (7:11), but the book simultaneously emphasizes God's immanence (the theophany in chs. 38–41), something that never occurs in Qohelet.

After all of Qohelet's searching and pondering what is profitable in life, he comes to the conclusion: "So I commend enjoyment, for there is nothing better for people under the sun than to eat, and drink, and enjoy themselves, for this will go with them in their toil through the days of life that God gives them

---

1. James L. Crenshaw, "Odd Book In: Ecclesiastes," *BRev* 6, no. 5 (1990): 28.

2. See Elias Bickerman, who includes it in his list of strangest books of the Hebrew Bible (*Four Strange Books of the Bible: Jonah, Daniel, Koheleth, Esther* [New York: Schocken, 1967]). James L. Crenshaw, in fact, calls it "the Bible's strangest book" (*Ecclesiastes* [OTL; Philadelphia: Westminster, 1987], 23).

3. Hans-Peter Müller, "Der unheimliche Gast: Zum Denken Kohelets," *ZTK* 84 (1987): 440.

4. Gerhard von Rad, *Old Testament Theology* (trans. D. M. G. Stalker; 2 vols.; New York: Harper & Row, 1962), 1:458.

5. C. L. Seow, *Ecclesiastes: A New Translation with Introduction and Commentary* (AB 18C; New York: Doubleday, 1997), 4.

6. Unless otherwise indicated, all scriptural citations are from the NRSV (1989).

under the sun" (8:15). This represents Qohelet's famous recurring carpe diem ethic found seven times in the book (2:24; 3:12–13, 22; 5:18––20; 8:15; 9:7–10; 11:7–10). The Hebrew word for "commend" (שׁבח) is usually used for praising God. Regarding this, Martin Rose states:

> What is said here seems meager compared to the great confessions of Israel. But what would one further say of this God who had not saved either Judah or Israel from national disaster, who had allowed his temple at Jerusalem to be destroyed, who had delivered the king, his anointed, his messiah, to the hostile power of the Babylonians and who had sent his people into exile and slavery. Here emerges the theme of the "hidden God," of "*deus absconditus*," and *even* after the Babylonian exile, there is no resplendent revival, nor any powerful manifestation of this God.[7] (my translation)

Similarly, in 1930 the famous Scandinavian scholar Johannes Pedersen said of Qohelet's deity, "Very nearly God is a power hostile to humans. The God of ancient Israel, king, protector of his people outside, guardian of its moral forces inside, has become a far and indifferent despot" (my translation).[8] Another Scandinavian scholar, Aarre Lauha, puts it quite succinctly, "Sein Gott ist nicht der Gott des israelitischen Glaubens."[9] Similarly, J. A. Loader refers to Qohelet's deity as a "remote God."[10]

Several scholars have noted that Qohelet's God appears capricious and despotic in relation to humanity.[11] An illustration is found in 6:1–2: "There is an evil that I have seen under the sun, and it lies heavy upon humankind: those to whom God gives wealth, possessions, and honor, so that they lack nothing of all that they desire, yet God does not enable them to enjoy these things, but a stranger enjoys them. This is vanity; it is a grievous ill." In 3:11, Qohelet describes a creative act upon humankind: "He has made everything suitable for its time; moreover he has put a sense of past and future into their minds,

---

7. Martin Rose, "De la 'crise de la sagesse' à la 'sagesse de la crise,'" *RTP* 131 (1999): 133.

8. Johannes Pedersen, "Scepticisme israélite," *RHPR* 10 (1930): 360.

9. Aarre Lauha, *Kohelet* (BKAT 19; Neukirchen-Vluyn: Neukirchener Verlag, 1978), 17; cf. R. B. Y. Scott, who states, "Such a God is not Yahweh, the covenant God of Israel" (*Proverbs. Ecclesiastes: Introduction, Translation, and Notes* [AB 18; Garden City, N.Y.: Doubleday, 1965], 191).

10. J. A. Loader, *Polar Structures in the Book of Qohelet* (BZAW 152; Berlin: de Gruyter, 1979), 124.

11. Duncan MacDonald describes Qohelet's God as "a capricious deity of no moral sense" (*The Hebrew Literary Genius: An Interpretation Being an Introduction to the Reading of the Old Testament* [Princeton: Princeton University Press, 1933], 213). Cf. Bickerman, who states that Qohelet's "God was as arbitrary and fickle as Luck" (*Strange Books*, 149).

yet they cannot find out what God had done from the beginning to the end." Concerning this verse, Crenshaw says:

> Whatever it is that God has placed in man's mind will do him no good, for God . . . has made him incapable of discovering it. Here we are approaching the demonic: this text is not far from others in the ancient Near East describing a god's jealousy lest human creatures achieve a status or power that threatens the deity, or from those accounts of a divine test with a stacked deck of cards.[12]

He summarizes Qohelet's conception of the deity by saying, "How perilously close he comes to depicting God as the force behind all things! Indeed, Qoheleth speaks as if God were indifferent power before which we must cower in fear, and often equates God's will with whatever happens."[13]

Some scholars have attempted to anesthetize Qohelet's heterodoxy, but to no avail.[14] It does not take a rocket scientist to perceive the book's heterodox character. The ancient rabbis were on to this and "sought to suppress the Book of Koheleth because they discovered therein words which savour of heresy" (*Qoh. Rab.* 1:3). The recurring carpe diem ethic in the book, which commends the enjoyment of life and making merry, was so troubling for the rabbis with their ascetic fixation on Torah-keeping that they allegorized it: "All the references to eating and drinking in this Book signify Torah and good deeds" (*Qoh. Rab.* 2:24; cf. the Targum [*Tg. Eccl.* 2:24]).[15] The book was canonized but almost ended up in the *genizah* ("storage"), where sacred books

---

12. James L. Crenshaw, "The Eternal Gospel (Eccl. 3:11)," in *Essays in Old Testament Ethics* (ed. James L. Crenshaw and John T. Willis; New York: Ktav, 1974), 43–44. As Joseph Blenkinsopp notes, "In his commentary Qoheleth accepts that there is a right time for every action, but denies to the human agent the knowedge requisite to act on it" ("Ecclesiastes 3.1–15: Another Interpretation," *JSOT* 66 [1995]: 61).

13. James L.Crenshaw, *Old Testament Wisdom: An Introduction* (Atlanta: John Knox, 1981), 137.

14. E.g., Franz Delitzsch labels the book "The Song of the Fear of God" ("Commentary on the Song of Songs and Ecclesiastes," in *Commentary on the Old Testament in Ten Volumes* [ed. C. F. Keil and F. Delitzsch; trans. M. G. Easton; Grand Rapids: Eerdmans, 1950], 6:183); cf. Stephan de Jong, "God in the Book of Qohelet: A Reappraisal of Qohelet's Place in Old Testament Theology," *VT* 47 (1997): 154–67; Tilmann Zimmer, *Zwischen Tod und Lebensglück: Eine Untersuchung zur Anthropologie Kohelets* (BZAW 286; Berlin: de Gruyter, 1999), 25–32, 109–111. A similar attempt is represented by C. L. Seow and his students, who characterize Qohelet as a realist as opposed to a pessimist (*Ecclesiastes*, e.g., ix, 54–69, 344, 370; Douglas B. Miller, "What the Preacher Forgot: The Rhetoric of Ecclesiastes," *CBQ* 62 [2000]: 220–21).

15. "There is nothing worthwhile for a man except that he eat and drink and enjoy himself *before the people, to obey the commandments of the Lord and to walk in straight paths before Him so that He will do good to him* for his labor" (*Tg. Eccl.* 2:24).

were kept that were not deemed fit for use in the synagogue.[16] The School of Hillel accepted the book as holy, while the School of Shammai rejected it (*m. 'Ed.* 5:3). The former accepted it mainly because it was believed to have been authored by Solomon but also because of the pious gloss that summarizes the book in 12:13: "The end of the matter; all has been heard. Fear God, and keep his commandments; for that is the whole duty of everyone."[17] This gloss, no doubt, was intended to soften the book's seeming heterodoxy. This effect is indicated in the Talmud, when the sages ultimately accepted the book because "its end is religious teaching" (*b. Šabb.* 30b). Of course, modern fundamentalists and evangelicals largely ignore the book except for this pious gloss and the book's usefulness at funerals (e.g., 3:1–2). Their suspicions about the rest of the book are accurate, and biblical scholars would do well simply to acknowledge this.

THE BOOK'S SKEPTICISM

Another facet of the book's disturbing nature is its skepticism about traditional doctrines. While Qohelet is skeptical about a number of things, the most shocking is his questioning of the doctrine of retribution, a fundamental principle underlying the Hebrew faith and especially the wisdom literature. This is the teaching that God punishes or rewards persons depending on their behavior.[18] A pious, righteous lifestyle will be rewarded with success and pros-

---

16. On the canonization of Qohelet, see R. B. Salters, "Qoheleth and the Canon," *ExpTim* 86 (1975): 339–42.

17. In this book I assume, as do most current Qohelet experts, that the book is largely the words of Qohelet except for a frame provided by an epilogist (1:1–2 [or 1:1–11]; 7:27 [brief remark]; 12:8–12). Qohelet 12:13–14 is assumed to be the words of a pious glossator distinct from the epilogist. See Michael V. Fox, *A Time to Tear Down & A Time to Build Up: A Rereading of Ecclesiastes* (Grand Rapids: Eerdmans, 1999), 364; Stuart Weeks, *An Introduction to the Study of Wisdom Literature* (T&T Clark Approaches to Biblical Studies; London: T&T Clark, 2010), 71–72; contra Crenshaw, who sees several glosses in the body of the book (2:26a; 3:17a; 8:12–13; 11:9b and possibly others) (*Ecclesiastes*, 48).

18. The Germans have a slightly different conceptualization of this that they call the *Tun-Ergehen-Zusammenhang* (act–consequence nexus), which assumes an almost deistic notion. God has established a natural process whereby good behavior is rewarded in life and bad behavior results in demise. But God is not viewed as directly intervening in the process. See Klaus Koch, "Is There a Doctrine of Retribution in the Old Testament?" in *Theodicy in the Old Testament* (ed. James L. Crenshaw; IRT 4; Philadelphia: Fortress, 1983), 57–87. Some scholars question the notion of a doctrine of retribution in Proverbs, at least in any rigid sense: Raymond C. Van Leeuwen, "Wealth and Poverty: System and Contradiction in Proverbs," *HS* 33 (1992): 25–36; Peter T. H. Hatton, *Contradiction in the Book of Proverbs: The Deep Waters of Counsel* (SOTSMS; Aldershot: Ashgate, 2008), 83–116.

perity, whereas wickedness will result in catastrophe and an early death. This was essentially the principle of cause and effect for the ancients and a form of rationality. This doctrine served as the basis for a sense of order in the universe, so that how one fares in life is not entirely haphazard (cf. Zophar's argument in Job 20). God, the ultimate source of the notion of order in the cosmos, is viewed as intricately involved in the connection between how one lives and how one fares. The doctrine served to reduce somewhat the mysteries of the cosmos and life and to make reality more predictable. This same doctrine is found also in the wisdom literature of ancient Egypt and Mesopotamia.

Qohelet questions its traditional formulation: "In my vain life I have seen everything; there are righteous people who perish in their righteousness, and there are wicked people who prolong their life in their evildoing" (7:15; cf. 3:16; 8:10, 14). Qohelet's observations create a profound tension for the wisdom corpus because the doctrine was so fundamental for the tradition. Qohelet's closest cousin, the book of Job (e.g. ch. 21), also questions the legitimacy of the doctrine but ends with an orthodox, not heterodox, stance (40:35; 42). J. A. Loader characterizes the different responses of Job and Qohelet to the problem of retribution: "Job answers the problem with a *warm and passionate turning to God and rest in a personal communion with him*. On the other hand Qoheleth coldly answers that the only thing to be done is to accept that anything can happen to man. *There is no rest or communion with God—only a tense acceptance of man's helplessness*."[19] Of course, skepticism of this doctrine is found also in ancient Near Eastern wisdom literature. But Qohelet's skepticism within a pious religious canon creates more tension than a skepticism that is found among scribal belles lettres, where it might be expected.

Beyond this doctrine, he seems to radically question the connection between behavior and fortune: "Again I saw that under the sun the race is not to the swift, nor the battle to the strong, nor bread to the wise, nor riches to the intelligent, nor favor to the skillful; but time and chance happen to them all" (9:11). One is made to wonder whether he sees any connection at all.

Again, Crenshaw has appropriately referred to the depiction of God in 3:11 as coming close to the demonic.[20] Most scholars believe that the reference to God creating everything "good" in its time is an allusion to the P creation account.[21] Thus, the verse forms a contrast between the positive account of the creation in P and Qohelet's more negative assessment of humanity's conflicted

---

19.   J. A. Loader, "Different Reactions of Job and Qoheleth to the Doctrine of Retribution," in *Studies in Wisdom Literature* (ed. W. C. van Wyk; Old Testament Studies: OTWSA 15, 16; Hercules, South Africa: N. H. W. Press, 1981), 47.

20.   Crenshaw, "Eternal Gospel," 43–44.

21.   See Lauha, *Kohelet*, 68.

state of desiring to know God's view of eternity and yet never grasping it. Of course, Qohelet's negative characterization of humanity's role in the created order (1:13; 2:22–23; 3:10, 18) certainly clashes with its role in P's account (and also the Psalms, e.g., Ps 8).

Instead of upholding traditional wisdom's teachings and assumptions, Qohelet appears to be critical of them throughout the book:

> Then I said to myself, "What happens to the fool will happen to me also; why then have I been so very wise?" And I said to myself that this also is vanity. For there is no enduring remembrance of the wise or of fools, seeing that in the days to come all will have been long forgotten. How can the wise die just like fools? (2:15–16)

> When I applied my mind to know wisdom, and to see the business that is done on earth, how one's eyes see sleep neither day nor night, then I saw all the work of God, that no one can find out what is happening under the sun. However much they may toil in seeking, they will not find it out. (8:16–17)

The degree of Qohelet's skepticism about the assumptions of traditional wisdom has caused German scholars to refer to it as a crisis of the wisdom movement, which is often seen to correlate with traumatic events.[22] Hans-Peter Müller speaks of a "Neige" or decline of traditional wisdom represented by Qohelet.[23]

Though skepticism exists in other places in the canon of the Hebrew Bible (the dialogue in Job, Agur [Prov 30:4], the laments in the Psalter, Lamentations, the prophets, etc.), it is not as systematic, comprehensive, acute, and final as in Qohelet.[24] Von Rad cites some other instances of skepticism

---

22. Frank Crüsemann, "The Unchangeable World: The 'Crisis of Wisdom' in Koheleth," in *God of the Lowly: Socio-Historical Interpretations of the Bible* (ed. Willy Schottroff and Wolfgang Stegemann; trans. M. J. O'Connell; Maryknoll, N.Y.: Orbis, 1984), 57–77; Hartmut Gese, "Die Krisis der Wersheit bei Kohelet," in *Les sagesses du Proche-Orient ancien* (Bibliothèque des centres d'études supérieures spécialisés; Paris: Presses Universitaires de France, 1963), 139–51; Martin A. Klopfenstein, "Die Skepsis des Kohelet," *TZ* 28 (1972): 102; Hans Heinrich Schmid, *Wesen und Geschichte der Weisheit: Eine Untersuchung zur altorientalischen und israelitischen Weisheitsliteratur* (BZAW 101; Berlin: de Gruyter, 1966), 173; Martin Hengel, *Judaism and Hellenism: Studies in Their Encounter in Palestine during the Early Hellenistic Period* (trans. John Bowden; 2 vols.; Philadelphia: Fortress, 1974; repr., Eugene, Ore.: Wipf & Stock, 2003), 1:115; Aarre Lauha, "Die Krise des religiösen Glaubens bei Kohelet," in *Wisdom in Israel and in the Ancient Near East* (ed. M. Noth and D. Winton Thomas; VTSup 3; Leiden: Brill, 1955), 183–91.

23. Müller, "Der unheimliche Gast," 441; idem, "Neige der althebräischen 'Weisheit': Zum Denken Qohäläts," *ZAW* 90 (1978): 238–63.

24. J. Jonathan Schraub describes the book of Job as "*the* book of unmitigated heresy," but his interpretation of Job's final statement in 42:6 as protestation is untenable ("For the

about understanding God's ways (Job 28, Prov 30:1–4, and Ps 90), but then concludes, "However, only with the Book of Ecclesiastes did this skepticism emerge broadly based and with a hitherto unheard of radicality and weight."[25] Compare the words of Martin Shields:

> The supposed tradition of skepticism or expressions of doubt elsewhere in the Hebrew Bible are not nearly as incessant or unremitting as the words of Qoheleth. . . . The simple truth is that, in spite of the existence of some expressions of doubt elsewhere in the Hebrew Bible, there is none that matches Qoheleth's words for a sustained denial of faith and doubt in the goodness of God.[26]

THE BOOK'S PESSIMISM

While pessimism is not necessarily a correlative of skepticism, in Qohelet they seem to be closely connected, as if two sides of the same coin. For example, in the passage cited above (2:15–16), Qohelet's questioning of the value of traditional wisdom leads him to a pessimistic conclusion. Though he views wisdom as more valuable than folly, death essentially vitiates its superiority, and because of this Qohelet says he hates life (2:17). The inclusion that frames the book ("Vanity of vanities . . . all is vanity") (1:2; 12:8) reinforces this. The concept of nothingness or uselessness dominates the book. The word for "vanity" (הֶבֶל) is onomatopoeic and literally means "breath" or "wind," connoting more abstractly the notion of emptiness or nothingness and also fleetingness.[27] It often signifies the futility of human effort (e.g., 2:11) and its conjunction with the frequently occurring "chasing after the wind" (seven times) further demonstrates this sense of futility, certainly a characteristic of pessimism. It is also the dominant motif of the book (seventy-three times) and its final conclusion.[28] The pessimistic declaration that everything is empty or futile or fleeting is directed more broadly at any human effort or toil or striving, and not just at the aspiration of the wisdom tradition, which seeks to grasp the order of the cosmos and essentially master it. It is devastatingly deconstructive of human ambition of any kind.

Sin We Have Committed by Theological Rationalizations: Rescuing Job from Normative Religion," *Sound* 86, nos. 3–4 [Fall/Winter 2003]: 431–62).

25. Von Rad, *Old Testament Theology*, 1:454.

26. Martin A. Shields, *The End of Wisdom: A Reappraisal of the Historical and Canonical Function of Ecclesiastes* (Winona Lake, Ind.: Eisenbrauns, 2006), 5.

27. On its onomatopoeic character, see K. Seybold, "הֶבֶל *hebhel*," *TDOT* 3:314.

28. For an intriguing explanation of its function as a symbol that unites the book, see Douglas B. Miller, *Symbol and Rhetoric in Ecclesiastes: The Place of Hebel in Qohelet's Work* (Academia Biblica 2; Atlanta: Society of Biblical Literature, 2002).

Many scholars assume that Qohelet's pessimism actually springs from his skepticism.[29] Crenshaw, who labels Qohelet both skeptic and pessimist, puts it this way:

> Once skeptics lose all hope of achieving the desired transformation, pessimism sets in, spawning sheer indifference to cherished convictions. Pessimists believe chaos has the upper hand and will retain control forever; they lack both a surge for transcendence and faith in human potential. Since they own no vision which acts as a corrective to the status quo, pessimists can muster no base upon which to stand and from which to criticize God and the world. The inevitable result is a sense of being overwhelmed by an oppressive reality.[30]

But whatever the relationship of pessimism to skepticism, they are obviously connected.

A major component of Qohelet's pessimism relates to his brooding over death. Qohelet appears obsessed with this topic (2:14–16; 3:2, 18–21; 4:2–3; 7:1–4; 9:2–6; 12:5–7).[31] Again, Job treats this topic (7:6–10; 14:1–17; 17:13–16) but does not devote the attention to it that Qohelet does. As Qohelet discusses death, he becomes quite poignant about its seeming injustice and gloomy prospects. About the wise and righteous, he says:

> Everything that confronts them is vanity, since the same fate comes to all, to the righteous and the wicked, to the good and the evil, to the clean and the unclean, to those who sacrifice and those who do not sacrifice. As are the good, so are the sinners; those who swear are like those who shun an oath. This is an evil in all that happens under the sun, that the same fate comes to everyone. . . . But whoever is joined with all the living has hope, for a living dog is better than a dead lion. The living know that they will die, but the dead know nothing; they have no more reward, and even the memory of them is lost. Their love and their hate and their envy have already perished; never again will they have any share in all that happens under the sun. (9:1b–6)

---

29. John F. Priest says, "Koheleth's skepticism is complete because he has lost all sense of any inner dynamic to history which might transcend the apparent present contradiction of the principles enunciated by religion and wisdom. This loss of the possibility of any meaning in history is what turns his skepticism into pessimism" ("Humanism, Skepticism, and Pessimism in Israel," *JAAR* 36 [1968]: 324). Cf. William H. U. Anderson, "Philosophical Considerations in a Genre Analysis of Qoheleth," *VT* 48 (1998): 295–97; Charles F. Forman, "The Pessimism of Ecclesiastes," *JSS* 3 (1958): 336–43.

30. James L. Crenshaw, "The Birth of Skepticism in Ancient Israel," in *The Divine Helmsman: Studies in God's Control of Human Events* (ed. James L. Crenshaw and Samuel Sandmel; New York: Ktav, 1980), 1–2.

31. The best discussion of Qohelet's view of death is Shannon Burkes's *Death in Qoheleth and Egyptian Biographies of the Late Period* (SBLDS 170; Atlanta: Scholars Press, 1999).

Though some have argued that the recurrent carpe diem ethic found throughout the book is its real message and, thus, that the book is not ultimately pessimistic, this seems rather apologetic.[32] The dark, somber melancholic mood of the book cannot be eclipsed by the brief and faint light expressed by this motif. Though he states it in the extreme, Crenshaw rightly detects the dark side to Qohelet's ethic:

> Qoheleth's positive counsel has little cause for exhilaration. The advice invariably occurs within contexts which emphasize life's vanity and attendant inequities, as well as those which stress God's control over human ability to enjoy life. Qoheleth's concept of divine gift is an expression for human limitation rather than an extolling of a generous God. The sources of pleasure—woman, wine, food, clothes, ointment, toil, and youth—are empty like life itself. In the end none accompanies the dead to Sheol.[33]

While pessimism is found in other places in the canon of the Hebrew Bible (Job 3, Lamentations, the laments in the Psalter, etc.), again, it is not as systematic, comprehensive, acute, and final as in Qohelet. The book, aside from its frame narrative (1:1–2; 12:8–12) and pious gloss (12:13–14), is consistently pessimistic. As John F. Priest has said, "The skepticism of Koheleth ends, however much some commentators cry to the contrary, as pessimism pure and simple."[34]

With this being the case, it is no wonder that Hebrew Bible theologians do not quite know what to do with the book; it is often ignored.[35] It is not con-

---

32. R. N. Whybray, "Qoheleth, Preacher of Joy," *JSOT* 23 (1982): 87–98; idem, *Ecclesiastes* (NCB; Grand Rapids: Eerdmans, 1989), 24–28; Robert Gordis, *Koheleth—The Man and His World: A Study of Ecclesiastes* (3rd ed.; New York: Schocken, 1968), 124; Graham Ogden, *Qoheleth* (Readings: A New Biblical Commentary; Sheffield: JSOT Press, 1987), 14–15, 21–22. Some scholars argue that Qohelet's pessimistic thoughts are used in irony as a foil for his theme of joy: Edwin M. Good, *Irony in the Old Testament* (Philadelphia: Westminster, 1965), 176–95; Timothy Polk, "The Wisdom of Irony: A Study of *Hebel* and Its Relation to Joy and the Fear of God in Ecclesiastes," *Studia Biblica et Theologica* 6 (1976): 3–17; Roland E. Murphy, "The 'Pensée' of Coheleth," *CBQ* 17 (1955): 304–14. William H. U. Anderson, to the contrary, considers the possibility that the carpe diem ethic is in fact ironic and not really Qohelet's solution to the problem ("Philosophical Considerations," 294; idem, "Ironic Correlations and Scepticism in the Joy Statements of Qoheleth?" *SJOT* 14 [2000]: 68–100).

33. Crenshaw, *Old Testament Wisdom*, 144.

34. Priest, "Humanism, Skepticism, and Pessimism," 323–24.

35. For example, in a very thick anthology on Old Testament theology, references to Qohelet were found on only one page (Ben C. Ollenburger, Elmer A. Martens, and Gerhard F. Hasel, eds., *The Flowering of Old Testament Theology: A Reader in Twentieth-Century Old Testament Theology, 1930–1990* [Sources for Biblical and Theological Study 1; Winona

sidered normative for Hebrew Bible theology. It merely occupies the negative and secondary role of corrective for traditional wisdom or the demonstration of wisdom's liabilities.[36] From this perspective, the book itself offers no positive message or contribution of its own.

Thus, Qohelet really is a "frightening guest" in the canon of the Hebrew Bible. How could a book so skeptical and pessimistic have become part of the Hebrew Bible? How could any Jew have accepted the book as divinely inspired? Why was the book ever preserved in the first place? What possible function did it have in the original community for which it was written? What possible function does the book have now in the canon of the Hebrew Bible? What made the author pessimistic and skeptical? How does one ultimately explain the dissonance the book creates within the canon?

These questions are all related and eventually lead to and revolve around the most critical and pressing issue in understanding the book: its canonicity. Shields provides a cogent and concise description of this problem:

> Although Qoheleth's words exhibit a predominantly negative assessment of life, an assessment due largely to the inevitability of death, and although he some-times appears to contradict himself, it is not these aspects of the book that are puzzling. It is, after all, not difficult to produce a text that has any or all of these features. What is most perplexing about Ecclesiastes is that a text of this sort is incorporated within a collection of writings that speak of a God who reveals and redeems, who chooses people and cares for them—themes not only absent from Qoheleth's words but frequently irreconcilable with them.[37]

In spite of this, the majority of modern commentators spend very little time addressing the problem of Ecclesiastes' inclusion in the Bible, and when they do, the reasons offered are largely unconvincing. I will offer an interpretation of Ecclesiastes that both acknowledges the unorthodox nature of Qohelet's words and manages to account for its acceptance among the canonical books of the Hebrew Bible.

Lake, Ind.: Eisenbrauns, 1992], 540). In Bernhard W. Anderson's *Contours of Old Testament Theology* ([Minneapolis: Fortress, 1999], 282–84), it gets only three pages.

36. Brevard Childs says, "Indeed Koheleth's sayings do not have an independent status, but function as a critical corrective, much as the book of James serves in the New Testament as an essential corrective to misunderstanding the Pauline letters" (*Introduction to the Old Testament as Scripture* [Philadelphia: Fortress, 1979], 588). Walther Zimmerli argues that Qohelet's value is in its assessment of the wisdom tradition as incomplete and insufficient ("The Place and Limit of the [*sic*] Wisdom in the Framework of the Old Testament Theology," *SJT* 17 [1964]: 157–58).

37. Shields, *End of Wisdom*, 1.

Shields is absolutely right in his assessment. Explaining away Qohelet's heterodoxy is the wrong, though popular, solution. Rather, embracing the book's heterodoxy, while simultaneously seeking the reasons why the book was still included in the canon is the only legitimate way to resolve this issue. Although Shields is to be applauded for his ability to discern succinctly the real issue and the way to resolve it, his own solution is faulty.[38] In this book, the issue will be tackled from a sociological perspective, which will be truly illuminating. But before this can be done, a review of the various explanations for the pessimistic and skeptical character of the book must be presented.

---

38. Shields counterintuitively argues that the frame narrator preserved Qohelet's words in order to provide a young audience an example of the bankruptcy of the wisdom tradition. While this is a possibility, it does not explain why one would go to the trouble to do that when a direct confrontation would have been more effective.

1

QOHELET'S HETERODOX CHARACTER: NON-SOCIAL-SCIENCE APPROACHES

IDEATIONAL APPROACHES

What one can call ideational approaches typically explain Qohelet's hetero-dox character as a strictly mental accomplishment or natural development of ideas, without much attention to sociohistorical factors. This way of explaining Qohelet's dissidence has certainly been the dominant one throughout the centuries. It represents the typically theological approach of an older generation of scholars, before the advent of the now popular sociological approach.[1] With the ideational perspective, the book is often depicted as a polemic against traditional wisdom (as represented by Proverbs and the friends of Job) and its unwarranted optimism and dogmatism, without considering the sociological dimensions to these literary works.

In America, James L. Crenshaw, the foremost expert on Qohelet, is representative of the ideational approach. In his commentary, the book of Qohelet is viewed as a polemic against traditional wisdom, with little socio-logical insight.[2] Michael V. Fox, another representative, instead of focusing on polemics, prefers to see Qohelet as simply tweaking traditional wisdom. But, again, his treatment lacks sociological perspective.[3] European scholars who refer to Qohelet representing a crisis of the wisdom tradition and believe that its assumptions and conceptualization have logically led to its bankruptcy are also representatives of this position. What is common to all of these approaches is an explanation of Qohelet's skepticism and pessimism as a natural inter-

---

1. On this contrast, see Crüsemann, "Unchangeable World," 61; cf. Robin Scroggs, "The Sociological Interpretation of the New Testament: The Present State of Research," *NTS* 26 (1980): 165–66.

2. Crenshaw, *Ecclesiastes*, 23–28, 49–50.

3. Fox, *Rereading of Ecclesiastes*, 26, 63, 91–92. Yet, strangely, Fox does attempt socio-logical inquiry into Proverbs, though without the use of social theory ("The Social Location of the Book of Proverbs," in *Texts, Temples, and Traditions* [ed. Michael V. Fox et al.; Winona Lake, Ind.: Eisenbrauns, 1996], 227–39).

nal development within the wisdom tradition itself: that is, ideational versus sociohistorical causation as an explanation. With this approach, Qohelet is often championed "as a break with tradition and thus as a landmark in the history of human thought."[4] Qohelet, thus, becomes a hero of free thinking over against the dogma of traditional wisdom, especially its doctrine of retribution. Crenshaw, in fact, connects his own personal religious skepticism with Qohelet's and views Qohelet in positive terms, in contrast to traditional wisdom's dogmatism.[5] According to this approach, Qohelet is assumed to have perceived the inadequacy of traditional wisdom's claims through the power of his reasoning capacities alone—a purely intellectual endeavor.

A connection between Qohelet's intellectual processes and the historical/social circumstances in which he found himself is never really pursued—a truly ahistorical approach. One could accurately describe this perspective as docetic. Since the roots of the change represented by Qohelet are sought in the development of ideas and theology, "the question of the reasons for the change is a priori excluded."[6] It is important to point out that many who take this position also, to some extent, point to historical factors, but these are never primary in their explanations of Qohelet's dissidence.

First, some German examples will be presented. In describing Qohelet's skepticism, Martin Kopfenstein speaks of the dogmatizing of traditional wisdom and Qohelet's polemic against it.[7] The source of Qohelet's skepticism stems from the legacy of ancient Israelite faith. From this legacy comes his conception of God as the all determining being, who acts according to his freewill and not according to the dictates of the wise. But Klopfenstein also speaks of the limits of Qohelet's skepticism and essentially makes him appear as a man of piety instead of as a skeptic.

Eberhard Wölfel maintains that Qohelet's skepticism and pessimism stem from the anthropocentric starting point of wisdom.[8] Qohelet represents the logical consequences to which wisdom leads. He shows that its utilitarian goals end in resignation because the means by which to reach them is precluded by the inaccessibility of the order of the world. Qohelet also demonstrates how the egoism/egocentrism of wisdom leads only to frustration. Wölfel concludes that the two dominating factors in Qohelet's skepticism and pessimism are utilitarianism and egoism.

---

4. Crüsemann, "Unchangeable World," 61.
5. Crenshaw, *Ecclesiastes*, esp. 53–54.
6. Crüsemann, "Unchangeable World," 61.
7. Klopfenstein, "Skepsis des Kohelet," 97–109.
8. Eberhard Wölfel, *Luther und die Skepsis: Eine Studie zur Kohelet-Exegeses Luthers* (Forschungen zur Geschichte und Lehre des Protestantismus 10/2; Munich: Kaiser, 1958), 84–88.

While Hartmut Gese admits the possibility that societal disorder is connected with skepticism/pessimism, as during the First Intermediate Period of Egypt and the Kassite period of Mesopotamia, the rest of his subsequent discussion of Qohelet essentially denies this.[9] He attempts to demonstrate that Qohelet's pessimism and skepticism about the discernment of the divine world order are not an aberration in wisdom but have been present from the beginning of the wisdom tradition. He does, though, point out a major difference between older wisdom and Qohelet: Qohelet speaks of a distancing/alienation of humanity from the world event, and this is a source of pessimism for him. But this is not seen as the concluding message of Qohelet. He admonishes humanity to give up this distancing by remaining open to time, fearing God, and placing oneself within his hands, for he is the one in control of all. Thus, Gese does not see Qohelet as a true pessimist or skeptic—instead Qohelet appears quite pious.

As an American example of the ideational approach, John Priest speaks of the main impetus for skepticism in ancient Israel: "The changes wrought by the Exile were of such a far-reaching nature that it is now possible for the legitimizations which had undergirded Israelite society in the pre-exilic period to be called into question."[10] But the rest of his discussion proceeds according to an ideational explanation. He attempts to determine how the door of skepticism was opened by changes made in Israel's theology.[11] This change involved a shift from a dynamic view of God and history to a more static and dogmatized one exemplified in Ezekiel and foreshadowed in Deuteronomy. Skepticism is viewed as naturally arising within the wisdom tradition to question such conceptualization. As for Qohelet, he becomes skeptical and pessimistic because he has lost any sense of meaning in history, any sense that God acts in history and that there is purpose to history.

Recently, a distinctive divide can be detected between two camps of Qohelet interpretation. The recent popularity of literary approaches, which purposefully ignore the historical background, is reflected in two works on Qohelet. Tremper Longman, in fact, does not include any sections on social or historical context in his commentary.[12] Eric Christianson reads the book as a narrative, in spite of the fact that the book is largely poetic.[13] These two can be considered heirs to Fox, a bona fide literary critic and the father of

---

9. Gese, "Krisis der Weisheit," 139–51.

10. Priest, "Humanism, Skepticism, and Pessimism," 319.

11. Ibid., 319–24.

12. Tremper Longman III, *The Book of Ecclesiastes* (NICOT; Grand Rapids: Eerdmans, 1998).

13. Eric S. Christianson, *A Time to Tell: Narrative Strategies in Ecclesiastes* (JSOTSup 280; Sheffield: Sheffield Academic Press, 1998).

narrative approaches to Qohelet, who argued years earlier that the real author is the framer narrator who has preserved the words of Qohelet as a persona to distance himself from their heterodox tendencies.[14] These represent the continuation of the ideational approach up to today. However, several recent commentaries include a sociohistorical section that at least considers social factors, and Richard Clifford's introduction to the wisdom literature includes a social location section for Ecclesiastes.[15]

CRITIQUE

A fundamental criticism of the ideational approach must come from a different paradigm, a new perspective. To maintain that Qohelet merely represents the development of ideas, that the change in wisdom represented by him is essentially an intellectual or theological process, seems simplistic and superficial. One brand of sociology, the sociology of knowledge, counters such an ideational approach. Going back to Marx and Engels and developed more fully by Karl Mannheim, its basic presupposition is that all knowledge or thought is intricately connected to one's social position.[16] As Marx and Engels famously wrote, "Men developing their material production and their material intercourse, alter, along with this their real existence their thinking and the products of their thinking. Life is not determined by consciousness, but consciousness by life."[17] Ideas do not simply float along detached from a person's particular situation and background or develop and exist in a vacuum.

---

14. Michael V. Fox, "Frame-Narrative and Composition in the Book of Qohelet," *HUCA* 48 (1977): 83–106.

15. Seow, *Ecclesiastes*, 21–36; Norbert Lohfink, *Qoheleth*, (trans. Sean McEvenue; CC; Minneapolis: Fortress, 2003), 4–6; William P. Brown, *Ecclesiastes* (IBC; Louisville: Westminster John Knox, 2000), 7–15; Thomas Krüger, *Qoheleth: A Commentary* (trans. O. C. Dean Jr.; Hermeneia; Minneapolis: Fortress, 2004), 19–26; Richard J. Clifford, *The Wisdom Literature* (IBT; Nashville: Abingdon, 1998), 99–101.

16. See Karl Mannheim, *Ideology and Utopia: An Introduction to the Sociology of Knowledge* (New York: Harcourt Brace, n.d.); Peter L. Berger and Thomas Luckmann, *The Social Construction of Reality: A Treatise in the Sociology of Knowledge* (Garden City, N.Y.: Doubleday Anchor, 1967). The most famous modern sociologist of knowledge is Michel Foucault, who showed how knowledge and power are always closely connected, especially in the school, home, and medical and penal fields (Michel Foucault, *Power/Knowledge: Selected Interviews & Other Writings 1971–1977* [ed. Colin Gordon; trans. Colin Gordon et al.; New York: Pantheon, 1980]). For a sociology-of-knowledge assessment of the Classicist controversy over the origins of Greek culture by a biblical scholar, see Jacques Berlinerblau, *Heresy in the University: The Black Athena Controversy and the Responsibilities of American Intellectuals* (New Brunswick, N.J.: Rutgers University Press, 1999).

17. Karl Marx and Frederick [Friedrich] Engels, *The German Ideology* (1845; repr., N.Y.: International Publishers, 1970), 47.

In other words, there is no such thing as "pure" intellect.[18] Thus, Qohelet's pessimism and skepticism are not to be accounted for by some purely intellectual or theological process.

To understand the source of Qohelet's worldview, one must delve below his conceptions and try to link them with a particular social situation.[19] All of the following analyses are in fact types of sociology of knowledge, though not in a developed sense. The broad sociological approach taken in this book is the sociology of knowledge. But the effort will be made to co-opt and assimilate other sociological perspectives.

However, as a caveat, it should be pointed out that the particular sociology-of-knowledge approach taken here does not see the superstructure (religion, law, politics, the arts, etc.) as completely or totally determined by the infrastructure or economy. This nuance was true for Marx, though his later disciples have turned Marxism into a distorted, vulgar version of his original ideas. Recent Marxists have in fact drifted away from the notion of total economic determination of ideas. For instance, the Western Marxist Fredric Jameson believes that the superstructure can actually react to and attempt to resolve the conflicts within the infrastructure.[20] In other words, the superstructure does not simply passively reflect the infrastructure but can actively respond to it. This more complicated way to explain the relationship of ideas and ideology to economy is typical of later Marxist approaches that have reacted to the old "vulgar materialism" that typified early Marxist theory.

Such an approach is also very Weberian. Sometimes Max Weber is misrepresented as countering the materialism of Marx with the other extreme of idealism.[21] In fact, Weber was very close to Marx in looking for connections between ideas and material interests. The term he uses for this is "elective affinity."[22] But he argues that ideas can emerge and remain largely unattached to economic conditions, though they often gravitate toward material interests. Weber saw a dialectic between material and ideational interests, with neither totally determining the other, though the emphasis falls on material conditions. In other words, Weber is essentially a nuanced Marx, who gave greater weight to the influence of ideas than did Marx. Weber famously says,

---

18. Louis Wirth, preface to Mannheim, *Ideology and Utopia*, xxv.

19. Cf. Crüsemann, "Unchangeable World," 59, 61.

20. Fredric Jameson, *The Political Unconscious: Narrative as a Socially Symbolic Act* (Ithaca, N.Y.: Cornell University Press, 1981).

21. For this corrective to popular interpretations of Weber, see Bryan S. Turner, *For Weber: Essays on the Sociology of Fate* (Boston: Routledge & Kegan Paul, 1981), 3–105.

22. Weber refers to the affinity between capitalism and Calvinistic asceticism (*The Protestant Ethic and the Spirit of Capitalism: The Revised 1920 Edition* [trans. Stephen Kalberg; Oxford: Oxford University Press, 2011], 72).

"Not ideas, but material and ideal interests, directly govern men's conduct. Yet very frequently the 'world images' that have been created by 'ideas' have, like switchmen, determined the tracks along which action has been pushed by the dynamic of interest."[23] The work on the sociology of knowledge developed by Peter Berger and Thomas Luckmann essentially assumes a Weberian perspective on this issue. The approach in this book will be essentially Weberian.

A major theme of the ideational approach is that Qohelet reacts to traditional wisdom because he perceives that it no longer fits reality. Some from this perspective suggest that traditional wisdom has become dogmatized and systematized, detached from reality. It is implied by this that Qohelet, on his own initiative and by the power of his own reasoning capacity, saw the inadequacy of traditional wisdom. The problem is believed to lie in traditional wisdom itself. Its formulation and dogmatization have caused it to lose touch with reality, and Qohelet was keen enough to recognize that fact.

Raymond Van Leeuwen has attempted to question the notion, assumed by many scholars, of a dogmatically held doctrine of retribution in Proverbs.[24] He is partly correct but fundamentally wrong. He has certainly demonstrated that the adherents to the doctrine were always aware of the many exceptions to the rule. In other words, there was built-in flexibility in the system. But what Van Leeuwen fails to acknowledge is that the exceptions would have been treated as just that—exceptions! This means that the rule of retribution was considered normative and dominant and, thus, the basis of rationality for the wisdom tradition, exceptions aside. Without the general working of retribution, the whole system fails and collapses, and another explanation would have to be sought. Even the "exceptions" get assimilated back into the retributive system because they are not really considered such but involve other categories; for example, dishonest wealth is distinguished from wealth gained honestly.[25] There is even a projected future retribution in Proverbs that Van Leeuwen acknowledges (e.g., 24:20; 28:20; 22:16).[26] Though he has demonstrated a creative flexibility to traditional wisdom, he has inadvertently and simultaneously demonstrated how thoroughgoing and fundamental retribution was for the early sages who composed Proverbs.

Van Leeuwen also fails to realize how tenaciously religious adherents hold to their beliefs even in the face of contradictory evidence. The social-psychological theory of cognitive dissonance demonstrates this tenacity and the creativity

---

23. Max Weber, "The Social Psychology of the World Religions," in *From Max Weber: Essays in Sociology* (trans. and ed. H. H. Gerth and C. Wright Mills; paperback ed.; New York: Oxford University Press, 1958), 280.

24. Van Leeuwen, "Wealth and Poverty," 25–36.

25. Ibid., 30.

26. Ibid., 31.

employed to explain away dissonance on the part of religious persons.[27] Religious persons are usually resistant to changing their beliefs, and they will ordinarily do many other things (mental acrobatics or rationalization) before they will change a belief. A fuller treatment of this theory will be offered below.

Van Leeuwen also fails to acknowledge that this ancient schema of retribution is patently false as far as the modern scientific perspective is concerned. All know that life's circumstances are not connected to individual piety or devotion to a particular deity. But it did provide payback for its adherents in that it explained so much of their reality and repressed chaotic and irrational elements. The ancients simply could not fathom that their own behavior and lifestyle would not have cosmic repercussions, that their behavior did not have connections with the larger world around them, including that of the gods. The tenacity and popularity of the doctrine are demonstrated in the friends of Job, whose adherence to the doctrine is no different than that in Proverbs. The doctrine continues in the New Testament when Jesus' disciples ask him in John 9 whether the blind man's parents or he himself had sinned to cause his malady. It is found today even in Hinduism with its notion of karma. Many Christians and especially evangelicals today also hold to the doctrine. It does have powerful explanatory power. It provides a sense of control over life and supports the notion of accountability. Its appeal is that it serves to make human life less subject to chance and the chaotic; it provides a powerful rationale or meaning for human activity.

There is yet another factor that Van Leeuwen does not consider. He never explains why scholars view the doctrine as dogmatic or why Job and Qohelet found it problematic. This can be attributed to the changed social conditions during the Persian and Ptolemaic periods, when skepticism about retribution emerged among the Jews with the composition of Job and Qohelet. With these changed conditions, though originally quite functional and explanatory, the doctrine now becomes problematic and a liability; it loses some of its payback value. Thus, it is not that the doctrine itself becomes more and more dogmatized or is more dogmatically adhered to but rather that the conditions under which it emerged changed, and this made it seem dogmatic because the exceptions were now becoming the rule and defending the doctrine became more and more difficult. In other words, there came a time when the doctrine's value or payoff began to be less than its liability, a point of diminishing returns.

This means that the doctrine has always been a dogma, and that there has never been a gradual process of dogmatization and inflexibility. Its dogmatic

---

27. On the theory used by a biblical scholar to interpret failed prophecies, see Robert P. Carroll, *When Prophecy Failed: Reactions and Responses to Failure in the Old Testament Prophetic Traditions* (London: SCM, 1979), 86–110; see also idem, "Ancient Israelite Prophecy and Dissonance Theory," *Numen* 24 (1977): 137–40.

character just became more obvious during the periods when Job and Qohelet were composed. The development of the doctrine of retribution is best understood under the broader notion of religious rationalization, and especially the effects of over-rationalization. Those effects will be discussed in more detail later. For now the conclusion can be drawn that the authors of Job and Qohelet would have perceived traditional wisdom as over-rationalized, not primarily because the tradition itself had become too rationalistic but rather because of the changed circumstances of the societies in which they lived, which undermined the original rationalization.

Weber describes a process of rationalization that is a tendency among the world's religions, with intellectuals as the key agents. Religions usually progress from a magical worldview to one where a deity is viewed as less and less capricious and more and more personal and reasonable, though this process is not uni-linear and regression is common.[28] The doctrine of retribution views God in this way as a reasonable deity who rewards righteous and pious behavior and punishes societal deviance. As has already been mentioned, it was the ancient principle of cause and effect for the ancient Near East. Moderns, of course, see this clearly as an over-rationalization of life. But in postexilic times, the ancients also began to notice its ineffectiveness. With the change in reality brought on by the exile and poor postexilic conditions for many of the subjugated Jews, it became increasingly difficult to maintain faith in the doctrine. In Qohelet's day it represented an over-rationalization of life, though those who continued to adhere to the doctrine should not really be called dogmatists because, as has been mentioned, the doctrine was an extremely powerful and illuminating notion that retains its popularity even today.

Non-Ideational Explanations for Qohelet's Heterodoxy

Assumption of a Weberian Approach

Before beginning to look at broadly sociological and then more narrowly social-scientific approaches to Qohelet, it is necessary to provide the sociological assumptions and position of this book. As already mentioned, it will take a largely Weberian approach.[29] This is a critical adoption, and at several points

---

28. On Weber's non-linear view, see Warren S. Goldstein, "The Dialectics of Religious Rationalization and Secularization: Max Weber and Ernst Bloch," *Critical Sociology* 31 (2005): 115–18.

29. For introductions to Weber, see Reinhard Bendix, *Max Weber: An Intellectual Portrait* (paperback ed.; Berkeley: University of California Press, 1977); Stephen Turner, ed., *The Cambridge Companion to Weber* (Cambridge: Cambridge University Press, 2000); Hans H. Gerth and C. Wright Mills, introduction to *From Max Weber: Essays in Sociology* (ed.

disagreement with Weber will be presented or new territory he did not cover will be charted. But, largely, Weber's theorization is extremely illuminating and powerful. His "big picture" approach and, especially his comparative-religion theorization will be especially helpful for understanding Qohelet and his heterodox character. There should, perhaps, be no need to defend a Weberian approach to a Hebrew Bible book. Weber, of course, was, along with Émile Durkheim and Karl Marx, one of the fathers of sociology.[30] In other words, he is one of the members of the sociological trinity. In addition to this, Hebrew Bible scholars are extremely fortunate that he wrote a treatise on the ancient Jews that starts with the Israelite confederacy and ends with Christianity and the Pharisees.[31] In addition, in the field of sociology, most of Weber's theories and analytical tools are still used today. There is even a current journal devoted to him from London: *Max Weber Studies*. Granted, most of his theorization has been modified, but, as a whole, Weber has fared well throughout the years in the field of social theory.

As has been said, Weber should be viewed as a nuanced Marx. Weber focused just as much as Marx did on how ideas are connected to economic class and power. However, for Weber, focusing almost exclusively on social class when considering social stratification is misdirected. Weber chose to highlight three principal variables of social stratification: wealth, power, and prestige or honor.[32] These variables usually correlate but not always. For example, a wealthy person might be powerful but lack the respect of his peers. Or a college professor might be esteemed for academic accomplishments but lack political power. For the upper class of ancient Judaism, prestige and power were important social commodities. The Jewish elite might be economically comfortable, but that was not enough. They also required power and prestige to enhance the honor and influence of their households.

Weber is also famous for his understanding of authority, of which he distinguishes three types: traditional, charismatic, and legal. Charismatic domination is "a belief in some extraordinary individual and the order that that individual stands for."[33] Prophets often display charismatic authority with their

---

and trans. H. H. Gerth and C. Wright Mills; paperback ed.; New York: Oxford University Press, 1958), 3–74.

30. For a comparison of the three, see Anthony Giddens, *Capitalism & Modern Social Theory: An Analysis of the Writings of Marx, Durkheim and Max Weber* (Cambridge: Cambridge University Press, 1971).

31. Max Weber, *Ancient Judaism* (trans. and ed. Hans H. Gerth and Don Martindale; paperback ed.; New York: Free Press, 1976).

32. Max Weber, *Economy and Society: An Outline of Interpretive Sociology* (ed. Guenther Roth and Claus Wittich; trans. Ephraim Fischoff et al.; 2 vols.; paperback ed.; New York: Bedminster, 1968; repr., Berekely: University of California, 1978), 1:302–7; 2:926–40.

33. Richard Swedberg, *The Max Weber Dictionary: Key Words and Central Concepts* (Stanford: Stanford Social Sciences, 2005), 64, s.v. "Domination (*Herrschaft*)."

ecstasy and magic. Traditional leadership is represented, say, by elders in a village or a king. Legal-rational authority is connected to legitimized official roles and legal codes found in a more highly stratified society. It is the most common today and is associated with the work of the bureaucracy and officials.

In Hebrew Bible studies, early on scholars drew on Weber often but in a piecemeal fashion. None adopted his focus on the interplay between materialist and idealist interests, which is what distinguishes Weber from Marx. None drew on his favorite and most comprehensive theory of rationalization. More recently, Norman K. Gottwald and the Marxist (or Materialist) school began to dominate the scene, at least in America.[34] Gottwald's monumental *Tribes of Yahweh* and his popular *Socio-Literary Introduction to the Hebrew Bible* have heavily influenced biblical sociology in America.[35] Walter Brueggemann proclaims this about *Tribes*:

> In this book we have a programmatic hypothesis which holds the potential of being an important historical moment in the discipline. Unless I greatly misjudge, the book holds promise of being a point of reference parallel in significance, potential, and authority to Wellhausen's *Prologemena* and Albright's *From Stone Age to Christianity*.[36]

---

34. Gottwald was president of the Society of Biblical Literature in 1992; see Roland Boer, "Twenty-Five Years of Marxist Biblical Criticism," *Currents in Biblical Research* 5 (2007): 298–321. The following is a representative sampling of Marxian Hebrew Bible scholars, with an exemplary work from each: Robert B.Coote and Keith W. Whitelam, "The Emergence of Israel: Social Transformation and State Formation Following the Decline in Late Bronze Age Trade," *Semeia* 37 (1986): 107–47; Naomi Steinberg, "The Deuteronomic Law Code and Politics of State Centralization," in *The Bible and the Politics of Exegesis* (ed. David Jobling, Peggy L. Day, and Gerald T. Sheppard; Cleveland: Pilgrim, 1991), 161–70; and, in the same volume, Marvin L. Chaney, "Debt Easement in Israelite History and Tradition," 127–39; Walter Brueggemann, *The Prophetic Imagination* (2nd ed.; Minneapolis: Fortress, 2001); Ronald Simkins, "Patronage and the Political Economy of Monarchic Israel," *Semeia* 87 (1999): 123–44; Frank S. Frick, "Sociological Criticism and Its Relation to Political and Social Hermeneutics: With a Special Look at Biblical Hermeneutics in South African Liberation Theology," in Jobling et al., *Bible and the Politics of Exegesis*, 225–238; and, in the same volume, David Jobling, "Feminism and 'Mode of Production' in Ancient Israel," 239–51; Itumeleng J. Mosala, "Social Scientific Approaches to the Bible: One Step Forward, Two Steps Back," *JTSA* 55 (1986): 15–30; and Gale Yee, "Ideological Criticism: Judges 17–21 and the Dismembered Body," in *Judges and Method: New Approaches in Biblical Studies* (ed. Gale Yee; Minneapolis: Fortress, 1995), 146–70.

35. The term "biblical sociology" comes from Jacques Berlinerblau ("The Present Crisis and Uneven Triumphs of Biblical Sociology: Responses to N. K. Gottwald, S. Mandell, P. Davies, M. Sneed, R. Simkins and N. Lemche," in *Concepts of Class in Ancient Israel* [ed. Mark Sneed; South Florida Studies in the History of Judaism: The Hebrew Scriptures and Their World 201; Atlanta: Scholars Press, 1999], 99).

36. Walter Brueggemann, "*The Tribes of Yahweh*: An Essay Review," *JAAR* 48 (1980): 443.

Brueggemann did not misjudge. But it is also significant that he does not cite Weber. Many biblical sociologists today assume a Marxist agenda without being explicit that their focus is almost entirely on economic influences to the exclusion of ideal ones. For example, most scholars who have analyzed Qohelet from a sociological standpoint assume a vulgar Marxist position, where Qohelet's thinking is viewed as largely determined by his economic circumstances.[37] Unfortunately, recent biblical sociologists have largely ignored Weber, with some exceptions, as shown below. However, the significance of Weber in the history of Hebrew Bible studies has been compellingly demonstrated in a significant book by A. D. H. Mayes.[38] His summary will not be repeated, but it should be mentioned that Albrecht Alt and Martin Noth particularly drew on Weber's concepts. As Mayes notes, the three main areas of influence Weber had on Hebrew Bible scholarship are the notion of charisma, the ideal type city-state, and Israel as an oath community.[39]

Weber's work on prophecy has also been very influential.[40] His view of the prophets is called the "religious genius" approach.[41] He refers to the prophets as "genteel intellectuals," who were socially detached individuals.[42] They were not connected with any institution or particular social class, and they had little social support. The prophets are characterized as loners who attacked the monarchy and the changes it brought, such as the class conflict that arose between peasant farmers and urban patricians. Weber forms a dichotomy pitting the solitary prophet with a concern for social justice against the professional priest with his cultic concerns.

---

37. See Mark Sneed, "Qohelet and His 'Vulgar' Critics: A Jamesonian Reading," *Bible and Critical Theory* 1/1 (2004): 1–11. http://www.relegere.org/index.php/bct/article/viewfile/17/5.

38. A. D. H. Mayes, *The Old Testament in Sociological Perspective* (London: Marshall Pickering, 1989), 18–27; cf. idem, "Sociology and the Old Testament," in *The World of Ancient Israel: Sociological, Anthropological and Political Perspectives: Essays by Members of the Society for Old Testament Study* (ed. Ronald E. Clements; Cambridge: Cambridge University Press, 1991), 39–41, 43–48, 52–55; cf. Victor Matthews, "Traversing the Social Landscape: The Value of the Social Science Approach to the Bible," in *Theology and the Social Sciences* (ed. Michael Horace Barnes; Annual Publication of the College Theology Society 46; Maryknoll, N.Y.: Orbis, 2000), 216, 218.

39. Mayes, *Sociological Perspective*, 36–77.

40. Ronald E. Clements uses Weber's notion of routinization and legitimization to explain why those responsible for the canon included the charismatic prophetic works ("Max Weber, Charisma and Biblical Prophecy," in *Prophecy and Prophets: The Diversity of Contemporary Issues in Scholarship* [ed. Yehoshua Gitay; SemeiaSt; Atlanta: Scholars Press, 1997], 89–108).

41. Peter L. Berger, "Charisma and Religious Innovation: The Social Location of the Prophets," *American Sociological Review* 28 (1963): 943.

42. Weber, *Ancient Judaism*, 279.

Before examining specifically explicit Weberian examples, a couple of scholars need to be noted. One could call George E. Mendenhall loosely Weberian, if one contrasts his with Gottwald's explanation of the origin of Yahwism. Though Gottwald explains his notion of an egalitarian Yahwism as essentially a reflection of the social location of the peasants that revolted against their Canaanite overlords, Mendenhall gives more place to the role of religious ideas (here Yahwism) to change Israelite society.[43] The other scholar is Mayes, who is clearly a Weberian but more from a theoretical standpoint than specific application.[44]

One explicitly Weberian example among many is Abraham Malamat, who uses Weber's notion of charisma to interpret the book of Judges.[45] He describes the judges as having charismatic authority—"deviating from the common or routine."[46] Foreign enemies and the wane of traditional authority (elders) created the opportunity for this type of charismatic authority in ancient Israel. "The authority of charismatic leadership, by nature, is not dependent on social class, nor on age-group or sex."[47] Examples include Deborah (Judges 4–5), the judge and prophetess, and Jephthah (Judges 10–12), youngest of his family and of "dubious descent."

Malamat has been criticized by Burke Long for not being systematic enough.[48] He wonders how the judges related to the elders and who installed them. Long notes that there seem to be two forms of authority in ancient Israel at the time: elder control (traditional authority) and charismatic judges.

---

43. See George E. Mendenhall, "The Hebrew Conquest of Palestine," in *Community, Identity, and Ideology: Social Science Approaches to the Hebrew Bible* (ed. Charles E. Carter and Carol L. Meyers; Winona Lake, Ind.: Eisenbrauns, 1999), 152–69 (repr. from *BA* 25 [1962]: 66–87); and, in the same volume, Norman K. Gottwald, "Domain Assumptions and Societal Models in the Study of Pre-Monarchic Israel," 170–81 (repr. from *Congress Volume: Edinburgh, 1974* [VTSup 28; Leiden: Brill, 1976]). Also in the same volume, A. D. H. Mayes views Gottwald's position as not solely materialistic because he sees the Israelites choosing Yawhism as the driving force behind social change ("Idealism and Materialism in Weber and Gottwald," 270 n. 36; repr. from *Proceedings of the Irish Biblical Association* 11 [1988]).

44. On theory, see Mayes, "Idealism and Materialism," 258–72; on application, see idem, *Judges* (OTG; Sheffield: JSOT Press, 1985; repr., Sheffield: Sheffield Academic Press, 1995), 78.

45. Abraham Malamat, "Charismatic Leadership in the Book of Judges," in *Community, Identity, and Ideology: Social Science Approaches to the Hebrew Bible* (ed. Charles E. Carter and Carol L. Meyers; Winona Lake, Ind.: Eisenbrauns, 1999), 293–310 (repr. from *Magnalia Dei—The Mighty Acts of God: Essays on the Bible and Archaeology in Memory of G. Ernest Wright* [ed. F. M. Cross, W. E. Lemke, and P. D. Miller; New York: Doubleday, 1976], 152–68).

46. Ibid., 300.

47. Ibid., 307.

48. Burke O. Long, "The Social World of Ancient Israel," *Int* 36 (1982): 246.

He then speculates on whether the elders gave up all their authority when a judge was commissioned. Recently, Timothy Willis has answered this question by arguing that Jephthah used both traditional and charismatic forms of authority during his stint as a judge.[49] He negotiates with the elders of Gilead to obtain the traditional status of a clan leader. But when faced with intertribal problems, he receives charismatic authority when he is filled with God's spirit before his battle with the Ammonites.

We can turn now to an example of modification of Weberian theory by biblical scholars, but first it is necessary to note the contribution of the famed sociologist of knowledge Peter Berger to this discussion. He criticizes Weber for being unduly influenced by the German biblical scholarship of the time.[50] He suggests that Weber's "religious genius" approach to the prophets can be essentially attributed to them. Berger shows how modern biblical scholarship, especially among the Scandinavians, supports the notion of an institution of prophecy with close connections to the cult (priesthood). Although critical of aspects of Weber's theorization, Berger believes that his views on charismatic authority and religious innovation hold true for the prophets. Stephen Cook essentially confirms Berger's conclusions about the social location of prophecy.[51] His main argument is that Hosea, though critical of the cult, does not reject it outright. He elicits cross-cultural comparison that involves the clash between new state cult systems and old ones. He then shows how Hosea criticizes the new form of prophecy from within the institution itself and not as an outsider.

However, Berger's and Cook's criticisms to some extent involve a misconception of Weber's notion of ideal type. Weber never intended his social profile of the Israelite prophet to fit every historical example. Weber's ideal type is an analytical tool necessary for sociological research and theorization. It reduces complex phenomena to simpler stereotypical traits. Weber's portrayal of prophets as loners and as anticultic certainly fits several of the Israelite prophets, especially Jeremiah. The question is not whether all the Israelite prophets fit this pattern but the extent to which any particular prophet did or did not. Though many prophets were socially marginal, no doubt, each needed a supportive and legitimizing audience. Recently, Thomas Overholt has illuminated this necessary audience-dependent facet of Israelite prophecy through anthropological cross-cultural comparison.[52] Thus, in actuality, even Weber's

---

49. Timothy M. Willis, "The Nature of Jephthah's Authority," *CBQ* 59 (1997): 33–44.

50. Berger, "Charisma," 940–50.

51. Stephen L. Cook, "The Lineage Roots of Hosea's Yahwism," *Semeia* 87 (1999): 145–61.

52. Thomas W. Overholt, "Prophecy: The Problem of Cross-Cultural Comparison," in *Community, Identity, and Ideology: Social Science Approaches to the Hebrew Bible* (ed.

conception of the ideal type of Israelite prophecy, when viewed appropriately, comes through basically unscathed.

This is enough of an introduction to allow criticism of the following non-ideational approaches. As the main thesis is presented, I will draw on Weber's notion of rationalization. I will not, however adopt all of Weber's notions or conclusions and will often modify them. It is important that one adopt a Weberian perspective that is critically applied. Applying Weber to Qohelet is also an intriguing enterprise because Weber never even refers to the book. He refers only to the wisdom books Proverbs, Job, and Ben Sira. One wonders why? Did he find the book puzzling? Did it not quite fit his theorization? At any rate, this gap in his work provides a wonderful opportunity to apply his theorization in a new, interesting, and provocative way. The challenge is a welcome one. Although I will embrace a Weberian approach, I will employ also insights from the social-psychological theory of cognitive dissonance, the psychology of pessimism, and genre and rhetorical criticism and integrate these insights into Weber's macro-sociological theorization. For now a return to reviewing non-ideational approaches is necessary.

BROAD SOCIOHISTORICAL EXPLANATIONS

In this category of explanations, social facets are engaged to explain Qohelet's heterodoxy. But none of these types of approaches draws on the social sciences explicitly or uses social theory to explain Qohelet's skepticism/pessimism. Sometimes this kind of perspective is known as social history.[53] Regularly, social-science approaches exclude social histories as examples of their methodology because of the lack of theory, though this is no verdict on their illumination or helpfulness. First there will be discussion of the two archetypal or pure types and then a look at hybrid examples.

SOCIOHISTORICAL CRISIS

A dominant explanation for the origin of skepticism/pessimism has been that of broad sociohistorical crises or periods of political chaos. Its basic premise is that pessimistic and skeptical literature can arise only during periods of social instability, such as during wars or periods of colonization. With this approach, the explanation for Qohelet's pessimism/skepticism is to be sought

---

Charles E. Carter and Carol L. Meyers; Winona Lake, Ind.: Eisenbrauns, 1999), 423–47 (repr. from *Semeia* 21 [1982]: 55–78).

53. See Mark Sneed, "Social Scientific Approach to the Hebrew Bible," *Religion Compass* 2 (2008): 290–91. DOI: 10.1111/j.1749-8171.2008.00072.x.

in the broad social and cultural milieu in which he lived. However, little attention is usually given to the social location of the author himself.

Still a related approach examines Qohelet via the broader sociohistorical
context and explains his heterodoxy as due to the encroachment of Hellenism
and exposure to Greek ideas. Technically, this is a type of crisis. A separate section will treat this approach because of its popularity and because it technically
is a fundamentally anthropological explanation known as diffusion.

Much of the pessimistic and skeptical literature in Egypt was once dated
to the First Intermediate Period after the collapse of the Old Kingdom. While
the actual dating of this literature was usually later than these periods, Egyptologists assumed that the earlier unstable period best accounted for its origins
(cf. the Kassite period for Mesopotamian literature).[54] For example, famed
Egyptologist A. H. Gardiner said this of the Egyptian work "The Admonitions
of Ipuwer": "The pessimism of Ipuwer was intended to be understood as the
direct and natural response to a real national calamity."[55] Egyptologists often
assumed the chaotic descriptions of the land in this literature to depict actual
historical events.[56]

> Crime is everywhere, there is no man of yesterday.
> ....
> Lo, poor men have become men of wealth,
>   He who could not afford sandals owns riches.
> ....
> Every town says, "Let us expel our rulers."
> ....
> Lo, the land turns like a potter's wheel,
> The robber owns riches, {the noble} is a thief.[57]

Compare Qohelet's words: "There is an evil that I have seen under the sun, as
great an error as if it proceeded from the ruler: folly is set in many high places,
and the rich sit in a low place. I have seen slaves on horseback, and princes
walking on foot like slaves" (10:5–6).

---

54. On the Kassite period, see Gese, "Krisis bei Kohelet," 140; Frank Crüsemann,
"Hiob und Kohelet: Ein Beitrag zum Verständis des Hiobbuches," in *Werden und Wirken
des Alten Testaments: Festschrift für Claus Westermann* (ed. Rainer Albertz et al.; Göttingen:
Vandenhoeck & Ruprecht, 1980), 390.

55. Alan Henderson Gardiner, *The Admonitions of an Egyptian Sage from a Hieratic
Papyrus in Leiden, Pap. Leiden 344 Recto* (1909; repr., Hildesheim: Georg Olms, 1969), 111.

56. John A. Wilson, introduction to "The Admonitions of Ipu-Wer," in *ANET*, 441; R.
O. Faulkner, introduction to "The Admonitions of an Egyptian Sage," in *LAE*, 210; William
W. Hallo and William Kelly Simpson, *The Ancient Near East: A History* (New York: Har-
court Brace Jovanovich, 1971), 235.

57. "The Admonitions of Ipuwer" (*AEL*, 1:151).

As for skepticism, two works have been treated in the same way. "A Dispute Over Suicide" involves a dialogue between a man and his soul on the advantages of suicide. John A. Wilson observes that the "Dispute" may date from the Intermediate Period "when the established order of life had broken down and men were groping for new values."[58] Because of the injustices of the land, the man welcomes death:

> None are righteous,
> The land is left to evildoers.
> ....
> Wrong roams the earth,
> And ends not.
> Death is before me today
> <Like> a sick man's recovery,
> Like going outdoors after confinement.
> Death is before me today
> Like the fragrance of myrrh,
> Like sitting under sail on a breezy day.[59]

The man wants to die and be resurrected. But his soul argues that what happens after death is at best uncertain and that maintenance of the dead by survivors cannot be relied on. One should, thus, avoid suicide and enjoy life while one has it: "Those who built in granite, who erected halls in excellent tombs of excellent construction—when the builders have become gods, their offering-stones are desolate, as if they were the dead who died on the riverbank for lack of survivor. . . . Listen to me! It is good for people to listen. Follow the feast day, forget worry!"[60] Here one sees the combination of pessimism, skepticism, and a carpe diem ethic, as in Qohelet.

"A Song of the Harper" also demonstrates these same sentiments. It claims to have been inscribed in the tomb of King Intef:

> The gods who were before rest in their tombs,
> Blessed nobles too are buried in their tombs.
> (Yet) those who build tombs,
> Their places are gone,
> What has become of them?
> ....
> Their walls have crumbled,
> Their places are gone,

---

58. John A. Wilson, introduction to "A Dispute Over Suicide" (*ANET*, 405).
59. "The Dispute between a Man and His Ba" (*AEL* 1:167–68).
60. Ibid., 165.

As though they had never been!
None comes from there,
To tell of their state,
To tell of their needs,
To calm our hearts,
Until we go where they have gone!
....
Refrain: Make Holiday,
Do not weary of it!
Lo, none is allowed to take his goods with him,
Lo, none who departs comes back again![61]

Wilson, again, connects this song with "the groping for value which followed the collapse of the Old Kingdom."[62]

The very general theory that connects social instability with this kind of literature also is applied to Qohelet in various ways. As already noted, Priest points out that the crisis of the exile opened the door for skepticism and pessimism in ancient Israel and is exemplified in the books of Job and Ecclesiastes.[63] Similarly, in addressing Qohelet's worldview, Johannes Pedersen refers to the disorienting effects that the exile and being under the power of foreign rulers had on Israelite culture and society.[64] He refers also to the dissolving effect that the rise of urbanism had on Israel's laws and norms. Recently and similarly, Craig G. Bartholomew writes, "The postexilic context of Israel, with what appeared to be the demise of the great Israelite experiment, must have led Qohelet and his educated contemporaries to question the reality of the Israelite vision of life into which they were born and nurtured."[65]

Some scholars appear to adhere to the historical-crisis approach but do not know how to apply it specifically to Qohelet. As already mentioned, Gese refers to this type of explanation but then proceeds along other lines.[66] Similarly, Hans H. Schmid follows this explanation in his treatment of pessimistic and skeptical texts in Egyptian wisdom of the First Intermediate Period and the Middle Kingdom, but not for Qohelet.[67]

---

61. "The Song from the Tomb of King Intef" (*AEL* 1:196).
62. John A. Wilson, introduction to "A Song of the Harper" (*ANET*, 467).
63. Priest, "Humanism, Skepticism, and Pessimism," 319–24.
64. Pedersen, "Scepticisme israélite," 347.
65. Craig G. Bartholomew, *Ecclesiastes* (Baker Commentary on the Old Testament; Grand Rapids: Baker, 2009), 59.
66. Gese, "Krisis bei Kohelet," 140.
67. Schmid, *Geschichte der Weisheit*, 40–68, 124–31.

Recently, C. L. Seow advocated the crisis approach, though he dates the book to the Persian period.[68] He describes Qohelet's descriptions of his society as a "topsy-turvy world" turned upside-down and connects this instability with Qohelet's particular theology.[69] While he recognizes the ancient Near Eastern topos, he argues that it reflects social reality in Qohelet, owing to "the volatile economy of his time."[70]

On balance, this interpretation is certainly superior to the ideational approach and is a necessary correction to the dominance of the latter approach. As Robert Carroll says, "*crisis produced critique*," and historical or social crisis goes a long way toward accounting for Qohelet's aberrant theology.[71] But the general sociohistorical background is only part of the equation. One also has to take account of the author's own social location and how it interacts with the broader sociohistorical circumstances. Did Qohelet's particular social status predispose him to his particular response? One needs to attend also to rival reactions to the same circumstances. This is especially true when one considers that catastrophe can strengthen faith as well as damage it, as found, for example, with the Deuteronomistic History, which explained the exile as due to Israel and Judah's violation of Deuteronomic law, and the Priestly material, whose subtle polemic against the Babylonian gods (Gen 1:1,14–19) may have been composed during the exile.[72] In other words, there needs to be an awareness of the complexity and diversification of a society's reaction to such

---

68. The consensus for the date of the book is the third century. In 1985, Norman K. Gottwald declared, "There is a solid consensus among scholars that Ecclesiastes belongs to the third century B.C.E., that is, to Ptolemaic Palestine" (*The Hebrew Bible: A Socio-Literary Introduction* [Philadelphia: Fortress, 1985], 580). However, in 1996, C. L. Seow challenged the consensus by arguing for a date in the Persian period with a linguistic argument ("Linguistic Evidence and the Dating of Qohelet," *JBL* 115 [1996]: 643–66). He notes the high number of Aramaisms, two Persian loanwords, and no Grecisms in the book. But his most significant piece of evidence is that the specific sense of שלט in Qohelet is technical and was current only for the Persian period and not later. Seow is answered by Dominic Rudman, who says, "By his own admission, however, almost all of the features of Qoheleth's vocabulary and syntax are common to both the Persian and Hellenistic eras" (*Determinism in the Book of Ecclesiastes* [JSOTSup 316; Sheffield: Sheffield Academic Press, 2001], 15); see idem, "A Note on the Dating of Ecclesiastes," *CBQ* 61 (1999): 47–52. He demonstrates that the technical meaning of שלט is found well into the Christian age.

69. C. L. Seow, "The Socioeconomic Context of 'The Preacher's' Hermeneutic," *PSB* 17 (1996): 186–7; cf. idem, "Theology When Everything Is out of Control," *Int* 55 (2001): 238–43.

70. Seow, "Socioeconomic Context," 187.

71. Carroll, *When Prophecy Failed*, 8.

72. On the resilience of faith during crisis, see Crenshaw, "Birth of Skepticism," 5.

a crisis.[73] It is difficult to imagine the entire society of Judah becoming uniformly pessimistic because of a broad sociohistorical crisis.

As for Qohelet's time, there is no evidence that supports the view that Ptolemaic Judah was socially tumultuous or unstable. Robert Harrison has shown that hellenization was slow to encroach on third-century Judah.[74] Many scholars, in fact, describe Ptolemaic Judah as rather placid, not socially anarchic.[75] Seow's attempt to describe Qohelet as reflecting what he purports to be the socially chaotic world of Persian Judah only weakens this whole line of argument. It shows how easily one can construe the data to fit one's own preconceived theory. But even if the evidence did suggest that Ptolemaic Judah was socially unstable, this would not mean that it is necessary and sufficient for explaining causation. The relationship between literature and its sociohistorical context is more complex than that. Rather, as we shall see later, Qohelet is disturbed by the continued subjugation of his people under the heavy hand of the Ptolemies. In other words, society was stable but unjustly so. As a result, scholars who point to colonization as a primary source for understanding Qohelet's pessimism and skepticism are correct, but it is not the only factor.

It should also be pointed out that several Egyptologists now question the old paradigm that saw the pessimistic and skeptical literature of the Middle Kingdom ultimately going back to the First Intermediate Period or that the period was really that anarchistic and socially chaotic. Social historians have pointed out that the bleak world description in these Egyptian sources is not to be taken as an actual reporting of events.[76] Miriam Lichtheim chides those who think that the First Intermediate Period was that chaotic:

---

73. Robert Gordis represents such an awareness when he proposes that the upper class in Israel was more prone to skepticism than the lower class ("The Social Background of Wisdom Literature," in *Poets, Prophets, and Sages: Essays in Biblical Interpretation* [ed. Robert Gordis; Bloomington: Indiana University Press, 1971], 177; repr. from *HUCA* 18 [1943–44]: 77–118).

74. C. Robert Harrison, "Hellenization in Syria-Palestine: The Case of Judea in the Third Century BCE," *BA* 57 (1994): 98–108.

75. Roger S. Bagnall, *The Administration of the Ptolemaic Possessions outside Egypt* (Columbia Studies in the Classical Tradition 4; Leiden: Brill, 1976), 9, 19; Bickerman, *Strange Books*, 74; Victor A. Tcherikover, "Hellenistic Age," in *The World History of the Jewish People* (ed. Abraham Schalit; 7 vols.; New Brunswick, N.J.: Rutgers University Press, 1972), 6:67–93.

76. Barry J. Kemp, "Old Kingdom, Middle Kingdom and Second Intermediate Period *c.* 2686–1552 BC," in B. G. Trigger, B. J. Kemp, D. O'Connor, and A. B. Lloyd, *Ancient Egypt: A Social History* (Cambridge: Cambridge University Press, 1983), 75–76, 115–116. Hallo and Simpson, while describing the period as anarchic, admit exaggeration (*Ancient Near East*, 237).

At no time did this brief interlude of local autonomy produce a social upheaval, a revolution designed to overthrow the hierarchic order of the society. Claims that such a revolution took place have absolutely no basis in the inscriptions of the period. They are conclusions mistakenly drawn from a single Middle Kingdom literary work, the *Admonitions of Ipuwer*. What the inscriptions of the First Intermediate Period show is the very opposite of social upheaval. In each nome the hierarchic fabric is intact and serves to promote the welfare of the region and its defense in times of trouble.[77]

As for "The Admonitions of Ipuwer," Lichtheim makes the case that the work simply expresses a typical topos of the day that she calls "national distress" or "social chaos."[78] It is significant that Egyptian skeptical/pessimistic literature retained its appeal and was preserved in the demonstrably peaceable period after the First Intermediate Period. It means that pessimism and skepticism might function in a way different from direct reflection of the historical context of the work in which they are found.

Wilson's assumption becomes problematic in the case of "A Song of the Harper," whose composition is dated to the New Kingdom. He believes that the work fits the collapse of the Old Kingdom and tries to circumvent this problem with this explanation: "However, the use of the text in the Eighteenth and Nineteenth Dynasties shows that this hedonism was an acceptable literary expression for some centuries."[79]

Having said all of this, Lichtheim does point out that the chaos that the Middle Kingdom works portray has some relation to historical reality, though greatly exaggerated. It revolves around the perennial problem of evil. In the Instructions of the Middle Kingdom, one finds

> a sage who laments the evil condition into which the country had fallen. This variation on the theme of Instructions can only have resulted from the growing recognition of the problematic nature of human life. All was not well on earth. Men frequently acted from evil impulses; the nation was often rent by civil war. The seemingly permanent order could be destroyed—and yet the gods did not intervene. Thus the Egyptian began to grapple with the problem of evil.[80]

That Lichtheim describes these poetic descriptions as "largely imaginary" means there is some sociohistorical basis for them.[81] But she argues that the extreme social inversion depicted is found in other literatures and is largely rhetorical.

---

77. *AEL* 1:83.
78. *AEL* 1:149–50.
79. Wilson, "Introduction to 'A Song of the Harper,'" 467.
80. *AEL* 1:9.
81. *AEL* 1:10.

Lichtheim cites an important work by the Russian S. Luria, who treats what he calls the "social revolution" theme (the title is significant: "The First Shall Be Last").[82] He demonstrates that it is a universal theme, with often messianic overtones. Luria focuses on ancient Egyptian literature and Attic comedy but also cites, for example, Vietnamese literature and the ancient king of Yadi. In discussing Ipuwer, Luria points out that there were disturbing elements during the collapse of the Old Kingdom such as aristocrats declassed and poor upstarts becoming wealthy, hungry mobs breaking open government storehouses, and even the burning of tax registries. But he concludes that the social inversion depicted in the piece is greatly exaggerated and has no historical basis. He concludes that the topsy-turvy motif is even contradictory in Ipuwer. He notes that although general barrenness and impoverishment in the land are depicted, the poor upstarts are wearing fine linen. What is significant here is that Luria does see at least some historical reality behind the depictions, though it has been highly hyperbolized.

Even Gardiner provides an example of a pessimistic Egyptian work that did not originate in a socially tumultuous time. The work is Khekheperresonbu, which is dated to the time of Sesostris II of the Twelfth Dynasty. Gardiner points out that the author treats "the wickedness of men, the corruption of society and his own grief and despondency."[83] He then writes:

Egypt had, by the time that Sesostris II came to the throne, long since recovered its old prosperity, and there is no evidence for any social or political disturbances at this flourishing moment in the Twelfth Dynasty. It follows that the pessimism of Khekhheperresonbu is of a quite general and literary quality, at the most an unconscious echo of that troubled period preceding the rise of the earlier Theban Empire which had first tinged Egyptian literature with melancholy.[84]

All of this is to say that Qohelet's description of a topsy-turvy world does not necessarily mean social volatility and anarchy. It does, however, mean that he is disturbed by the actions of the Ptolemies and/or their Jewish collaborators in their governing of his country. Qohelet's frustration does not appear to be based on this alone but rather on the fact that persons who seem to be undeserving, according to traditional understanding, are enjoying prosperity (cf. 7:15; 8:14). This clash between social reality and Jewish expectations seems

---

82. S. Luria, "Die Ersten werden die Letzen sein (Zur 'sozialen Revolution' im Altertum)," *Klio* n.F. 4 (1929): 1–27. For a discussion of the topsy-turvy motif in Proverbs, see Raymond C. Van Leeuwen, "Proverbs 30:21–23 and the Biblical World Upside Down," *JBL* 105 (1986): 599–610.

83. Gardiner, *Admonitions*, 110.

84. Ibid., 111.

to be the real problem underlying Qohelet's malaise. Thus, Weber's perspective rings true: economic and social interests intersect with ideas (Jewish values). In addition, there is the problem with the view assumed by this approach that literature passively reflects its social context. It might also react to it, attempting to mollify it, change it in some way. In today's parlance one would call that being "proactive" versus passive.

Finally, it should be noted that Qohelet's perplexity concerning the problem of evil reflects an ongoing Israelite tradition that also echoes a difficulty faced by all religious traditions. The book of Job also questions the doctrine of retribution, as we have mentioned, and it was probably written during the Persian period. Of course, problems with retributive theology were experienced on a national level by the Deuteronomistic Historian(s) and later even by the Chronicler. Thus, the problem of evil is a universal and perennial phenomenon that is not necessarily connected with social upheaval or anarchy. Social change can cause it to erupt, but it is not the sole cause of the problem. Again, there is no archaeological or literary evidence to suggest that the Ptolemaic period was any more socially unstable than the earlier Assyrian, Babylonian, or Persian periods.

SOCIAL-LOCATION APPROACH

The other purist approach is the social-location perspective. It is the opposite of the sociohistorical-crisis perspective, which focuses on the general milieu. Instead, the social-location approach considers the social status of the author or the audience and, in dealing with social class, often has a dialectic dimension that connects particular classes with particular ideologies and views the classes as being in conflict with each other, while one dominates the other. The premier example is Robert Gordis and his famous article "The Social Background of Wisdom Literature."[85] It is monumental because it represents the first substantial sociological interpretation of wisdom literature. He argues that the sages who wrote wisdom literature were part of the upper class or aristocracy and that this is the social basis for the skepticism found in Job and Qohelet.[86] Skepticism is feasible only for the well-to-do because it "is a state of mind possible only for those who observe and dislike evil, but are not its direct victims."[87] Contrary to other biblical traditions, the sages were not interested in countering the present state of the society, though it might be unpleas-

---

85. Gordis, "Social Background," 160–97.
86. Ibid., 173, 177–79. For treatments that identify Qohelet as upper class that are less sociological, see Bickerman, *Strange Books*, 160–65; R. N. Whybray, *The Intellectual Tradition in the Old Testament* (BZAW 135; Berlin: de Gruyter, 1974), 69.
87. Gordis, "Social Background," 177.

ant; nor did they escape these conditions via apocalyptic thought. Despite the injustice in society, the sages were supporters of the status quo and were unwilling to make changes. Thus, their skepticism derives from two factors: "an awareness of evil and an absence of compulsion to modify conditions."[88]

Gordis never cites any evidence for his sociology of skepticism; it is presented as a general rule and, as such, it rings true. Skepticism seems to emerge from the upper classes, which are more educated and, as leisured persons, have the advantage of time and opportunity to question traditional tenets. They can become, then, more astute observers of society and have the time to contemplate the meaning of life, whereas the poor and manual workers by necessity focus on more mundane and practical matters of survival!

However, Gordis's characterization would not apply to what sociologists call deviants or those who form a counter-culture, those who do not play by the rules of society. Modern examples include gangs and criminals, who seem never to have bought into the worldview of mainstream society. In fact, they define themselves in opposition to conventional norms and values. They usually come from the poorer social classes. In ancient Israel, examples might include a segment of the wicked and the foolish and witches (part of popular versus official religion). They are skeptical in the sense that they never really accepted mainstream theology and norms, whereas a skeptic like Qohelet has turned his back on these. Thus, skepticism in mainstream society would have an affinity with the upper classes, while beyond its borders skepticism is prevalent in marginal groups. Thus, skepticism, while having an affinity with certain classes and groups, is, technically, not class specific.

Crenshaw's famous article "The Birth of Skepticism in Ancient Israel" should be mentioned here.[89] He attempts to counter the argument that skepticism in ancient Israel arose among the elite, not the populace. He tries to show that skepticism was an integral part of Israelite faith from its early inception on and that it was always there in the background, because of the inherent clash between claims about God and the realities of human experience. He argues that skepticism was widespread, not confined to small circles.

However, the examples that Crenshaw gives (Psalms, Gideon, etc.) are only brief instances of doubt and do not really parallel what one finds in the sustained and consistent skepticism of Qohelet and Job. It should also be pointed out that Qohelet represents literary skepticism, which by its nature is an elite phenomenon, since only a small fraction of the population could read and write. Thus, very few in Jewish society would have had access to literary works. Generally, then, one can say that Gordis is correct about the social location of

---

88. Ibid., 178.
89. Crenshaw, "Birth of Skepticism," 1–19; cf. idem, "Popular Questioning of the Justice of God in Ancient Israel," *ZAW* 82 (1970): 380–95.

the skeptic, and it seems to fit Qohelet. But considering the above discussion of deviants and the reality that skepticism is not entirely class specific, Crenshaw also is partially correct.

But the significant question is whether Qohelet is a skeptic only because of his own particular social location as an elite individual or whether the circumstances of the Ptolemaic period also have a bearing on his disposition? In general, most elites do not succumb to skepticism. In fact, Gordis refers to a split among the wisdom sages, with Qohelet forming his own skeptical school over against other more conservative schools, both groups apparently members of the same upper class.[90]

Gordis connects the upper classes, who themselves suffered no direct oppression, with skepticism, and the lower classes, who did suffer oppression, with apocalypticism. This connection is highly significant because it shows how rival thought systems are related socially. The idea behind this is that the upper classes, though critical of the status quo, were comfortable enough to accept it as it was, while the lower classes were not, since they were the direct recipients of the oppression. Thus, they projected a utopian world in the future that would compensate for their present misery.

However, this needs to be nuanced. Stephen Cook has demonstrated that apocalyptic thinking or its modern equivalent, millennialism, is not always found among economically deprived or marginal groups.[91] In the Hebrew Bible, he finds the proto-apocalyptic groups consisting of privileged priests who had considerable power and certainly were not peripheral to their own society. His evidence and conclusions go against the dominant and mainstream interpretation of apocalyptic literature in the Hebrew Bible, including the notable John Collins and, of course, Paul Hanson. There is a caveat to this, however. The upper-class priests' apocalyptic thinking seems to be in reaction to their social status as a colonized people. Thus, Collins responds to Cook by redefining deprivation as relative: the priests or groups who produced the apocalyptic literature perceived themselves as deprived, though they were not economically deprived.[92] Thus, deprivation can carry more than one sense. One could say they were politically, not economically, deprived. Though Cook's attempts to demolish any connection between apocalypticism and deprivation is an overreaction, his thesis is significant in that it forces scholars to acknowledge that apocalyptic or utopian thinking is not limited exclusively

---

90. Gordis, *Koheleth*, 28, 77.

91. Stephen L. Cook, *Prophecy & Apocalypticism: The Postexilic Social Setting* (Minneapolis: Fortress, 1995), 211; cf. idem, *The Apocalyptic Literature* (IBT; Nashville: Abingdon, 2003), 19–38.

92. John J. Collins, *The Apocalyptic Imagination: An Introduction to Jewish Apocalyptic Literature* (2nd ed.; Biblical Resource Series; Grand Rapids: Eerdmans, 1998), 24 n. 69, 38.

to the lower class or the economically deprived, though it certainly has an affinity to these groups.[93] In essence, upper-class Judean priests who adopted apocalyptic thinking became an underclass in relation to their colonizers. Thus, Cook helps scholars nuance the thesis of deprivation, but it is still generally true that those with power and wealth in a society do not usually wish for a radical cataclysmic change in that society since they enjoy its privileges and benefits. Thus, it is still generally true that the closer persons are to power and privilege, the less likely they are to turn to utopian thinking.

Gordis is certainly on to something with his connection of skepticism with the upper classes. However, again, things are more complicated than that. An upper-class status is not a necessary and sufficient explanation for the rise of skepticism.

Another example of the social-location approach is Walter Brueggemann, who, in his famous *Prophetic Imagination*, makes several references to Qohelet.[94] Qohelet simply becomes one element in an arsenal for his main thesis that the prophets reacted against the Israelite monarchy because it had reestablished the oppressive regime that early Israel had fled when Moses led it out of Egypt. Brueggemann argues that the monarchy represents a return to Egypt and the assimilation of pagan and bureaucratic structures. He contrasts the dynamic covenantal relationship of the early Israelites under Moses, when they were sojourners and egalitarian, with the static, hierarchical, and eternal covenant relationship of the Davidic dynasty and its permanent placement at Zion. Brueggemann contrasts the religion of early Israel, which was mysterious, dynamic, and open to the transcendent, with that of the conformist and complacent Egyptian regime. The prophets, Brueggemann argues, represent a return to this openness in the midst of the stymieing and stultifying Israelite monarchy. They are counter-cultural and nonconformist. The prophets represent hope and a change of the status quo. The monarchy is connected with the status quo, wealth, greed, and boredom. These, Brueggemann argues, led to pessimism and the loss of hope. Though Qohelet was not alive during the days of the Israelite monarchy, Brueggemann sees him, especially in view of the Solomonic fiction early in the book, as simply a continuation of the same program. Thus, it is no surprise to find that Qohelet's worldview was pessimistic.

In another work, Brueggemann argues that the wisdom literature, whose origins are to be found with Solomon, is a prime example of upper-class conceptualizations and values that are intricately connected with the monarchy.

---

93. Similarly, Dominic Rudman, though largely positive in his critique, says, "Cook may perhaps be criticized for pushing the pendulum too far in the other direction" (review of Cook, *Prophecy & Apocalypticism*, *BibInt* 7 [1999]: 455).

94. Brueggemann, *Prophetic Imagination*, 41, 60–61.

The wisdom literature, according to Brueggemann, is simply the rationalization of life in service of the monarchy.[95] It represents the monarchy's ability to gain further control over life with new knowledge and understanding and was part of a movement that served to enhance the monarchy's bureaucratic control over Israel and the growth and increase of Israelite political power at the expense of its neighbors. Toward the end of the article, Brueggemann focuses on the social facets associated with the problem of theodicy. He argues that both Job and Qohelet represent attempts to solve this problem, but he points out that in all such attempts there have always been winners and losers. The upper class wins in this case: the wealth of the upper class is legitimized. This type of legitimization is similar to Weber's notion of what has been called anthropodicy or sociodicy, where the problem of disparity in the current wealth distribution is explained and rationalized so that the wealthy do not feel guilty in the enjoyment of a comfortable lifestyle.[96]

Again, like Gordis, Brueggemann is on to something when he connects Qohelet's pessimism and boredom to an upper-class location and to the royal tradition. However, as is the case with skepticism, pessimism may have an affinity with the upper classes, but it surely cannot be solely confined to this class. Connecting pessimism with a particular social class is not a necessary and sufficient explanation for the onset of pessimism in Qohelet. Things are more complicated than that.

However, locating Qohelet within the aristocracy or upper class is not totally without problems. There are several scholars who are hesitant to locate Qohelet within this group. Thomas Krüger avoids explicitly designating Qohelet's social status but seems not to see him as aristocratic, since he criticizes royal power.[97] While reluctant to peg Qohelet's own social location, Seow discerns it for Qohelet's audience: more middle class than upper.[98] Harrison also designates Qohelet's audience as a member of this class, but his analysis will be discussed in the next section. Similarly, Crenshaw, who represents the ideational approach, is also reluctant to identify Qohelet as privileged, only his students.[99]

Relating Qohelet or his audience to a middle class is significant in that it forces scholars to complicate the blunt designation of aristocrat. What does

---

95. Walter A. Brueggemann, "The Social Significance of Solomon as a Patron of Wisdom," in *The Sage in Israel and the Ancient Near East* (ed. John G. Gammie and Leo G. Perdue; Winona Lake, Ind.: Eisenbrauns, 1990), 117–32.

96. Weber, *The Sociology of Religion* (trans. Ephraim Fischoff; paperback ed.; Boston: Beacon, 1991), 107; see Swedberg, *Max Weber Dictionary*, 274, s.v. "Theodicy (*Theodizee*)."

97. E.g., Krüger, *Qoheleth*, 115.

98. Seow, *Ecclesiastes*, 27–28, 37.

99. Crenshaw, *Ecclesiastes*, 50.

it mean to be an aristocrat and were aristocrats all cut from the same cloth? How could an aristocrat critique the status quo? Basically, a more nuanced approach is needed.

At this point two problems with locating Qohelet in a middle class will be mentioned, but fuller analysis of Qohelet's social location will have to wait for a later chapter. First, I have argued that concern for the oppressed in Proverbs and its criticism of the status quo are not incompatible with aristocratic interests.[100] Second, I have also argued that to speak of a middle class in the days of ancient Israel is somewhat anachronistic.[101] There was no middle class in ancient Israel at least from a modern standpoint. A class able to sustain itself independent of the aristocracy first emerged only with the Industrial Revolution—what became known as the *bourgeoisie,* which itself quickly became as powerful as the old aristocracy. In the ancient world, where stratification was more pronounced, there were essentially only two significant classes: the upper and the lower, though this can be nuanced somewhat, as shall be seen.

HYBRID EXPLANATIONS

Leaving the purist approaches aside, it is now time to examine the more typical hybrid approaches that incorporate both an interest in the broader historical context of the book of Qoheleth and in the social location of its author and/or audience. These often also explore the relation between the social classes of the time of the book's composition. The point is to see how both social facets interact to produce the pessimism/skepticism of Qohelet. But, like the above, these explanations never integrate these facets into a comprehensive social theory or draw on the social sciences in any explicit way.

Similarly to Gordis, Martin Hengel describes Qohelet as having a conservative and aristocratic attitude.[102] In his interpretation, Qohelet exhibits a "cool detachment" from the injustices brought against the people and a lack of initiative to solve these problems.[103] He refers to this as Qohelet's "bourgeois ethic."[104] Hengel is also famous for his argument that Qohelet's skepticism reflects heavy influence from Hellenism, an approach to be discussed soon. Hengel explains Qohelet's lack of apocalypticism, which could have provided

---

100. Mark Sneed, "The Class Culture of Proverbs: Eliminating Stereotypes," *SJOT* 10 (1996): 296–308.

101. See Mark Sneed, "A Middle Class in Ancient Israel?" in *Concepts of Class in Ancient Israel* (ed. Mark Sneed; South Florida Studies in the History of Judaism: The Hebrew Scriptures and Their World 201; Atlanta: Scholars Press, 1999), 53–69.

102. Hengel, *Judaism and Hellenism,* 1:115–30.

103. Ibid., 1:117.

104. Ibid., 1:126, citing Kurt Galling, "Kohelet-Studien," *ZAW* 50 (1932): 292.

a solution to many of the injustices he describes by anticipating the impending consummation of God's kingdom, by observing that apocalypticism was an idea that was not available to Qohelet at the time. This is why his philosophy had to remain pessimistic. Finally, he also views Qohelet's aristocratic conservatism as the reason for his failure to reject the faith of his ancestors and completely transform the Hebrew deity into the Greek notion of Fate. This is interesting because inversely Gordis saw Qohelet's aristocratic conservatism as the impetus for his skepticism, not its inhibitor.

Similarly, Norbert Lohfink includes Qohelet in an upper class that was becoming increasingly hellenized.[105] He believes that Qohelet was the head of a school and had read Greek philosophical literature. In a recent work, Leo Perdue argues that the book's skepticism reflects exposure to Greek skepticism, but he also sees Qohelet as part of a rapid hellenization of an upper class that was open to new ideas and influences.[106] To Perdue's credit, archaeologists note that, in the Greek world, the upper class was generally more exposed to Hellenism than the lower.[107] Thus, Qohelet's class location would predispose him to Hellenistic influences not found among the masses.

However, as shall soon be seen, evidence that Qohelet's skepticism reflects the influence of Greek skepticism, whether popular or philosophical, is difficult to demonstrate. Not all of the upper class became so hellenized; some resisted this influence. The question of how hellenized Ptolemaic Judah became is hotly contested.

Anton Schoors has produced an extremely perceptive article on the sociohistorical background to Qohelet's skepticism and pessimism. He essentially argues that these characteristics of the book of Qohelet are ultimately due to the rapidly changing society in which he lived.[108] Looking at both the textual and archaeological evidence of the Ptolemaic period, Schoors speculates that the underlying social problem of the book and the source of its author's sense of absurdity is the rising status of Jewish Hellenists in contrast to the diminishing economic status of Torah adherents. He further defines this poor class: "the leading theocratic supporters of the Torah, who belonged mostly to the lower clergy and the Levites and whose conservative stand appeared in the works of the Chronist and Ben Sira."[109]

---

105. Lohfink, *Qoheleth*, 4–11.

106. Leo G. Perdue, *The Sword and the Stylus: An Introduction to Wisdom in the Age of Empires* (Grand Rapids: Eerdmans, 2008), 232–43.

107. Lee I. Levine, *Judaism and Hellenism in Antiquity: Conflict or Confluence?* (Seattle: University of Washington Press, 1998; repr., Peabody, Mass.: Hendrickson, 1999), 23–24.

108. Anton Schoors, "Qoheleth: A Book in a Changing Society," *OTE* 9 (1996): 68–87.

109. Ibid., 74.

However, Schoors never specifically locates the author of the book socially. Schoors is interested only in how Qohelet reacts to the social situation. He hints at Qohelet's detached character as an intellectual in these matters. Qohelet acutely observes the many injustices of his time. "However, he does not really criticize these abuses. In his reflections they are not a problem in their own right but they only illustrate the absurdity of human existence."[110]

Schoors can be commended for his allusion to Qohelet's status as an intellectual, the importance of which will be discussed later. He can be criticized, though, for considering the broad sociohistorical background to the book more than the author's own social position. Also, categorizing all the devout Torah adherents as lower class and all the upper class as Hellenists is a great exaggeration. Members of the upper class were sometimes resistant to Hellenism. Ben Sira and the Chronicler were not likely poor, and Ben Sira praises the powerful high priest of his day, Onias II, who was a devoted fan of the Torah (50:1–24).

To summarize, most scholars who discuss Qohelet's social location in a non-sociologically sophisticated way place him firmly in the upper class. A few are hesitant to make this claim. At this point, it will be said only that these two positions can be brought together in a nuanced way. These scholars all acknowledge some type of historical crisis that interacts with Qohelet's or his audience's social status, especially the oppressive cruelty of the Ptolemies and the social change associated with Hellenism. While this kind of approach is helpful to some extent, it does not go into enough detail and is not comprehensive enough to be as illuminating as it might be. For this approach, its lack of the use of the social sciences or social theory leaves the explanations rather deficient and sometimes superficial.

DIFFUSION EXPLANATIONS

A long-standing popular explanation of societal change found in anthropology is the theory of diffusion.[111] Diffusion is the notion that societal changes can best be explained by one culture's exposure to another. New ideas can then be explained as having spread from one locale to another. This explanation for change in religious ideas is in fact a very old one. Hecataeus states that when the Jews "became subject to foreign rule, as a result of their mingling with men of other nations (both under Persian rule and under that of the Macedo-

---

110. Ibid., 68.
111. For a comparison of diffusion and evolution theories in anthropology, see J. W. Rogerson, *Anthropology and the Old Testament* (1978; repr., Biblical Seminar; Sheffield: JSOT Press, 1984), 22–45.

nians who overthrew the Persians), many of their traditional practices were disturbed" (Diodorus Siculus, *Bibliotheca Historica* 40.3.8).

Throughout the years, by far the most popular non-ideational explanation for Qohelet's heterodoxy is that he was heavily influenced by outside sources, especially Greek thinking. Biblical scholars who have turned to this approach do not seem to be aware that it is an anthropological theory. For this reason it is included here as only a broad approach, though it technically is a type of social-science explanation. As recently as 2008, Leo Perdue adopted this explanation, "In his skeptical views of God, wisdom, and human existence, Qoheleth appears to have drawn on similar Greek and Egyptian traditions of wisdom, religious teachings, and philosophy vibrant during his time as a teacher. At least his book takes its place in a world in which skepticism was regnant in the cultural climate."[112]

Similarly, the 2009 commentary by Craig Bartholomew maintains that Qohelet's epistemology is inherently Greek, not ancient Near Eastern.[113] This explanation was a popular one with the early commentaries on Qohelet.[114] The classic work for this position is that by Rainer Braun who concludes that Qohelet was influenced by Greek popular philosophy.[115] Of course, Hengel is famous for taking this approach as well.[116] For a while, this position lost its dominance following Crenshaw's 1976 verdict: "Greek presence in Qoheleth no longer functions as the decisive key to understanding its contents."[117] But it has become popular again recently. In 2001 Dominic Rudman stated, "The question of whether Qoheleth shows traces of Greek thought refuses to go away."[118] In 2000, rejecting clear Mesopotamian or Egyptian influences, Karel van der Toorn concluded that Qohelet "owes an unmistakable debt to the spirit of Greek popular philosophy."[119] Even recent archaeologists such as Lee Levine

---

112. Perdue, *Sword and Stylus*, 200.

113. Bartholomew, *Ecclesiastes*, 54–59.

114. Cf. Harry Ranston, *Ecclesiastes and the Early Greek Wisdom Literature* (London: Epworth, 1925); Robert H. Pfeiffer, "The Peculiar Skepticism of Ecclesiastes," *JBL* 53 (1934): 100–109.

115. Rainer Braun, *Kohelet und die frühhellenistische Popularphilosophie* (BZAW 130; Berlin: de Gruyter, 1973), 167–68.

116. Hengel, *Judaism and Hellenism*, 1:115–28.

117. James L. Crenshaw, foreword to *Studies in Ancient Israelite Wisdom* (ed. James L. Crenshaw; Library of Biblical Studies; New York: Ktav, 1976), 8.

118. Rudman, *Determinism in Ecclesiastes*, 25. See my critique of his argument for the influence of stoic thinking on Qohelet (review of Dominic Rudman, *Determinism in the Book of Ecclesiastes*, *JBL* 121 [2002]: 549–51).

119. Karel van der Toorn, "Did Ecclesiastes Copy Gilgamesh?" *BRev* 16, no. 1 (February 2000): 30; cf. idem, "Echoes of Gilgamesh in the Book of Qohelet? A Reassessment of

are still resorting to this explanation for Qohelet's skepticism.[120] Peter Machinist of Harvard should be mentioned as well.[121] He argues that Qohelet's concept of fate reflects Greek influence and is actually of a higher level of rationality, what he calls "second order" thinking, than other uses of the concept in the Hebrew Bible. In Qohelet's usage, he reflects on the reasoning process itself, typical of the Greek philosophers but not of ancient Near Eastern intellectuals. Similarly, even Michael Fox seems to jump on the bandwagon here and describes Qohelet's epistemology as empirical. He notes, "Qoheleth's epistemology is, as far as I can tell, foreign to the ancient Near East, but is paralleled in his Hellenistic environment."[122] While he does not view Qohelet as having studied Greek philosophy or aligned himself with a particular school, he says, "He does, however, incorporate the fundamental tenet of Greek philosophy— the autonomy of individual reason, which is to say, the belief that individuals can and should proceed with their own observations and reasoning powers on a quest for knowledge and that this may lead to discovery of truths previously unknown."[123]

In response, the notion that change in thinking emerges with exposure to outside influences is certainly true. But if there is evidence for indigenous and internal change, the resorting to foreign influence as an explanation should take second place. As an example, it used to be thought that apocalypticism was

---

the Intellectual Sources of Qohelet," in *Veenhof Anniversary Volume: Studies Presented to Klaas R. Veenhof on the Occasion of His Sixty-fifth Birthday* (ed. W. H. van Soldt et al.; Uitgaven van het Nederlands Historisch-Archaeologisch Instituut te Istanbul 89; Leiden: Nederlands Instituut voor het Nabije Oosten, 2001), 513–14. See also Russell Peck, an English professor at the University of Rochester, who, in his World Literature class, uses Ecclesiastes as a "pivotal text between Hebraic and Hellenistic traditions" ("Ecclesiastes as a Pivotal Biblical and Literary Text," *Association of Departments of English Bulletin* 81 [1985]: 43). As mentioned already, Lohfink seems to suggest that Qohelet had actually studied Greek literature (*Qoheleth*, 6).

120. Levine, *Judaism and Hellenism*, 38.

121. Peter Machinist, "Fate, *miqreh*, and Reason: Some Reflections on Qohelet and Biblical Thought," in *Solving Riddles and Untying Knots: Biblical, Epigraphic, and Semitic Studies in Honor of Jonas C. Greenfield* (ed. Ziony Zevit, Seymour Gitin, and Michael Sokoloff; Winona Lake, Ind.: Eisenbrauns, 1995), 159–75. L. Schwienhorst-Schönberger also speaks of this type of reflexivity in Qohelet's treatment of the possibility of happiness for the individual but especially in reference to 7:15–18 ("Via media: Koh 7, 15–18 und die griechisch-hellenistische Philosophie," in *Qohelet in the Context of Wisdom* [ed. Anton Schoors; BETL 136; Leuven: Leuven University Press and Peeters, 1998], 182–83; 195–202).

122. Michael V. Fox, "Wisdom in Qoheleth," in *In Search of Wisdom* (ed. Leo G. Perdue, Bernard Brandon Scott, and William Johnston Wiseman; Louisville: Westminster John Knox, 1993), 122.

123. Ibid., 123.

explained by the outside influence of Zoroastrianism on Israelite society. Now, however, Stephen Cook has applied a more sophisticated social-science methodology to explain the emergence of this movement.[124] While acknowledging that there may have been some Persian influence, Cook depicts the emergence of the movement as primarily indigenous and shows how apocalypticism and millennialism are related and represent a cross-cultural phenomenon.[125] Similarly, numerous scholars have argued that Qohelet's skepticism and pessimism are more easily explained as Semitic in nature and not Hellenistic.[126] Charles Forman notes, "There is nothing in Ecclesiastes demanding a frame of reference beyond the bounds of Semitic thought . . . his pessimism springs from Semitic soil."[127] He further states:

> That Greek literature or philosophy is the source of Koheleth's striking departures from traditional thought is an *unwarranted* argument. Koheleth is more at home in Israelite thought than has been generally supposed. He is first of all a Hebrew— though not orthodox—and he shares the same frame of reference and point of departure as his compatriots and co-religionists. His unorthodox conclusions do *not* take him out of an *essentially* Hebrew context; they merely emphasize a *less apparent aspect* of the thought of the Old Testament.[128]

There is a body of ancient Near Eastern pessimistic and skeptical literature that appeared on the scene long before the Greeks. If Ronald Williams is correct, then the beginning of pessimistic literature actually goes back to the twenty-second century B.C.E. with "The Admonitions of Ipuwer."[129] The genre's popularity quickly spread throughout the ancient Near East. In ancient Egypt, during the Middle Kingdom (2040–1650 B.C.E.), several pessimistic and skeptical works were composed.[130] In addition to the three already mentioned, "The Instruction of King Amenemhet I" is pessimistic advice of a king to his son to watch his back. "The Prophecies of Nerferti" and "The Complaints of Khakheperre-Sonb" present dark, unjust, and chaotic worlds similar to Qohelet. One might compare the story of the "Eloquent Peasant," also from the same period, whose protagonist pessimistically complains of personal injustice done by an oppressor. During the New King-

---

124. Cook, *Apocalyptic Literature*, 31–38.

125. Ibid., 79–87.

126. One of the most articulate is Pedersen, "Scepticisme israélite," 338–44.

127. Forman, "Pessimism of Ecclesiastes," 336.

128. Ibid., 339.

129. Ronald J. Williams, "The Sage in Egyptian Literature," in *The Sage in Israel and the Ancient Near East* (ed. John G. Gammie and Leo G. Perdue; Winona Lake, Ind.: Eisenbrauns, 1990), 20.

130. These dates of the Egyptian works are from *AEL*, vols. 1–2.

dom (1550–1080 B.C.E.) a work emerged entitled "The Instruction of Any," in which a young scribe is skeptical of the value of his father's (Any) teaching for his own generation.

In addition, from Mesopotamia comes "The Gilgamesh Epic" (beginning of the second millennium B.C.E.), which treats the theme of the vanity of human effort in view of death. In the "Dialogue of Pessimism" (early first millennium B.C.E.), one finds a satirical portrait of a master and a slave who debate the meaning of life and resign themselves to the fact that it is beyond human reach. "The Babylonian Theodicy" (1000 B.C.E.), also known as the "Babylonian Ecclesiastes," involves a dialogue between a pious sage and a skeptical sufferer concerning the problem of evil that ends in a compromise. Further, one might compare this with "The Sumerian Job" (2000 B.C.E.) and "I Will Praise the Lord of Wisdom," (Cassite Period: 1530–1160 B.C.E.), also known as "The Babylonian Job," in which a righteous sufferer expresses horror at his plight and pleads with his deity to intervene until he does. In "The Counsels of Pessimism" (1700–1650 B.C.E.), the protagonist declares that all is vanity but counsels fulfilling certain obligations and enjoying life. In addition, recently Bendt Alster has published a chapter on Sumerian wisdom literature devoted to the theme of vanity: "Nothing Is of Value" (*niŋ-nam nu-kal*), "The Ballade of Early Rulers," "Proverbs from Ugarit," "Enlil and Namzitarra," and "The Underworld Vision of 'Gilgameš, Enkidu, and the Netherworld.'"[131]

In characterizing ancient Near Eastern pessimistic literature, William H. U. Anderson states,

> What all these works have in common is a sense of frustration with the way God and life in the world are; there is a sense of futility in life in the pursuit of materialism, pleasure and life after death. . . . Finally, the overall mood, tone and ethos of the books put them in the genre category of pessimistic literature because ultimately they remain indifferent to cherished traditional beliefs and emotionally disturbed by these axioms of life which give life only a negative value.[132]

As Crenshaw puts it, there is "a sense of being overwhelmed by an oppressive reality."[133] This listing of Semitic instances of skepticism and pessimism is not intended to suggest that Qohelet had personally read all of these works or that the tone of his book comes directly from them. Rather, it is to indicate that the genre is ancient and Semitic and that it would have been familiar to Jewish intellectuals of Qohelet's day. Qohelet merely represents a Jewish variation of it.

---

131. Bendt Alster, *Wisdom of Ancient Sumer* (Bethesda, Md.: CDL, 2005), 265–341.
132. Anderson, "Genre Analysis of Qoheleth," 300.
133. Crenshaw, "Birth of Skepticism," 2.

Harrison makes an important distinction for this discussion: being influenced by Greek ideas versus responding to social changes brought on by the Greeks. After examining the archaeological record and material culture of Ptolemaic Judah, he concludes, "Although Qohelet's work itself betrays little if any overt Hellenistic influence, the rapid progress of Hellenistic culture all around Judea would have been difficult to ignore in the third century BCE." He adds, "It seems increasingly clear that Qoheleth and his students were just at the cusp of important cultural changes." [134] He seems to be arguing that Qohelet's pessimism emerges from the social changes that Hellenism brought to Judah and not from Greek literary sources. Social changes would not necessarily show up in the archaeological evidence. A fuller treatment of the archaeological and literary evidence for the degree of hellenization in Ptolemaic Judah will be discussed later.

The fact is that there is no definite evidence that Qohelet has drunk deeply from the well of Hellenism. In 1995, Carol Newsom aptly referred to "the controversial and unproven assumption that there was in fact strong Hellenistic cultural influence on Ecclesiastes." Some of Qohelet's terminology and concepts might betray Greek influence, but his skepticism and pessimism certainly do not. Rather, they reflect a long-standing oriental, not occidental, tradition. Jonathan Barnes, an expert on Greek philosophical skepticism, closely analyzes Qohelet and concludes that his thinking is not skeptical in the Greek sense of the term and "owes nothing to Greek philosophy." [135] Some have attempted to water this argument down to a softer form: Qohelet has been influenced by the spirit of Hellenism. [136] But, as Newsom states, "Unfortunately, we know very little about the extent to which Hellenistic popular philosophy and culture was available in the mid-third century BCE." [137]

Crenshaw has also persuasively argued that Fox's characterization of Qohelet's epistemology as empirical is inaccurate. [138] Many of Qohelet's sentiments are not verifiable by observation. For example, he asks

---

134. C. Robert Harrison, "Qoheleth among the Sociologists," *BibInt* 5 (1997): 165.

135. Jonathan Barnes, "L'Ecclésiaste et le scepticisme grec," *RTP* 131 (1999): 103–14; cf. William H. U. Anderson, "What Is Scepticism and Can It Be Found in the Hebrew Bible?" *SJOT* 13 (1999): 225–57.

136. Hengel, *Judaism and Hellenism*, 1:116; van der Toorn, "Did Ecclesiastes Copy?" 30; Bartholomew, *Ecclesiastes*, 58.

137. Carol A. Newsom, "Job and Ecclesiastes," in *Old Testament Interpretation: Past, Present, and Future* (ed. James L. Mays, David L. Petersen, and Kent H. Richards; Nashville: Abingdon, 1995), 185.

138. James L. Crenshaw, "Qoheleth's Understanding of Intellectual Inquiry," in *Qohelet in the Context of Wisdom* (ed. Anton Schoors; BETL 136; Leuven: Leuven University Press and Peeters, 1998), 212–13.

What empirical facts conveyed the following insights: that God has appointed a time for judgment, dislikes fools, will punish rash vows, created the world good/appropriate, dwells in heaven, creates the embryo within the mother's womb, chases the past, tests people in order to make them fear, gives human beings unpleasant business, keeps them preoccupied with joy, made men and women upright, has already approved one's actions, and rewards those who fear/worship the deity.[139]

Also, contrary to Machinist, second-order thinking existed among the ancient Mesopotamians long before the Greeks.[140] Martin Rose has argued convincingly that the wisdom literature of the ancient Sumerians, the Jews, and the Greek philosophers involves the same empirically based form of reasoning: observation, reflection, and then judgment.[141] He argues that Qohelet does not represent a crisis of wisdom literature but rather wisdom literature especially adapted to a crisis situation. He demonstrates that Qohelet's rational methodology is identical to that found among the Sumerians, the Greek philosophers, and Proverbs. His pessimistic theology is explained as due to the negative circumstances of the Jews after the exile involving continued subjugation to foreign powers and not to a change in methodological thinking.

In conclusion, in view of the lack of definite evidence that Qohelet's skepticism and pessimism show Hellenistic influence, it is best to appeal to Ockham's razor and find these traits compatible with the Semitic conceptuality and traditions. Again, this does not mean that Qohelet had read the Gilgamesh Epic or other works, but simply that his pessimism about human striving was part of the stock and trade of the ancient Near Eastern Semitic intellectual world, as had been his skepticism about traditional teachings.

But being satisfied with simply demonstrating that Qohelet's thinking certainly fits Semitic mentality and conceptions and, thus, represents internal development rather than outside influence is not enough. As shall be seen, connecting the *social changes* brought on by the Ptolemaic regime and their hegemony over Judah with Israelite and Jewish *conceptuality and ideation* promises brighter prospects for explaining Qohelet's pessimism and skepticism, and places one firmly within a Weberian perspective.

Before finishing this section, a brief look at two approaches that technically represent the diffusion approach but go in the opposite direction is necessary. Instead of seeing Qohelet as influenced by Hellenism, these approaches see him as reacting against it. Lee I. Levine proposes that Hellenistic influence

---

139. Ibid., 213.
140. Giorgio Buccellati, "Wisdom and Not: The Case of Mesopotamia," *JAOS* 101 (1981): 44.
141. Rose, "'Sagesse de la crise,'" 115–34.

should be defined to include also resistance to it.[142] This is probably because in resisting something, one's exposure to it will have some kind of effect and create changes. If so, then Stephan de Jong needs to be included when he argues that Qohelet is largely reacting to Hellenistic cultural values.[143] De Jong agues that Qohelet attempts, in his book, to counter the ambitious spirit of Hellenistic culture that had been embraced by Jewish aristocrats. Qohelet's condemnation of human striving, de Jong argues, is ultimately cast against the Hellenistic culture and its striving for dominance and superiority. He views the depiction of Solomon early in the book as actually a cipher for the folly of the Hellenistic kings. In this ambitious atmosphere, Qohelet warns young Jewish aristocrats that money will not automatically bring happiness. De Jong is careful to point out that Qohelet does not reject the Hellenistic world in toto, but rather he prepares his students to navigate it more effectively and to become successful in their careers.

As part of the scholarly examination of this period, de Jong's analysis is extremely important because it puts a new twist on the issue of Hellenistic influence on Qohelet. In a counterintuitive move, de Jong shows that, instead of Qohelet passively assimilating Hellenistic culture, in fact he represents largely a resistance to it, especially its values. In other words, de Jong shows how Qohelet can be considered a form of resistance literature, which is an important concept in postcolonial approaches, which shall be discussed later.

A serious flaw in de Jong's analysis, however, is his essential reduction of all of Qohelet's critique to resistance to hellenization. While one can certainly see aspects of the book that might be polemical toward Hellenistic culture, it is more natural to view Qohelet as primarily critiquing aspects of his own Jewish culture. In fact, this has been the dominant assumption of Qohelet interpretation throughout the ages. Qohelet has been viewed as a polemic against traditional Israelite wisdom. As von Rad noted famously years ago, "Ecclesiastes is a polemical book."[144] Of course, many of the values of Hellenistic culture overlapped with Jewish ones. Competition, the striving for wealth, the value of wisdom, and so on, are indications of this. Thus, the criticism of these values could go in both directions. But, essentially, de Jong reduces the book to Hellenistic categories. There is no clear indication that Hellenism is Qohelet's main target. While the dangers of materialism, which he sees as a largely Hellenistic vice, is a topic in Qohelet (e.g., 5:10–17), it certainly is a minor one and not the focus of the book as a whole.

---

142. Levine, *Judaism and Hellenism*, 27.
143. Stephan de Jong, "Qohelet and the Ambitious Spirit of the Ptolemaic Period," *JSOT* 61 (1994): 85–96.
144. Von Rad, *Old Testament Theology* 1:457.

R. N. Whybray makes a similar argument.[145] He describes Qohelet as an apologist who attempts to rescue the Jewish faith from demise because it had become problematic. He describes the Ptolemaic period as one of disorientation due to exposer to an alien culture and a sense of powerlessness connected with the oppressive Ptolemaic presence, which was unlike that of the Persians.[146] Whybray sees Qohelet writing his book as a theologian to young students in order to enable them to endure this crisis and to ride it out, while preserving their faith. Whybray attempts to show that, while Qohelet might be to some degree unorthodox, his thinking operates within the parameters of the Hebrew Bible tradition. In Qohelet's declaration of general injustice in the land, Whybray asserts that Qohelet blames humans for this (7:29). He then states, "Qoheleth never blames God for this state of affairs, and there can be no doubt of his indignation at human wickedness."[147] But then he later qualifies this indignation when he says that Qohelet "was far from being a social reformer, still less a denunciatory prophet. He was above all an observer and a commentator on the way of the world, though not a cynical one."[148] He consistently refuses to view Qohelet's conception of God as impersonal and indifferent to human conditions, and based on the motif of fear of God motif and 8:12–13, he concludes that Qohelet held a "confidence, albeit a puzzled one, in God's good intentions towards the human race."[149]

Ultimately, one can see Whybray himself as the apologist who attempts to rescue Qohelet from the numerous scholarly claims that he was radical and heterodox. His assessment that Qohelet was an apologist of sorts and a theologian who attempted to reconfigure the Jewish faith in changing times is largely true. But Whybray puts a too-positive spin on the book, which means that he simply explains away the darker elements. His view that Qohelet's conception of God is positive and personable and that he has good intentions for humanity will not stand, if one looks honestly at what Qohelet says about the deity. It is probably for this reason that the colloquium that discussed his manuscript was reluctant to embrace Whybray's thesis entirely.[150]

---

145. R. N. Whybray, "Qoheleth as a Theologian," in *Qohelet in the Context of Wisdom* (ed. Anton Schoors; BETL 136; Leuven: Leuven University Press and Peeters, 1998), 239–65.

146. Ibid., 243–44, citing Martin Hengel, *Judentum und Hellenismus: Studien zu ihrer Begegnung unter besonderer Berücksichtigung Palästinas bis zur Mitte des 2. Jh. v. Chr.* (WUNT 10; Tübingen: J. C. B. Mohr, 1969), 210–237 and Bernhard Lang, *Ist der Mensch hilflos? Zum Buch Kohelet* (Theologische Meditationen 53; Zurich: Benziger, 1979), 66–67.

147. Whybray, "Qoheleth as a Theologian," 252.

148. Ibid., 259.

149. Ibid., 252.

150. Anton Schoors, introduction to *Qohelet in the Context of Wisdom* (ed. Anton Schoors; BETL 136; Leuven: Leuven University Press and Peeters, 1998), 7–8.

Qohelet has many things to say about the deity that are not entirely positive. For example, in 1:13 he describes God's allotment of human activity as "an unhappy business." Qohelet says that the inevitability of death is God's way of showing humans that they are no better than animals (3:18). While Qohelet sometimes blames humanity for injustices, he also blames God for misfortune (7:14). In 4:1, Qohelet refers to the oppressed and their lack of power with no one to comfort them. Qohelet was certainly not happy with everything that God did, though he resigned himself to it.

EVOLUTIONARY EXPLANATIONS

In anthropology, evolutionary explanations for changes in culture are the very reverse and antithesis of the diffusion theory. This is the view that changes in society can best be explained as due not to foreign exposure but to a natural process that can be found in other cultures on the same stage of evolutionary development. The true father of this approach to Qohelet is certainly Johannes Pedersen. In a 1930 article, he describes Qohelet as belonging to a very late stage of development in Israel and states, "Pessimism and skepticism belong to advanced periods of the life of a people."[151] Similarly, in 1912 Henry Breasted said this about the skepticism of the Middle Kingdom in Egypt:

> Scepticism means a long experience with inherited beliefs, much rumination on what has heretofore received unthinking acquiescence, a conscious recognition of personal power to believe or disbelieve, and thus a distinct step forward in the development of self-consciousness and personal initiative. It is only a people of ripe civilization who develop skepticism. It is never found under primitive conditions. It was a momentous thousand years of intellectual progress, therefore, of which these skeptics of the Feudal Age represented the culmination.[152]

Forman also accepts this position, citing both Pedersen and Breasted.[153]

But its most classic expression is found in Schmid's treatment of Qohelet in his famous *Wesen und Geschichte der Weisheit*. While Schmid invests great effort in demonstrating that Egyptian wisdom was shaped, changed, and, thus, essentially determined by its historical, social, and intellectual context, this methodology is strangely absent from his examination of Qohelet.[154] Instead, Schmid places Qohelet within his evolutionary theory of the development of

---

151. Pedersen, "Scepticisme israélite," 331.
152. James Henry Breasted, *Development of Religion and Thought in Ancient Egypt* (1912; repr., paperback ed.; Philadelphia: University of Pennsylvania, 1972), 181.
153. Forman, "Pessimism of Ecclesiastes," 342–43.
154. Schmid, *Geschichte der Weisheit*, 36–84. See especially his treatments of the First Intermediate Period and the Middle Kingdom, where pessimistic and skeptical motifs

wisdom.[155] This theory, summarized, is that wisdom, whether Egyptian, Mesopotamian, or Israelite, goes through three stages of development. There is the beginning stage, when wisdom is flexible and conforms to reality. Then wisdom becomes dogmatized and inflexible. The third stage involves a "crisis" wherein wisdom attempts to deal with the dogmatized stage. Qohelet represents this last crisis stage, and his skepticism springs from his reaction to a dogmatized, systematized wisdom. The pessimistic approach of Qohelet, Schmid concludes, stems from his detached, unhistorical relation to the world event. In other words, before the world, Qohelet is an "observer standing outside."[156]

Schmid's schema of increasing dogmatism and resistance is too Hegelian and idealistic. It is as if the process of dogmatization is inherent in the ideas themselves and humans are largely irrelevant to the process. As said in connection with Van Leeuwen, wisdom and its retributive theology are technically dogmatic from their inception. There is no evidence of an increasing dogmatization within the tradition itself. Resistance to wisdom orthodoxy is due to changes in the original social conditions that eventually undermine it. Further, Schmid does not pay enough attention to social factors, especially Qohelet's own social location or the location of the Israelite wisdom writers in general. As shall be seen, an evolutionary perspective can be better approached from Weber's notion of rationalization. In addition, Schmid artificially detaches the Israelite wisdom tradition from the others (prophetic, historical, etc.) and from the history of the Israelite faith.

Finally, Crenshaw deserves mention here. He attempts to counter the evolutionary approach to skepticism by attacking the idea that skepticism emerges only late in the development of societies.[157] He argues that certain Hebrew dogmas contained within themselves the seeds for skepticism and that skepticism is, thus, a natural development within the history of Israelite religious thinking.

However, in the history of Israelite religion, Job and Qohelet do in fact represent late developments. As mentioned earlier, Crenshaw's examples of early skepticisms are only spurts of doubt and do not involve the sustained and developed skepticism of Qohelet. While Crenshaw is correct that skepticism is always a possibility when any new conception or notion is advanced in

---

appear (pp. 40–68). This is often portrayed as a period of social and political chaos, and Schmid attempts to demonstrate how the Egyptian wisdom of the period reflects this.

155. Schmid, *Geschichte der Weisheit*, 186–95. J. A. Loader assumes Schmid's thesis and applies it to Qohelet but also does not bring any sociohistorical dimension to the discussion (*Polar Structures*, 124–31).

156. Schmid, *Geschichte der Weisheit*, 189, citing Lauha, "Krise des religiösen Glaubens," 188; cf. Gese, "Krisis der Weisheit," 141–51.

157. Crenshaw, "Birth of Skepticism," 1–19.

a society, that the seeds of skepticism are inherently sown into any new idea that becomes popular, once that thinking wins sway in a particular society, sustained skepticism is often held at bay for long periods of time. For example, Christianity, once established as the official religion, was able to prevent any serious and sustained skepticism for over a millennium, until the Renaissance. Crenshaw, thus, fails to account for the fact that, once religious dogmas are conceived and held, their tenacity is considerable. Van Leeuwen also fails on this count.

But, in the end, although the evolutionary approach has much promise, it needs to include social factors that help to explain the development of retributive theology and Qohelet's reaction to it. In addition, it needs a "big picture" approach that relates the doctrine to other central tenets of Israelite faith and its historical development. In other words, this approach, though anthropological, can have a docetic and idealistic character that needs to take on flesh and blood. This is where Weber has much to contribute, as shall be seen.

Psychological Explanations

In conclusion and before examining a variety of social-science approaches, we look at psychological explanations. Though one could categorize psychology as a social science, because it focuses primarily on the individual, psychological approaches will be treated here instead of in the next chapter. There have been a few psychological approaches to explain the aberrant character of Qohelet.

Frank Zimmerman explains the often noted contradictory nature of the book as the product of Qohelet's self-doubt and obsessive-compulsive disorder.[158] In another work, Zimmerman psychoanalyzes the poem about old age in ch. 12 and concludes this about Qohelet, "It was the sense of inadequacy, of incompetence, and finally of failure to measure up sexually, that gave rise to his pessimism and cynicism."[159] Aarre Lauha also must be included in this approach. He attempts to illuminate the nature of Qohelet's skepticism by a comparison with Job.[160] Both authors deny the validity of the doctrine of retribution, and this questioning of it has become possible because of their "observance of the facts and experienced disappointments."[161] But the difference between them is that Qohelet essentially loses his religious faith and makes this problem into a philosophical issue. While Lauha admits that the histori-

---

158. Frank Zimmermann, *The Inner World of Qoheleth: With Translation and Commentary* (New York: Ktav, 1973), 5–8, 12–13.
159. Frank Zimmermann, "The Book of Ecclesiastes in the Light of Some Psychoanalytic Observations," *American Imago* 5 (1948): 305.
160. Lauha, "Krise des religiösen Glaubens," 183–91.
161. Ibid., 184.

cal situation and Hellenistic influence may partially explain the differences between Qohelet and Job, ultimately it is due to a difference in personality types. Lauha uses evaluative descriptions when referring to this: Qohelet gives up and does not fight as Job did. It is very apparent that Lauha champions the position of Job against Qohelet.

The supreme example of psychological approaches is provided by Bernhard Lang. Basically, Lang believes that Qohelet is deeply depressed, and this is expressed in the melancholic mood of the book.[162] This is key to his and many other social-science approaches: Qohelet's worldview is described negatively as pathological and maladaptive, which, of course, means that Qohelet can be easily dismissed theologically. Lang and others will essentially dismiss Qohelet's message as bourgeois and, thus, as unworthy of consideration.

Lang looks to the "newer" psychology to diagnose Qohelet. The depressed are described as feeling helpless and becoming passive, retreating into their homes. Perhaps they have lost their jobs and have basically given up the fight of life. They view the world as hostile and threatening. But Lang stresses that these are maladaptive strategies, whereas the balanced person never gives up being active and fighting the battle.

Lang also draws on the psychological theory of Günter Hole, who points out how depressed persons often lose a relationship with God.[163] Intellectually, they still believe in God, but they have no real personal relationship with him. Lang also refers to the psychologist H. Tellenbach, who sees Ecclesiastes, along with Goethe's Werther and Kierkegaard, as examples of a melancholic person who, in his isolation, no longer encounters God.[164] Lang also interprets Qohelet's carpe diem ethic as an addictive, hedonistic compensation for his frustration.[165] It is like a narcotic addiction: "The feasts are his aspirin."

Finally, Bartholomew has used Jungian theory to interpret Qohelet's conflicted nature.[166] He argues that the dialectic in the book is the result of Qohelet's progressive struggle between his ego and his Self. His early struggle involves his immature focus on his ego, but he eventually submits at the end of the book to the Self, who in Jungian theory is associated with God. Bartholomew also connects Qohelet's conflicted character with a midlife crisis,

162. Bernhard Lang, "Ist der Mensch hilflos? Das biblische Buch Kohelet, neu und kritisch gelesen," TQ 159 (1979): 119–20.

163. Lang, "Ist der Mensch hilflos?" 120, citing Günter Hole, Der Glaube bei Depressiven (Stuttgart: Enke, 1977).

164. Lang, "Ist der Mensch hilflos?" 120 n. 21, citing H. Tellenbach, "Gestalten der Melancholie," Jahrbook für Psychologie, Psychotherapie und medizinische Anthropologie 7 (1960): 9–26.

165. Lang, "Ist der Mensch hilflos?" 120.

166. Bartholomew, Ecclesiastes, 377–82.

a common popular-level interpretation of the book, often found on Internet sites.

An important distinction needs to be made between melancholy/depression and literary pessimism. Literary pessimism certainly draws on these dark moods but uses them for rhetorical effect, as shall be seen in the case of Qohelet. But even if Qohelet is depressed to a degree, this approach fails to explain how the book found support beyond Qohelet as an individual. In other words, that the book was preserved and eventually canonized means that Qohelet's dark world was significant and meaningful for a group of persons, perhaps a large number, not just an individual. Now if the psychological approach can be projected from the individual onto larger groups and communities, then it has possibilities. Of course, there is a whole subfield of psychology, social psychology, that does exactly this kind of thing. This, in fact, is what Lang does when he simultaneously embraces a Marxist interpretation. He projects the psychology of the depressed individual onto the Jewish aristocrats of Ptolemaic Judah. The next chapter will analyze other social-science approaches that attempt to explain Qohelet's malaise and heterodoxy and go beyond investigating his psyche alone.

2

EXPLAINING QOHELET'S HETERODOX CHARACTER:
SOCIAL-SCIENCE APPROACHES

MARXIAN APPROACHES

The following are more sophisticated analyses of Qohelet's heterodox character that incorporate social theory and insights from the social sciences into the interpretation. Marxist approaches will be discussed first. As will be seen, almost all biblical scholars who have taken a Marxist approach to Qohelet are rather "vulgar," seeing his worldview as merely a direct reflection of his social position, the superstructure merely mirroring the infrastructure.

Marxist theorists usually look to a person's social class as the most significant influence on his/her thinking and belief structure. Thus, one's social class, in conjunction with the general social milieu, is key to Marxist analyses. Though Marxist assumptions have come under heavy criticism for their vulgarity, Marxist biblical analyses, in general, are often quite sophisticated and show attention to detail that many bourgeois (non-Marxist) interpretations lack.[1]

Picking up Lang again, he incorporates both a psychology of pessimism and a sociology of skepticism into his Marxist analysis. In his discussion of Qohelet's skepticism, Lang presents a sociology of skepticism from the philosopher and social scientist Max Horkheimer, a Neo-Marxist of the famous Frankfurt School. This is Lang's summation of Horkheimer's "Montaigne and the Function of Skepticism":

> The skeptic is, as a rule, a member of the higher bourgeoisie or aristocracy. He knows no financial cares and can educate himself broadly. Into the most diverse spheres of life, he has insight. He is very sensitive to the suffering of man, to the uncertainty of all things—but misfortune does not personally touch him. He belongs to the *happy few*, retreats to his possessions, deplores the circumstances of the world and attempts, if all goes well, to lead a comfortable life in a corner.

---

1. For an exemplary anthology of Marxist biblical interpreters who also integrate feminist concerns, see Roland Boer and Jorunn Økland, eds., *Marxist Feminist Criticism of the Bible* (Bible in the Modern World 14; Sheffield: Sheffield Phoenix, 2008).

He does not engage in politics because this is only trouble for him or even could drag him into misfortune.[2] (my translation)

Lang's summation, however, is not an entirely accurate reflection of Hork-heimer's portrayal of the French renaissance skeptic Montaigne.[3] Montaigne actually did participate in politics. He was mayor of Bordeaux and very politi-cally astute. He was Catholic but was able to work with the Protestants to pro-mote peace. It is true that he did retreat into his library and did not travel abroad, but Montaigne was a very political being. As shall be seen, Qohelet was also a political being, and his profession as a scribal scholar and teacher had very real political effects.

A few words are in order about Horkheimer and his article on Montaigne. As already mentioned, Horkheimer was Neo- or Post-Marxist. He estab-lished the Frankfurt School, which attempted to merge philosophy with social science.[4] It tried to correct the weaknesses in Marxism by adopting and adapt-ing bourgeois ideas coming from the likes of Nietzsche and Weber.

Horkheimer shows how the skepticism that emerged in the Greek period and the Renaissance had similar origins.[5] Greek philosophical skepticism emerged in the midst of the deterioration of the polis and the emergence of the Hellenistic kingdoms after Alexander the Great, a shift from democracy to monarchy.[6] There was much social turmoil that Horkheimer argues con-tributed to the questioning of the tried and true Greek way of life. Similarly, skepticism during the Renaissance emerged in the transition from the dete-rioration of the aristocracy and the emergence of the powerful bourgeoisie, and in Montaigne's milieu absolutism had developed. In the midst of such social flux, skeptics questioned the certainty and validity of many traditional notions. They preferred to hesitate, delaying making any definitive conclusions about reality and refusing to believe in anything dogmatically. They are char-acterized as being very tolerant.

Horkheimer is certainly critical of aspects of Montaigne's skepticism and places it within the social matrices of the bourgeoisie.[7] He points out that

---

2. Lang, "Ist der Mensch hilflos?" 118.

3. See Max Horkheimer's discussion of Montaigne ("Montaigne and the Function of Skepticism," in *Between Philosophy and Social Science: Selected Early Writings* [trans. G. Frederick Hunter, Matthew S. Kramer, and John Torpey; Cambridge, Mass.: MIT Press, 1993], 265–311, esp. 266–77; repr. from *Zeitschrift für Sozialforschung* 7 [1938]).

4. For a discussion of the Frankfurt School and Weber's relationship to it, see B. Turner, *For Weber*, 61–105.

5. Horkheimer, "Function of Skepticism," 265–311, esp. 266–77.

6. Ibid., 265–66, citing Jacob Burckhardt, *Griechische Kulturgeschichte*, vol. 4 (vol. 8 of idem, *Gesammelte Werke* (Basel: Schwabe, 1978), 492–93.

7. See Horkheimer, "Function of Skepticism," 269–82.

Montaigne was aware of oppression and suffering but refused to do anything about it for fear of disturbing the peace and stability of the society. However, Horkheimer also praises Montaigne's liberal humanism and his questioning of traditional notions.[8] In the article, what Horkheimer is really trying to do is contrast Montaigne's renaissance skepticism with another brand emerging during the development of fascism in Germany.[9] While he is sympathetic to Montaigne's lack of resistance in his historical context, he is less understanding of the liberal skeptics of the twentieth century who were turning their backs on the rise of fascism in the name of tolerance.

Lang's characterization of the skeptics as spineless opportunists is not entirely accurate. His negative assessment of Qohelet's skepticism is apparent. He views Qohelet as a rich aristocrat who refused to help the poor and oppressed of his time for fear of damaging his own comfortable life situation. As evidence of Qohelet's aristocratic status, Lang notes how Qohelet ignorantly believes that the hungry poor sleep well (5:11).

Lang's introduction of Horkheimer's sociology of skepticism is very significant for this discussion because such sociologies are hard to come by. The quality of Horkheimer's argumentation is extremely high. Lang's connecting Montaigne with Qohelet is important. Interestingly, Lang points out that Montaigne was a fan of Qohelet and even inscribed citations of the biblical book on the walls of his library![10]

Lang integrates his sociology of skepticism and psychology of helplessness into a brief sociohistorical analysis of Ptolemaic Judah. He points out that the sources for this period are scarce, but they reveal deplorable positions for the Jewish aristocracy of the period. Basically, the Jewish elite became depoliticized by the Ptolemies, who ruled with an iron hand and economically drained the province that included Judah. Decision making was out of Jewish hands, and therefore the Jewish elite felt powerless. While they may have had economic opportunities during this time, the sources point to non-Jewish players who profited the most. The sense of powerlessness reflected in Qohelet mirrors this political and economic situation in Ptolemaic Judah.

While seeing many positive aspects to Qohelet's teaching, Lang ultimately rejects the book as a viable theological option. He points out that critical theory (developed by Horkheimer and the Frankfurt School) assesses skepticism as an essentially cowardly position that does not contribute to societal changes

---

8. See ibid., 292–93.

9. See ibid., 292–311.

10. Lang, "Ist der Mensch hilflos?" 119 n. 17, citing M. Gauna, "Les épicuriens bibliques de la Renaissance," in *Association Guillaume Budé, Actes du VIIIᵉ Congrès (Paris 1968)* (Paris: Société d'édition "Les Belles Lettres," 1969), 685–95.

but reaffirms the status quo.[11] Lang quotes Theodor Adorno, who collaborated with Horkheimer, who discusses Qohelet's "everything is vanity" motif:

> The "everything is vanity," according to which, since the time of Solomon, the great theologians judged immanence, is too abstract for transcending immanence. Where humans are assured of the indifference of their existence, they raise no protest; as long as they do not change their opinion about existence, the other is also vanity. Whoever accuses existence, indiscriminately and without perspective, with the possibility of nothingness lends his support for an apathetic business. The sermon about the vanity of immanence secretly liquidates also transcendence, which is solely fed by the experiences of immanence. . . . Only if "what is" can be changed, is the "what is" not everything.[12] (my translation)

Lang is to be commended for an extremely perceptive and penetrating analysis. His integration of the sociology of skepticism, psychology of helplessness, critical theory, and a sociohistorical analysis of Ptolemaic Judah is exemplary. However, there are a number of problems. First, there is no evidence that the Jewish aristocracy was depoliticized by the Ptolemies any more than by the Persians. The Jews had neither king nor independence under the Persians. The subjugation under the Ptolemies did not change this. But economically, the Jewish aristocracy, especially the upper-level priests, were able to flourish during this period. As a matter of fact, the Ptolemies relied on the indigenous aristocracy for their tax-farming system. More will be said about this later. However, that the continuing subjugation of the Jews by foreign powers would, no doubt, have had a cumulative deleterious effect on their psyche is, of course, a reasonable supposition. Certainly, they continued to feel powerless under the iron grip of the Ptolemies.

Second, simply describing Qohelet as a rich aristocrat is not sufficiently nuanced. As will be shown, he was also an intellectual, who creatively attempted to solve the problem of evil with literary pessimism.

Third, as already hinted, Lang's depiction of Qohelet's skepticism/pessimism as pathological and spineless is problematic. One can rightly criticize Qohelet and his group of followers for not really addressing the plight of the poor, though there is probably an element of hypocrisy in doing that for most Western academics. However, considering the incredible power that the Ptolemies wielded over Judah, a little more sympathy is appropriate. In addition, as will be shown, Qohelet's pessimism is not pathological but, in fact, displays

---

11. On critical theory, see G. Frederick Hunter, introduction to Horkheimer, *Between Philosophy and Social Science: Selected Early Writings* (trans. G. Frederick Hunter, Matthew S. Kramer, and John Torpey; Cambridge, Mass.: MIT Press, 1993), vii–x.

12. Lang, "Ist der Mensch hilflos?" 123 n. 27, citing Theodor W. Adorno, *Gesammelte Schriften VI* (Frankfurt: Suhrkamp, 1973), 390–91.

positive features that enabled many of the Judean elite to survive the hostile circumstances of the period. In other words, it will be shown how both Qohelet's skepticism and pessimism were coping mechanisms for the elite to survive such a threatening period for the tiny Judean nation.

Norman Gottwald, of course, represents the epitome of Marxian biblical interpreters. His treatment of Qohelet is especially nuanced, though it is brief, owing to the nature of an introduction.[13] Gottwald notes Qohelet's "socioreligious setting" in the oppressive Ptolemaic kingdom and his "class-privileged position" as a sage.[14] Qohelet sympathizes with the poor and oppressed but does nothing because of his desire to to preserve his privileges. In this trapped situation, Qohelet finds himself in a context "where God and government are distanced from the people."[15] Qohelet is powerless to influence either of these power structures. But Gottwald also speaks of Qohelet's attempt to preserve his own sanity in this situation by working, enjoying family, worshiping correctly, and preaching the irrationality of life.

Gottwald seems to be situating Qohelet in what some Marxists generally refer to as class contradiction.[16] As a matter of fact, he uses this terminology in connection with the authors of Proverbs.[17] Class contradiction is a situation in which the sympathies of a particular stratum do not quite square with its class position. Though some Marxists categorize intellectuals in this way, it is significant that Gottwald never refers to Qohelet as an intellectual.

This is an excellent, though brief, analysis of Qohelet. Though there is a detectable underlying criticism of Qohelet's inactivity in response to the plight of the poor, Gottwald seems sympathetic to him. It should be noted that Gottwald's interpretation does not constitute a totally "vulgar" approach. It is true that he does emphasize that Qohelet's mood directly reflects the social circumstances of his time: God and the Ptolemaic king are powerful and aloof, while Qohelet and the Jews are powerless. In essence, Qohelet's concept of the capricious and powerful deity Gottwald sees as simply a reflection of the powerful and despotic Ptolemaic king, a mere homology of him. But he also shows how Qohelet reacts to this condition, that Qohelet is not totally passive in confronting the situation: he enjoys his family, and so on. Thus, the work of Qohelet not only reflects the author's sociohistorical background but attempts to act on it, resolving its contradictions.

---

13. Gottwald, *Socio-Literary Introduction*, 579–82.

14. Ibid., 581–82.

15. Ibid., 582.

16. See Erik Olin Wright, "Class Boundaries in Advanced Capitalist Societies," *New Left Review* 98 (1976): 3–41; idem, "Intellectuals and the Working Class," *Insurgent Sociologist* 8 (1978): 5–18.

17. Gottwald, *Socio-Literary Introduction*, 574.

Further, the notion of God as distanced is not entirely correct for Qohelet. Qohelet seems to see God involved in all aspects of one's life or in everything that happens, as Crenshaw has noted.[18] Qohelet continually attributes both good and bad events to God's doing (7:14): it may be that the carpe diem ethic is a gift of God (5:19), and the wealthy man's loss of all his possessions is likewise an act of God (6:1–2). Perhaps "distanced" more appropriately describes Qohelet's relationship to his deity, an impersonal deity with which he has only an intellectual relationship. The reality is that Qohelet views his deity as very transcendent and yet simultaneously very immanent. Sovereignty is the chief characteristic of God that Qohelet really emphasizes, as will be seen.

Another Marxist approach is represented by my article entitled "Qohelet and His 'Vulgar' Critics: A Jamesonian Reading."[19] The methodology used is that of the Neo-Marxist Fredric Jameson, who views both art and literature as an aggressive response to relieve the underlying social contradictions in hierarchical societies.[20] The superstructure reacts to and compensates for deficiencies in the base. It aesthetically and imaginatively resolves social contradictions. Jameson draws on Freud and sees art and literature as a dominant means whereby a society represses underlying social contradictions. Literature serves to smooth over these underlying tensions and enables both oppressor and oppressed to live together more manageably. The methods of repression Jameson calls "strategies of containment."[21] This process is easier than actually changing the social reality itself as it exists, which would be largely unthinkable for most persons.

The famous example Jameson uses is taken from Claude Lévi-Strauss's fieldwork with the Caduveo Indians (South America).[22] Their women use art

---

18. Crenshaw, *Old Testament Wisdom*, 137.

19. Sneed, "'Vulgar' Critics."

20. See Jameson, *Political Unconscious*, 17–102.

21. See ibid., 10, 53–54.

22. Ibid., 77–79. Many biblical scholars have drawn on Jameson for interpreting biblical texts: see, e.g., Tina Pippin, "Eros and the End: Reading for Gender in the Apocalypse of John," *Semeia* 59 (1992): 194; Yee, "Ideological Criticism," 149; David Jobling, "Deconstruction and the Political Analysis of Biblical Texts: A Jamesonian Reading of Psalm 72," *Semeia* 59 (1992): 95–127; David J. A. Clines, *Interested Parties: The Ideology of Writers and Readers of the Hebrew Bible* (JSOTSup 205: Gender, Culture, Theory 1; Sheffield: Sheffield Academic Press, 1995), 10, 132; Carol A. Newsom, "Knowing and Doing: The Social Symbolics of Knowledge at Qumran," *Semeia* 59 (1992): 141; Roland Boer, *Jameson and Jeroboam* (SemeiaSt; Atlanta: Scholars, 1996); David Penchansky, *The Betrayal of God: Ideological Conflict in Job* (Louisville: Westminster John Knox, 1990), 10–18. For introductions to Jameson's thought, see William C. Dowling, *Jameson, Althusser, Marx: An Introduction to the Political Unconscious* (Ithaca, N.Y.: Cornell University Press, 1984); Adam Roberts, *Fredric Jameson* (Routledge Critical Thinkers; London: Routledge, 2000); Ian Buchanan,

(facial paint) to repress the hierarchical caste society they live in. "Caduveo decorations are patterns organized along an axis running obliquely to that of the face."[23] This formal contradiction begs for explanation. Jameson does this by comparing the facial art of this people with that of its neighbors, the Guana and Bororo, who use a nonaesthetic solution to mitigate the inequalities of their caste system. The castes are divided into moieities, providing the illusion of egalitarianism. The Caduveo people, on the contrary, have no moiety system and so resort to art to help reduce the social tension.

Jamesonian analysis begins by closely searching for formal or logical contradictions in the text. These are essentially battle scars that betray the underlying societal tensions. It is a scar, but it also points to the attempted solution that the text produces for mitigating the tension.

Jameson's methodology is technically a type of ideological criticism, which originated as Marxist literary criticism.[24] It is usually viewed as a type of postmodern approach.[25] It is always suspicious of a text and looks for contradictions that reveal ideological interests. Ideological critics define "ideology" in various ways, but most see it as the ideals and values and, essentially, worldview of the upper class that allow both oppressor and oppressed to live comfortably in society. This ideology dupes the poor into not wanting to revolt, and it assuages the conscience of the upper class, who might otherwise feel guilty in their oppressive acts.

Including an example of ideological criticism as a type of social-science approach might be a stretch, but really it is a subset that has developed its own unique methodology and has become somewhat independent, drawing heavily on philosophy as it has matured.

In the article, the fundamental formal contradiction that I see in Qohelet is its mixed or hybrid form. Is the book poetry or prose? It seems to be a mixture of both: Qohelet attempts to cast his reflections in narrative form, but they are largely structured poetically. As Robert Alter describes it, Qohelet's literary

---

Fredric Jameson (Live Theory; London: Continuum, 2006). For an introduction to Jameson for biblical scholars, see Roland Boer, "Jameson," in *Handbook of Postmodern Biblical Interpretation* (ed. A. K. M. Adam; St. Louis: Chalice, 2000), 138–43.

23. Dowling, *Jameson, Althusser, Marx*, 119.

24. See esp. Terry Eagleton, *Marxism and Literary Criticism* (Berkeley: University of California Press, 1976); idem, *Ideology: An Introduction* (London: Verso, 1991); Raymond Williams, *Marxism and Literature* (paperback ed.; Marxist Introductions; Oxford: Oxford University Press, 1977).

25. For introductions to ideological criticism in biblical studies, see George Aichele et al., *The Postmodern Bible: The Bible and Culture Collective* (New Haven: Yale University Press, 1995), 272–308; Beverly J. Stratton, "Ideology," in *Handbook of Postmodern Biblical Interpretation* (ed. A. K. M. Adam; St. Louis: Chalice, 2000), 120–27.

style is a kind of "cadenced prose."[26] This ambiguity and hesitancy about form are interpreted as reflecting Qohelet's hesitancy about the issue of Hellenism that had recently confronted the Jews. The question was how much should Jews resist or assimilate the Hellenistic culture? Qohelet takes a middle-of-the-road approach and avoids strong resistance as exemplified by the Hasidim, who adhere to scrupulous adherence to the Torah and resistance to any Hellenistic encroachment into their society. But he also resists complete abandonment of the Torah by the radical Hellenistic Jews of his day.

In other words, Qohelet's formal contradiction is a reflection of his aesthetic resolution of the problem of Hellenism during his era. The hybrid mixture of poetry and prose is a reflection of his solution to become a hybrid Jew who is open to Hellenism but not interested in totally abandoning the ancestral faith. He represents a group of moderate Jewish Hellenists who were simply trying to survive such a critical period. This middle-of-the-road strategy is then demonstrated by examining 7:15–18, which contains an ethic of moderation that avoids extremes. The passage represents Qohelet's more general attempt to make the ancient faith more malleable to the new developments and challenges of Hellenism.

How the social problem is solved along class lines is then shown. Qohelet should technically be located socially within the Judean aristocracy—more specifically, in the retainer class that served the rulers—and his resolution of the problem of Hellenism was only one of several strategies among upper-class factions.

I show that while Qohelet rejects the traditionally formulated doctrine of retribution, he refashions it with his notion of God-fearing (3:14; 5:6; 7:18; 8:12–13). Though God no longer rewards and punishes behavior along traditional lines of understanding, encompassed in the terms the wise/righteous versus the foolish/wicked, he still rewards and punishes along more mysterious lines. The God-fearer/non–God-fearer becomes the new dichotomy Qohelet uses to speak in terms of retribution. The concept of God-fearer involves respect for the mystery of God, who does not reward along traditional lines; thus, the God-fearer lives cautiously, avoiding extremes. God-fearers know that they cannot manipulate God. They usually fare well in life, though there are no guarantees. Thus, God-fearers become the new righteous and wise, while the non–God-fearers become the new fools and wicked. The logical result of this is that it legitimizes the well-to-do status of some and justifies the poor status of others. In other words, it legitimizes Qohelet and the class to which he belongs—a genuine anthropodicy! Thus, Qohelet's new doctrine of retribution is every bit as elitist as the old version!

---

26. Robert Alter, *The Art of Biblical Poetry* (New York: Basic Books, 1985), 167.

Further, Qohelet essentially occludes the poor as real participants in his society. When the poor are referenced (e.g., 4:1–2), they really only serve as data to demonstrate the oppressive and irrational character of the world. Qohelet feels no compunction to counsel assistance for them. He appears totally oblivious to the fact that his leisure lifestyle of study and writing is dependent on the back-breaking work of Judean peasants.

Connected with this legitimization is detachment from any responsibility toward the poor. This is achieved primarily through the strong sense of fatalism that permeates the book. Qohelet 9:12 is typical: "For also no one knows the time of tragedy. Like fish caught in a cruel net and like birds caught in a trap, so humans, like them, are snared by an evil time as it falls upon them suddenly." Against fate, little can be done: "What is bent cannot be straightened, and to what is lacking, nothing can be added" (1:15).

In other words, Qohelet's work not only addresses a very broad and general social problem of the domination by the Ptolemies and the encroachment of Hellenism, that is, the Jewish aristocracy's lower-class position in relation to the Ptolemies, but it also addresses the internal problem of the Jewish aristocracy's relation to the poor of their own people.

My article is a penetrating and interesting analysis that is counterintuitive. It represents a good mix of social theory, exegesis, and social history. However, Jameson's fixation on generic and formal resolution is speculative. My application of this to Qohelet as the hybrid mixture of poetic and narrative features is fascinating but also rather speculative. Although a more concrete social-science analysis of Qohelet is possible, my essay does a good job of treating all the social variables: Qohelet's general milieu, his social location, their connection, and his faction and its ideology in relationship to other factions. The article also shows how Qohelet's reaction to Hellenism and the social problems of his day is not passive but rather an aggressive approach to solving the problems. In other words, one finds here a more dialectical approach to the problem of the relation of the superstructure to the infrastructure—what one might call Weberian! The article represents a paradigm for social-science approaches. But the biggest problem is that there is not enough evidence to suggest that Hellenism had actually encroached vigorously on Ptolemaic Judah. This means the detection of a blending of Greek and Semitic thinking in Qohelet is problematic.

Another Marxist approach is represented by John Rogerson, who uses Theodor Adorno's negative dialectic to interpret Qohelet.[27] Before looking at

---

27. J. W. Rogerson, "The Potential of the Negative: Approaching the Old Testament through the Work of Adorno," in *Rethinking Contexts, Rereading Texts: Contributions of the Social Sciences to Biblical Interpretation* (ed. M. Daniel Carroll R.; JSOTSup 299; Sheffield: Sheffield Academic Press, 2000), 24–47.

particular biblical texts, Rogerson briefly describes Adorno's methodology of negative dialectic.[28] Adorno is critical of human rationality. He believes that rationality originally emerges in the human battle with overcoming and dominating nature, as when the humans used irrigation to grow crops in arid regions. But this inevitably meant the domination of humans over other humans. Thus, rationality is inherently related to domination. Adorno criticizes the rationality of the Enlightenment and capitalism for involving this feature, yet he realizes one cannot escape it. By negative dialectic, one has to understand Adorno's pessimism. Adorno argues that one should be honest about the world's deplorable social condition and realize that things are not really going to get any better in the future. But in this dark honesty and pessimism, one should still reject the status quo. In this rejection is a hidden spark of hope, even if it is but a fantasy that is never realized. Rogerson applies this to the biblical text by recognizing a negative dialectic in it where one finds the support of the status quo and simultaneously a critique of it, warts and all.

For example, Rogerson discusses a tension in the Song of Songs between social norms and values that would prevent the young lovers from consummating anything outside of marriage and the fantasy of the lovers somehow to transcend these restrictions.[29] Rogerson sees this fantasy as a rejection of the current status quo and its hierarchic controls. Here he sees a hidden redemptive quality in the text that hermeneutically can be grasped.

Rogerson turns his attention also to Qohelet.[30] He sees a clear negative dialectic. On the one hand, Qohelet frequently notes and bemoans the injustices of his world (9:11; 3:16; 4:1, etc.). On the other hand, he seems still to maintain the hope that God will somehow judge and compensate for those injustices (3:17), and he even admonishes the reader to trust God (5:1–7). Qohelet has some positive statements about God (3:11, 13; 5:19–20; 8:12). This more optimistic perspective, Rogerson points out, comes from traditional wisdom, which Qohelet seems to still embrace. Though pointing out that Adorno is less optimistic about Qohelet, Rogerson himself sees a redemptive element in the book here. Qohelet's ultimate rejection of the world as it is provides hope in the conjuring up of an alternative world. Rogerson, then, is rather sympathetic with Qohelet and points out, citing Adorno, that simply to dismiss ancient societies for being patriarchal or socially stratified is a form of domination itself.

---

28. Rogerson, "Potential of the Negative," 26–32. For an introduction to Adorno by a biblical scholar, see Roland Boer, *Marxist Criticism of the Bible* (London: T&T Clark, 2003), 159–68.

29. Rogerson, "Potential of the Negative," 35–39.

30. Ibid., 42–47.

Rogerson is to be commended for using a provocative Neo-Marxist like Adorno. Adorno was in fact a member of the Frankfurt School and actually collaborated with Horkheimer. Rogerson's use of Adorno is interesting as a hermeneutical move that helps make Qohelet more relevant for today's society. However, his acceptance of Qohelet's descriptions of divine judgment as compatible with traditional wisdom is problematic. Qohelet uses traditional language in untraditional ways. Language in Qohelet about God's judgment is not the traditional notion that God will bring justice as previously understood according to Jewish expectations. Rather, Qohelet believes that God is the supreme sovereign and master judge, but God's standards of evaluation and verdict are beyond mortal ken and understanding. Thus, God will bring about justice according to the divine standards and timetable, not according to humanity's. In other words, Qohelet speaks of God judging, but there is a deep element of mystery and irrationality connected to it. This will be spelled out more fully later.

In addition, Rogerson does not really address Qohelet's own social location or connect it with the injustices of his society, which is unexpected considering Adorno's Marxist position. Finally, the utopian element that Rogerson sees in Qohelet is not really there. It is present only in the negation of the world that Qohelet laments. Thus, Rogerson's move is primarily hermeneutical, and here is a double-edged sword. Hermeneutically, although it makes Qohelet more adaptable to today's world, it is not true to Qohelet's message. Again, one finds here the attempt to tone down Qohelet's melancholic mood and heterodoxy and give the book a more positive spin. But, ultimately, this is an inappropriate move. Qohelet, contrary to the many conservative commentators, was a consistent pessimist, through and through.

The final Marxian example of what might appear at first to be a Weberian approach is Hans-Peter Müller, whose position is almost identical to Lang's.[31] Müller maintains that Qohelet belonged among the well-to-do bourgeoisie or nobility, which has been depoliticized and disenfranchised by "the Diadochi and their native collaborators" such as Tobias and his son Joseph. Müller maintains that Qohelet's pessimism springs from such removal of power, and he cites Weber to support his claim. Weber describes how depoliticized ruling classes tend to withdraw from political activity and focus on their own intellectual development; he maintains that redemption/deliverance teachings derive from such a situation.[32] Müller maintains that the depoliticized class to which Qohelet belonged, finding itself in such a situation, sought a way out via

---

31. Müller, "Neige," 256–58.

32. Ibid., 258 n. 112, citing Max Weber, *Wirtschaft und Gesellschaft: Grundriss der verstehendedn Soziologie* (2 vols.; Tübingen: Mohr, 1956), 1:306.

the search for pleasure and also through their own "economic expansion." But when satisfaction did not occur, pessimism emerged. Similarly to Lang, Müller emphasizes that Qohelet's coping mechanism, his way out of such miserable conditions, is the enjoyment of life.[33] Qohelet abandons the search for "cosmic order," characteristic of traditional wisdom, and turns instead to pleasure. But Qohelet also takes an ambivalent attitude toward the value of pleasure and realizes the limitations of even this last remaining purpose for life: ultimately, it too is "unreachable" and disappointing, and death cancels it out.

Müller's analysis is significant for including Weber in his interpretation and his correlating of social class, crisis, and religious ideas. But his argument that the Judean aristocracy's depoliticization was anything new in the Ptolemaic period is erroneous, as was mentioned in connection with Lang, though the continued depoliticization of the Jews by foreign empires certainly was catastrophic psychologically for the Jewish aristocracy. Müller's failure to identify Qohelet as an intellectual aristocrat means that his analysis is blunted, yet overall his analysis is highly illuminating and original. It should be noted that his publication preceded both Lang's and Crüsemann's, and his depoliticization theory has essentially been co-opted by Lang and elaborated. Further, though Müller cites Weber, his approach is essentially Marxian. Qohelet's pessimism, according to Müller, is a direct result of his déclassé status as a former aristocrat. In other words, Qohelet's worldview is directly caused by an economic and political societal change. This is perhaps the most crudely "vulgar" Marxist interpretation of Qohelet's worldview ever. For Müller, there is no possibility of an ideational element that might have influenced or been determinative in Qohelet's pessimistic outlook.

POSTCOLONIAL APPROACHES

Postcolonial approaches are included in this analysis because they are technically a subset of social-science approaches.[34] They involve a heavy focus on social class and domination by colonial powers and often draw on social theory. This type of interpretation arose out of the colonial experiences that many indigenous people experienced under British rule in India or Australia or under American colonization.[35] These theorists focus on how the nonindig-

---

33. See Müller, "Neige," 258–59; idem, "Der unheimliche Gast," 445–46, 449, 451–52; idem, "Theonome Skepsis und Lebensfreude—Zu Koh 1:12–3:15," *BZ* n.F. 30 (1986): 2, 7.

34. For an introduction to postcolonial biblical criticism, see Uriah Y. Kim, *Decolonizing Josiah: Toward a Postcolonial Reading of the Deuteronomistic History* (Sheffield: Sheffield Phoenix, 2005), 1–47.

35. For an interesting Native American perspective on the conquest of Canaan by the

enous elite control and attempt to assimilate the indigenous people. The native people then either assimilate or offer subtle and covert forms of resistance. This methodology is especially significant for biblical studies, since most of the biblical material, at least in its literary form, was produced and preserved during periods of colonial dominance by foreign powers such as the Babylonians, the Persians, the Greeks, and the Romans.

Postcolonial theorists often draw on the concept of hegemony to explain how colonial powers subjugate indigenous peoples. This concept goes back to the Italian Neo-Marxist Antonio Gramsci.[36] Gramsci theorizes that dominant powers maintain their coercion over subjugated people either through physical force and/or hegemony, which is similar to the notion of ideology. Hegemony is a sort of ideational subjugation in which the dominant social class legitimizes its domination and persuades the lower class to accept its situation.[37] This is done often subliminally but also more overtly in propaganda. Even the dominant class is largely unconscious of this hegemonic process. In other words, hegemony allows both oppressor and oppressed to remain unaware of the social dimensions of their existence and allows each to live comfortably with the other.

One of the most famous postcolonial biblical scholars, the Indian R. S. Sugirtharajah, incorporates a brief discussion of Qohelet and includes it under the subheading of decoding texts.[38] Drawing on the British culture critic, Stuart Hall, he sees four types of codes latent in texts.[39] One type of code is what he calls the hegemonic code, concerning which he says:

> The function of the hegemonic code, turned to our postcolonial purpose . . . is to legitimize, consolidate, and promote the dominant values and ideological interests of the ruling class. It tends to embrace colonial and monarchical models and patriarchal practices, and to praise, prescribe, and perpetuate them as sources of good governance.

Israelites, see Robert Allen Warrior, "A Native American Perspective: Canaanites, Cowboys, and Indians," in *Biblical Studies Alternatively: An Introductory Reader* (ed. Susanne Scholz; Upper Saddle River, N.J.: Prentice Hall, 2003), 400–405; repr. from *Christianity & Crisis* 49 (September 1989).

36. For an introduction to Gramsci, see James Joll, *Antonio Gramsci* (Modern Masters; New York: Viking, 1977); Ann Showstack Sasson, *Gramsci's Politics* (2nd ed.; Minneapolis: University of Minnesota Press, 1987). Roland Boer takes a Gramscian approach to Moses' leadership (*Marxist Criticism of the Bible*, 42–64).

37. See Benedetto Fontana, *Hegemony & Power: On the Relation between Gramsci and Machiavelli* (Minneapolis: University of Minnesota Press, 1993).

38. R. S. Sugirtharajah, *Postcolonial Criticism and Biblical Interpretation* (Oxford: Oxford University Press, 2002), 80–81.

39. Ibid., 79, citing Stuart Hall, *Encoding and Decoding in the Television Discourse* (Birmingham: Centre for Cultural Studies University of Birmingham, 1973), 16–18.

He also speaks of an oppositional code where the voice of the marginal surfaces to contest the dominant voice. He includes Ecclesiastes in the hegemonic category and describes it as reflecting "the view of the establishment." Sugirtharajah describes behind its pages a newly developing Jewish elite who took advantage of Ptolemaic policies to exploit their own people. He describes this group as materialistic to the core, and he includes Qohelet among its numbers. Sugirtharajah takes 2:4–8 literally as Qohelet's own economic endeavors. He sees Qohelet's advice to be a royal loyalist (10:20) and his adage that "money answers everything" (10:19) as evidence of his entrenchment within the hegemonic perspective. Concerning the poor, Sugirtharajah says that Qohelet has only bad news: "Nothing can change their situation (4:1–3; 5:12)."

Sugirtharajah is correct that Qohelet is an aristocrat, but, again, this is not sufficiently nuanced. Sugirtharajah fails to point out where Qohelet is critical of the status quo, as when he labels what a ruler does as erroneous (10:5–7). While Qohelet seems to resign himself to the status quo, this does not mean he endorses it. Also, taking 2:4–8 literally as largely autobiographical is rather unsophisticated and naïve. Sugirtharajah fails to perceive the nature of this passage as a literary device used for rhetorical purposes. Thus, while there is truth in Sugirtharajah's characterization of the book as elitist, his analysis is too simplistic. Qohelet is more complex than his assessment suggests.

It is interesting that the next example of a postcolonial approach to Qohelet takes the very opposite tack of Sugirtharajah! Elsa Tamez is a Mexican biblical scholar who puts a positive spin on the book.[40] She characterizes Qohelet as a renegade aristocrat who turns on his own social class and perceives the illusive nature of the Ptolemaic lifestyle and grasp for dominance.[41] She focuses on Qohelet's notion of "nothing new under the sun," and this is basically Qohelet's criticism of the Ptolemies and their Jewish cronies. She also does something new and interesting—using utopian theory hermeneutically to apply the book to Christians today.[42] She draws on the work of utopian scholar Franz Hinkelammert and argues that even those who see themselves as anti-utopian and realistic have a hidden utopia underneath.[43] Thus, in spite of Qohelet's pessimism, she sees a glimmer of hope in his work that questions the status quo.

40. Elsa Tamez, *When the Horizons Close: Rereading Ecclesiastes* (trans. Margaret Wilde; Maryknoll, N.Y.: Orbis, 2000).

41. Ibid., 10–13.

42. Ibid., 17–18.

43. Ibid., 17, citing Franz Hinkelammert, *Crítica a la razón utópica* (San José: DEI, 1984) and idem, "El cautiverio de la utopia: Las utopias conservadoras del capitalismo actual, el neoliberalismo y la dialéctica de las alternativas," *Pasos* 50 (Nov.–Dec. 1993): 1–14.

Tamez's more complicated view of Qohelet is to be commended. She recognizes that Qohelet is not simply the typical aristocrat. Her application of utopian theory to the book is important, though she fails to integrate studies on dystopia, its opposite, which is more germane to Qohelet.[44] Still, her class analysis needs to be further nuanced. Qohelet's disenchantment with the status quo stems from the oppressive character of the Ptolemaic regime, not solely from criticism of his own countrymen. While Tamez's notion of a renegade aristocrat is provocative, it seems a little strained and anachronistic for Qohelet. It is doubtful that Qohelet turned against his own class wholesale. It should be noted that Tamez's analysis is similar to Rogerson's Adornian interpretation of Qohelet. Both turn a negative outlook into something more positive. While this is hermeneutically helpful, it is ultimately not true to Qohelet. He did not fully embrace the status quo, but he did resign himself to it. Both Rogerson and Tamez fail to fully appreciate Qohelet's pessimism and essentially, just like other interpreters, explain it away.

DURKHEIMIAN APPROACHES

Émile Durkheim was one of the founding fathers of sociology, a member of the holy trinity, along with Marx and Weber.[45] Durkheim is most famous for his legitimization of the field of sociology. He demonstrated this with his famous book *Suicide*.[46] Suicide, even today, is treated as an individual phenomenon and appropriately studied and treated by psychologists or psychiatrists. However, Durkheim demonstrated that suicide cannot be reduced to a psychological malady. By studying records of suicides in France, Durkheim found that they increased during times of social and economic instability, as during sudden shifts in economic development.[47] He describes these as periods of anomie, when the usual normative constraints of society are disrupted during rapid social and economic change.[48] During this time, people become frustrated, confused, and question their sense of meaning in life. That is why suicide increases. Another factor is the social location of the suicidal. He

---

44. For a definition of dystopia and its relation to utopia and how this plays out in the Hebrew Bible, see Ehud Ben Zvi, ed., *Utopia and Dystopia in Prophetic Literature* (Publications of the Finnish Exegetical Society 92; Göttingen: Vandenhoeck & Ruprecht, 2006).

45. Again, for a penetrating contrast of all three, see Giddens, *Capitalism & Modern Social Theory*.

46. Émile Durkheim, *Suicide: A Study in Sociology* (trans. John A. Spaulding and George Simpson; paperback ed.; New York: Free Press, 1966).

47. Ibid., 252–54, 285–86.

48. Ibid., 241–76.

found that Catholics had fewer incidences of suicide than Protestants.[49] Thus, Durkheim demonstrated that social factors have a bearing on this supposedly individual phenomenon. From his research, he proposed that suicide was inversely correlated to the degree of integration of an individual in a particular society. The more integrated a person is (membership in clubs or religious organizations, married, etc.), the less likely that person is to commit suicide. From this study, the concepts of anomie and alienation have become a dominant part of modern sociological theory and experimentation.

Durkheim is branded as a functionalist, which is in opposition to conflict theories of social stratification.[50] Functionalists view society and its hierarchal structure as functioning like an organism. Each body part of the organism serves to enable it to survive and, thus, function and maintain equilibrium within its system. Functionalism has been criticized for being elitist because it never judges the hierarchical nature of society but assumes it to be natural; thus, indirectly functionalism supports the status quo. In addition, functionalists are criticized for viewing a society as static rather than dynamic and for believing that any change in society must be neutralized so that equilibrium might be restored. To the contrary, conflict theorists view society as dynamic and constantly changing, and they always question the forms of society that develop, especially hierarchical ones.

Without a doubt, one of the most sophisticated social science analyses of Qohelet is that of Frank Crüsemann: "The Unchangeable World: The 'Crisis of Wisdom' in Koheleth."[51] He is always the one scholar almost everyone cites and critiques when discussing the social location of Qohelet. As one begins to read his article, one might guess that his approach is Marxist. He quotes a brief note from Georg Lukács, a Neo-Marxist, to support his particular methodology, and he relies heavily on Hans Kippenberg, whose social history of ancient Israel appears to be essentially Marxist.[52] Though the article is largely a social class analysis of Ptolemaic Judah, Crüsemann's dominant explanation for Qohelet's pessimism and skepticism is actually quite Durkheimian, with the use of the concept of alienation.

---

49. See ibid., 152–70.

50. For an accessible discussion of these approaches, see James W. Vander Zanden, *Sociology: The Core* (New York: McGraw-Hill, 1990), 161–65.

51. Crüsemann, "Unchangeable World," 57–77.

52. Ibid., 59, citing Georg Lukács, *History and Class Consciousness: Studies in Marxist Dialectics* (trans. Rodney Livingston; Cambridge, Mass.: MIT Press, 1971), 50. He frequently cites Hans G. Kippenberg, *Religion und Klassenbildung im antiken Judäa: Eine religionssoziologische Studie zum Verhältnis von Tradition und gesellschaftlicher Entwicklung* (SUNT 14; Göttingen: Vandenhoeck & Ruprecht, 1978), 255ff.

In another work, Crüsemann speaks of "depoliticization and demilitarization of early ruling classes" in reference to the effects of the exile and subsequent periods, but this concept plays little role in his discussion of the source of Qohelet's particular worldview.[53] Crüsemann's basic argument is that what is at the source of Qohelet's pessimism/skepticism is the alienation that occurred in Israelite society because of the Ptolemaic circumstances.

Crüsemann's discussion of "the collapse of the act-consequence connection" (similar to the doctrine of retribution) presents the main thesis.[54] Following Kippenberg, he describes how the ancient Israelite kinship or segmentary society created solidarity among all classes of Israelites.[55] Under such conditions, one can easily see how a connection between act and consequence would be seen as self-evident and would fit that particular reality. But after the exile and especially during the Ptolemaic period, this all changed. A new "rich class of aristocrats" emerged who collaborated with the Hellenistic rulers and taxed the people. The economy changed to one based on money. There was increased pressure for productivity. These drastic changes created insecurity. The aristocrats alienated themselves from the rest of Israelite society and took advantage of the new circumstances to increase their own wealth at the expense of the poorer Israelites.

These circumstances broke down the ancient solidarity of Israel and, at the same time, the basis for the act–consequence connection. Thus, Judean society became generally alienated, and Qohelet and the rich class to which he belonged became alienated from the rest, the poorer Judeans. Thus, this disintegration of solidarity is the basis of Qohelet's skepticism/pessimism.

Crüsemann places Qohelet along the trajectory of an increasingly hellenized Jewish aristocracy that eventually broke away from the ancestral faith and entirely embraced the Greek world. He contrasts this class with the poor one that eventually turned to apocalypticism and the notion that God would intervene in history and bring justice, even on behalf of the dead.[56] The poorer Judeans had preserved the segmentary ways of life and resisted the oppressive hellenized upper class.

Crüsemann draws on anthropology for his alienation theory. In his discussion of Qohelet's obsession with death, he states, citing a work based on anthropological theory: "Degree of individualization and experience of death

---

53. Crüsemann, "Hiob," 390–91.

54. Crüsemann, "Unchangeable World," 59–64.

55. Ibid., 62 n. 33, citing Kippenberg, *Religion und Klassenbildung in antiken Judäa*, 55–78.

56. Crüsemann, "Unchangeable World," 73–74.

are correlative."[57] He then states, "It is the breakdown of supportive group identity in the class to which Koheleth belongs and the focusing of attention on the isolated individual and his or her 'gain' that give death a fascination that eclipses everything else."

Crüsemann's work is exhilarating and extremely sophisticated. It is to be commended as one of the most thorough and comprehensive treatments of Qohelet's social matrix. His attention to general social conditions, the social location of Qohelet, and the class antagonism of the period leaves few areas untouched. That he does not appeal to depoliticization of the native aristocracy as a significant key to understanding Qohelet's pessimism, as did Lang and Müller, is highly significant. As already pointed out, there was no new deprivation of the Jewish upper class in Judah with the arrival of the Greeks.

However, there are serious weaknesses in Crüsemann's interpretation. First, the breakdown of segmentary society in ancient Israel did not start with the Ptolemaic period or even the postexilic period. Many scholars have noted that the Israelite monarchy began the process of undermining the ancestral tribal and segmentary society. The taxation by Solomon weakened the traditional tribal boundaries. Gale Yee and Ronald Simkins both argue that the command for a husband to leave his parents and marry his wife (Gen 2:24) is an ideological ploy of the monarchy to subvert the traditional extended family and replace it with the nuclear family.[58] As Walter Brueggemann has demonstrated, the Israelite monarchy was detrimental to the earlier Mosaic form of religion, which was tribal, more egalitarian, and dynamic in its view of the deity as mysterious and having no permanent home.[59] The covenant with God was conditioned on the obedience of the people. In contrast, the monarchic form viewed the covenant as unconditional. God was viewed as static and bound to king and Zion (versus Sinai), instead of a transitory God who moved along with the Israelites in the wilderness. Here the covenant with God was eternal.

Second, Crüsemann's appeal to Qohelet's obsession with death as an indication of the degree of alienation or disintegration in his society or characteristic of the social class to which he belonged is problematic. While it may be true that death has for Qohelet an uncharacteristic fascination not seen before in Jewish thinking, his apparent obsession with death has a rhetorical dimension not largely recognized. Again and again, he uses death to point out the

57. Ibid., 68, citing W. Fuchs[-Heinritz], *Todesbilder in der modernen Gesellschaft* (Frankfurt: Suhrkamp, 1969), 30. Fuchs is accepting the results of the work of Lucien Lévy-Bruhl, Bronislaw Malinowski, and others (77 n. 73).

58. Simkins, "Political Economy," 123–44; Gale A. Yee, "Gender, Class, and the Social-Scientific Study of Genesis 2–3," *Semeia* 87 (1999): 177–92.

59. Brueggemann, *Prophetic Imagination*.

inadequacy of traditional wisdom (e.g., 2:14–15) or humanity's futile attempts to pursue what is beyond mortal grasp (e.g., 9:11–12). Qohelet uses death to prioritize life so that the more significant elements could be appreciated. In other words, Qohelet's frequent allusions to death are not pathological or maladaptive but the opposite. They represent an attempt to take a more balanced view of life and its priorities. Few scholars have appreciated this rhetorical dimension of his discussions of death. This will be treated more fully later.

Third, this leads to a more serious flaw in Crüsemann's argument. If Qohelet's society had become less integrated and generally alienated, would this not also have affected the other classes and not just the aristocracy? Alienation goes both ways, in other words. If the problem was only the upper class's alienation from the other classes who preserved the segmentary ways of life, would the aristocracy not have formed its own solidarity that would have mitigated the effects of alienation? Would the embrace of Hellenism and its religious and philosophical traditions not have provided the aristocracy with new coping mechanisms that would have replaced the ancestral faith and have mitigated the effects of any alienation?

Fourth, the notion that Qohelet embraced Hellenism with open arms cannot be maintained. While it may seem logical to connect Qohelet's heterodox character with the popularity of Jewish assimilation of Hellenism, this is a non sequitur. His heterodoxy has no direct connection with Hellenism; it is a heterodoxy born and bred within Semitic parameters and constraints. Rather, it should be viewed as his reaction to the changes brought on by the Ptolemaic empire, not assimilation to it.

A more purist Durkheimian approach is represented by my dissertation completed in 1990.[60] It represents the attempt to apply Durkheim's concept of anomie to the book of Ecclesiastes. The idea of anomie in Ptolemaic Judah is used to explain Qohelet's skepticism and pessimism. It represents the first book-length work devoted to a social-science approach to Qohelet (it precedes Harrison's dissertation at Duke by a year[61]). In it, Durkheim's concept was integrated into a broad sociology-of-knowledge approach, particularly that of Luckmann and Berger, which focuses on how the commonsense worldview is socially constructed and maintained.

The dissertation contains Marxist elements, such as the use of Gottwald and the focus on determining the social class of Qohelet, as well as Weberian ones, such as the focus on the status group (scribe) to whom Qohelet belonged. But the dominant interpretive element is Durkheimian. The main

---

60. Mark Sneed, "The Social Location of Qoheleth's Thought: Anomie and Alienation in Ptolemaic Jerusalem" (Ph.D. diss., Drew University, 1990).

61. C. Robert Harrison, "Qoheleth in Social-Historical Perspective" (Ph.D. diss., Duke University, 1991).

thesis is that Qohelet's pessimism and skepticism are symptoms that stem from the declassed position of the professional group to whom he belonged: the scribes. Basically, Qohelet's pessimism is the result of his social location as a disenfranchised intellectual. The scribes of the Ptolemaic period had somehow suffered a loss in economic status, though not a loss of vocation, and a loss of prestige. This link is made by interpreting 9:13–16 as autobiographical. Here a poor wise man saves a small city by his wisdom and then is forgotten. The anecdote, it is argued, indicates that the scribes in Qohelet's day were no longer respected and treated with dignity by society at large. This is the ultimate source of Qohelet's melancholy.

This particular interpretation is integrated into a broader sociology-of-knowledge approach. Luckmann and Berger also treat anomie and use it to explain the function of a symbolic universe or worldview, their notion of a normative and regulative phenomenon that keeps chaos and meaninglessness at bay. They argue that our commonsense knowledge about the world is socially constructed.[62] A worldview may differ from culture to culture, but all worldviews serve to give any individual in a society a sense of purpose and meaning in life and help impose order and systematization upon a world that is inherently chaotic and irrational. A symbolic universe or, in the case of a religion, a sacred canopy, protects its adherents from such onslaughts as the uncertainty of death and exposure to a host of disorienting phenomena. However, sometimes this protection or "nomic" function does not work, and cracks or tears appear in this canopy as a result of crises such as exposure to a foreign culture.[63] Because of this, the individual is exposed to anomie or a sense of deregulation and chaos.[64]

I connect the detection of a sense of anomie felt by Qohelet to the German scholars who speak of a crisis of wisdom represented by Qohelet. Qohelet had shown the ultimate bankruptcy of the wisdom tradition and its inability to cope with and explain the failure of the act–consequence connection. I interpret this to be the failure of Qohelet's symbolic universe; that is, the wisdom tradition, and his book, with its sense of meaninglessness and vanity, is viewed as a direct expression of the anomie in his society. Scholars who translate הֶבֶל as "absurdity" and "meaninglessness" further support the notion that Qohelet suffers from anomie.

The collapse of traditional wisdom is then connected to Durkheim's theory that during periods of rapid economic change, the levels of suicide increase due to exposure of anomie. This, according to Durkheim, can occur in two ways.

---

62. Berger and Luckmann, *Social Construction of Reality*, 92–128.

63. See Peter Berger, *The Sacred Canopy: Elements of a Sociological Theory of Religion* (paperback ed.; New York: Anchor, 1969), 53–80.

64. Berger and Luckmann, *Social Construction of Reality*, 101–102.

A society can collapse, economically, as in the stock market crash of 1929 in which businessmen jumped out of skyscrapers to their death because they had lost everything. This is called the anomie of deprivation.[65] But deregulation or anomie can occur also in dramatic economic upsurges. Durkheim showed that instances of suicide increased during periods of rapid growth of economic prosperity. Today this is exemplified individually when people win the lottery, cannot control their greed, and want more and more. They find out that life after the lottery is not what they expected and eventually wish they had never won the money. This is known as the anomie of affluence.[66] Durkheim's thesis then is that rapid economic and social changes create a situation of anomie or deregulation, in which persons who are usually constrained by social forces and mores and are satisfied with their lives find themselves unregulated and, thus, dissatisfied with life, unconstrained and unable to cope with it. It is during these periods of social and economic anarchy that the suicide rates increase until equilibrium can be restored.

I connect the concept of anomie with rapid social changes brought on by the Ptolemaic period and, specifically, with the scribal group to which Qohelet belonged. This group, it is argued, is suddenly declassed and concomitantly loses prestige, a situation that does not occur among the other social groups and the Jewish aristocracy. I draw on the notion of relative deprivation to explain the scribes' melancholic response to this as represented by Qohelet. Though Qohelet and his status group have not lost their jobs and are still fairly comfortable, they feel relatively deprived by their loss of prestige and the diminution of economic potentialities.

Qohelet is socially located in a middle class and is an intellectual. I discuss the sociology of intellectuals and show how they occupy a complex and conflicted social location. They usually do not hold positions of much power. Qohelet has a comfortable lifestyle, though he is not "filthy rich." His implicit criticism of the king (8:3) and the wealthy (10:20) shows that his worldview is not typically aristocratic.

My discussion of the modern use of the concept of anomie in sociology treats especially its popularity during the 1960s and '70s and criticism of it. I explore also the closely related and extremely significant concept of alienation, which is especially illuminating for modern society. Qohelet is shown to display symptoms of alienation similar to moderns.

Finally, while I view the book of Qohelet largely as passively reflecting the anomie of Ptolemaic Judah, I note instances of resistance in which the book attempts to compensate for the anomie. I agree with Lang that Qohelet's carpe

---

65. Durkheim, *Suicide*, 252, 285.
66. Ibid., 252–54, 285–86.

diem ethic evidences this resistance, but Qohelet's criticism of the aristocracy and monarchy are intellectual forms of resistance to the regime that have an air of intellectual superiority. Moreover, the very writing of his book is a form of resistance and compensation in the face of such oppression. It is also a way to impress Qohelet's colleagues.

My dissertation is an extremely significant contribution to the sociological study of Qohelet, though it has been almost completely ignored. It is an excellent blend of social theory, social history, and exegesis. The incorporation of the sociology of knowledge as the broad framework for exploring this issue is helpful and highly illuminating. The use of the notion of anomie to explain Qohelet's pessimism and skepticism is innovative and also highly creative. The history of research is also quite comprehensive, which includes the important German contribution to this issue.[67]

However, there are significant weaknesses. First of all, the attempt to connect Qohelet's anomic worldview with economic and social deprivation via the parable in 9:13–16 is faulty. It should be noted that the wise man in the parable is poor, which is not the social status of Qohelet for which I argue. Second, that the book of Qohelet reflects the effects of anomie is doubtful. As will be shown later, Qohelet's pessimism is not a psychological malady or pathology but a rhetorical strategy to deal with the problem of evil and irrationality in the world. Third, though there are references to compensation for (carpe diem ethic) and resistance to (intellectual superiority) the social problems reflected in the book, on the whole the book is viewed as a rather passive reflection of its sociohistorical context. As will be shown later, Qohelet is reactive and responsive to his circumstances, not passive. His pessimism is functional, not reflective. Finally, the main criticism of the dissertation is the degree of speculation involved. Whether there was anomie in Ptolemaic Judah is difficult to determine, but showing that Qohelet's literary pessimism is being used rhetorically is much less speculative to prove.

Grand Theories

Harrison's dissertation at Duke and his summary of it in an article in *Biblical Interpretation* in 1997 represent a major contribution to the issue.[68] It should be noted that in the article, he does not reference my dissertation of 1990. While not using the concept of anomie, he does ultimately explain Qohelet's pessimism/skepticism as a "sociology of uncertainty."[69] Harrison does not

---

67. In contrast, it is interesting that in Harrison's 1997 article "Qoheleth among the Sociologists," he fails to cite any German sociological interpreters except Crüsemann.
68. Harrison, "Social-Historical Perspective."
69. Harrison, "Among the Sociologists," 179.

believe that Qohelet has necessarily been influenced by Greek thinking but rather is reacting to social changes brought on by the encroachment of Hellenism. Basically, this uncertainty is created by the rapid social change that he sees occurring during this time. He interprets 10:7 literally as revealing a "world turned upside down."[70]

Methodologically, Harrison is suspicious of using literary texts to reconstruct their social world because they are "too inherently biased to serve as the sole data upon which to base any reconstruction of the ancient world."[71] He turns to integrating literary and archaeological sources and interpreting them with comparative and historical sociology. While he claims that his analysis does not represent grand macro-social theory, in that he is eclectic, his work squarely belongs to this genre because his interpretive tools are drawn from grand theorists (Immanuel Wallerstein, Robert Wuthnow, S. N. Eisenstadt, and Karl Jaspers).[72] This is characterized by using very broad strokes for interpretation that focus on the politics and economics of empires and their peripheral territories.

As an example, Harrison draws on Jaspers's notion of an axial or revolutionary age that occurred during the first millennium, in which there arose a tension "between transcendental and mundane orders."[73] This occurred in ancient Greece, Israel, India, Iran, and China. Eisenstadt then develops this idea and sees another period of intense religious activity when what he calls a "secondary breakthrough" occurs within this schema when postexilic Judaism encounters Greek culture.[74] Harrison then applies this to Qohelet and argues that, after sociological breakdown and disorientation occurred during this period, Qohelet essentially picks up the pieces and tries to reformulate the Jewish religious traditions.

As far as Qohelet's social location, Harrison is reticent, but he speaks of his audience as middle class.[75] Harrison speaks of a newly developing middle class or petite bourgeoisie of this time that consisted of traders, craftsmen, and businessmen. This emerging new class, Harrison argues, actually contrib-

70. Ibid., 178.

71. Ibid., 161.

72. Ibid., 166–78.

73. Ibid., 175, citing S. N. Eisenstadt, "The Axial Age Breakthroughs: Their Characteristics and Origins," in *The Origins and Diversity of Axial Age Civilizations* (ed. S. N. Eisenstadt; SUNY Series in Near Eastern Studies; Albany: State University of New York Press, 1986), 1.

74. Harrison, "Among the Sociologists," 176, citing Eisenstadt, "The Secondary Breakthrough in Ancient Israelite Civilization: The Second Commonwealth and Christianity," in Eisenstadt, *Origins and Diversity of Axial Age Civilizations*, 227–40.

75. Harrison, "Among the Sociologists," 164–65, 171.

uted to the social instability of the time since it essentially sidetracked the old aristocracy.

While Harrison usually describes the book of Qohelet as merely passively reflecting such socially turbulent times, at several points he significantly argues that Qohelet is attempting to shore up and adapt the old faith so that it can withstand these difficult times. Drawing on sociologist of religion Robert Wuthnow, Harrison makes one of his most fascinating proposals: Qohelet, in response to the chaos of his time, makes the Jewish faith more flexible by his creating and combining ideological elements as he sees fit. In other words, Qohelet reshuffles the deck of Jewish tradition. He describes this as "an important 'decoupling mechanism' that made traditional Yahwism flexible enough to withstand the pressures of the Hellenistic Age."[76] This, of course, creates an inconsistency in Qohelet, and this is how Harrison explains away the famous contradictions in Qohelet. Harrison concludes, "Qoheleth's biblically unusual theology and anthropology also represent a significant attempt to adapt to rapidly changing social circumstances. Qoheleth stands as a prominent example of someone trying valiantly to maintain faith in crisis."[77] This is very similar to Whybray's argument that Qohelet was ultimately an apologist for the Jewish faith in the midst of the Hellenistic crisis.

Overall, Harrison's analysis is very sophisticated and should be seen as a paradigm of integrating social theory, social history, and exegesis. His expertise in archaeology and grand theory makes his analysis penetrating and profound; however, there are several weaknesses. His reliance on grand theory is helpful and illuminating but not to the extent that he claims. It may be generally helpful to know that Qohelet lived in an age when religious ideas were undergoing rapid change and new conceptions were emerging, but the degree of illumination is minimal. His reliance on grand theory is also rather speculative. As Carol Newsom said in criticism of Harrison's argument in his dissertation: "There is something of an *a priori* quality in the application of such a theoretical model to a particular case. It is just as difficult to show the connections between large scale changes in economic and social structures and ideas as it is to show the influence of Hellenistic culture on a Judean writer of the third century BCE."[78] In essence, she is showing that Harrison's argumentation is no better than the infusion theorists who explain Qohelet's alleged heterodoxy as due to Greek influence. Both are rather speculative. In the area

---

76. Harrison, "Among the Sociologists," 171, citing Robert Wuthnow, "World Order and Religious Movements," in *Studies of the Modern World System* (ed. A. Bergesen; New York: Academic Press, 1980), 489–91.

77. Harrison, "Among the Sociologists," 179.

78. Newsom, "Job and Ecclesiastes," 186.

of sociology, Stephen Kalberg has demonstrated the superiority of Weber's multicausal methodology to the deductive nature of World Systems Theory (Wallerstein, etc.).[79]

Harrison has failed to treat the perennial nature of the problem of evil as exemplified in Qohelet. What made the Ptolemaic period more unstable socially or involved more rapid change than in the other periods when this issue erupted? In addition, Harrison's hesitancy in locating Qohelet socially in lieu of focusing on the broader social context serves to flatten his analysis. Harrison fails to realize that Qohelet's work was produced in the midst of class antagonism and represents the interests of a particular class in opposition to the others. In essence, Harrison is a functionalist. He seems to view social classes in rather static ways, as if classes can exist relatively independent of each other. This notion of free-floating social classes serves to exculpate social classes from any blame in the deplorable conditions of the poor. Also typically functionalistic, Harrison never discusses Qohelet's apparent aloofness concerning the plight of the poor, nor does he engage in any criticism of it.

Another problem is Harrison's view of archaeology and grand theory as somehow less biased than literary texts. In fact, however, whenever Harrison cites Qohelet, he is nowhere suspicious of his sociohistorical accuracy. The reality is that bias clings as tenaciously to archaeological and sociological interpretation as it does to literary texts. A healthy bit of skepticism regarding Qohelet's depictions of reality would have been appropriate.[80] Harrison never considers that Qohelet's depictions might involve exaggeration or rhetoric.

In spite of these criticisms, Harrison's notion that Qohelet is attempting to make the Jewish faith more malleable to the crisis his contemporaries were facing is very much on target and serves to distinguish his work from that of others. He does not view literary works as merely passive reflections of their sociohistorical circumstances but as potentially aggressive reactions against and compensation for the circumstances.

Shannon Burkes represents another example of the application of grand theory to explain Qohelet's pessimism/skepticism.[81] Burkes focuses on Qohelet's seeming obsession with death as the key to understanding his aberrant

---

79. Stephen Kalberg, "Weber's Critique of Recent Comparative-Historical Sociology and a Reconstruction of His Analysis of Confucianism in China," *Current Perspectives in Social Theory* 19 (1999): 207–46.

80. On the need for skepticism regarding the social transparency of biblical texts, see Berlinerblau, "Uneven Triumphs," 104–107, 110. For a concern for the same kind of skepticism in ancient Near Eastern studies, see idem, *Heresy in the University*, 29–38.

81. See Burkes, *Death in Qohelet*, 236–43.

character. She shows how the Egyptian tomb biographies written around the same time as Qohelet, which she dates to the Ptolemaic period, reflect the same kind of fascination with death that Qohelet demonstrates. A similar phenomenon occurred also among the Greeks during this time period.

She draws on the historian of religion Jonathan Z. Smith to explain this apparently ubiquitous phenomenon occurring along the Mediterranean basin.[82] Smith speaks of two kinds of religions: locative and utopian. The locative religions are the archaic ones in which the limits of humanity versus the divine are accepted and embraced and in which the gods keep chaos at bay. Examples include the Epic of Gilgamesh, in which the hero eventually succumbs to the irresistible conclusion that humans are not immortal and that they must resign themselves to such limitations. The Greek tragic hero does the same. Smith theorizes, however, that during the Hellenistic period, a radical revaluation occurred. The seemingly beneficent and necessary limitations placed on humanity began to be viewed as oppressive and restrictive. The goal of the individual, then, no longer fits into the cosmic scheme of things but resists it. Instead of being the tragic hero who failed, the hero now succeeds to grasp immortality. Now, instead of facing the terror of chaos, the threat is other humans, demons, evil, and death. Here the sage is replaced by the savior who seeks escape. Smith connects this radical questioning of traditional values with the disintegration of the polis in Greece and the loss of native kingship when Alexander the Great conquered the world. Smith connects this disintegration of traditional society with the notion of anomie as well.

Burkes then connects Smith's theory with Qohelet. She acknowledges that Qohelet seems stuck between locative and utopian options. She especially focuses on Qohelet's fascination with death, which she connects with Smith's theory and a similar angst that she finds in the Egyptian tomb biographies composed during the Hellenistic period.

It is illuminating to connect Qohelet's thinking about death and his reflection of anomie with similar expressions in Egypt and throughout the Mediterranean basin during the Hellenistic invasion. However, it still is very speculative, which is typical of grand theories. It also does not address the perennial character of the problem of theodicy and anomie that occurred during the Assyrian, Babylonian, and Persian periods. As pointed out in the discussion of Crüsemann, Burkes fails to appreciate the rhetorical dimension of Qohelet's discussions of death. In a certain sense, death serves positively to help him prioritize his life and focus on what is really important such as family

---

82. Burkes, *Death in Qohelet*, 237, citing Jonathan Z. Smith, *Map Is Not Territory: Studies in the History of Religions* (SJLA 23; Leiden: Brill, 1978), 101–86.

and the simple pleasures instead of constantly striving for the impossible and being disappointed.

ANTHROPOLOGICAL APPROACH

Thomas Bolin has a recent article that uses anthropology and comparative literature to explain Qohelet's apparently unconventional thinking.[83] Bolin's main intention for the article is to show that Qohelet is not some radically heterodox skeptic whose thinking departs greatly from normative Hebrew thinking. He attempts to demonstrate this by drawing on the anthropologist René Girard, who sees an inherent "mimetic rivalry" in religions between God and humanity.[84] This is akin to the Oedipus complex where the son admires his father and wants to become more like him, but when he does, he ends up becoming his rival. In the same way, often in religions humans know they are distinct from the deity, yet they want to become like the deity, mimic the deity, but this inevitably leads to a rivalry between mortals and the immortal.

Bolin applies this to Qohelet. He maintains that the best translation of הֶבֶל is "transience" and that what Qohelet is trying to do is to get humanity to recognize its profound difference from the deity and resign itself to its mortal and fallible possibilities. He then demonstrates how this motif is a major theme in the ancient Near East and the Hebrew Bible by examining the Epic of Gilgamesh and Adapa and then Genesis 2–3. He also finds this conceptuality in the Greek tragedies, where the hero finally succumbs to demise because of overreaching the bounds of mortals. Qohelet is merely echoing this theme and emphasizing the great gulf between God and humanity.

If Bolin is correct, then there is no need to search for Greek conceptuality to explain Qohelet's skepticism and pessimism. Rather, Qohelet is reflecting a universal theme found throughout ancient religion. It means that Qohelet is merely returning to an earlier and more basic understanding of the divine–human relationship as understood in the ancient Near East.

Bolin's article is extremely illuminating and powerful. He goes a long way toward mitigating the notion that Qohelet is radically heterodox by drawing him into the wider arena of ancient Near Eastern conceptuality. However, for the Hebrew Bible, the degree of Qohelet's skepticism/pessimism is unchar-

---

83. Thomas Bolin, "Rivalry and Resignation: Girard and Qoheleth on the Divine–Human Relationship," *Bib* 86 (2005): 245–59.

84. Ibid., 253, citing René Girard, *Deceit, Desire, and the Novel: Self and Other in Literary Structure* (Baltimore: Johns Hopkins University Press, 1965); and idem, *Things Hidden since the Foundation of the World* (Baltimore: Johns Hopkins University Press, 1978), 283–431; and idem, *Violence and the Sacred* (Baltimore: Johns Hopkins University Press, 1977), 143–92.

acteristic. Thus, Bolin has not adequately treated Qohelet's anomalous character within the book's canonical context. Moreover, though Bolin draws on an anthropological theory to explain Qohelet's dissidence, his explanation is hardly sociological. There is no discussion of Qohelet's social location or the broader sociohistorical milieu of the author or how this motif resolves the societal problems of Qohelet's day. Of course, that was not the focus and intent of his article.

CONCLUSION

This concludes the review of the various attempts to explain Qohelet's heterodox nature. The ideational approach attempts to explain Qohelet's pessimism and skepticism in terms of his own cognitive ability to see the inadequacies of traditional wisdom. Some even see skepticism built into the ideational process itself, a natural development of thought. The non-ideational approaches include a gamut of perspectives that explain Qohelet's idiosyncratic character as due to other factors such as his psychological state or the general sociohistorical background or his specific social location or the class antagonism in his society. Some see the non-ideational factors as determinative in producing Qohelet's malaise. Others see a more complex dialectical process in which Qohelet's intellect interacts with these social and psychological variables. The most important non-ideational explanations are the social-science ones, which go beyond merely recounting social facets contributing to Qohelet's worldview. They incorporate sophisticated social theories, models, and sociological analytical tools to explain Qohelet's pessimism and skepticism. Important components of this type of approach are textual analysis, social history of the period, and the integration of a theory. But a problem with many of these is that they have been largely micro-sociological. They do not provide the "big picture" of how Qohelet's thinking fits in with the larger social environment or theological landscape. Or, with the Marxian interpretations, the analytical tools they use are often too blunt, focusing on social class to the neglect of other social variables. Often sociological interpretations focus on the wrong things: materialism, Hellenism, or loss of status, instead of on Qohelet's frustration with traditional wisdom and his polemic against it.

Basically, all of the sociological elements that could have contributed to Qohelet's dark perspective have been touched on in this review. What is necessary now is simply to reconfigure them. In the following, there will be no claim to present any totally new data per se. Rather, the originality is that the analysis will be more comprehensive and the theorization broader and deeper than previous attempts. Drawing on Weber will enable this to be done.

The basic methodology will be the following. First, I present a sociological analysis of Ptolemaic Judah and a determination of Qohelet's social location.

Second, I offer a literary-critical reading of the book of Qohelet as a whole that draws out its theology and anthropology. The following sociological theorization is directly dependent on this reading. This procedure provides some degree of objectivity, showing that the analysis is ultimately very text oriented and driven. Third, drawing primarily on Weber as master theorist, while simultaneously incorporating other theorists, I mainly interpret Qohelet using his concept of rationalization, which provides the "big picture" approach just mentioned and links nicely with the literary reading.

3

QOHELET'S SOCIOHISTORICAL CONTEXT

The purpose of this chapter is to provide a brief and broad social history of Ptolemaic Judah, which will include a class analysis of the society. This necessitates analyzing the Ptolemaic political and economic system into which Judah was integrated. It is important to emphasize that primary sources are few for the period, both for Ptolemaic Egypt and Judah. Therefore, I draw on secondary sources by experts to synthesize the material and make it meaningful. Priority is given to experts on the Ptolemaic kingdom and not just Qohelet specialists. These procedures help mitigate the typical circularity that biblical scholars fall victim to when they correlate the Ptolemaic political and social history with the text of Qohelet to illuminate both. Instead, the social history and class analysis of Ptolemaic Judah will be presented first, and then the next chapter will explore how Qohelet may reflect this history and then determine the social location of Qohelet and his audience. Significantly, these two chapters will form the basis for the integration of the literary reading and incorporation of social theory.

BRIEF HISTORY OF THE PTOLEMAIC KINGDOM
(THIRD CENTURY B.C.E.)

By 323 B.C.E., Alexander the Great had conquered much of the civilized world, reaching even into India.[1] When he died, he left behind a feeble-minded brother and an unborn son. A crisis emerged immediately over the succession of power in the empire.[2] Perdiccas, who was first in rank after Alexander,

---

1. Josef Wiesehöfer counters the argument that Alexander conquered Persia because of its moral decadence or decline. Instead it was due "to the outstanding military and tactical skill of its military opponent" ("The Achaemenid Empire in the Fourth Century B.C.E.: A Period of Decline?" in *Judah and the Judeans in the Fourth Century B.C.E.* [ed. Oded Lipschits, Gary N. Knoppers, and Rainer Albertz; Winona Lake, Ind.: Eisenbrauns, 2007], 11–30, esp. 28).

2. John D. Granger argues that while Alexander was superb as a military leader and conqueror, he failed to prepare for a successor and to install an adequate administration for all the satrapies of his empire. In many ways, he followed in the footsteps of his father, who

ruled as regent for Alexander's half-brother Arrhidaeus, who became Philip III of Macedon, and then as regent for both Philip and Alexander's infant son Alexander IV of Macedon. Perdiccas appointed Ptolemy, one of Alexander's closest companions, to be satrap of Egypt. As the empire disintegrated, Ptolemy established himself as ruler in his own right. Perdiccas invaded Egypt in 321 B.C.E., but Ptolemy defeated him.

In 305 B.C.E., Ptolemy took the title of king and became Ptolemy I Soter ("Savior") and founded the Ptolemaic dynasty, which would last for nearly three hundred years. The males of the dynasty took the name Ptolemy, while the queens preferred the names Cleopatra and Berenice. The Ptolemaic kings adopted the Egyptian custom of marrying their sisters, who often co-ruled. This incestuous polity served eventually to contribute to the disintegration of the kingdom.

The early Ptolemies catered to the Egyptian religion and customs, even building new temples for their gods. "The priests enjoyed considerable political power, not least because their good will was evidently seen by the Ptolemies as the key to acquiescence of the Egyptian population."[3] During the reign of Ptolemy II and Ptolemy III, thousands of Greek veterans were awarded land grants (as part of a cleruchy) for coming to Egypt. However, "the Greeks always remained a privileged minority in Ptolemaic Egypt," rarely admitting native Egyptians into the higher levels of Greek culture.[4] The presence of cleruchs in Egypt did three things. First, obviously it provided a military reserve for necessary maneuvers. Second, it provided a convenient police force in case of revolts.[5] Third, and perhaps most important, it tended to instill loyalty in would-be mercenaries because they had land and family now in Egypt.[6]

---

failed to perceive the value of administration in the maintenance of his kingdom (*Alexander the Great Failure* [London: Hamblin Continuum, 2007], esp. 34). By contrast, according to Richard A. Billows, Antigonus the One-Eyed understood the value of administration and with ingenuity and flexibility essentially adopted and adapted the Persian satrapy system in Syria to his ends. Billows believes that Antigonus represents the model of how the Hellenistic kingdoms should have been run (*Antigonos the One-Eyed and the Creation of the Hellenistic State* [Hellenistic Culture and Society; paperback ed.; Berkeley: University of California Press, 1997], 5–6, 237–85).

3. Alan B. Lloyd, "The Ptolemaic Period (332–30 BC)," in *The Oxford History of Ancient Egypt* (ed. Ian Shaw; paperback and new ed.; Oxford: Oxford University Press, 2003), 407.

4. F. W. Walbank, "Monarchies and Monarchic Ideas," in *The Cambridge Ancient History,* vol. 7, part 1, *The Hellenistic World* (ed. F. W. Walbank et al.; 2nd ed.; Cambridge: Cambridge University Press, 1984), 68–70.

5. E. G. Turner, "Ptolemaic Egypt," in *The Cambridge Ancient History,* vol. 7, part 1, *The Hellenistic World* (ed. F. W. Walbank et al.; 2nd ed.; Cambridge: Cambridge University Press, 1984), 125.

6. Ibid., 124.

The Ptolemies' benefactions to the Egyptian religion and traditions and their simultaneous installation of cleruchies demonstrate the two most important aspects of the maintenance of power: force and persuasion (consent). The use of both is what the Italian Western Marxist Gramsci calls hegemony.[7] An undue reliance on either to the exclusion of the other will result in the loss of power. Military force has the liability of being very expensive, while propaganda will only go so far. Ultimately, the potentate cannot depend completely on the spontaneous goodwill of his subjects. The balancing of these factors is critical for the domination of any peoples. Kings who are too brutal often have to contend with revolts.[8]

The early reign of Ptolemy I was dominated by the Wars of the Diadochi ("heirs") between the various successor states within the empire. In a short time, he gained control of Libya, Coele-Syria (including Judah), and Cyprus. When Antigonus, who ruled Syria, tried to unite the empire, Ptolemy joined in a coalition against him.[9] In 312 B.C.E., allied with Seleucus, the ruler of Babylonia, he defeated Antigonus's son, Demetrius, at Gaza.[10] Peace was established in 311. But war broke out again, and Ptolemy joined the coalition against Antigonus again in 302. But instead of being there at Antigonus's defeat at Ipsus, he secured Coele-Syria and Palestine for himself, setting the scene for the future Syrian Wars between the Ptolemies and Seleucids over control of this area: First Syrian War (274–271 B.C.E.), Second (260–253), Third (246–241), and the Fourth (219–217).[11] The Ptolemies wanted control of this entire region

---

7. See Antonio Gramsci, *Selections from the Prison Notes* (ed. and trans. Quintin Hoare and Geoffrey Nowell Smith; 1971; repr., New York: International Publishers, 2003), 80 n. 49.

8. A. B. Bosworth counters the view that the Hellenistic kings were able to claim kingship mainly due to their military and financial achievements. Bosworth contrasts the generosity and reciprocity of Alexander to the brutality of Demetrius; military achievements must be balanced with euergetism (*The Legacy of Alexander: Politics, Warfare, and Propaganda under the Successors* [Oxford: Oxford University Press, 2008], 246–78). Cf. Billows, who attempts to soften the brutal reputation of Antigonus (*Antigonos*, 10–12). The king was not only to be victorious but also to bring peace from outside threat and justice within his territory, and be generous and magnanimous (Walbank, "Monarchic Ideas," 81–84). Sitta von Reden points out that Ptolemaic catering to the priesthood was ultimately to prevent revolts (*Money in Ptolemaic Egypt: From the Macedonian Conquest to the End of the Third Century BC* [paperback ed.; Cambridge: Cambridge University Press, 2010], 23).

9. On Antigonus, see Édouard Will, "The Succession to Alexander," in *The Cambridge Ancient History*, vol. 7, part 1, *The Hellenistic World* (ed. F. W. Walbank et al.; 2nd ed.; Cambridge: Cambridge University Press, 1984), 39–61. On his underrated significance among the Diadochi, see Bosworth, *Legacy of Alexander*, v, 98–168.

10. On the rise of Seleucus, see Bosworth, *Legacy of Alexander*, 210–45.

11. See H. Heinen, "The Syrian-Egyptian Wars and Asia Minor," in *The Cambridge Ancient History*, vol. 7, part 1, *The Hellenistic World* (ed. F. W. Walbank et al.; 2nd ed.;

for two main reasons: financial (tribute via agricultural products and control of trade routes through this region) and military (the zone served as a buffer between the Ptolemies and Seleucids).[12] The Ptolemies also needed the Phoenician naval resources and the Lebanon timber for shipbuilding.[13] Ptolemy I died in 283 at the age of eighty-four.

Ptolemy II (Philadelphus) started his reign with the First Syrian War and demonstrated his mastery over the eastern Mediterranean. He spent lavishly to transform Alexandria into the cultural and intellectual center of the Hellenistic world. It was exploited "as the major showcase for Ptolemaic wealth and splendour and by the same token as the most significant non-military means by which the Ptolemies could vie with and surpass their rivals."[14] He is famous for inaugurating the Ptolemaieia, a four-yearly festival intended to rival the Olympics, with athletes, artists, and exotic animals.[15] In an account of the first inaugural event (279 B.C.E.), Callixeinus of Rhodes asks "What kingdom, my fellow diners, has ever been so rich in gold?"(Athenaeus, *Learned Banqueters* 5.203b). Ptolemy III Euergetes ("the Benefactor") succeeded his father in 246 and the kingdom reached its zenith of power during the Third Syrian War, with his march into the Seleucid realm as far as Babylonia and Thrace.[16] During his reign, he controlled most of the coasts of Asia Minor and Greece. In 221, Ptolemy III died, and he was succeeded by Ptolemy IV Philopator, a weak and corrupt king, easily influenced by others who really controlled the government. This period marks the beginning of the decline of the Ptolemaic kingdom. Eventually, the Seleucid king Antiochus III retook Coele-Syria from the Ptolemies in 198 after the Battle of Panias in the Galilee region.

PTOLEMAIC ADMINISTRATION

An important principle of the Ptolemaic administration is that the king considered all of his conquered territory to be his rightful property, which some have referred to as "royal absolutism" or a "totalitarian" principle.[17] The phrase

---

Cambridge: Cambridge University Press, 1984), 412–45, and the chronological table (pp. 493–511).

12. See ibid., 440–41.

13. Lloyd, "Ptolemaic Period," 392–3.

14. See ibid., 399–400.

15. See ibid., 401–2; E. G. Turner, "Ptolemaic Egypt," 138–39.

16. The first Ptolemy's epithet as "Soter" and the third's as "Euergetes" indicates how they wanted to be perceived: "The rulers had absolute power over these communities, but they courteously heard the representations of city embassies and gave grants of freedom, autonomy, exemption from tribute or garrison, and graciously received acclamations of saviour, benefactor, or even god manifest" (Bosworth, *Legacy of Alexander*, 4–5).

17. Kippenberg, *Religion und Klassenbildung,* 79; Gottwald, *Socio-Literary Introduc-*

the Diadochi used was "spear-won" territory, which gave them the right to view it as their very own.[18] This was true theoretically, but in reality private land existed.[19] There were two broad categories of land: crown land worked by royal tenants, who paid a yearly rent, and "remitted land" which fell into a number of categories: temple land, land held by cleruchs, "land held in gift" assigned to servants of the crown as stipend for their offices, private land, and city land held by a few Greek poleis.[20]

Egyptian temples were not simply cult centers but also had an economic function: they produced textiles and sponsored artists.[21] But industries they formerly controlled before the Ptolemies, such as textile, beer, and oil, now became state monopolies.[22] The state also monopolized salt.[23]

How far the principle of royal absolutism extended to Ptolemaic Judah is another matter. Some hold that it would apply more readily to Egypt than to the other territories like Palestine, since the Ptolemies "had to take time-honored local tradition into account."[24] The Ptolemies feared inciting the people's anger by taking their land.[25] However, some see the amount of crown land in Palestine as more extensive. Shimon Applebaum argues that during this period at least half the territory of Judah constituted state domain.[26] Elias Bickerman believes that the crown land in Palestine was maximal: Transjordan, Galilee, and the valley of the upper Jordan, with the cities of Lydda, Ekron, and perhaps Jamnia.[27] On the crown land, tenant farmers "paid their rent in kind, perhaps one-third of the yield of their sown crops and one-half of their fruits."[28]

---

tion, 442; Victor Tcherikover, "Hellenistic Palestine," in *The Hellenistic Age* (ed. Abraham Schalit; WHJP 6; New Brunswick, N.J.: Rutgers University Press, 1972), 93; cf. E. G. Turner, "Ptolemaic Egypt," 148.

18. See Walbank, "Monarchic Ideas," 66; Lloyd, "Ptolemaic Period," 402.

19. Lloyd, "Ptolemaic Period," 404–5.

20. Ibid.

21. Ibid., 406–7.

22. Von Reden, *Money in Ptolemaic Egypt*, 23.

23. Peter Schäfer, *The History of the Jews in the Greco-Roman World* (London: Taylor & Francis, 2003), 14.

24. Tcherikover, "Hellenistic Palestine," 93.

25. Ibid.

26. Shimon Applebaum, "Josephus and the Economic Causes of the Jewish War," in *Josephus, the Bible, and History* (ed. Louis H. Feldman and Gohei Hata; Detroit: Wayne State University Press, 1989), 238.

27. Elias Bickerman, *The Jews in the Greek Age* (Cambridge, Mass.: Harvard University Press, 1988), 73.

28. Ibid.

Bickerman also points out that numerous military colonies, often on crown land inherited from the Persians, were stationed in Palestine.[29] Especially significant among these was the cleruchy of the Tobiads who lived in Birta in Transjordan. Tobias was a "wealthy sheikh" who was probably counted on to resist any Seleucid invasion.[30] Garrisons were also placed in various cities such as Gaza and Beth-Zur and in the Negev.[31] From the Zenon papyri, it is also known that a high Ptolemaic official, Apollonios, owned a large wine-growing estate in Galilee (Bet Anat), an example of a *dorea* or "gift land," on which the owner had to pay taxes.[32]

Outside the crown lands and the Greek and Phoenician cities, the native towns and tribes of Syria and Phoenicia lived according to their customary laws.[33] The Ptolemies avoided interfering with them, being concerned only with security and revenue. Jerusalem was, thus, a subject town. There is a lot of uncertainty about whether there was a royal governor in the city or a garrison.[34] There were Ptolemaic officials who visited Jerusalem, such as Zenon (*C.P.J.* 2a.). Some certainly lived there, if royal officials actually collected the taxes under the supervision of the tax-farmer.[35] Thus, there was some degree of Greek presence in the city. But Roger Bagnall reveals a principle in Ptolemaic Egypt that seems to fit the circumstances of Jerusalem: "Let the cities run their own affairs so long as they satisfy whatever obligations they have to the crown."[36] It seems that Jerusalem was able to carry on as it had in Persian times, as long as it paid its taxes.[37] This laissez-faire approach fits with the general tendency of the Ptolemaic governance of Egypt: a deliberate unwillingness to interfere with institutions as they existed—a desire to avoid change. The Egyptian nome structure and bureaucracy were taken over with few changes as far as dealings with the native population were concerned. The natural evolution of bureaucracy was not prevented, but formal reforms must have been

---

29. Ibid., 71–73.

30. Tcherikover, "Hellenistic Palestine," 64–65.

31. Bickerman, *Greek Age*, 72.

32. Heinen, "Syrian-Egyptian Wars," 441.

33. Bickerman, *Greek Age*, 74.

34. Heinen believes that there was a garrison ("Syrian-Egyptian Wars," 441); Bickerman does not (*Greek Age*, 74). During the Fourth Syrian War, the Ptolemaic general Scopas installed a garrison in Jerusalem, but it was removed by Antiochus III after he reclaimed the city (Josephus, *Ant.* 12.133).

35. See Bagnall, *Ptolemaic Possessions*, 19. Schäfer believes that a "Temple President" oversaw finances at the Jerusalem temple, similar to the Egyptian practice (*History of the Jews*, 14, 16).

36. Bagnall, *Ptolemaic Possessions*, 9.

37. Cf. Gottwald, *Socio-Literary Introduction*, 442.

exceptions. Change was usually limited to rationalization and tightening the system for the sake of higher income.[38] But how independent were the Jews as whole? Bickerman aptly concludes: "The Jews of Judaea constituted a more or less self-governing *ethnos*, the law of Moses was their law, and their Temple was sacrosanct."[39] It was only when the high priest Onias refused to pay the tribute for Judah that Ptolemy III threatened to make Judah a cleruchy (Josephus, *Ant.* 12.159). Thus, the Jews as a people were generally free as long as taxes were paid.

The Ptolemaic administrative system involved a layering of bureaucracy. In Egypt, next to the king was the *dioketes*, "the minister of finance and economic affairs," who was "the real administrator of the kingdom."[40] Egypt was divided up into three layers in ascending order: the village, the toparchy (tax district), and the nome.[41] Each nome had an *oikonomos* who, along with his subordinates, had collectors, auditors, and checking clerks, and a *strategos* (military commander).[42] The basic unit of government in Syria/Phoenicia and presumably Palestine was the *hyparchy*, a territorial district, which was supervised by an *oikonomos*.[43] This district was divided up into villages whose administrative office was known as a *komarch*.[44] A *strategos* probably governed the whole province of Syria/Phoenicia with both military and civil authority.[45]

PTOLEMAIC TAXATION

What kept this administration running, as well as the military, of course, was the taxation. The success of the Ptolemies in their Syrian Wars and the ostentatious splendor of the Ptolemaieias were due in large part to the taxation in Egypt.[46] In contrast to the censuses that the pharaohs had conducted earlier

---

38. Bagnall, *Ptolemaic Possessions*, 9.

39. Bickerman, *Greek Age*, 74; cf. Tcherikover, "Hellenistic Palestine," 67–68, 79, 93. Those who see less autonomy include Peter Schäfer, "The Hellenistic and Maccabaean Periods," in *Israelite and Judean History* (ed. John H. Hayes and J. Maxwell Miller; OTL; Philadelphia: Westminster, 1977), 572; Hengel, *Judaism and Hellenism*, 1:24–25.

40. Schäfer, "Maccabaean Periods," 572.

41. See E. G. Turner, "Ptolemaic Egypt," 146.

42. See Schäfer, *History of the Jews*, 13, 15.

43. See Kippenberg, *Religion und Klassenbildung*, 79; Bagnall, *Ptolemaic Possessions*, 19; Schäfer, *History of the Jews*, 13.

44. See Kippenberg, *Religion und Klassenbildung*, 79; Bagnall, *Ptolemaic Possessions*, 19.

45. See Bickerman, *Greek Age*, 70; Heinen, "Syrian-Egyptian Wars," 440.

46. Dorothy Thompson, "The Infrastructure of Splendour: Census and Taxes in Ptolemaic Egypt," in *Hellenistic Constructs: Essays in Culture, History, and Historiography* (ed.

in Egypt to assess the labor force available for royal building projects, the Ptolemies' censuses were primarily for fiscal purposes.[47] Unlike states that tax either the land or the people, for example, the Romans, the Ptolemies taxed both.[48] The royal absolutist principle was the underlying legitimization for the famous tax system of the Ptolemaic kingdom: the king had the right to a certain percentage of the harvest yield.[49] It should be kept in mind, however, that "the art of taxation consists in so plucking the goose as to get the most feathers for the least hissing" (Jean Baptiste Colbert).[50]

Fundamental to the efficiency of the Ptolemaic tax system was the use of "intermediaries—tax-farmers, managers of gift estates, temple personnel and tenants—who were not only responsible for full payment of the tax, but also for the form in which it reached the treasury."[51] Most Egyptian taxation served local needs because transportation costs to Alexandria were too high.[52] Instead of one large type of tax, there were many small taxes levied on the Egyptians that constituted the particular burden: bath, salt (or poll), obol, trade, and animal taxes.[53] Certain professions and ethnicities were exempted from the salt tax by Philadelphus: schoolteachers, coaches, artists, victorious athletes at the Alexandrian festivals, Hellenes, and Persians.[54] In addition, censuses have been recovered that are organized according to occupations (e.g., beekeepers, weavers, or gooseherds), where differential taxation applied.[55]

The most famous of the intermediaries was the tax-farmer. Kippenberg describes this tax-farming system as *Staatspacht*, "government lease," where private citizens are actually leased the right to collect royal taxes and share in the profit.[56] In Egypt, these were usually Greek entrepreneurs who took advantage of the difficulty of paying cash taxes, but the main criterion was how well they were familiar with the trade to be taxed, often belonging to it.[57] The tax-farmer himself did not actually collect the taxes, though he could

---

Paul Cartledge, Peter Garnsey, and Erich Gruen; Hellenistic Culture and Society 26; Berkeley: University of California Press, 1997), 257.

47. Ibid., 243–44.

48. Ibid., 244.

49. Kippenberg, *Religion und Klassenbildung*, 79.

50. Gerhard E. Lenski, *Power and Privilege: A Theory of Social Stratification* (New York: McGraw-Hill, 1966; Chapel Hill: University of North Carolina Press, 1984), 243.

51. Von Reden, *Money in Ptolemaic Egypt*, 85.

52. Ibid., 87.

53. Ibid., 103; Thompson, "Census and Taxes," 245.

54. Thompson, "Census and Taxes," 247.

55. Ibid., 251.

56. Kippenberg, *Religion und Klassenbildung*, 78–79.

57. Von Reden, *Money in Ptolemaic Egypt*, 107–8.

monitor it. Tax-farmers were aristocratic private citizens who joined with the Ptolemaic administration in exploiting their own people.[58]

Egyptian taxation under the Ptolemies was greatly aided by the introduction of coinage,[59] which also aided the administration as a whole: "Because of the convenience of its collection and transportation, as well as reduction of other costs, coinage increased the efficiency of the administration and royal surplus extraction."[60] Furthermore, coinage served to centralize Ptolemaic Egypt and provided the ideological self-representation of the king and his power.[61] It was also responsible, however, for a massive increase in debt among the people.[62]

In the provinces, "the job of collection belongs to the royal officials of the village and *hyparchia*."[63] The tax-farming position was apparently lucrative and highly sought-after, as is seen in the reference made by Josephus to prominent men coming to Alexandria to bid for such positions: "But it so happened that at that time all the chief men and magistrates of the cities of Syria and Palestine were coming there to bid for the tax-farming rights which the king used to sell every year to the wealthy men in each city" (Josephus, *Ant.* 12.165 [Marcus, LCL]). The high priest was responsible for the payment of a tribute of twenty talents of silver to the Ptolemaic dynasty (Josephus, *Ant.* 12.158). According to Josephus, the high priest had received and maintained the office of *prostasia*, ("exercising authority," "leader or ruler," "guardian" [LSJ, 1526]) "chief magistracy" or representation of the Jewish people, and high priesthood through the payment of this tribute (Josephus, *Ant.* 12.161 [Marcus, LCL]). The high priest may have served as "general contractor responsible to the Ptolemies for the revenue of that region."[64] The position of *prostasia* was perhaps like a "petty monarch," though Bickerman sees the office of high priest as no pontificate.[65] Ralph Marcus sees the title as largely synonymous with the high priesthood and not a technical term denoting a civil office (Josephus, *Ant.* 12.161, d [Marcus, LCL]). In addition to the tribute, it appears that the Jews in Ptolemaic times were required to pay personal taxes (poll, salt, and crown

---

58. Kippenberg argues that this compromising aristocracy separated itself from the rest of Jewish society and was responsible for the later revolt by the common people against its exploitative measures (*Religion und Klassenbildung*, 78–93).

59. Thompson, "Census and Taxes," 297.

60. Ibid., 296.

61. Ibid. 296.

62. Ibid., 298.

63. Bagnall, *Ptolemaic Possessions*, 19.

64. M. Rostovtzeff, *The Social and Economic History of the Hellenistic World* (3 vols; Oxford: Clarendon, 1941), 1:349.

65. Tcherikover, "Hellenistic Palestine," 59; Bickerman, *Greek Age*, 143.

taxes).[66] In the following decree, Antiochus III, the Seleucid king who confiscated Judah from the Ptolemies after the Battle of Panias, does as new despots often do and performs a *mišarum* act to give tax breaks for both the elite and the general citizenry of Jerusalem:

> And all the members of the nation shall have a form of government in accordance with the laws of their country, and the senate, the priests, and scribes of the temple and the temple-singers shall be relieved from the poll-tax and the crown-tax and the salt tax which they pay. And, in order that the city may the more quickly be inhabited, I grant both to the present inhabitants and to those who may return before the month of Heperberetaios exemption from taxes for three years. We shall also relieve them in the future from the third part of their tribute, so that their losses may be made good. (Josephus, *Ant.* 12.142–44[Marcus, LCL])

This leads one naturally to the question of the extent of the tax burden that the Jews faced under the Ptolemies. Some argue that the tax burden of this period appears to have been greater than in Persian times.[67] As Rostovtzeff argues:

> It seems reasonable to suppose that the early Ptolemies (probably Philadelphus) organized Judaea and probably other parts of Palestine for purposes of taxation more strictly than before. As might be expected, the rural population, which was probably treated in the same way as that of Egypt and Syria, resented the new system and hated the new taxes and their collectors, while the privileged city population was satisfied with the new régime and became rapidly Hellenized.[68]

The oppressiveness of the tax burden may also be indicated in two instances of rebellion. One is found in a letter (258 B.C.E.) by a local official, Alexandros, to Oryas. The incident reported involves a local Jewish prince, Jeddous, who refused to pay the money he owed to Zenon (taxes/debt?). Straton is a messenger of Zenon:

> I have received your letter, to which you added a copy of the letter by Zenon to Jeddous saying that unless he gave the money to Straton, Zenon's man, we were to hand over his pledge to him (Straton). I happened to be unwell as a result of taking some medicine, so I sent a lad, a servant of mine, with Straton, and wrote a letter to Jeddous. When they returned they said that he had taken no notice of my letter, but had attacked them and thrown them out of the village. So I am writing to you (for your information). (*CPJ* 6)

---

66. This is argued by Rostovtzeff, *Economic History*, 1:349; Hengel, *Judaism and Hellenism*, 1:28; Kippenberg, *Religion und Klassenbildung*, 90–91; contra Tcherikover, "Hellenistic Palestine," 83–84. Bickerman leaves the question undecided (*Greek Age*, 74).

67. Cf. Gottwald, *Socio-Literary Introduction*, 442.

68. Rostovtzeff, *Economic History*, 1:350.

This points to Jewish discontent with Ptolemaic taxation, but it also seems to show that the Ptolemies were limited in enforcing their policies.[69] Note that Jeddous feels he can get away with thwarting these minor officials. It also indicates that the Ptolemies had to take time-honored traditions and customs into consideration.

A second example is the refusal to pay the tribute by Onias, the high priest (Josephus, *Ant.* 12.158). It appears that Onias had had enough of Ptolemaic rule with its heavy financial extraction, and he anticipated a change in regime (Seleucid).[70] Josephus blames Onias's refusal to pay on his being "small-minded and passionately fond of money" (Josephus, *Ant.* 12.158 [Marcus, LCL]). More likely this is Josephus's persistent attempt to discredit the Oniads (Zadokites), whom Josephus saw as rivals of the Hasmoneans, of whom he was a direct descendant, for the high priesthood.[71] But, at any rate, these two incidents represent Jewish elites who felt and resisted the oppressive character of the Ptolemaic bureaucracy.

The tax burden was perhaps greatest under the tax-farming of Joseph Tobias, as was mentioned earlier. Joseph outbid his tax-farming competitors in Alexandria, the capital, where the auction was held:

> When the sum of taxes from Coele-Syria and from Phoenicia and Judaea with Samaria added up to eight thousand talents, Joseph came forward and accused the bidders of having made an agreement to offer the king a low price for the taxes, whereas he for his part promised to give double that amount and send over to the king the property of those who had been remiss toward his house; for this right was sold along with that of farming the taxes. Thereupon the king, who heard him gladly, said that he would confirm the sale of the tax-farming rights to him, as he was likely to increase his revenue. . . . This gave great pains to those who had come to Egypt from the cities, for they considered themselves slighted. And so they returned with discomfiture to their respective provinces. (Josephus, *Ant.* 12.175–77, 179 [Marcus, LCL])

Joseph, thus, doubles the taxes that Syria/Phoenicia bid from eight to sixteen thousand talents. If this statistic is true, surely this would have had catastrophic consequences for all of this area. The resentment against such a measure is

---

69. Tcherikover also points to a similar situation when Zenon had to write five letters and repay to retrieve two escaped slave girls ("Hellenistic Palestine," 65).

70. Gottwald, *Socio-Literary Introduction,* 442; Hengel, *Judaism and Hellenism,* 1:27; Schäfer, "Maccabaean Periods," 573; Jonathan A. Goldstein, "The Tales of the Tobiads," in *Christianity, Judaism and Other Greco-Roman Cults: Studies for Morton Smith at Sixty,* vol. 3, *Judaism before 70* (ed. Jacob Neusner; SJLA 12; Leiden: Brill, 1975; repr., Eugene, Ore.: Wipf & Stock, n.d.), 97–98.

71. See Goldstein, "Tales of the Tobiads," 85, 121.

reflected in the resistance to Joseph's newly acquired power and economic exploitation:

> Then Joseph, after getting from the king two thousand foot-soldiers—for he had asked to have some assistance, in order that he might be able to use force with any in the cities who treated him with contempt—and borrowing five hundred talents in Alexandria from the friends of the king, set out for Syria. And coming to Ascalon, he demanded tribute from the people of the city, but they not only refused to give him anything, but even insulted him to boot; he therefore arrested some twenty of their principal men and put them to death, and sent their property, which all together was worth a thousand talents, to the king, informing him of what had happened. (Josephus, *Ant.* 12.180–81 [Marcus, LCL])

Schäfer argues:

> There is nothing to indicate that he extracted double taxes only from non-Jewish cities such as Ashkelon and Scythopolis and that he spared his Jewish co-religionists. We must, on the contrary, begin with the assumption that the policies of the Tobiads played an important role in sharpening the social differences in Palestine and thus also in giving rise to apocalyptic tendencies and revolutionary movements.[72]

Similarly, Kippenberg theorizes that Joseph assumed the office of *prostasia* and then speculates that the newly set amount of tribute could not be paid via the temple treasury, so a produce tax was installed.[73] This deficit problem was compensated for by two strategies: enslavement of family members beyond that needed for cultivation and emphasis placed on highly profitable businesses in Judah such as olive production.[74]

---

72. Schäfer, "Maccabaean Periods," 574. On the rift that developed between the upper and lower classes during this period, see Crüsemann, "Unchangeable World," 62–74; Kippenberg, *Religion und Klassenbildung,* 78–93; Tcherikover, "Hellenistic Palestine," 110–14; Hengel, *Judaism and Hellensim,* 1:49–50; Rostovtzeff, *Economic History,* 1:349–50; Samuel K. Eddy, *The King Is Dead: Studies in the Near Eastern Resistance to Hellenism 334–31 b.c.* (Lincoln: University of Nebraska Press, 1961), 196–99; Gottwald, *Socio-Literary Introduction,* 442–43; Menahem Stern, "Aspects of Jewish Society: The Priesthood and Other Classes," in *The Jewish People in the First Century: Historical Geography, Political History, Social, Cultural and Religious Life and Institutions* (ed. S. Safrai and M. Stern; CRINT 1/2; Assen: Van Gorcum, 1976), 561–65. On the rise of apocalyptic groups during this period, see Crüsemann, "Unchangeable World," 63–65, 68–69, 74; Hengel, *Judaism and Hellenism,* 1:49–50. For the connection between apocalyptic thought and social position, see Paul D. Hanson, *The Dawn of Apocalyptic* (Philadelphia: Fortress, 1975), 231–18, 282, 409; Crüsemann, "Hiob," 386, 389–92.

73. Kippenberg, *Religion und Klassenbildung,* 81–82.

74. Ibid., 82. On the intensification of agriculture in Judah during this period, see Crüsemann, "Unchangeable World," 62–63; Gottwald, *Socio-Literary Introduction,* 443.

However, Kippenberg's thesis assumes the historicity of the amount of Joseph's bid at sixteen thousand talents. Jonathan Goldstein believes that this figure is an exaggeration.[75] Schäfer's assumption that Joseph would not have placed the greater tax burden on the non-Judeans does not make sense because it would have served to undermine Joseph's position among the Jews. Though the tribute amount is probably exaggerated, Schäfer's point that this development exacerbated the rift between the wealthy and the poor peasants is, of course, probably correct. Rostovtzeff's similar note that the upper classes suffered much less than the poor under the Ptolemies is also probably very close to the truth. In fact, the tax-farmers would have prospered during this time.

But how did the taxation under the Ptolemies compare with that of the Persians? This is difficult to answer. Bickerman believes that when Alexander conquered Palestine, everything remained the same: "The rulers of the people, the tribute, the status of the Temple, all remained as they had been under the Persian kings."[76] Several archaeologists have pointed to continuity between the late Persian and early Greek period in Palestine in terms of administration, culture, and ethnicity.[77] Aramaic ostraca from fourth-century Idumea show the same system of tax collection for the early Hellenistic period as for the Persian era; there were land taxes (tribute), taxes on craftsmen and trade, taxes on slave trade, a poll tax, and corvée, and it was probably the same for Judah as a whole.[78] It is therefore reasonable to conclude that Ptolemaic taxation was probably very similar to that in the Persian period until the time of Joseph's twenty-two-year tenure as provincial tax-collector (227/224 to 205/202 B.C.E.), when the tribute for Judah may have increased.[79]

As in Egypt, coinage in Ptolemaic Judah was connected with the tax system. Archaeological finds in Palestine suggest that Ptolemy II increased coinage to four to five times that of his father, which may indicate an economic

---

75. Goldstein, "Tales of the Tobiads," 102.

76. Bickerman, *Greek Age*, 6.

77. Oded Lipschits and Oren Tal, "The Settlement Archaeology of the Province of Judah: A Case Study," in *Judah and the Judeans in the Fourth Century B.C.E.* (ed. Oded Lipschits, Gary N. Knoppers, and Rainer Albertz; Winona Lake, Ind.: Eisenbrauns, 2007), 47–48; and, in the same volume, Oded Lipschits and David Vanderhooft, "Yehud Stamp Impressions in the Fourth Century B.C.E.: A Time of Administrative Consolidation?" 84–85; Esther Eshel, "The Onomasticon of Mareshah in the Persian and Hellenistic Periods," 154; and cf. this article with Amos Kloner and Ian Stern, "Idumea in the Late Persian Period (Fourth Century B.C.E.)," 139–44.

78. André Lemaire, "Administration in Fourth-Century B.C.E Judah in Light of Epigraphy and Numismatics," in *Judah and the Judeans in the Fourth Century B.C.E.* (ed. Oded Lipschits, Gary N. Knoppers, and Rainer Albertz; Winona Lake, Ind.: Eisenbrauns, 2007), 56–61.

79. For the dating, see Goldstein, "Tales of the Tobiads," 101.

boom.[80] With him, minted money was finally established in Palestine and bartering was superseded.[81] Judah was allowed to mint its own coins during the Ptolemaic period, unlike Samaria, because of the latter's revolt against Alexander the Great.[82] These are called Yehud coins and were used in the same late-Persian period denominations.[83] They were minted until the late 260s during the reign of Ptolemy II. In the Persian period, a poll tax was paid with coins, and the temple became a bank of sorts as a result.[84] The high priest was the minting authority, as shown by a coin found perhaps dating to the late fourth century with the inscription "Yochanan, the priest."[85] This may point to the economic and political power of the high priest in Hellenistic times; "Yaddua" (the high priest under Darius III) may have been Yochanan's son and successor, who welcomed Alexander in "Saphein" (Josephus, *Ant.* 11.326).[86]

GENERAL BENEFITS OF PTOLEMAIC GOVERNANCE OF JUDAH

Though the Ptolemaic taxation of subjugated peoples was oppressive, there were some benefits brought by the kingdom. First, there was peace from foreign aggression. Bickerman says eloquently, "Under the wings of the Ptolemaic eagle, the Holy Land enjoyed the blessings of peace throughout the century."[87] Connected with this were internal peace and security: law and order. As the Islamic ulema said, "A hundred years of despotism are better than one day of anarchy."[88] In addition, a period of great economic productivity and political significance for Judah appears to be reflected in Josephus's eulogy of Joseph Tobias, who outbid his competitors: "And then also died Hyrcanus' father Joseph, who had been an excellent and high-minded man and had brought the Jewish people from poverty and a state of weakness to more splendid opportunities of life during the twenty-two years when he controlled the taxes of Syria, Phoenicia and Samaria" (Josephus, *Ant.* 12.224 [Marcus, LCL]). The archaeological evidence seems to confirm this, at least as far as the Tobiads are

---

80. Hengel, *Judaism and Hellenism*, 1:43.

81. Ibid., 44.

82. See Magen Yitzhak, "The Dating of the First Phase of the Samaritan Temple on Mount Gerizim in Light of the Archaeological Evidence," in *Judah and the Judeans in the Fourth Century* B.C.E. (ed. Oded Lipschits, Gary N. Knoppers, and Rainer Albertz; Winona Lake, Ind.: Eisenbrauns, 2007), 181–82.

83. Lipschits and Tal, "Settlement Archaeology," 47.

84. Lemaire, "Fourth-Century B.C.E. Judah," 59–60.

85. Ibid., 55, 60.

86. Ibid., 54, 60.

87. Bickerman, *Greek Age*, 70; cf. Tcherikover, "Hellenistic Palestine," 59.

88. Lenski, *Power and Privilege*, 296 n. 188, citing a personal conversation with Robert Bellah.

concerned. A Tobiad temple, palace, or mausoleum has been discovered in Iraq al Amir, Jordan, which indicates the great wealth the family accumulated.[89] But how did Judah fare as a whole? Techrikover believes that Joseph benefited himself and his family and not the Jews as a whole.[90] Bickerman points to the many discovered Rhodian stamped jars that contained imported Greek wine and olive oil, luxury items, as evidence for "a raised standard of living in Ptolemaic Palestine."[91]

The *Letter of Aristeas* has been cited as evidence for such a profitable period.[92] Aristeas supposedly was an official in Ptolemy II's court, who was sent as an emissary to visit the high priest Eleazar to discuss sending seventy-two scholars to translate the Hebrew Torah into Greek (the Septuagint). Aristeas writes to his brother Philocrates.[93] The following is a description by the emissaries of Jerusalem and its surroundings:

> The diligence of their agriculturists is indeed great. Their country is plentifully wooded with numerous olive trees, and rich in cereal crops and pulse, and also in vines and honey. Date palms and other fruit trees are beyond reckoning among them. They have plentiful cattle of all varieties, and their pastures are lush. Hence they recognized that the rural districts required a dense population, and they laid the city and the villages out in proportion. A great volume of spices, precious stones, and gold is brought into the region by the Arabs. For the country is adapted for commerce as well as agriculture, and the city is rich in crafts and lacks none of the things imported by sea. It also has harbors well situated to supply its needs, those at Ascalon, Joppa, and Gaza, and likewise Ptolemais, which was founded by the king. It is centrally located with reference to the places just mentioned, and not far distant from them. The country enjoys everything in abundance, being well watered everywhere and possessing great security. Around it flows the river called Jordan, whose stream never fails. Originally the country comprised no less than six million aroura (but afterwards the neighboring peoples encroached upon it), and six hundred thousand men each became holders of hundred-aroura lots. About the time of harvest the river rises, like the Nile, and irrigates much of the land. The stream empties into another river in the district of Ptolemais, and this flows into the sea. Other mountain torrents, as they are

---

89. See Hengel, *Judaism and Hellenism*, 1:272–77. Stephen G. Rosenberg argues that the main structure is a mausoleum in Hellenistic style ("Qasr al-Abd: A Mausoleum of the Tobiad Family?" *BAIAS* 19–20 [2001–02]: 157–75).

90. Tcherikover, "Hellenistic Palestine," 142.

91. Bickerman, *Greek Age*, 75.

92. Claude Orrieux, "Les papyrus de Zénon et la préhistoire du mouvement maccabéen," in *Hellenica et Judaica* (ed. A. Caquot, M. Hadas-Lebel, and J. Riaud; Leuven: Peeters, 1986), 331.

93. See Moses Hadas, introduction to *Aristeas to Philocrates (Letter of Aristeas)* (ed. and trans. by M. Hadas; Dropsie College Edition: Jewish Apocryphal Literature; New York: Harper, 1951), 1–2.

called, flow down and take in the parts about Gaza and the district of Azotus. The country is encircled by natural defenses, so that it is hard to penetrate and impracticable for large numbers, because the passes are narrow, being flanked by steep cliffs and deep ravines; the whole mountain range which surrounds the entire country is rugged. (*Ep. Arist.* 112–18 [Hadas])

But the credibility of the letter is suspect in that it is dated to 130 B.C.E. and was perhaps written by an Alexandrian Jew.[94] Also, as Moses Hadas surmises, "All references to the country in Aristeas envisage a remote and idealized Biblical Palestine and seem purposely to ignore contemporary reality."[95]

The letter also contains additional evidence of the benefits of Ptolemaic rule. It portrays Ptolemy II as beneficent. He freed thousands of Jewish slaves, perhaps pro-Seleucid, who had been enslaved by his father and brought to Egypt, as well as other enslaved Egyptian Jews (*Ep. Arist.* 12–16). "It is also consistent with Philadelphus's intellectual curiosity that he would have given strong royal support to his chief librarian's request for a Greek translation of the sacred texts, especially the laws, of his Jewish subjects."[96]

Drawing on literary evidence, Bickerman also argues for a two- or three-fold increase in the Palestinian population during the third century, but the settlement archaeology of Judah for this period does not substantiate this.[97] Thus, the evidence is mixed.

But, of course, these responses assume that the Tobiad tales are historical.[98] The bias of Josephus is legendary, so another important question is how much of the story is true?[99] As Goldstein has asked, why would Josephus include a tale like this (including a similar tale about Hyrcanus, Joseph's son) in which the

---

94. Hadas, "Introduction," 54, 65. Lipschits and Tal believe that the letter may reflect Hasmonean conditions more than Ptolemaic ("Settlement Archaeology," 41 n. 6).

95. Hadas, "Introduction," 64.

96. Leonard J. Greenspoon, "Between Alexandria and Antioch: Jews and Judaism in the Hellenistic Period," in *The Oxford History of the Biblical World* (ed. Michael D. Coogan; New York: Oxford University Press, 1998), 426.

97. Bickerman, *Greek Age*, 152; Lipschits and Tal, "Settlement Archaeology," 34–41.

98. Susan Niditch largely questions the historicity of the tales, showing how the stories reflect biblical stories such as the Joseph narrative and folklore patterns such as the displacement of an elder by a younger person (son) ("Father-Son Folktale Patterns and Tyrant Typologies in Josephus' Ant. 12:160–222," *JJS* 32 [1981]: 47–55).

99. Gottfried Mader gives the intended audience and two purposes of Josephus's *Jewish War*, which are probably similar for his *Jewish Antiquities*: writing to Romans/Greeks and Hellenistic Jews to curb anti-Semitism and to show the Romans in a more positive light (*Josephus and the Politics of Historiography: Apologetic and Impression Management in the Bellum Judaicum* [Mnemosyne: Supplementum 205; Leiden: Brill, 2000], 152–56). He shows that the air of objectivity in Josephus's work is due to his imitation of a Thucydidean-Polybian pattern (52–54). By contrasting Josephus with 1 Maccabees, his source, Louis H.

characters display unethical qualities (bribery and wenching), when Josephus was a strict Pharisee?[100] Several explanations have been given. Tcherikover sees Joseph's heroic portrayal as due to his introduction of new elements into Jewish society.[101] Bickerman maintains that Joseph demonstrates the superiority of Jewish intellectualism because he essentially outwits Ptolemy.[102] Perhaps it was Joseph's loyalty to the Ptolemies that Josephus most admired, especially in his attempt to portray the Jews as nonthreatening to those in power (for him, the Romans). But the fact that Josephus's source was probably by a pro-Ptolemaic Jew who resided in Egypt during the second or first century seriously calls into question the accuracy of Josephus's account of Ptolemaic conditions.[103] Nevertheless, Josephus may be recounting actual events. Therefore there seems to be no compelling reason to reject the Tobiad romance as largely fictive, even if particular features are. Louis Feldman's advice is apropos regarding the credibility of Josephus's accounts: "Suspect but respect."[104]

Bickerman points out another related development.[105] The Ptolemies greatly valued the wine and olive oil of Palestine (Egypt did not have extensive olive groves). This means that the exportation of these commodities could have made many Jews rich. He points out, however, that this factor made a small vineyard or olive orchard as profitable as four or five grain fields just as large. The negative effect of this development is emphasized by Gottwald, who points out that this intensification was "chiefly for export products such as wine and oil rather than for grain and vegetable production for the native populace."[106] He adds, "State monopolies on these exports, joined with heavy taxation framed by self-serving local officials, created a debilitating pressure on the majority of the rural populace."[107] In other words, the "more splendid

---

Feldman shows how Josephus depicts the Hasmoneans as Greek leaders and heroes (*Studies in Hellenistic Judaism* [AGJU 30; Leiden: Brill, 1996], 137–63).

100. Goldstein, "Tales of the Tobiads," 86, 88.

101. Tcherikover, "Hellenistic Palestine," 131.

102. Bickerman, *Greek Age*, 175.

103. Goldstein, "Tales of the Tobiads," 107, 116; Dov Gera, "On the Credibility of the History of the Tobiads (Josephus, *Antiquities*, 12, 156–222, 228–236)," in *Greece and Rome in Eretz Israel: Collected Essays* (ed. A. Kasher, U. Rappaport, and G. Fuks; Jerusalem: Yad Izhak Ben-Zvi/Israel Exploration Society, 1999), 38. Robert Doran argues that Hyrcanus was not really pro-Ptolemaic and that the struggle over Jerusalem before the accession of Antiochus was largely a fight between rich families and not a pro-Seleucid versus pro-Ptolemaic battle ("Parties and Politics in Pre-Hasmonean Jerusalem: A Closer Look at 2 Macc 3:11," *SBL 1982 Seminar Papers*, 105–11).

104. Feldman, *Hellenistic Judaism*, 6.

105. Bickerman, *Greek Age*, 151.

106. Gottwald, *Socio-Literary Introduction*, 581.

107. Ibid., 443.

opportunities of life" that Josephus mentions would have been reserved for a small elite. This social rift was true also for the Egyptian poor under the Ptolemies: "In most cases the peasantry was evidently operating at the level of marginal subsistence, and its lot could easily be intolerable, particularly in times of internal political disruption, which were increasingly common from the end of the third century BC."[108]

SOCIAL STRATIFICATION IN PTOLEMAIC JERUSALEM

PRIESTS

The mention of the tribute and the high priest's control of its payment in Josephus's account of Onias's refusal to pay (*Ant.* 12.142) reveals something of the power of the high priest, as well as the relationship between Jerusalem and Egypt. It obviously reveals the status of the high priest as a leader and representative of the Jews. In contrast to governors and high priests who were in charge during the Persian period, under the Ptolemies the high priest appears to have ruled alone.[109] The Jews were considered an *ethnos* by the Greeks (Antiochus III refers to the Palestinian Jews as a "nation" [Josephus, *Ant.* 12.142]).[110] Hecataeus of Abdera identifies the high priest's powerful position as the representative of the *ethnos* to the Ptolemaic kingdom (Diodorus [first century B.C.E.] cites Hecataeus):

> For this reason the Jews never had a king, and authority [*prostaisan*] over the people is regularly vested in whichever priest is regarded as superior to his colleagues in wisdom and virtue. They call this man the high priest, and believe that he acts as a messenger to them of God's commandments. It is he, we are told, who in their assemblies and other gatherings announces what is ordained, and the Jews are so docile in such matters that straightway they fall to the ground and do reverence to the high priest when he expounds the commandments to them. (Diodorus Siculus, *Bibliotheca Historica* 40.3.5–6 [Walton, LCL])

Josephus refers to him as *tou laou tēn prostasian* "representative of the people" (*Ant.* 12.161).

---

108. Lloyd, "Ptolemaic Period," 410.

109. Lemaire lists the officials of fourth-century Judah: governors, high priests, a prefect (tax-collector), judges, and a treasurer ("Fourth-Century B.C.E. Judah," 54–56). On the Samaritan governors, some simultaneously high priests, see Hanan Eshel, "The Governors of Samaria in the Fifth and Fourth Centuries B.C.E.," in *Judah and the Judeans in the Fourth Century B.C.E.* (ed. Oded Lipschits, Gary N. Knoppers, and Rainer Albertz; Winona Lake, Ind.: Eisenbrauns, 2007), 223–34.

110. For the Greek concept of *ethnos*, see Hengel, *Judaism and Hellenism*, 1:24; Kippenberg, *Religion und Klassenbildung*, 82; Bickerman, *Greek Age*, 74.

Obviously, power was linked to control of the payment of this tribute. According to Josephus, the high priest had received and maintained the office of *prostasia* and high priest through the payment of tribute (*Ant.* 12.161). As Rostovtzeff suggests, the high priest may have served as "general contractor" of Ptolemaic revenue for the region.[111] Though the reliability of the *Letter of Aristeas* is questionable, as has already been indicated, it purports to describe the lofty position of the high priest in the time of Ptolemy II (Philadelphus)[112]:

> We were struck with great astonishment when we beheld Eleazar at his ministration, and his apparel, and the visible glory conferred by his being garbed in the "coat" which he wears and the stones that adorn his person. For there are "bells of gold" upon the "skirts of the robe" giving out a peculiar musical sound, and on either side of these are "pomegranates" broidered "with flowers," marvelously colorful. He was girt with a rich and magnificent "girdle," woven with most beautiful colors. And "upon his breast" he wears what is called the "oracle," in which are set "twelve stones" of various species, soldered with gold, with "the names" of the heads of the tribes, according to their original constitution, each of them flashing forth indescribably with the natural color of its own peculiar character. Upon his head he has the "tiara" as it is called, and on top of this the inimitable "mitre," bearing "engraven" in sacred letters upon a "plate of gold" set between his eyebrows the name of God filled with glory. He is adjudged worthy of these things in his ministrations. The total effect of the whole arouses awe and emotional excitement, so that one would think he had passed to some other sphere outside the world. I venture to affirm positively that any man who witnessed the spectacle I have recounted will experience amazement and astonishment indescribable, and his mind will be deeply moved at the sanctity attaching to every detail. (*Ep. Arist.* 96–99 [Hadas])

Ben Sira similarly reflects the same awe of the high priest in Seleucid times (second century B.C.E.):

> The leader of his brothers and the pride of his people
> Was the high priest, Simon son of Onias,
> Who in his life repaired the house, and in his time fortified the temple.
> He laid the foundations for the high double walls,
> The high retaining walls for the temple enclosure.
> In his days a water cistern was dug,
> A reservoir like the sea in circumference.
> He considered how to save his people from ruin,
> And fortified the city against siege.
> How glorious he was, surrounded by the people,
> As he came out of the house of the curtain.

---

111. Rostovtzeff, *Economic History*, 1:349.
112. See Tcherikover, "Hellenistic Palestine," 54, 106–8.

Like the morning star among the clouds,
Like the the full moon at the festal season;
Like the sun shining on the temple of the Most High. (Sir 50:1–7)

Tcherikover makes an interesting observation concerning the priests during this period: "It is worth noting that out of the whole population of Jerusalem Hecataeus took note of only one social group—the priest, which indicates that in his time the priestly class was the only one which could attract a stranger."[113] Tcherikover also maintains that "their class was the strongest and the wealthiest among the classes of Jerusalem."[114] Aristeas also describes this stratum:

> In its exhibition of strength and its orderly and silent performances the ministration of the priests could in no way be surpassed. All of them, self-bidden, carry out labors involving great toil, and each has his appointed charge. Their service is unceasing, some attending to the wood, others the oil, others the fine wheat flour, others the business of spices, and still others the portions of the flesh for burnt offering, employing extraordinary strength in this task. For with both hands they grasp the legs of the calves, almost all of which weigh more than two talents each, and then with marvelous deftness they fling them to a considerable height with their two hands, and they never fail of spacing the victim correctly. . . . Complete silence prevails, so that one might suppose that not a person was present in the place, though those performing the service amount of some seven hundred— beside the great multitude of persons bringing sacrifices to be offered—but everything is done with reverence and in a manner worthy of the great divinity. (*Ep. Arist.* 92–95 [Hadas])

The power of this professional group is exemplified also in a decree by Antiochus III concerning the temple and Jerusalem:

> And out of reverence for the temple he also published a proclamation throughout the entire kingdom, of which the contents were as follows. "It is unlawful for any foreigner to enter the enclosure of the temple which is forbidden to the Jews, except to those of them who are accustomed to enter after purifying themselves in accordance with the law of the country. Nor shall anyone bring into the city the flesh of horses or of mules or of wild or tame asses, or of leopards, foxes or hares or, in general, of any animals forbidden to the Jews. . . . But only the sacrificial animals known to their ancestors and necessary for the propitiation of God shall they be permitted to use. And the person who violates any of these statutes shall pay to the priests a fine of three thousand drachmas of silver." (Josephus, *Ant.* 12.145–46 [Marcus, LCL])

Josephus describes the form of government among the Jews as a "theocracy" (Josephus, *Ag. Ap.* 2.165). However, it was in reality a "hierocracy," ruled by priests.

---

113. Ibid., 106.
114. Ibid., 120.

To summarize, the high priest appears to have had considerable power, and the priests in general would have shared in this power. They perhaps monopolized political power during much of the Ptolemaic period, except possibly during the time of Joseph Tobias (227/224 to 205/202 B.C.E.), assuming he obtained the office of magistracy. Because of this, the priests were the professional group that attracted the attention of foreigners.

However, one should not be satisfied with grouping all the priests within one monolithic body. There certainly was hierarchical structure to the priesthood, as the office of high priest indicates. One should speak of a higher and lower clergy.[115] Only the higher-order priests, who stood in close relationship to the high priest, were able to live an aristocratic style of life. Of course, one can divide the priests still further between the Zadokites and the Levites, the latter, of course, with much lower status. One could also divide the stratification of priests into urban versus rural priests.[116] It is significant that the Maccabean revolt was started by a country priest from Modiin, not from the upper class priests in Jerusalem. On the whole, then, one can speak of a priestly aristocracy in Jerusalem that governed Judah. As one would expect, only a small number of individuals in Jerusalem probably enjoyed the rich benefits of the oppressive Ptolemaic system. In fact, probably only a small number of priests were truly rich and powerful.

Just as the Ptolemies had catered to the native priesthood in Egypt to keep the people in line, so the Ptolemies were smart to maintain a symbiotic relationship with the Judean priesthood. This relationship represents the typical strategy used by empires to subjugate foreign peoples: the imperial powers collaborate with the native priesthood and aristocracy. Both parties, of course, get something out of it. The higher powers are able to rule indirectly by relying on the priesthood to keep order and control and collect taxes.[117] The priesthood also serves to legitimize the governing elite to the masses, a not insignificant contribution.[118] But the priesthood also benefits. Although the status and power of priests are dependent on the governing class, they often receive various tax exemptions and are enabled to prosper economically because of their position.[119] The priesthood could also rely on the governing stratum for military response to heresy.[120]

The stereotypical collaboration of empire and indigenous priestly aristocracy is most illuminatingly portrayed by Richard Horsley, who shows how the

115. Cf. Lenski, *Power and Privilege,* 258.
116. See Bickerman, *Greek Age,* 154.
117. Cf. Lenski, *Power and Privilege,* 260.
118. Ibid.
119. Ibid., 257–58.
120. Ibid., 261.

Judean high priests collaborated with the Romans in subjugating their own people.[121] The priests became incredibly wealthy as a result of this symbiotic relationship and were even resistant to the Zealots and their messianic ideology when they revolted against Rome. The aristocratic priests agreed only reluctantly to help the revolutionaries when there was no other option. They primarily served as a moderating influence on the rebels, hoping that they could forestall the Roman destruction of the land. Josephus, himself a member of the upper class, also sided with the priests. Thus, as Gerhard Lenski notes, though priests could actually mediate the interests of the masses to governing powers, "Many members of the priestly class were grasping, mercenary, self-seeking, cruel, tyrannical, and exploitative."[122]

The typical role of priests as mediators between the political elite and the masses means that they were not always simply lackeys for the dominating powers, which complicates the relationship between the three. The priesthood is often very popular with the masses because it does so many things for the people: absolution from sin, promise of an afterlife, provision with a meaningful worldview, and so on. Sometimes the priests' relationship with the political elite goes sour, and often the priests get the worse end of the deal, with the consequence of the confiscation of wealth and lands by the political elite, which would naturally align the priests more with the masses.[123] Of course, this brings to mind Joseph Tobias's possible usurpation of the office of *prostasia* from the high priest, as a result of Joseph's astute political maneuverings.

The inherent priestly bias toward the poor is demonstrated with reference to Judaism by a fact noted by Lenski: "Though technically most of the prophets were not priests, and, in fact, criticized the priestly class no less than the others, it was the priestly class which was the basic transmitter of the Mosaic tradition and its concept of Yahweh's concern for justice and righteousness."[124] This view fits with Weber's notion of the priests' routinization of the prophetic charisma and provision for practical application of prophetic norms.[125] But, of course, the lower rung of priests would be expected to be more sympathetic to the poor than the higher orders. As already stated, it is certainly no coinci-

---

121. Richard A. Horsley, "High Priests and the Politics of Roman Palestine," *JSJ* 17 (1986): 23–55.

122. Lenski, *Power and Privilege*, 266; cf. Applebaum, "Economic Causes," 254.

123. Cf. Lenski, *Power and Privilege*, 259.

124. Lenski, *Power and Privilege*, 264.

125. Weber, *Ancient Judaism*, 173–80, 380–82. On how prophetic charisma was routinized by the emergence of written prophecy, see Clements, "Max Weber, Charisma," 89–108.

dence that the Maccabean revolt began with country priests, not their upper-class counterparts.[126]

Competing with the priests but certainly not dominating them was another social stratum, what might be called a secular aristocracy. Tcherikover surmises, "There is no doubt that they were the strongest class after the priests."[127] In fact, if it were not for the Ptolemies, this body would most likely have reigned supreme. As Bickerman notes:

> The primary reason for the ascendancy of the priesthood in the Hellenistic period was the tendency of Macedonian rulers to distrust the secular aristocracy of the conquered peoples. The result was that the native clergy, who could neither be eliminated nor disposed, became the leading privileged group among the native population and their natural spokesmen.[128]

Tcherikover points out that this class is actually older than the priests and was present in the Persian period, represented by the *ḥōrîm* (nobles) and *sĕgānîm* (rulers) of Nehemiah 5.[129] Ben Sira apparently refers to this class as "lords" (mostly *śārîm* and *nĕdîbîm* in Hebrew).[130] He says that the wise scribe "serves among the great and appears before rulers" (39:4).

Especially representative of this secular aristocracy is the Tobiad family. They are mentioned in Ezra 2:59–60 as not being able to prove their Israelite descent, though this may be a separatist slur.[131] In Neh 4:3, Tobiah, the Ammonite, is mentioned as a resister of Nehemiah's construction project. The Tobiad

---

126. Martin Hengel sees an enduring postexilic social divide: "The more 'liberal' aristocracy stood against the minor clergy of the Levites and pious peasantry" ("Judaism and Hellenism Revisited," in *Hellenism in the Land of Israel* [ed. John J. Collins and Gregory E. Sterling; CJAS 13; Notre Dame: University of Notre Dame Press, 2001], 13); cf. Tcherikover, "Hellenistic Palestine," 192.

127. Tcherikover, "Hellenistic Palestine," 120.

128. Bickerman, *Greek Age*, 141. But he sees the most powerful group to be still the secular aristocrats, particularly the members of the Popular Assembly that he sees ruling Jerusalem (p. 154).

129. Tcherikover, "Hellenistic Palestine," 121.

130. See Bickerman, *Greek Age*, 154.

131. Orrieux argues that the Tobias of the Zenon papyri was a Judean governor of Ammonite territory ("Les papyrus de Zénon," 322). Gary N. Knoppers views him as a Judean or Transjordan Israelite who is being slurred by Nehemiah, who takes a separatist policy toward those he deems semi-Jews ("Nehemiah and Sanballat: The Enemy Without or Within?" in *Judah and the Judeans in the Fourth Century B.C.E.* [ed. Oded Lipschits, Gary N. Knoppers, and Rainer Albertz; Winona Lake, Ind.: Eisenbrauns, 2007], 305–31).

family's connection with the Ptolemies is evidenced in the Zenon papyri where Tobias writes two letters to Apollonios, the *diokētēs*, and the superior of Zenon:

> Toubias to Apollonios greeting. If you and all your affairs are flourishing, and everything else is as you wish it, many thanks to the gods! I too have been well, and thought of you at all times, as was right. I have sent to you Aineias bringing a eunuch and four boys, house-slaves and of good stock, two of whom are uncircumcised. I append descriptions of the boys for your information. (*CPJ* 4)

> Toubias to Apollonios greeting. On the tenth of Xandikos I sent Aineias our servant, bringing the gifts for the king which you wrote and asked me to send in the month of Xandikos: two horses, six dogs, one wild mule out of an ass, two white Arab donkeys, two wild mules' foals, one wild ass's foal. They are all tame. I have also sent you the letter which I have written to the king about the gifts, together with a copy for your information. (*CPJ* 5)

These letters reveal the family's great wealth. As Orrieux says, "Tobias is rich, very rich indeed" (my translation).[132] He points out the well-bred slaves and exotic animals that Tobias offers to Apollonius and states that "in the Ptolemaic empire, the great fortunes belonged to the dignitaries of the regime, military and civilian high functionaries" (my translation).[133]

But might the reference to the gods ("thanks to the gods!") in the letter reveal the extent of Hellenistic tendencies of the Tobiad family, as some have suggested? Or is it simply accommodation to the Greek style of letter writing and Apollonius's Greek polytheism? Hengel argues that the two letters demonstrate "a very lax view of the law."[134] He points out that though a Greek secretary no doubt penned the letter, Tobias was responsible for its content. Hengel also believes that the reference to the two uncircumcised slaves indicates Tobias's laxness concerning the commandment of circumcision, and he notes that the post-Maccabean period forbade the sale of Jewish slaves to foreigners. Similarly, Tcherikover envisions a trajectory of hellenization that begins superficially with the first Tobiads and progresses to a "thoroughgoing Hellenistic reform" two generations later.[135]

Orrieux is more cautious.[136] He admits that the polytheistic address is a little shocking but notes that the uncircumcised slaves may not have belonged to Tobias's own household. He also says it is unfair to judge Tobias by rabbinic standards regarding the sale of Jewish slaves. Admitting Hengel's description

---

132. Orrieux, "Les papyrus de Zénon," 327.
133. Ibid.
134. Hengel, *Judaism and Hellenism*, 1:268.
135. Tchrikover, "Hellenistic Palestine," 71, 140.
136. Orrieux, "Les papyrus de Zénon," 330.

of the general tone of the story of Joseph as "secular and nationalistic," Orrieux qualifies, "Nothing is allowed to suspect the least religious laxity; all the wrong resides with the brothers of Hyrcanus, fallen into the Seleucid party and, by ricochet, into apostasy" (my translation).[137] Further, John Collins notes that when the Jews began to interact with Hellenism, they had no problem with identifying Yahweh with pagan deities like Zeus, but they drew the line at worshiping them and their cults.[138] That might explain Tobias's lack of scruples in making his polytheistic greeting.

The story of the rise to power of the son of Tobias, Joseph, recorded in detail in Josephus, reveals a period of change in Jerusalem and the province (227/224 to 205/202 B.C.E.). Joseph was also the son of the sister of the high priest Onias (Josephus, *Ant.* 12.160). His mother informed him of the arrival of the Ptolemaic envoy sent because Onias had refused to pay the tribute, and Joseph condemned him for his foolish action and asked if he could go to Ptolemy on behalf of the nation (Josephus, *Ant.* 12.160–63). Joseph then brilliantly "buttered up" Ptolemy and outwitted the wealthy men of Syria, Samaria, and Phoenicia by revealing their scheme to offer a low bid for the right of tax-farming. He doubled the amount they offered and received their positions and power to collect from those who had not paid (Josephus, *Ant.* 12.164–79). He had thereby created a new system whereby the fragmented power of the individual tax-farmers was consolidated into one position.[139]

Joseph's powerful position is demonstrated in his treatment of those who refused to pay taxes owed: twenty principal men of Ashkelon were executed (Joseph had two thousand foot soldiers given him by Ptolemy to carry out such activities) (Josephus, *Ant.* 12.180–81). Josephus indicates the extent of Joseph's power and wealth:

> Thereupon Ptolemy, who admired his spirit and commended his actions, permitted him to do whatever he wished. . . . Having thus collected great sums of money and made permanent the power which he now had, thinking it prudent to preserve the source and foundation of his present good fortune by means of the wealth which he had himself and acquired. (*Ant.* 12.182, 84 [Marcus, LCL])

Joseph and his family now represented a new secular power structure in Jerusalem that competed with the priests.[140] Schäfer believes that Joseph assumed the office of *prostasia* when he won tax-farming rights and that this

---

137. Ibid., 331.
138. John J. Collins, "Cult and Culture: The Limits of Hellenization in Judea," in *Hellenism in the Land of Israel* (ed. John J. Collins and Gregory E. Sterling; CJAS 13; Notre Dame, Ind.: University of Notre Dame Press, 2001), 41–42.
139. Tcherikover, "Hellenistic Palestine," 99.
140. Cf. Kippenberg, who theorizes the development of a secular aristocracy in Judah

began the "reign" of the Tobiads, who "were for all practical purposes the rulers of Judaea."[141] But this is an assumption. There is no clear indication that Joseph assumed the office and then "deprived Onias of part of his official rank" (Josephus, *Ant.* 12.161, d [Marcus, LCL]). Thus, one cannot properly speak of a depoliticized priesthood, though the high priest may have lost his tax-farming privileges. Joseph simply became a new player in the politics of the province, and certainly the Tobiad family became a leading and influential family in Jerusalem after this affair, as well as incredibly wealthy. The priests no doubt continued as a governing body and still held sway over the masses.

Finally, in connection with the secular aristocracy, discussion of another political entity is necessary. In a decree of Antiochus III there is a reference to the important political groups of Jerusalem surviving after the end of the Ptolemaic period: "the senate [*gerousia*], the priests, the scribes of the temple and the temple-singers" (Josephus, *Ant.* 12.142 [Marcus, LCL]). Antiochus frees these groups from personal taxes. Kippenberg notes that when comparing this list with the parallel one in Ezra 7:21–24 (Persian period [398 B.C.E.]), a new group emerges: the senate.[142] What is this organization? Kippenberg argues that this group included members of the class of aristocrats and governors, which formed the 150-member committee under Nehemiah but did not lead the community.[143] Kippenberg argues that Antiochus was attempting to strengthen the secular aristocracy by giving the *gerousia* political power and freeing it from taxes—this is the beginning of the emancipation of the aristocracy from the hierocracy, according to Kippenberg.

During the time of Joseph Tobiad, this council perhaps gained additional strength when the Tobiads sided with them against the priests. Antiochus may not in fact have been attempting to grant additional powers to this group but rather was recognizing the already higher-ranking status of the *gerousia*, which had been attained during the reign of Joseph. Contrary to Kippenberg, Bickerman sees Antiochus's decree as actually setting back the secular aristocracy in that the council was given a tax exemption, not the aristocracy as a whole, while the entire priesthood was exempted (cf. Ezra 7:24).[144]

---

during the Ptolemaic and Seleucid periods; this aristocracy became oppressive for the general populace (*Religion und Klassenbildung*, 78–93).

141. Schäfer, "Maccabaean Periods," 575; cf. Hengel, *Judaism and Hellenism*, 1:270.

142. Kippenberg, *Religion und Klassenbildung*, 83.

143. Ibid., 83–4.

144. Bickerman, *Greek Age*, 141.

Temple Scribes and Temple Singers

"The scribes of the temple and the temple-singers" (Josephus, *Ant.* 12.142 [Marcus, LCL]) were also freed from taxes by Antiochus III, and this reveals something of their status in the Jerusalem community. Kippenberg theorizes that these scribes were "a special group of Levites" (my translation).[145] Their high status is most likely residual and connected with their bond with both the priesthood and the temple, which were privileged by the Ptolemies and later by the Seleucids. That they are found at the end of this list indicates that they were probably not ranked as highly as the priests or the council. This lower ranking further indicates their membership within a special class of the ancient agrarian cultures: retainers.

Lenski's description of this stratum is especially illuminating. He points out that every governing class employs "a small army of officials, professional soldiers, household servants, and personal retainers."[146] The word "retainer" shows that this class is essentially hired or created to serve the interests of the governing class. This means that the essence of this class is "its dependence on the political elite."[147] Again, a mutually beneficial relationship is usually found between these two strata. In return for their service to the political elite, the retainer stratum was "separated from, and elevated above, the mass of common people, and to a limited degree shared in the economic surplus."[148] In fact, Lenski points out that some of this stratum could actually become wealthier than some of the governing elite, who also desperately needed the retainer stratum for numerical reasons.[149] The governing stratum usually made up only 1 to 2 percent of the population, while the retainer stratum was 5 percent. The addition of the retainers strengthened the numbers of the governing stratum and helped them to maintain their control over the other 93 percent.

Also, in terms of exploitation, the governing elite needed the retainers:

> Collectively the retainer class was also important because it performed the crucial task of mediating relations between the governing class and the common people. It was the retainers who actually performed most of the work involved in effecting the transfer of the economic surplus from the producers to the political elite.[150]

The retainer stratum then served as a buffer for the ruling elite in that it distanced them from the masses. Rarely did the commoners come in contact with

---

145. Kippenberg, *Religion und Klassenbildung*, 84.
146. Lenski, *Power and Privilege*, 243.
147. Ibid.
148. Ibid., 244.
149. Ibid., 245–46.
150. Ibid., 246.

the governing class. The retainers did the bidding of the political elite, so that peasant anger was more often directed against them instead of at the upper class. Thus, for political reasons, the retainer class was invaluable and a necessity for the governing class.

However, the governing class was always wary of the retainers, particularly army officers, because of the danger of a coup d'état.[151] Thus, the governing class made sure that the retainers were highly rewarded, perhaps even admitting them into their own numbers. Civil officials also were known for assassinations but did not pose the degree of threat that soldiers did. Often civil retainers worked their way up in rank, eventually becoming part of the highest class themselves.

The temple scribes mentioned in Antiochus's decree, then, are properly retainers because they served the needs of the priestly aristocracy in Jerusalem. But were temple scribes the only kind of scribe in ancient Israel and Judaism? More fundamentally, who were the scribes and what was their primary role in society? Anthony Saldarini notes that the Hebrew word for scribe, סֹפֵר, is from the Semitic root *spr*, "originally meaning a written message which was sent, then meaning 'writing,' and finally meaning 'writer.' . . . The word 'scribe' in Hebrew, Greek, and other languages had a wide range of meaning that changed over time and could denote several social roles. The closest English equivalent is the term 'secretary.'"[152] In the ancient Near East, the term "scribe" "refers to roles from that of a typist to a cabinet officer at the highest level of government." The base of the scribes was at the royal court or temple.

> Their duties included administrating and keeping records of tax collection, forced labor, military activities, commodities, and building projects. For example, in Egypt they supervised land measurement after the annual Nile flood; drafted correspondence, contracts, and treaties; and at the highest level kept the royal annals, collected laws, preserved sacred traditions, and were experts in astronomy, omens, and other religious rites and activities.

In ancient Mesopotamia, scribes were the glue that kept the empire together.[153] Thus, their training was considered to be paramount for the functioning of the empire.

In reference to the Jews, Bickerman sees the scribe's most basic role as that of a penman but also a legist or notary "who drew up contracts, bills of

---

151. Ibid., 247–48.

152. Anthony J. Saldarini, "Scribes," *ABD* 5:1012.

153. David M. Carr, *Writing on the Tablet of the Heart: Origins of Scripture and Literature* (Oxford: Oxford University Press, 2005), 33.

divorce, and other deeds."[154] Bickerman distinguishes these technicians from what he characterizes as the true Jewish sages like Qohelet, Ben Sira, and later the rabbis. However, the sages whom Ben Sira describes (chs. 38–39), he calls scribes.[155] Moreover, the scribes in the New Testament were certainly more than technicians.

The most definitive work on the role of scribes in the Second Temple period is that of Christine Schams. She defines the fundamental scribal role as reading and writing expertise but includes other roles. Referring to סֹפֵר and its Aramaic equivalent, she concludes: "The Semitic terms designate a variety of functions and positions on various levels of the government and administration relating to reading and writing expertise, but they can also be associated with expertise in Jewish law, instruction, wisdom, the interpretation of dreams and authorship of books."[156] She contrasts this broad usage with the typical Greek usage of the term *grammateus*, which designated a professional writer and official only. But she nuances Bickerman in distinguishing scribes who became Torah scholars and others that did not. Her basic model is that the dominant role of scribes as reading/writing experts allowed some to specialize and become legal experts and others Scripture experts. For example, she explains the development of the latter: "As experts of written things they were probably also expected to explain textually difficult passages of the Scripture."[157]

As for the Ptolemaic period, she notes that the temple scribes referenced in Antiochus's decree probably had functions relating to the temple such as record keeping, copying, and legal documentation.[158] She also documents the role of village scribes in Egypt at this time. They registered tax information, composed records/documents for villagers archiving them, and served as mediators with higher authorities; some may have not been well educated.[159] As for Judah, she conjectures that Ptolemy I increased the status of scribes there because of the increased need for written records, and scribes were found in all levels of administration.[160] Similarly, Bickerman states, "Down to the shepherd in the wilderness of Judah, everyone was entangled in the red

---

154. Bickerman, *Greek Age*, 162.

155. Ibid., 163–76.

156. Christine Schams, *Jewish Scribes in the Second Temple Period* (JSOTSup 291; Sheffield: Sheffield Academic Press, 1998), 285.

157. Ibid., 303. Raymond F. Person argues that ancient Israelite scribes copied their texts "with an oral mindset," which means they were not just copyists but also performers ("The Ancient Israelite Scribe as Performer," *JBL* 117 [1998]: 601–9, esp. 602).

158. Schams, *Jewish Scribes*, 90.

159. Ibid., 135–36.

160. Ibid., 291.

tape of the Greek fiscal system and needed the help of a professional scribe"; this was necessitated by the bilingual demands of the Greek administration.[161] Schams speculates that these scribes were paid by the foreign administration and were powerful officials, and that some where scholars and intellectuals.[162]

In ancient Israel, scribes assumed various roles. Along with priests, they taught the people the law (Ezra 7:6, 10; Neh 8). According to Mark Christian, middle-level, levitical scribes stood as liaisons between the urban elite and the rural villagers and helped produce the laws in Deuteronomy, which do not reflect simply the interests of the upper class.[163] Some scribes, for example, the chief scribe, were high-level officials under a king (2 Kgs 22; Jer 36:10), what one might call royal scribes.[164] In 2 Sam 8:15–18, a scribe Seraiah is listed along with David, his commander, main priests, and David's son. Some scribes served as royal courtiers like Jonathan, David's uncle, who gave advice to him (1 Chr 27:32). The famous scribe Ahiqar held a similar position in the seventh century under King Esarhaddon of Assyria. During the exile, when literary expression was the only form of power for Israelite elites, "priesthood and scribalism became inextricably linked."[165] One might refer to prophetic scribes such as Baruch, who recorded prophetic oracles for prophets or wrote about them.[166]

Like the Egyptian "The Satire of the Trades," Ben Sira praises the scribal profession as being far superior to other trades. While he applauds the necessity of farmers and craftsmen, he states, "The wisdom of the scribe depends on the opportunity of leisure; only the one who has little business can become wise" (38:24). Wisdom here is defined not as a way of living but as intellectual prowess and love of literature. In comparison to the manual laborer, Ben Sira states,

---

161. Bickerman, *Greek Age*, 162.

162. Schams, *Jewish Scribes*, 313.

163. Mark A. Christian, "Priestly Power that Empowers: Michel Foucault, Middle-Tier Levites, and the Sociology of 'Popular Religious Groups' in Israel," *Journal of Hebrew Studies* 9, Article 1 (2009): 1–81, online at http://www.arts.ualberta.ca/JHS/Articles/article _103.pdf (accessed March 18, 2009).

164. For a discussion of the different types of Mesopotamian scribes, see A. Leo Oppenheim, "The Intellectual in Mesopotamian Society," *Daedalus* 104 (1975): 37–46. On the types of scribes in the Hebrew Bible, see Karel van der Toorn, *Scribal Culture and the Making of the Hebrew Bible* (Cambridge, Mass.: Harvard University Press, 2007), 75–108.

165. Mark Leuchter, "Zadokites, Deuteronomists, and the Exilic Debate over Scribal Authority," *Journal of Hebrew Studies* 7, Article 10 (2007): 5–18, here 17, online at http://www.arts.ualberta.ca/JHS/Articles/article_71.pdf (accessed March 18, 2009).

166. See David L. Petersen, "The Nature of Prophetic Literature," in *Prophecy and Prophets: The Diversity of Contemporary Issues in Scholarship* (ed. Yehoshua Gitay; SemeiaSt; Atlanta: Scholars Press, 1997), 31–32.

How different the one who devotes himself to the study of the law of the Most High! He seeks out the wisdom of all the ancients, and is concerned with prophecies; he preserves the saying of the famous and penetrates the subtleties of parables; he seeks out the hidden meanings of proverbs and is at home with the obscurities of parables. He serves among the great and appears before rulers; he travels in foreign lands. (38:34–39:6)

Of course, Ben Sira is mostly speaking of high-level scribes. The importance of this lengthy treatment of scribes will become apparent in the next chapter, where Qohelet is indentified as a scribal scholar, another variety of scribe that reflects more the ancient Near Eastern version. His audience would eventually serve in a variety of roles; as retainers and in general, they should be classified as the lowest rung of the aristocracy or, alternatively, an upper middle class.

A MIDDLE CLASS (OR STRATUM)

A class that has always seemed to be able to escape complete control by the ruler and governing class has been the merchants.[167] Merchants are often of humble origin, especially younger sons who could not inherit their father's land.[168] Sometimes the class emerged from the ranks of peasants. Because of their lack of status, merchants usually have an "inferiority complex," which they compensate for by adopting the lifestyle of nobles and marrying into this class.[169] Many merchants of ancient times became extremely wealthy and powerful. The governing class usually allowed the merchant class to remain somewhat independent because the governing class needed the luxury items that only the merchants could provide and because of the high risk involved in the merchants' pursuits, as well as the nontraditional character of their role.[170] The importation of Greek wines and olive oil in Rhodian jars, already mentioned, points to the presence of this class during this period.[171] Harrison speculates that a new mercantile middle class (or petite bourgeoisie) emerged in Ptolemaic Palestine.[172]

---

167. Lenski, *Power and Privilege*, 248.
168. Ibid., 249. Cf. Lawrence E. Stager, who argues that noble Israelite males who were not firstborn had to fend for themselves and seek positions in the military, government, or priesthood to maintain their honorable status ("The Archaeology of the Family in Ancient Israel," *BASOR* 260 [1985]: 1–35).
169. Lenski, *Power and Privilege*, 250.
170. Ibid., 250–53.
171. Bickerman, *Greek Age*, 75.
172. Harrison, "Among the Sociologists," 164–65, 171.

The Lower Classes

The largest class by far in the ancient world and particularly in ancient Judah was that of the peasantry. As has been mentioned, this class bore the brunt of the Ptolemaic tax burden. In addition, peasants living on crown land may have been required to return a third of their yield in crops and half of their fruit to the king. This is not quite as bad as during the Tokugawa period in Japan, when 30 to 70 percent of the crop was paid in taxes.[173] As for the non-tenant peasants, there is much that cannot be determined with certainty.[174] Was the twenty-talent yearly tribute for Judah drawn from the land taxes or poll taxes? Were peasants required to tithe to sustain the priesthood in addition to paying their part of this tribute? Idumean records of the fourth century under the Persians show a quarter land tax.[175] Thus, it is reasonable to suppose that peasants of the Ptolemaic period who owned land paid a land tax to a comparable percentage.

As for the general state of the peasants, Bickerman views Gen 49:14 as aptly revealing:

> Issachar is a strong donkey,
> Lying down between the sheepfolds;
> He saw that a resting place was good,
> And that the land was pleasant;
> So he bowed his shoulder to the burden,
> And he became a slave at forced labor. (Gen 49:14–15)[176]

He suggests that this may be why Ben Sira advises against abandoning husbandry (7:15).[177] As Lenski remarks, "The great majority of peasants who lived in the various agrarian societies of the past apparently lived at, or close to, the subsistence level."[178] He further notes, "The great majority of the political elite sought to use the energies of the peasantry to the full, while depriving them of all but the basic necessities of life. The only real disagreement concerned the problem of how this might best be done."[179] Peasants reacted to their oppression in one of two ways: nonviolently or violently. With the nonviolent approach, "their efforts consisted of little more than attempts to evade taxes, rents, labor services, and other obligations, usually concealment of a portion

---

173. Lenski, *Power and Privilege*, 267.
174. See Bickerman, *Greek Age*, 74–45.
175. Lemaire, "Fourth-Century B.C.E. Judah," 56–57.
176. Bickerman, *Greek Age*, 154.
177. Ibid., 155.
178. Lenski, *Power and Privilege*, 271.
179. Ibid., 270.

of the harvest, working slowly and sometimes carelessly as well."[180] The phrase "foot-dragging peasants" comes to mind. The other, more extreme means was revolt.[181] Again, one thinks of the lower-rung country priests (Maccabees) and peasants who initiated the revolt against the Seleucids.

The only exception to the generally deplorable economic condition of the peasants was when peasants formed the militia of a society, in which case they ranked as powerful citizens.[182] This was true for Israel during the days of the judges. Pointing to the song of Deborah, Weber theorizes that the tribal peasants were warriors with the power to fight.[183] The ability to fight is connected to rights and privileges. As Yuko Takahashi states, "In the ancient world, political rights, such as judicial and administrative rights, were connected with military ability, particularly the ability to be a self-equipped warrior."[184]

In order to explain how the peasantry ended up oppressed and without many rights, a brief summary of Weber's view of the origin and evolution of social class antagonism in ancient Israel will be helpful.[185] Weber starts with Israel's beginnings.[186] He speaks of three classes in the land of Canaan. He never really theorizes on the earliest origins of Israel outside of the land as in the story of the exodus. He merely begins with the Israelites in the land. He first speaks of the Bedouin as always a significant social class in the struggles of the Israelites, but he does not see the Israelites as part of this class or emerging from them. Rather, the Israelites had constantly to repulse the Bedouin. The Israelites emerge from the relationship between two other classes: small cattle breeders and landed peasants. He discusses their mutual and conflicted relationship. The cattle breeders had to negotiate grazing rights with the peasants who controlled the land. The herders were considered *gērîm*, or foreigners, not in the sense of non-Israelites but as a guest people without rights. The herders and the peasants often had to band together to fight a common enemy like the Bedouin. Weber speaks of sibs and the high importance of family relations and tribes that cut across these class relationships. One tribal member became a

---

180. Ibid., 273.

181. See ibid., 274.

182. See ibid., 270, 275.

183. Weber, *Ancient Judaism*, 23.

184. Yuko Takahashi, "A Study on Max Weber's *Ancient Judaism*: Theoretical Framework and Methodology," *Max Weber Studies* 7 (2008): 217.

185. This summary is drawn from Weber's *Ancient Judaism*. Other helpful summaries are Hans H. Gerth and Don Martindale, preface to Weber, *Ancient Judaism*, ix–xxvii; John Love, "Max Weber's *Ancient Judaism*," in *The Cambridge Companion to Weber* (ed. Stephen Turner; Cambridge: Cambridge University Press, 2000), 200–220; B. S. Turner, *For Weber*, 158–66; Bendix, *Max Weber*, 200–256. The best general introduction to Weber's sociology of religion is Talcott Parsons, introduction to Weber, *Sociology of Religion*, xxix–lxxvii.

186. See Weber, *Ancient Judaism*, 3–27.

gēr once he crossed into the territory of another tribe. This *gēr* status is eventually transferred by Weber to the Israelites as a whole people who become pariah people when they are subjugated by the great powers (Egypt, Mesopotamia, Syria, etc.).[187] Weber applies the notion also to the tribe of Levi, which was preeminently a *gēr* people, without land and holy.

Weber then speaks of another typical synchronic class relationship that developed as social stratification began to emerge. This is the class antagonism between urban patricians and indebted peasants living outside the city.[188] Cities began to emerge as significant centers of power. Certain sibs would control them and would become wealthier than other sibs and the poorer peasants outside the cities. The powerful urban patricians would work to impoverish these peasants and make them indebted to them, forcing them to sell their own children to pay off these debts, as in Nehemiah 5.[189] Through this process, the peasants essentially became urbanized plebs.[190]

---

187. Weber's use of this term to describe Judaism is problematic. In fact, Hans Derks comes very close to accusing him of being anti-Semitic ("Nomads, Jews, and Pariahs: Max Weber and Anti-Judaism," *The European Legacy* 4 [1999]: 42–43). But Weber did not use it pejoratively; see Love, "Weber's *Ancient Judaism*," 210–12; Swedberg, *Max Weber Dictionary*, 194, s.v. "Pariah People (*Pariavolk*)"; Efraim Shmueli, "The Novelties of the Bible and the Problem of Theodicy in Max Weber's *Ancient Judaism*," *JQR* 60 (1969): 181–82. Weber takes the term's application to the Untouchables in Hinduism's caste system, where ghetto segregation was involuntary, and applies it to the Jews. He qualifies the notion by noting that the Jews' segregation and ritual separation was voluntary. Wolfgang Schluchter argues that Weber's use of the term represents a projection of a medieval notion (ghetto) back on to the Jews because he needed a fundamental break with Judaism through Paul and Christianity, a revolution from segregation to the universalism of Christianity ("The Approach of Max Weber's Sociology of Religion as Exemplified in His Study of Ancient Judaism," *ASSR* 127 [2004]: 49–50). Jack Barbalet acknowledges that Weber was not anti-Semitic but criticizes him for not contributing to a sociology of anti-Semitism ("Max Weber and Judaism: An Insight into the Methodology of *The Protestant Ethic and the Spirit of Capitalism*," *Max Weber Studies* 6 [2006]: 61). Gerth and Mills point out that Weber referred to the Germans as pariah people after the devastation of WWI ("Introduction," 27).

188. George M. Soares-Prabhu argues that there is a social class of poor in the Hebrew Bible but not strictly in the Marxist sense of non-ownership of the means of production. Rather "biblical poverty has a broader sociological and even a religious meaning" ("Class in the Bible: The Biblical Poor a Social Class?" in *Voices from the Margin: Interpreting the Bible in the Third World* [ed. R. S. Sugirtharajah; Maryknoll, N.Y.: Orbis, 1991], 147–71, esp. 170).

189. See Norman K. Gottwald, "The Expropriated and the Expropriators in Nehemiah 5," in *Concepts of Class in Ancient Israel* (ed. Mark Sneed; South Florida Studies in the History of Judaism: The Hebrew Scriptures and Their World 201; Atlanta: Scholars Press, 1999), 1–19.

190. See Goldstein, "Religious Rationalization," 122. Bernhard Lang believes that the Israelite patricians were absentee landlords, which constituted what might be called rent capitalism. He also points out that their urban residency contributed to their developing an

Then another level of social class antagonism arose with the emergence of the monarchy.[191] This institution was viewed as inevitable on account of the threat of the Philistines, but most peasants, whether wealthy or poor, resented the new taxes and oppressive forces. In effect, the peasantry became demilitarized at this point and lost most of its power.[192] An anti-royalist sentiment emerged that was taken up by the classical prophets who preached against these oppressive features and argued that this amounted to a return to slavery in Egypt. Weber speaks of a new class of governmental officials connected with the monarchy that are represented in the high poetry of Song of Songs, Proverbs, and the book of Job.[193] He describes the wisdom literature as having an international air that smacks of the aristocracy. Against these upper-class intellectuals and the monarchical powers, Weber speak of a class of plebs, by which he means not the destitute but those who were depoliticized by the monarchy, like the old sibs, wealthy peasants, and classical prophets. He detects anti-royalist sentiments in the intellectuals who wrote Deuteronomy, placing limits on the king's power.

Weber's evolutionary trajectory of social class antagonism in ancient Israel appears to be generally sound, though his particular detection of this in the biblical literature is faulty, which will be discussed later. In fact, his essentially dualistic approach is similar to Gottwald's own Marxian theorization about these matters.[194]

The generally demilitarized and oppressed condition of the peasantry no doubt continued under the Ptolemies. Ptolemy II's decree against the enslavement of free citizens in Syria may confirm the degree of indebtedness many peasants experienced during this time:

> And also, in the future, the sale of native free persons or allowing them to pledge themselves should never be allowed under any circumstances. Exempted are those surrendered by the administration of the Syrian and Phoenician state revenue into the compulsory auction process, to which also belongs personal

---

exploitative rather than benevolent patron–client relationship ("The Social Organization of Peasant Poverty in Biblical Israel," in *Anthropological Approaches to the Old Testament* [ed. Bernhard Lang; IRT 8; Philadelphia: Fortress; London: SPCK, 1985], 86, 88).

191. See Weber, *Ancient Judaism*, 194–218.

192. Takahashi shows how Weber's theorization here involves an implicit contrast with a reverse process of democratization in the ancient Greek cities ("Weber's *Ancient Judaism*," 213–29).

193. See Weber, *Sociology of Religion*, 112, 127.

194. See Norman K. Gottwald, "Social Class as an Analytic and Hermeneutical Category in Biblical Studies," *JBL* 112 (1993): 3–22; idem, "Sociology (Ancient Israel)," *ABD* 6:83.

impounding, as stands written in the law about state lease. (*Papyrus Rainer* R 12–22; my translation)[195]

Of course, it is significant that in the decree Ptolemy allows the enslavement of persons who owed money to the crown![196] The Jews, of course, had had slaves before the Greeks, but the latter had introduced the practice of selling them for export.[197] The purpose of this ancient Greco-Roman practice is explained by Lang: "to prevent the development of a poor and dependent class of proletarians in the community, debtors are disposed of by selling them abroad."[198] Slave trading is reflected in the counter-decree of Antiochus III after he had taken control of Judah: "And as for those who were carried off from the city and are slaves, we herewith set them free, both them and the children born to them, and order their property to be restored to them" (Josephus, *Ant.* 12.144 [Marcus, LCL]).

Ranked below the peasant but above the slave is the artisan. In most ancient agrarian societies, artisans were recruited from dispossessed peasants, and noninheriting sons were hired by the merchant class.[199] Like peasants, artisans sometimes rebelled against those who had authority over them.[200] Bickerman believes that Ben Sira sees the craftsmen of his day as forming a middle class, but this is probably due to Ben Sira's not wanting to denigrate them in his comparison of the vocations.[201] Sirach notes that though artisans neither sit on the judge's bench nor partake in the popular assembly, their work plays an essential role in the maintenance of society (38:33).

THE DEGREE OF HELLENIZATION IN PTOLEMAIC JUDAH

Before discussing the extent of hellenization during this period, a few remarks about why the Jews would be tempted to embrace aspects of Hellenistic culture are in order. Tcherikover puts it succinctly: "the advantages of Hellenism over Judaism."[202] Leonard Greesnpoon observes:

---

195. Kippenberg, *Religion und Klassenbildung*, 79, citing H. Liebesny, "Ein Erlaß des Königs Ptolemaios II. Philadelphos über die Declaration von Vieh und Sklaven in Syrien und Phönizien," *Aegyptus* 16 (1936): 257–88.
196. Bickerman, *Greek Age*, 76.
197. Ibid.
198. Lang, "Peasant Poverty," 95.
199. Lenski, *Power and Privilege*, 278–79.
200. Ibid., 279.
201. Bickerman, *Greek Age*, 154.
202. Tcherikover, "Hellenistic Palestine," 118.

Hellenism posed a unique challenge. It incorporated a worldview and way of life that appeared to avoid the excesses and unacceptable features of earlier outsiders' religions and cultures; at the same time it offered elevated concepts that would join Jews to the rest of the culturally and economically advantaged of the known world.[203]

Bickerman notes that Hellenism's secularity was psychologically appealing; it had no priestly caste and had an "intelligentsia independent of both palace and temple."[204]

It has already been noted that the Tobiad romances reveal no clear instances of hellenization. Harrison attempts to discern how much Hellenistic cultural influence is indicated archaeologically in third-century B.C.E. Judah.[205] He looks at the Yehud coins minted in the third century, monumental architecture, and other artifacts and concludes that third-century Judah was hardly affected by Hellenism. Because of the images on the coins (e.g., the Athenian owl, Ptolemy I, his wife Berenice, Ptolemy II, the Ptolemaic eagle, a bird, and a roaring winged lion), one might surmise that this is an indication of vigorous hellenization. But Harrison speculates that the Jewish authorities might have disagreed.[206] Harrison points out that this practice is a continuation of the Persian-period policy and that the Hebrew inscriptions on the coins are probably a concession.[207] Harrison concludes that "the Yehud coins are witness to the vitality of Judean traditions that 'Judaized' Attic and Hellenistic numismatic conventions with appropriate symbolism and inscriptions."

The material culture certainly does not reflect Hellenistic influence. The reality is that in third-century Ptolemaic Judah, there had not been enough time for Hellenism to penetrate very far. In the Persian period, the hinterland, in contrast to the coastline, became hellenized at a much slower rate.[208] But even during the third century, when the hinterland was becoming rapidly hellenized, Judah was still remarkably insular.[209] The Jerusalem people would have been exposed to a possible garrison of Greek soldiers, officials, and merchants, but this is hardly enough to suggest a penetrating Greek presence in the city.

---

203. Greenspoon, "Alexandria and Antioch," 422.
204. Bickerman, *Greek Age*, 79.
205. Harrison, "Hellenization in Syria-Palestine," 98–108.
206. Ibid., 100.
207. Ibid., 101.
208. See Ephraim Stern, "Between Persia and Greece: Trade, Administration and Warfare in the Persian and Hellenistic Periods (539–63 BCE)," in *The Archaeology of Society in the Holy Land* (ed. Thomas E. Levy; New York: Facts on File, 1995), 444. Harrison makes this same contrast ("Hellenization in Syria-Palestine," 102–6).
209. Harrison, "Hellenization in Syria-Palestine," 102–6.

Social class also affects the degree of hellenization. Archaeologist Lee Levine points out that, in the Greek world, the upper class was generally more exposed to Hellenism than the lower.[210] Immediately prior to the Maccabean revolt, one can see the divide between the wealthy hellenizers like the high priest Jason, who converted Jerusalem into a polis with gymnasium and ephebeion (2 Macc 4), and the poorer pious resisters, but even here the degree of hellenization by the elite was not total.[211] The Hasmoneans were certainly not against hellenization, with their adoption of Greek names and customs.[212] As has been indicated, the Jews could refer to Yahweh as Zeus but drew the line when it came to engaging in foreign cultic practices.

But hellenization does not always work in a passive assimilating way. Active resistance to Hellenistic ideas or a creative adaptation of them is also a variety of hellenization, as indicated by the Yehud coins.[213] Even Ben Sira, though showing signs of hellenization, essentially resists the then-prevalent Greek notion of life after death.[214] It was not until the Wisdom of Solomon that this doctrine began to be more and more acceptable.[215] This more dynamic way to view hellenization is demonstrated by Gregg Gardner, who shows how Jews creatively adapted the Greek concept of euergetism during the second century. The Greek concept involved benefactors to a city being given gifts, such as an honorary decree, "statues in his/her image, crowns, and/or seats of honor at games and festivals."[216] The Jews adopted and adapted this form and practice. For example, the honorary decree for Simon Maccabee (143/2–135/4 B.C.E.) is presented in 1 Macc 14:25–29 and is strikingly similar to Greek form and practice, but the deviations are significant.[217] "Although Simon is given various symbols of authority and titles, crowns are conspicuously absent."[218]

---

210. Levine, *Judaism and Hellenism*, 23–24; cf. Tcherikover, "Hellenistic Palestine," 142.

211. John Collins argues that his reforms were not really over any principles but over power and profit—not for religious reform ("Limits of Hellenization," 46, 51–52; cf. Tcherikover, "Hellenistic Palestine," 166–67).

212. See Bickerman, *Greek Age*, 302; cf. Collins, preface to *Hellenization in the Land of Israel* (ed. John J. Collins and Gregory E. Sterling; CJAS 13; Notre Dame, Ind.: University of Notre Dame Press, 2001), xii.

213. See Levine, *Judaism and Hellenism*, 27–28.

214. Cf. ibid., 39.

215. For a discussion of how the wisdom tradition adapts to the problem of theodicy over time and eventually embraces the notion of immortality, see Jack T. Sanders, "Wisdom, Theodicy, Death, and the Evolution of Intellectual Traditions," *JSJ* 36 (2005): 263–77.

216. Gregg Gardner, "Jewish Leadership and Hellenistic Civic Benefaction in the Second Century B.C.E.," *JBL* 126 (2007): 328.

217. Ibid., 332–37.

218. Ibid., 336.

Also missing are statues, references to games and festivals, and the title "savior of the people." The result is that "the decree for Simon seamlessly blended traditions that were native to both Jew and Greek, and the result proved to be an innovation both within and without Judea."[219] After presenting this and other examples, he concludes,

> The present argument supports the growing consensus that stresses the Jews' active engagement with Greek culture, a dynamic interaction that often produced innovation. This position departs from that which assumes the Jews' passive reception of Greek ways and understands Judaism and Hellenism as irreconcilable forces for which the adoption of one necessitates the abrogation of the other. In contradistinction, the new, growing consensus holds that a native culture can be preserved through the proactive restructuring of alien custom, enabling Judeans to integrate into the wider world while retaining their distinctive identity.[220]

CONCLUSION

During the third century B.C.E., Judah was under the dominance of the Ptolemies as part of a kingdom that once formed part of Alexander the Great's empire. Palestine was important for the Ptolemies not only because of its economic opportunities (agricultural goods, taxation, and trade routes) but also because it served as a buffer between them and the Seleucid kingdom.

The Ptolemies were careful to balance power and persuasion (good will) in order to control the Egyptian populace and extract as much surplus from Egypt as possible. They developed a special relationship with the Egyptian priesthood, who helped them control the masses and, in turn, were benefited by tax exemptions and other privileges. The Ptolemies taxed both people and land and inflicted the Egyptians with a whole host of small taxes that were surely disproportionately burdensome for the lower classes. Tax-farmers were ubiquitous.

The Ptolemies no doubt exerted a similar control over Judah, though perhaps less stringent owing to the distance between the areas. Judah was governed by the high priest, and the Jerusalem priests constituted the indigenous aristocracy who collaborated with the Ptolemies to retain their power (as a hierocracy) and increase their wealth, especially via tax-farming, at the expense of the common people. In turn, the priests helped control the masses and supervised the collection of the tribute for the Ptolemies. As long as Judah paid its tribute, it was semi-autonomous. How extensively the Jews were taxed

---

219. Ibid., 337.
220. Ibid., 342–43.

cannot be known. It was at least as much as during the Persian period, and probably more. As typical for all societies, the poor would have suffered the most, while the rich became richer. But the land benefited from peace and order and a rise in the standard of living, though again, not necessarily for the poor.

The priests had to compete with an emerging secular aristocracy represented by the Tobiad family and the senate. The priests' status was due in part to the Ptolemies' intention to suppress any power such a secular aristocracy might develop. The retainer class ranks next, with scribes, temple singers, and lower clergy (Levites) forming a lower upper class that served the priesthood. Merchants formed a kind of middle class or layer. The peasants were the majority class, with artisans ranked below them, and then slaves, all forming Judah's underclass.

There is no clear indication of heavy hellenization of Judah during the third century; it was superficial at best. Jews were fascinated with the new and strange culture that promised economic and political advantages, though there were limits to what they would incorporate. Their engagement with it was dynamic, not passive.

4

QOHELET AND HIS AUDIENCE'S SOCIAL LOCATION

Now that the social history of the period and class analysis of Judean society have been delineated, it is appropriate to show where Qohelet possibly alludes to this history and then where he and his audience should be located socially. With the former, there is a significant caveat. Qohelet is part of a mode of literature called wisdom literature. By its very nature, wisdom literature is resistant to such investigation.[1] That is because it is focused not on recording and interpreting events in the past but rather on the cognitive and moral development of its audience. It may refer to historical events but only as they serve educative and ethical purposes. Wisdom literature is also centered on the individual and his/her concerns and not on national or international issues.

This does not mean that the writers of wisdom literature were antihistorical, as some scholars have maintained.[2] In fact, many were quite likely also authors of historical material and other genres.[3] Rather, it means that when these writers were composing wisdom literature, their primary concern was not history per se. What makes a genre (or more broadly, mode of litera-

---

1. See Mark Sneed, "The Social Location of Qoheleth," *HS* 39 (1998): 47.
2. Crenshaw, *Old Testament Wisdom*, 29; Gerhard von Rad, *Wisdom in Israel* (trans. James D. Martin; London: SCM, 1972; repr., Nashville: Abingdon, 1988), 314; Joseph Blenkinsopp, *Sage, Priest, Prophet: Religious and Intellectual Leadership in Ancient Israel* (Library of Ancient Israel; Louisville: Westminster John Knox, 1995), 52; Zimmerli, "Limit of the Wisdom," 147.
3. Moshe Weinfeld argues that wisdom scribes authored Deuteronomy ("Deuteronomy—The Present State of Inquiry," *JBL* 86 [1967]: 256). John L. McKenzie concludes that the wisdom writers were also the authors of the historical material ("Reflections on Wisdom," *JBL* 86 [1967]: 4–9); see Mark Sneed, "Is the 'Wisdom Tradition' a Tradition?" *CBQ* 73 (2011): 63–64. Several scholars explain the wisdom elements in nonwisdom books as due to a common wisdom matrix and/or training for biblical authors: Kenton L. Sparks, *Ancient Texts for the Study of the Hebrew Bible: A Guide to the Background Literature* (Peabody, Mass.: Hendrickson, 2005), 56; Richard Clifford, "Introduction to the Wisdom Literature," *NIB* 5:1, 7; David M. Carr, "Wisdom and Apocalpticism: Different Types of Educational/Enculturational Literature" (paper presented at the annual meeting of the Society of Biblical Literature, San Antonio, Texas, November 21, 2004).

ture) a genre are certain characteristics that distinguish it from other genres. Genres do not represent total worldviews but are only partial ways to look at the world.[4] They deal with pieces of reality, not the full gamut. Thus, it should not be surprising that wisdom literature is not primarily historical in nature. Wisdom literature is focused on what the Germans call *Lebenskind*, that is, "the art of living," the skill of living life successfully. As such, it is inherently focused on the typical and repetitive and not the specific or particular, especially unique events. It provides guides and rules for effective behavior and action that have been passed down for generations. This means that it focuses on general patterns of behavior and the stereotypical, the universal, the cyclical, not the idiosyncratic or linear. Sometimes wisdom literature becomes philosophical, as when treating the problem of evil (e.g., in Qohelet and Job), but even here the primary focus is always advice for practical, daily living.

Though wisdom literature represents the culmination of wisdom and knowledge gathered over many generations (i.e., it is in many ways transgenerational or transhistorical), one would also expect that this body of knowledge would reflect at times specifics or idiosyncrasies of its own milieu. Thus, the wisdom literature is conflicted and has a dualistic nature. It is both historical and ahistorical, both the result of the culmination of gathering of wisdom over a long period of time and, thus, timeless, and the product of its own specific milieu, primarily synchronic but also diachronic to an extent. Thus, when Leo Perdue states, "The literature of the sages did not transcend its historical and social setting," he is overstating the case.[5]

The duality is reflected also in a related phenomenon of wisdom literature: its transcendence of nationality and ethnicity and simultaneous reflection of parochial values. Scholars have often noted the international character of wisdom literature.[6] The values and norms expressed in Israelite wisdom are very similar to those found in Egyptian and Mesopotamian wisdom literature. Weber, in fact, argues that this characteristic is an indication of this literature's upper-class status.[7] Ancient Near Eastern wisdom literature shares many similarities with wisdom literature found throughout the world, for example,

---

4. "World" rather than "worldview" is the more appropriate term; see John Frow, *Genre* (New Critical Idiom; London: Routledge, 2005), 75–77, 85–87.

5. Perdue, *Sword and Stylus*, 3; see the recent review by Benjamin G. Wright III (review of Leo G. Perdue, *The Sword and the Stylus: An Introduction to Wisdom in the Age of Empires*, *RBL* 06/2009: n.p., online at http://www.bookreviews.org/pdf/6647_7205.pdf (accessed June 16, 2009).

6. E.g., Blenkinsopp, *Sage, Priest, Prophet*, 33–34; Crenshaw, *Old Testament Wisdom*, 72.

7. Weber, *Sociology of Religion*, 127.

Greek and Indian wisdom.[8] This is because all of these literatures focus on the rules for a successful life, which are probably similar across cultures. Yet wisdom literature never totally transcends its own particular culture and milieu and will contain certain parochial flavors. For instance, Jewish monotheism is definitely ubiquitous in Israelite/Jewish wisdom literature in contrast to the polytheistic Egyptian or Mesopotamian wisdom literature.

The transhistorical character of wisdom literature is true also for Qohelet. His proverbial material represents the accumulated wisdom of many generations, but when he cites this material in his argumentation, he does so in a particular sociohistorical context. Qohelet is addressing conditions of his own time, though he continually cites proverbial material that is in many ways timeless. Thus, as is true generally for the wisdom literature, the book of Qohelet reflects a strange combination of dominant ahistorical elements with some historical ones. Though the book also reflects the typical international character of wisdom literature generally, it simultaneously contains distinctive Jewish features. We turn now to the historical features of Qohelet.

POSSIBLE ALLUSIONS TO THE MILIEU IN QOHELET

Several scholars have viewed the account of "The Royal Experiment" in 1:12–2:26 as a veiled reference to the aspirations and materialistic lifestyle of the Ptolemies or of contemporary aristocratic Jews.[9] Lauha compares this account with the one in 1 Kings (4:23, 26; 8:63; 10:5, 26–29; 11:3) and shows that there are many elements in this depiction that do not match up.[10] He concludes that this is a portrait of an "ideal king of fantasy, the prototype of wisdom and wealth." He compares it to the types of stories found in the "Arabian Nights." Thus, instead of viewing this narrative as an allusion to contemporary lifestyles or even specifically to Solomon, it is the portrayal of an idealized king in Solomonic garb used by Qohelet to make his point that all human striving, even royal, is ultimately futile and unsatisfactory.[11]

---

8. For an analysis of both Eastern and Western ancient wisdom literature, see Wanda Ostrowska Kaufmann, *The Anthropology of Wisdom Literature* (Westport, Conn.: Bergin & Garvey, 1996).

9. De Jong, "Ambitious Spirit," 92; Lohfink, *Qoheleth*, 50; Krüger, *Qoheleth*, 66; Applebaum, "Economic Causes," 238.

10. Aarre Lauha, "Kohelets Verhältnis zur Geschichte," in *Die Botschaft und die Boten: Festschrift für Hans Walter Wolff zum 70. Geburtstag* (ed. Jörg Jeremias and Lothar Perlit; Neukirchen-Vluyn: Neukirchener Verlag, 1981), 395.

11. Aron Pinker believes that 2:12b is the advice of the king to his successor to be wise even though this carries with it liabilities. He sees the issue of royal succession and continuity to be a perennial concern even for Qohelet's time ("Qohelet 2,12b," *BZ* 53 [2009]: 94–105).

The references to injustice and oppression in 3:16; 4:1; 7:15; and 8:14 are certainly compatible with this time but are too generic to be specifically limited to this period. Moreover, the account in Qoh 1:12–2:26 can be interpreted as referring to either the Ptolemies or the Jewish collaborators or both. The problem of evil raised in the former verses, of course, was a perennial issue for the Jews ever since the exilic period. Historically, it certainly was not a new or idiosyncratic issue for the Jews.

Another possible allusion is in 4:13–16, which depicts a young, poor upstart who came from prison and replaces an older foolish king and enjoys popular support but later is rejected by the same fickle masses. Lauha notes that some have seen in this story an allusion to Nimrod and Abraham (Targum), Saul and David, Solomon and Jeroboam, Hyrcanus and Alexander Jannaius, and Achaius and Antiochus III, and so on.[12] He maintains that the closest biblical story may be that of Joseph, who came from prison to become second in command to the pharaoh. However, there is no fickle crowd in the story. Lauha concludes appropriately that this anecdote is popular pseudo-history that does not allude to any specific historical event but is a prototypical picture that demonstrates another vanity Qohelet wants to expose. Other scholars essentially concur, seeing not a specific historical reference but primarily a narrative with didactic intent.[13]

Ecclesiastes 5:7 contains another possible historical allusion, where Qohelet describes the corruption of a layering of officials. Lauha explains the verse as a general observation about colonialism that would have been especially true of the situation in Ptolemaic Judah.[14] The Ptolemaic king was too far away to deal with injustices by royal officials to the vassals. But, again, this description cannot be limited to the Ptolemaic regime. As Schäfer points out

---

12. Lauha, "Verhältnis zur Geschichte," 396–97.

13. Pinker believes that this pericope contains a *gute-Sprüche* unit, which teaches that innate intelligence is superior to maturity and experience, and an observation unit, which confirms this: the heir of an old but foolish king will be innately no better ("Qohelet 4,13–16," *SJOT* 22 [2008]: 176–94). Graham S. Ogden sees two segments as well with the first unit referring to someone like Joseph or David, who rose from deprived circumstances to great heights, with the second showing that superior wisdom is unappreciated ("Historical Allusion in Qoheleth IV 13–16?" *VT* 30 [1980]: 309–15). Michael V. Fox sees the anecdote treating the issue of the transfer of power: the first part shows the power of wisdom, the second its failure ("What Happens in Qohelet 4:13–16," *Journal of Hebrew Scriptures* 1, article 4 [1996–97]: n.p., online at http://www.arts.ualberta.ca/JHS/Articles/article4.pdf [accessed April 20, 2011]). Ze'ev Weisman sees the anecdote as quasi-historical and used by the author "to persuade his audience that there is no history: the causality operating in it is paradoxical, and memory, the thread connecting various events in history, is nothing more than illusion" ("Elements of Political Satire in Koheleth 4,13–16; 9,13–16," *ZAW* 111 [1999]: 554).

14. Lauha, "Verhältnis zur Geschichte," 399.

concerning this verse, "This might equally well refer to exploitation by the Ptolemies and their accomplices, the Jewish priests and lay nobility, headed by the Tobiad family."[15]

Another possibility is 6:1–3, where Qohelet describes a wealthy citizen whose possessions are confiscated and given to a stranger, and who receives no proper burial. Lauha views this unit as one of two in which there is "political agitation because of the foreign, powerful regime" (my translation).[16] Lauha sees here a situation of a "political judicial murder." The Ptolemaic authorities have suspected the man of political intrigue, seized his property, and murdered him. Lauha even sees the man as a personal acquaintance of Qohelet because of his emotional reaction to the incident: a stillborn is better off than he (v. 3)! But might not the Jewish aristocracy resort to the same type of confiscation, as, for instance, in the story of Naboth's vineyard (1 Kgs 21)? Marie Maussion interprets this passage contextually and sees this individual as Qohelet's idiosyncratic "sinner" (2:26), who attempts to amass wealth through arduous labor but fails to enjoy the simple pleasures of life.[17] Her interpretation puts the blame more on the individual than on God or the political authorities, which would tend to make this anecdote less particular and more generic.

Another possibility is 8:2–4, in which Qohelet advises his audience to obey the king's command and not hasten to leave his presence, emphasizing the powerful position of the king. Lauha interprets the oath to God as a loyalty oath to the Ptolemies that Qohelet advises them not to break.[18] Lauha points out that Ptolemy I demanded that the Jerusalem citizens take this oath after the death of Alexander the Great (Josephus, *Ant.* 12.1). Lauha sees the political context as one where the Jews might decide to support the Seleucid ruler during one of the many battles between the Ptolemies and the Seleucids. "Evil matter" (v. 3) would then mean getting involved in such political intrigue. Others treat the "evil matter" as not a loyalty issue but escaping from a difficult situation where the king has become angry.[19] This would mean that the verse is more generic than Lauha indicates.[20]

---

15. Schäfer, *History of the Jews*, 21.

16. Lauha, "Verhältnis zur Geschichte," 400.

17. Marie Maussion, "Qohélet VI 1–2: 'Dieu ne permet pas . . .'" *VT* 55 (2005): 501–10.

18. Lauha, "Verhältnis zur Geschichte," 398.

19. See Crenshaw, *Ecclesiastes*, 150–51; Fox, *Rereading of Ecclesiastes*, 276–778; Bartholomew, *Ecclesiastes*, 281.

20. Scott C. Jones makes an interesting argument that v. 1 belongs to this section and that the whole unit is about the liabilities of mantic wisdom in the context of the court. He sees פשר referring to mantic speculation about the future ("Qohelet's Courtly Wisdom: Ecclesiastes 8:1–9," *CBQ* 68 [2006]: 211–28).

Lauha sees a possible historical allusion also in the famous critically difficult 8:10.[21] With minor text-critical emendations, Lauha translates the verse as follows: "Then I saw sinners draw near and enter the Holy Place. As they returned, they boasted in the city that they had done this" (my translation). Lauha considers these to be heathen representatives of the government entering the sacred site, which is categorically forbidden by Jewish law. While Lauha admits that there is no record of such an event for the Ptolemaic period (unlike the Seleucid period), he claims that it has the "impression of the historical authenticity of a recorded event." More likely, as Kay Weißflog translates it, assuming the MT's קבר: "Then I saw the godless—buried, although they entered and had walked away from the Holy Place and boasted that they had done so" (my translation of Weißflog), what is problematic is that the wicked receive proper burial when, in fact, they should be cursed according to Deut 28:26 and left exposed to the beasts and birds.[22] Thus, once again, this verse is probably more generic than Lauha indicates.

Lauha examines 9:14–16, where a poor wise man has the potential to deliver a small city from a great king who has besieged it, but because he is poor his advice is not sought and, so, the city falls.[23] Lauha believes that the closest parallel would be Archemides in Syracuse. Again, he concludes that this is a prototypical picture that serves as paradigmatic for the teaching that wisdom, though powerful, has its liabilities.[24] This is one way to interpret or translate the story. Others see the city delivered but the sage forgotten because of his poverty.[25] The point, however, would still be the same, and Lauha's conclusion seems sound that the story is not historical but prototypical.

Lauha also discusses 10:5–7, which has already been cited as an example of the topsy-turvy motif often found in pessimistic literature.[26] Here a ruler has made a slave rich and a rich person a slave. Lauha again does not see Qohelet referring to a specific evident. Rather, he explains that it is typical for a foreign subjugator to install formerly low-ranking individuals in high positions

---

21. Lauha, "Verhältnis zur Geschichte," 401.

22. Kay Weißflog, "Worum geht es in Kohelet 8,10?" *BN* 131 (2006): 39–45. Pinker has a very complicated and untenable solution to the text-critical problem: he sees a pious scribe correcting an original text by Qohelet where he expresses his frustration that wicked persons have repented but have been forgotten ("The Doings of the Wicked in Qohelet 8:10," *Journal of Hebrew Studies* 8, article 6 [2008]: 1–22, online at http://www.arts.ualberta.ca/JHS/Articles/article_83.pdf [accessed April 20, 2011]).

23. Lauha, "Verhältnis zur Geschichte," 397–98; cf. Crenshaw, *Ecclesiastes*, 165.

24. Weisman notes the collective forgetfulness of the city dwellers that makes history inhuman ("Satire in Koheleth," 559).

25. See NRSV translation; Fox, *Rereading of Ecclesiastes*, 299–300; Bartholomew, *Ecclesiastes*, 313–14.

26. Lauha, "Verhältnis zur Geschichte," 399.

to gain their loyalty. But once again this action could as likely have been insti-
gated by the Jewish aristocracy, with the high priest benefiting his favorites.
Lauha then considers 10:16–17, where Qohelet bemoans a land where a
king and his officials party inappropriately early in the morning.[27] Some have
suggested that this may refer to Ptolemy V and Antiochus III or the drunken
king Pharaoh Amasis. However, again Lauha sees no reference to "some definite historical persons but a question of types and principal aspects" (my
translation).

Three conclusions can be drawn from this discussion. First, the difficulty
in seeing clear historical allusions in Qohelet is due to the book's classification
as wisdom literature, which is more interested in repeatable patterns of behavior than specific events because of its primarily didactic function. Second, it is
easy to see that Qohelet observes oppression and corruption in the land, but
whether it is the Ptolemaic period or some other is impossible to demonstrate.
Third, Qohelet's observations about injustice could be attributable to the Ptolemaic regime and/or its Jewish aristocratic collaborators.

Hellenistic Influence in Qohelet

There is no definitive and clear evidence of Greek ideas or values in Qohelet.
As already indicated, it is simpler to attribute Qohelet's pessimism and skepticism to his usage of established Semitic genres than to exposure to Greek ideas.
If anything, his skepticism about the notion of life after death in 3:21 and his
refusal to countenance this idea as a solution to the problem of theodicy certainly indicate that Qohelet should be viewed as countering Hellenistic ideas
rather than embracing them.[28] Of course, resistance to Hellenism is in fact a
form of Hellenism, but only in that sense can Qohelet be described as showing
Hellenistic influence. Even if Qohelet was a member of the upper class and
consequently was probably more exposed to Greek ideas than the masses, this
does not necessitate that he more easily accepted them. Rather than viewing
Qohelet's skepticism and pessimism as directly influenced by Greek ideas, one
should see them as part of his strategic response to changes in Jewish society
and culture brought on by Ptolemaic domination, as will be shown.

Qohelet: Aristocrat or Middle Class?

Determining Qohelet's social location is not easy to do, mainly because of his
ambivalence about power and wealth. This ambivalence is indicated in scholars' inability to agree on where to locate Qohelet socially. Of course, no one

---

27. Lauha, "Verhältnis zur Geschichte," 399–400.
28. See J. T. Sanders, "Wisdom, Theodicy, Death," 269–70.

places him among the oppressed peasantry; however, determining his location more precisely—either in an upper class or a middle class—is the subject
of debate among scholars. Most commentators locate him in the upper class.
Gordis speaks of him among the "upper classes." Bickerman describes him as
a sage who addresses a rich mercantile class. Whybray views him as a disillusioned man of wealth. Hengel describes him as a member of the bourgeoisie which still had an "aristocratic stamp." Crüsemann locates Qohelet within
the hellenizing urban aristocracy. Müller describes him as one who is "formerly upper class," and similarly Lang calls him a "rich aristocrat" who has
lost power and status. Gottwald speaks of Qohelet's "class privilege" as a sage
who feels powerless before the government and God; as a Marxist, Gottwald
views Qohelet as an aristocrat, since there are only two classes to which one
may belong, and he certainly was not poor. [29]

But a minority of scholars classifies him as more middle class. Crenshaw is
hesitant to locate Qohelet, but apparently it would be in the middle class, while
he assigns Qohelet's students to the upper class. Similarly, Harrison, Seow, and
Krüger all also seem to imply that Qohelet belonged to the middle class or at
least his audience did.[30] This refusal to lump Qohelet with the aristocracy is
significant.

There is truth in both positions. The reality is that Qohelet reflects both
elitism and less-than-aristocratic concerns, values, and ideas. In other words,
his social location is more complex than a simple assignment to the aristocracy as it is usually understood. But this does not necessarily mean placing
him in the middle class. In the following I will argue that he should be viewed
as occupying the lowest rung of the aristocracy, a member of the retainer class,
which served the higher aristocrats yet shared their privileged lifestyle, though
not to the same degree. In addition, his membership in the scribal guild and
identity as an intellectual are also important components of a complicated
social location. The latter category will explain his creativity in solving the
problem of theodicy in a particular way.

As already mentioned, it is somewhat anachronistic to speak of a middle
class in ancient Israel.[31] Again, this is because a middle class or bourgeoisie that
was independent of the aristocracy did not properly develop until the Industrial Revolution of the modern era. Thus, Harrison's reference to a middle class

---

29. Gordis, "Social Background," 175–79; Bickerman, *Strange Books,* 160–65;
Whybray, *Intellectual Tradition,* 69; cf. idem, *Ecclesiastes,* 12; Hengel, *Judaism and Hellenism,* 1:126–27; Crüsemann, "Unchangeable World," 58, 65–69, 72–74; Müller, "Neige,"
258; Lang, "Ist der Mensch hilflos?" 118; Gottwald, *Socio-Literary Introduction,* 582.

30. Crenshaw, *Ecclesiastes,* 50, 143; Harrison, "Among the Sociologists," 164–65, 171;
Seow, *Ecclesiastes,* 27–28; Krüger, *Qoheleth,* 115..

31. See Sneed, "Middle Class," 53–69.

or petite bourgeoisie in Ptolemaic times to which Qohelet's audience belonged is faulty on this score, though perhaps one could speak of a middle layer or stratum. This "layer" would be parasitically attached to the aristocracy. The layer, then, would not be independent in any sense. The lack of autonomy suggests that this stratum should be viewed as a lower rung of the aristocracy rather than as a middle class or layer. The merchants would constitute the only true middle class, but it was probably very small. Only in this case is Harrison correct.

In Weber's discussion of the class affiliation of Jewish intellectuals, he speaks of a petite bourgeoisie that included the rabbis, but he never includes the wisdom writers in that class.[32] Weber views the authors of wisdom literature, including Ben Sira, as members of the upper class or anti-plebian class, which had its origins in royalist, particularly Solomonic circles, though he never specifically cites Qohelet.[33] For example, Weber contrasts the retributive and salvific religious orientation of the oppressed Jews who yearned for a messiah with the anti-theodical book of Job where the problem of evil is not solved and, instead, submission to the absolute sovereignty of God is commended. He attributes the book to an upper or anti-plebian class.[34] He refers to Proverbs and Job as products of scribal intellectualism, which he says "is sometimes apolitical and always aristocratic and anti-plebian."[35] He connects Job, the "Solomonic" books, and Ben Sira with upper classes that reflect an international perspective.

From these comments, one can conclude the following concerning Weber's determination of the social location of the wisdom literature. The authors were aristocrats but held no fundamental power. Their religious perspective might not be retributive, as in Job. The authors were exposed to other cultures and ideas through their literature. As will be shown, all of Weber's instincts are essentially correct. But before examining Qohelet's complex social location, a discussion of Weber's dualistic trajectory of Jewish intellectualism is necessary.

Weber's Theorization about Plebian/ Upper-Class Intellectuality

As already mentioned, Weber believes the primary or fundamental social class conflict in ancient Judah was patrician versus plebs. He sees these two trajectories reflected in the literature. Weber sees a "Yahwistic" plebeian intellectualism reflected in Deuteronomy, the Deuteronomistic History, and especially

---

32. Weber, *Ancient Judaism*, 31–36, 388, 414.
33. See ibid., 194–97.
34. Weber, *Sociology of Religion*, 112.
35. Ibid., 127.

the prophets, who were never plebian themselves and yet resisted the Israelite monarchy, seeing it as a return to the oppressiveness of Egypt.[36] He contrasts the ability of Israelite intellectuals to oppose the monarchy with the typical repression of prophecy in Egypt and Mesopotamia.[37] Weber views this as due to the smaller size of Israel and the inability of the Israelite monarchy to attain enough power to repress such opposition. Further, Weber describes the religion of the prophets as very rationalistic because it rejected irrational magic and a cultic emphasis, focusing on God's rational commands found in the covenant. This rationalistic intellectual development Weber sees as due to Israel's being on the perimeter of great powers and not located within them. Only those on the perimeter of great empires, Weber argues, can become conscious of new ideas and develop revolutionary ideas as the Israelite prophets did.[38]

Weber also explains how this rationalization of Israelite religion involved the development of theodicy. He connects the development of theodicy in ancient Israel with the devastation of the land and people of Israel by the more powerful Egyptians, Assyrians, and then Babylonians and the consequent bafflement over why God had abandoned them.[39] The prophets explained that God had used these foreign powers to punish his people because they had not kept his commandments and been loyal to him. Eventually, as subjugation of the Jews persisted, the theodicy developed where deprivation took on a positive quality—one suffers unjustly for God, and one day God will avenge the Jews' enemies and exalt his people. Thus, messianic notions developed that were connected with the conception of the Jews as a pariah people who waited for the messiah.[40] The Jewish religion, thus, always remained a retributive and salvation religion, with hope in God's justice pushed farther and farther into the future.

Weber's instinctive detection of the Deuteronomic/istic anti-royalist tendencies is highly significant but needs qualification. There are certainly what one might describe as "democratic" features of the work that several recent scholars have attempted to explain. For example, Eric Seibert argues that the authors who composed the Solomonic narrative in 1 Kgs 1–11 were subversive scribes who worked under the authority of kings and yet subtly criticized them through irony and other methods.[41] Though no doubt scribes had some

---

36. See Weber, *Ancient Judaism*, 205–18.
37. See ibid., 195–97, 207–9.
38. See ibid., 206–7.
39. See ibid., 297–335.
40. See ibid., 336–55.
41. Eric A. Seibert, *Subversive Scribes and the Solomonic Narrative: A Rereading of 1 Kings 1–11* (Library of Hebrew Bible/Old Testament Studies 436; New York: T & T Clark, 2006).

independence with respect to the king, Seibert's explanation is too far-fetched and overly complicated.[42] Better is Crüsemann's speculation that the "people of the land" or wealthy farmers underwrote the Deuteronomic code and the Deuteronomistic History when Josiah was an infant and attempted to democratize the old urban aristocratic Book of the Covenant with greater concern for the poor.[43] Or, as Thomas Römer suggests, the law of kingship in Deut 17:14–20 and other royal-critical materials (1 Sam 8–12) were added during the exile when the king could not suppress them.[44] Others emphasize an inherent tension in the materials. Tamis Rentería argues that the Elijah and Elisha accounts are essentially peasant stories that Jehu and his court co-opt to legitimize his coup of the Omrides.[45] Wesley Bergen argues that Elisha's literary role is ambiguous: he represents an alternative to the monarchy, which the dominant voice attempts to repress.[46]

Weber's description of the Deuteronomic/istic authors as plebs and anti-monarchic is problematic in light of more recent work on the function of Deuteronomy and the Deuteronomistic History as a whole. Most North American scholars today see an early version of the Deuteronomistic History serving as propaganda to legitimize Josiah's reign and his political and religious centralizing reforms.[47] Thus, this makes it difficult to characterize the work as anti-monarchic. As a matter of fact, it is doubtful whether the anti-monarchic or pro-monarchic dichotomy is helpful.[48] This modern concern was prob-

---

42. On the independence of ancient Near Eastern scribes, see Thomas Römer, *The So-Called Deuteronomistic History: A Sociological, Historical and Literary Introduction* (paperback ed.; London: T&T Clark, 2007), 47.

43. Frank Crüsemann, *The Torah: Theology and Social History of Old Testament Law* (trans. Allan W. Mahnke; Minneapolis: Fortress, 1996), 201–75; cf. Joseph Blenkinsopp, *Wisdom and Law in the Old Testament: The Ordering of Life in Israel and early Judaism* (Oxford Bible; Oxford: Oxford University Press, 1983), 97–100.

44. Römer, *Deuteronomistic History*, 139–43.

45. Tamis Hoover Rentería, "The Elijah/Elisha Stories: A Socio-Cultural Analysis of Prophets and People in Ninth-Century b.c.e. Israel," in *Elijah and Elisha in Socioliterary Perspective* (ed. Robert B. Coote; SemeiaSt; Atlanta: Scholars Press, 1992), 75–126. Similarly, Roland Boer has described the Jeroboam narrative (1 Kgs 11–14) as involving the co-option of critical prophetic material to legitimize a declassed ruling class (the Deuteronomists) (*Jameson and Jeroboam*, 165–66).

46. Wesley J. Bergen, "The Prophetic Alternative: Elisha and the Israelite Monarchy," in *Elijah and Elisha in Socioliterary Perspective* (ed. Robert B. Coote; Semeia St.; Atlanta: Scholars Press, 1992), 127–37.

47. See Frank Moore Cross, *Canaanite Myth and Hebrew Epic: Essays in the History of the Religion of Israel* (1973; repr., paperback ed.; Cambridge, Mass.: Harvard University Press, 1997), 274–89.

48. Gerald Eddie Gerbrandt, *Kingship According to the Deuteronomistic History* (SBLDS 87; Atlanta: Scholars Press, 1986), 41.

ably not a burning issue for the Deuteronomist(s). Rather, a better question is "what kind of kingship he saw as ideal for Israel, or what role kingship was expected to play for Israel." According to Gerald Gerbrandt, the king was to assume the role of covenant administrator.[49] But Marvin Sweeney goes too far when he states that the law of kingship in Deut 17:14–20 "merely defines the means by which royal authority is exercised; it does not restrict the power of the king to rule."[50] Any limitation on what the king could or could not do entails a limitation of his power, however relative.

Most post-Weber scholars view the authors of at least the Josianic version of Deuteronomy and the Deuteronomistic History as royal scribes.[51] This means that Weber's positing of a literate plebian intellectuality in ancient Israel and Judah is problematic. In the world of the ancient Near East, true literacy was confined to a small percentage of the population. Sophisticated literary writing had to take place solely within the confines of the palace or the temple. Thus, instead of a viable literary plebian intellectuality, there were scribes (royal, priestly, or prophetic) who were sympathetic to the plight of the plebs, perhaps mainly due to prophetic influence.[52] The latter explanation certainly fits with Weber's emphasis on the role of ideas and not just material interests for bringing about change. The recognition of the scribal membership within the retainer class also helps explain this plebian sympathy. The scribes were essentially lower-level aristocrats or aristocratic retainers, as already discussed. There was a stratum above the retainers and the masses below them. Thus, they were more predisposed to be sympathetic with the oppressed than would be their superiors.

But Weber's theorization need not be completely dismissed. The complexity of the scribal social location can allow Weber's basic theorization to remain useful. A "plebian" and anti-plebian literary intellectuality can be maintained

---

49. Ibid., 102.

50. Marvin A. Sweeney, "The Critique of Solomon in the Josianic Edition of the Deuteronomistic History," *JBL* 114 (1995): 615.

51. Weinfeld, "Deuteronomy," 256; Römer, *Deuteronomistic History*, 45–47. Patricia Dutcher-Walls deals with the problem of identifying the specific authorship of the Deuteronomistic History by positing an upper-class factional alliance of prophets, officials, priests, and gentry ("The Social Location of the Deuteronomists: A Sociological Study of Factional Politics in Late Pre-Exilic Judah," *JSOT* 52 [1991]: 91). However, à la Ockham's razor, it is simpler to point to royal scribes as the actual authors, though certainly various factions would have subscribed to the work's ideology.

52. Jacques Berlinerblau notes the difficulty in retrieving the popular voice from elitist texts ("The 'Popular Religion' Paradigm in Old Testament Research: A Sociological Critique," *JSOT* 60 [1993]: 3–26). For his own methodology for properly retrieving this voice, see idem, *The Vow and the 'Popular Religious Groups' of Ancient Israel: A Philological and Sociological Inquiry* (JSOTSup 210; Sheffield: Sheffield Academic Press, 1996).

within the same class. Not all scribes display the plebian sympathy of the Deuteronomist(s).[53] A scribe could just as easily assimilate more fully the ethos of his superiors. The wisdom tradition seems to reflect this more aristocratically oriented type of scribal perspective. David Pleins has demonstrated that the wisdom lexical repertoire concerning poverty in Proverbs reflects a more elitist perspective than that of the prophetic literature.[54] While the prophetic literature focuses on social justice concerning poverty and valorizes the status as almost virtuous, the concern in Proverbs is more on how to avoid poverty. I have also shown that the concern for the poor in Proverbs is not incompatible with upper-class interests and reflects the perspective of noblesse oblige.[55]

Thus, though Qohelet was a member of the same social class as the Deuteronomists, he shares neither their plebian flare nor their prophetic passion. Weber's characterization of the wisdom literature as anti-plebian certainly fits Qohelet. While he has sympathy for the poor, it is always from an aristocratic perspective. Apparently, the complex social location of the retainer class allowed its members to be oriented either to the stratum above or to that below them. The Deuteronomists took the latter route, whereas the wisdom writers took the former.

QOHELET'S ARISTOCRATIC SIDE

Returning to our discussion of Qohelet's complex social location, on the one hand, Qohelet reflects what might be considered an aristocratic air. He has the leisure to read and write. The true ability to read and write, or functional literacy—not simply the ability to read and write simple phrases—was probably confined to a very small minority in the ancient world.[56] Qohelet's ability to produce the quality literature that the book represents puts him into an even smaller elite circle. In ancient agrarian societies, literacy drove a wedge between the governing class and the governed.[57] This resulted in a high intel-

---

53. As a complication of this portrayal of the Deuteronomistic tradition, note Steinberg, who argues that Deut 19–25, which ostensibly seems to elevate the rights of women, in fact ultimately serves the needs of the state ("Deuteronomic Law Code," 161–70).

54. J. David Pleins, "Poverty in the Social World of the Wise," *JSOT* 37 (1987): 61–78. Cf. Frank S. Frick, who analyzes the same repertoire of the Deuteronomistic History and concludes that the authors were not very interested in social justice ("*Cui Bono?*—History in the Service of Political Nationalism: The Deuteronomistic History as Political Propaganda," *Semeia* 66 [1994]: 79–92).

55. Sneed, "Culture of Proverbs," 296–308.

56. See Christopher A. Rollston, *Writing and Literacy in the World of Ancient Israel: Epigraphic Evidence from the Iron Age* (Arcaheology and Biblical Studies 11; Atlanta: Society of Biblical Literature, 2010).

57. Lenski, *Power and Privilege*, 208.

lectual tradition associated with sacred literature, great works of literature, and high standards of honor and etiquette, contrasted with a low intellectual tradition associated with practical matters and a parochial mind-set.

Writing is intricately connected with power and social inequality. It was invented in ancient Sumer essentially to keep financial records of business transactions at the temples.[58] In ancient agrarian societies, it was an instrument of social control as well as a business aid. It increased the efficiency of political administration, and "it has become the foundation of every true bureaucracy."[59]

Qohelet also refers to the poor and the oppressed as if he were neither. In 4:1, he refers to the tears of the oppressed who have no power. But the reference has the feel of a detached observer, not a participant. In 9:13–16, Qohelet presents the anecdote about a poor wise man who saved a city with his wisdom but was soon forgotten, but it is unlikely that this is in any way autobiographical. In 5:12, Qohelet refers to the sleep of laborers as sweet, whether they go to bed hungry or not, in contrast to the worried sleep of the wealthy.[60] Lang describes the reference to the sweet sleep of manual laborers as ignorant, and Müller refers to it as "a romantic transfiguration of the life of labor."[61] Similarly, David Clines finds the depiction of the poor in Job to be unrealistic and, in fact, a "glamourization" of poverty.[62] This is because, with the book of Job, one has a wealthy author attempting to describe the poor, whom he really does not know or understand.[63]

In addition, Qohelet's horror at the declassing of formerly rich and wealthy citizens and their replacement with fools and slaves (10:5–6) reveals that Qohelet is fundamentally an aristocrat who believes that high social stratification is a good thing and its inversion a great evil. In fact, typical of the wisdom literature, Qohelet seems to have no problem with kingship itself, only the abuses he sees in the Ptolemaic system and/or among the Jewish collaborators.

Incisively, Müller lists several indicators of what he views as evidence of Qohelet's upper-class status. [64] The reference to wisdom providing security like money (7:12) points to Qohelet's belonging probably to the well-to-do.

---

58. Ibid., 207; see Giuseppe Visicato, *The Power and the Writing: The Early Scribes of Mesopotamia* (Bethesda, Md.: CDL, 2000).

59. Lenski, *Power and Privilege*, 207.

60. Contrast this with the "'Teaching of Khety," where the jeweler is described as working all day on one piece of jewelry, and "when he lies down at dusk, his back aches and his thighs cramp" (Victor Matthews and Don C. Benjamin, *Old Testament Parallels* [3rd ed.; New York: Paulist Press, 2006], 291).

61. Lang, "Ist der Mensch hilflos?" 118; Müller, "Neige," 257.

62. Clines, *Interested Parties*, 128.

63. Ibid., 124–28.

64. Müller actually uses the term "bourgeoisie" but in the Marxist sense of the new upper class emerging after the Industrial Revolution ("Neige," 256–57).

Müller makes the interesting observation that the allusions to Solomon's great building projects and wealth in 1:12–2:12 represent "a dream of the well-to-do 'bourgeoisie'" (my translation). He also points out that 7:19 and 8:10 indicate an urban milieu, specifically Jerusalem, "where the mercantile activities of the Phoenician-Hellenistic civilization desired to concentrate." Qohelet 11:1–4, which is also interpreted as advice to invest in mercantile trade or some other industry, seems to suggest Qohelet's privileged social position. Moreover, Qohelet's concerns often have an aristocratic flavor to them: the problem of inheritance (2:18–23), the problem of competitors (4:4), business risks (5:13), insomnia due to being overemployed and oversatiated (2:23; 5:11). But in the end, business aspirations (5:10–12; 6:3, 7) do not satisfy, nor do "the pleasures to be had for money" (10:19).

But, in fairness, it must be pointed out that all of these observations and warnings could have come from a member of a lower class who could acutely observe the numerous problems of the rich without having to be one himself. Could not Qohelet's observation that the wealthy are not really happy be the fantasy of a member of the lower class who would like to think so?

Though in 4:1 Qohelet is touched by the tears of the oppressed, he shows much more emotional reaction to the declassing of aristocrats in 10:5–7, and his reaction to the nobleman toppled in 6:1–6 includes his assessment that a stillborn child is better off than he![65] This indicates that in these instances the problem of evil has struck a nerve because it has hit a little closer to home!

Additionally, Qohelet's citation of an aphorism (7:21–22) that assumes the reader might overhear his slaves indicates that he and his audience were usually slave owners and, by definition, should be classified as upper class or, at least, well-to-do. Another indication that the author is connected to the upper crust is his counseling of the reader to keep the king's edict because of an oath (8:2). This oath of loyalty would most likely not have been required of the poor but only officials and leaders. Further, 8:2–5 seems to reflect a court setting: Qohelet assumes that his students might actually stand in the presence of the king or at least before officials or authority figures, and 10:4 indicates the role of a governmental official with a reference to "post," literarily in Hebrew "place." Thus, Qohelet assumes that his audience will be government officials who need to be very cautious in their dealings with the king and/or his royal officials.

QOHELET'S PROLETARIAN SIDE

Though Qohelet has an aristocratic flare, he also refers to the rich and powerful as if he were neither. In 5:13, he refers to the owners of riches that are lost

---

65. Lauha, "Verhältnis zur Geschichte," 400.

in a bad business adventure as if this were impossible for himself. In 10:20, he warns against cursing the king and the rich because they might get wind of it. Qohelet generally exudes a sense of powerlessness before the king, rulers, and high officials (5:8–9; 8:2–5; 10:5–6).

Qohelet also demonstrates sympathy for the poor, which does not seem compatible with genuine aristocratic interests. Müller points out that the book contains instances of solidarity with the poor.[66] He refers to the deprivation of justice (3:16), the oppression of the poor (4:1), and extortion and bribery (7:7). His reference to the romantic depiction of the sleep of the poor in 5:11 has already been mentioned.

Müller concludes, "Apparently, from the perspective of Qohelet, there was an even more powerful class in society, which promised solidarity against downward profit" (my translation).[67] As has already been noted, this class consisted of the royal Ptolemaic officials and Jews who collaborated with them. Müller then very compactly cites passages that seem to indicate the negative relationship between this class and the class to whom Qohelet belonged. He believes that the parable in 9:13–16 (cf. 10:1b) about the poor wise man who has the knowledge to defeat the great king but is forgotten symbolizes the political position withheld by this dominant class from the class to which Qohelet belonged. Similar to Lauha, he sees the wicked in 8:10 who violate the holy place in Jerusalem as the dominant class, while the righteous are forgotten in the city. In 7:19, a proverb about one wise man being greater than ten rulers, Müller sees Qohelet's own class raising claim to a power actually assumed by a powerful minority, and he views 10:6–7 in the same way, where foolish and lower class upstarts are given positions of nobility. He sees an upper-class hierarchy in 5:7 and 10:20 (a bird will tell what one says about the rich and powerful in private). In 10:4 and 8:2–4, Qohelet warns to be careful before rulers and the Diadochi kings, especially when the latter are old stubborn fools or children (4:13–16). Finally, 5:8b (Heb.), which speaks of the advantage a king might supply in connection with land, probably criticizes monarchic policy, though the Hebrew is difficult.[68]

Müller is correct in his recognition of an aristocratic flare to Qohelet and yet simultaneously sympathy for the poor. But, as has already been argued, this ambivalence is not due to a recent or new depolitization of the Jewish upper class under the Ptolemies. A degree of depoliticization was characteristic of both the Persian and Ptolemaic periods in that during these periods the Jews were subjugated or colonized by empires.

---

66. Müller, "Neige," 257.
67. Ibid.
68. Charles F. Whitley notes the pairing of "land" and "field," which also occurs in Ugaritic literature; he interprets the verse to suggest "the benefits of land to a people and a field to a king" ("Koheleth and Ugaritic Parallels," *UF* 11 [1979]: 816).

Why does Qohelet reflect ambivalence about wealth and power? Two factors can explain such tension. The first is Qohelet's social position as a member of a colonized nation. Qohelet's solidarity with the poor, then, can be explained as the result of the Jewish upper class's position vis-à-vis the Ptolemies as a lower class. Thus, the social hierarchy is quite complicated. Among the Jews, their highest echelon constituted an indigenous upper class and enjoyed many privileges and power. But in relation to the Ptolemies, this stratum was indeed a lower class. Qohelet's sympathy with the poor can then be partly explained as not due to some new loss of status and power but a result of the frustration of the continued subjugated position, actually for centuries, of the Jewish elite as a segment of colonized people. Thus, one can say that Qohelet and the class to which he belonged have status inconsistency. On the one hand, they are aristocrats, but, on the other, they are subjugated colonials. They are probably not economically deprived but suffer from a continual lack of prestige and power that they believe their class and nation as a whole deserve. The reference to Solomon in the first two chapters probably represents a nostalgic yearning for the days of glory when Israel was independent and at its height of power.

Müller goes on to explain Qohelet's pessimism as due to this new declassed situation. As already noted, he tries to justify his thesis by appealing to Weber's comparative and historical observation that an aristocratic or bourgeois class of one nation that is depoliticized by another often retreats into intellectual pursuits, which typically results in salvation teaching. Of course, again, there was no new declassing of the Jewish aristocrats during the Ptolemaic period. But this notion is generally true for the Jews during and after the exile. Much of the present Hebrew Bible was produced and finalized during colonial periods. There was much intellectual creativity during these periods and the development of messianic hopes, with the concomitant emphasis on salvation and retribution, especially in the prophetic and apocalyptic works. Weber argues that salvation religions always involve some type of distress, often actual oppression and suffering, which indicates the need and desire to be delivered or saved from such.[69] This may take the form of resentment and hope for a messianic figure, who will someday bring about compensation for such suffering. Salvific religions generally take two forms: either flight from the world (mysticism) or mastery of it (asceticism), which means making the world conform to God's will externally and internally (disciplining of the body).[70]

---

69. See Weber, *Sociology of Religion*, 107.

70. See Max Weber, "Religious Rejections of the World and Their Directions," in *From Max Weber: Essays in Sociology* (ed. and trans. Hans H. Gerth and C. Wright Mills; paperback ed.; New York: Oxford University Press, 1958), 323–59; see Stephen Kalberg, introduction to Weber, *Protestant Ethic and the Spirit of Capitalism*, 35–37.

Qohelet certainly stands within this broad tradition as a member of an oppressed nation, but salvific and retributive elements are quite muted in the book. In other words, it is a bit of a stretch to describe Qohelet's theology as salvific or retributive. Since his status is as a colonial subject, the nonsalvific character of the book cannot be attributed directly to his membership in the upper class, though its possibility as a response to the problem of evil is, as will be shown.

Qohelet's situation is more complicated than simple oppression. Deprivation can take more than one form.[71] Qohelet is not oppressed physically or economically. His oppression is more subtle: social and psychological, which is just as real but of a different type. While Qohelet is "oppressed" in this sense, he does not resort to the utopian impulse. Qohelet has been described as anti-apocalyptic and rightly so. Many scholars have noted Qohelet's epigram of "there is nothing new under sun" (1:9) as polemical against the proto-apocalypticism of, say, Isaiah, who speaks of God creating new things among Israel (42:9).[72] Further, Qohelet's skepticism about life after death in 3:21 points to the same polemic, as a notion of resurrection is found in Dan 12:2 (mid-second century B.C.E.).[73] Weber views Israel's resistance to the concept of resurrection as a rejection of anything Egyptian and especially their gods of the dead, and this fits mainline Jewish orthodoxy of the time.[74] Qohelet is then simply being Jewish here. He is not happy with the status quo, but he does not believe there will be change anytime soon, at least not in apocalyptic terms.

---

71. On the notion of relative deprivation, see Robert Nisbet, *The Social Bond: An Introduction to the Study of Society* (New York: Knopf, 1970), 270; David Aberle, "A Note on Relative Deprivation Theory as Applied to Millenarian and Other Cult Movements," in *Reader in Comparative Religion: An Anthropological Approach* (ed. William A. Lessa and Evon Z. Vogt; 2nd ed.; New York: Harper & Row, 1965), 538. For its application in biblical studies, see Collins, *Apocalyptic Imagination*, 24 n. 69, 38. Eep Talstra creatively tries to bring Deutero-Isaiah and Qohelet together in spite of their differences concerning new things by arguing that both operate through creation theology instead of salvation history ("Second Isaiah and Qohelet: Could One Get Them on Speaking Terms?" in *The New Things: Eschatology in Old Testament Prophecy* [ed. F. Postma, K. Spronk, and E. Talstra; ACEPT Supplement 3; Maastricht: Shaker, 2002], 225–36).

72. See Thomas Krüger, "Dekonstruktion und Rekonstruktion prophetischer Eschatologie im Qohelet-Buch," in *"Jedes Ding hat seine Zeit . . .": Studien zur israelitischen und altorientalischen Weisheit* (ed. Anja A. Diesel et al.; BZAW 241; Berlin: de Gruyter, 1996), 107–29. Ironically, Nicholas Perrin finds the frame narrative of Qohelet to contain messianic features, such as the "one shepherd" (12:11) ("Messianism in the Narrative Frame of Ecclesiastes?" *RB* 108 [2001]: 37–60). Scholars have noted that 12:14 may refer to an eschatological judgment (Seow, *Ecclesiastes*, 395; Lauha, *Kohelet*, 223).

73. On the date of Daniel in its final form, see Paul L. Redditt, *Daniel* (NCB; Sheffield: Sheffield Academic Press, 1999), 4–6.

74. Weber, *Ancient Judaism*, 144–46.

The second way to explain Qohelet's ambivalence about wealth and power, which has already been anticipated, is in reference to his membership in the retainer class attached to the priestly aristocracy. Qohelet's feeling of powerlessness then can be explained as due to his class's occupation of the lowest rung of the indigenous aristocracy. In that position, it would make sense for Qohelet to be critical of the powers immediately above his own class, much as the lower class criticizes those above it. The fullest discussion of this explanation will now ensue.

Qohelet's Scribal Audience

Attention now will shift to Qohelet's status-group membership, which will further demonstrate the complexity of his social location. A good way to get at this is to discern his audience. There are a few indicators of Qohelet's audience. In 11:9, Qohelet identifies the audience as בָּחוּר or young unmarried males; this coheres with the frame narrator's "my son" in 12:12. Further, notable is "days of your youth," which is used twice (11:9; 12:1), "while you are young" (11:9), and "youth and the dawn of life" (11:10). The misogynistic advice about women as seductive traps (7:26–28) also implies a male and young audience. Qohelet assumes that his audience will appear before the king (8:2–5) or a ruler (10:4). Qohelet 5:10 assumes that the audience will regularly see oppression of the poor—the poor being a group different from them—which fits the role of a governmental official. As Gordis has noted, the carpe diem ethic in Qohelet would be a bitter mockery for the truly destitute, especially in ch. 9, where expensive white linen clothes are mentioned.[75]

As Crenshaw has indicated, the audience assumed by Qohelet was probably advanced in instruction level.[76] The work was not intended for the masses or even immature elite youth. The book of Proverbs may have been used in the beginning stages of scribal training before advancing to such books as Job and Qohelet, though Stuart Weeks argues that the high aesthetic quality of Prov 1–9 indicates that an intellectually advanced audience was in view here as well.[77] Qohelet also taught a wider audience at times, according to the frame narrator (12:9). All of this fits with the dominant view that the wisdom literature, especially Proverbs, is to be connected with the training of young scribes.[78]

---

75. Gordis, "Social Background," 179.

76. James L. Crenshaw, "Unresolved Issues in Wisdom Literature," in *An Introduction to Wisdom Literature and the Psalms* (ed. H. W. Ballard Jr. and W. D. Tucker Jr.; Macon, Ga.: Mercer University Press, 2000), 218.

77. Stuart Weeks, *Instruction and Imagery in Proverbs 1–9* (Oxford: Oxford University Press, 2007).

78. See Saldarini, "Scribes," 1012; cf. Carr, *Origins of Scripture*, 126–34.

Qohelet and the Scribal Status Group

Qohelet is never identified as a scribe, but this can be maintained as a reasonable assumption. He is identified by the frame narrator as חָכָם, "wise" (12:9). As Ben Sira indicates, all the scribes probably considered themselves wise, but surely not all of them were labeled this way. Qohelet was no run-of-the-mill scribe, accountant, or copyist, but a high ranking one, who actually produced literature (12:9). In other words, Qohelet was a scribal scholar; חָכָם was probably the Hebrew term to distinguish such a scribe from others in the status group. Michael Fishbane argues that the technical jargon in 12:9–12 about the typical activities of Qohelet and the wise (e.g., "weighing and studying and arranging many proverbs" [v. 9]) indicates the scribal profession.[79]

Also in 12:9, one finds that Qohelet not only instructed young elite scribes but also "taught the people," which means he may have worked outside the academy on occasion, as a service to the masses.[80] Thus, Qohelet was primarily a teacher and a scholar. The scholarly emphasis of wisdom is reflected in the prologue to Proverbs, where one learns that the book was not solely, even though mainly, intended for the young. Those already "wise" and "discerning" could also benefit from the book (1:5). Instead of just learning basic knowledge and cleverness, these can acquire skill in understanding "a proverb and a figure, the words of the wise and their riddles." Here one sees the aesthetic and artistic quality of wisdom that the Israelite/Jewish scholars would relish.

The scribes of ancient Israel, whether royal or temple scribes after the exilic period, would have formed what Weber calls a status group. This concept is important because it complicates the typically blunt Marxist type of analysis that focuses on social or economic class when examining social stratification to the exclusion of other variables. Stratification is more complex than that. The scribes were a professional group or guild bound by common education and vocation. Their cohesiveness relates more to prestige or honor (or the lack thereof) than their common economic role in Israelite society.

A status group is a social body that is born and preserved on the basis of esteem versus economic factors.[81] Among such groups, "a specific *style of life*

---

79. Michael Fishbane, *Biblical Interpretation in Ancient Israel* (Oxford: Clarendon, 1988), 29–32.

80. Though some scholars debate the existence of schools in ancient Israel or Judah prior to the time of Ben Sira or later, it is not an unreasonable assumption; see Ronald R. Clark Jr., "Schools, Scholars, and Students: The Wisdom School *Sitz im Leben* and Proverbs," *ResQ* 47 (2005): 161–77. David Jamieson-Drake argues that there is no archaeological evidence for the existence of schools in ancient Israel until the eighth century (*Scribes and Schools in Monarchic Judah: A Socio-Archaeological Approach* [JSOTSup 109; Sheffield: Almond, 1991]).

81. Weber, *Economy and Society*, 2:932–38; see Swedberg, *Max Weber Dictionary*, 268–70, s.v. "Status (*Stand*)."

is expected from all those who wish to belong to the circle."[82] Typical class categories today would include entrepreneurs and laborers. Status group categories would include lawyers, doctors, and even Mormons. They can be guilds,
religious sects, and minority groups.[83] Status groups often have an in-group
and out-group ethic, whereby outsiders are treated differently than persons
belonging to the group, and often marriage is forbidden outside it. The members often have their own distinctive worldview. There is cohesiveness to status
groups that one does not find in classes, and members have a strong camaraderie and a sense of purpose. Weber sometimes refers to the Diaspora Jews as
a status group. They treated Gentiles differently than their own when it came
to business practices; they forbid marriage to Gentiles; and they practiced an
exclusivist diet (kosher).[84] He refers to them as a "pariah" people who were
always discriminated against but learned to specialize in certain vocations like
financing and jewelry to compensate for this and survive. The castes in India
are types of status groups; for example, the Brahmins could not marry below
their caste.[85] The Chinese bureaucratic literati formed a status group.[86] In
ancient Israel, the priests were a type of status group, with restrictions on possible marriage candidates, though one could also view them as a class because
of their position of power, as we saw above in chapter 3.

Brian Kovacs has done an interesting analysis of the ethic, social psychology, and worldview of the scribes who produced the sentence collections
in Proverbs, which relates to the notion of status group. He argues that the
intended audience of the *māšāl* collections in Proverbs is not the masses or
even the wealthy and powerful.[87] Rather, the collections reflect a professional
code or in-group ethic intended for Israelite scribes.

Kovacs detects a paternalism and concern for the widow, the poor, and the
oppressed (e.g., mention of slaves with a touch of irony [17:2; 29:19]), which he
describes as noblesse oblige.[88] He concludes that the wise "are responsible and
dutiful citizens who act to uphold the proper social order." He also detects an
emphasis with the wise on the disposition or intentionality of a person and not
just actions as paramount in assessing a person's character.[89] The wise under-

82. Weber, *Economy and Society*, 2:932.

83. See Swedberg, *Max Weber Dictionary*, 270.

84. See Weber, *Ancient Judaism*, 336–55; see Swedberg, *Max Weber Dictionary*, 193–4,
s.v. "Pariah People."

85. On Weber's analysis of Indian religion, see Bendix, *Max Weber*, 142–99.

86. On Weber's analysis of Chinese religion, see ibid., 98–141.

87. Brian W. Kovacs, "Is There a Class-Ethic in Proverbs?" in *Essays in Old Testament
Ethics* (ed. James L. Crenshaw and John T. Willis; New York: Ktav, 1974), 173–89.

88. Ibid., 178.

89. Ibid., 178–82.

stand their own social responsibility toward the poor as more intentionality than the actual practical attempt to bring justice to the oppressed. He states,

> Like those in almost every society, the Hebrew intelligentsia were probably administrators and teachers, a group separate from the rich or the powerful— sometimes counselors whose power consisted solely in the adroitness of their speech, but not statesmen. . . . While they could plead for social justice, they had neither the wealth nor the power to bring it about themselves.[90]

He points out that the wise do not slavishly support the status quo. For example, the wise slave will rule the foolish son (17:2). He then concludes,

> Thus, even if the wise man is oriented toward the acknowledged Hebrew goods-of-life (long life, success, progeny, and recognition), he may not seek them directly nor by the path of his own planning. Only by pursuing wisdom for its own sake, so that it is good and valuable in its own right, rather than instrumentally, by means of the discipline of restraint, can he succeed. It is only a slight exaggeration to say that the wise could seek success only by giving it up.[91]

Kovacs also discusses the importance of propriety, the appropriateness of time and place (e.g., 15:23), and an ethic of restraint (e.g., 16:20–30).[92] All of these point to "the implication that the wise were advisors and administrators but that fundamental power, and thus consequences, lay with others." Finally, Kovacs concludes,

> The mashal collections come from a distinct social group and retain marks of that origin. More strictly, the wise perceived a gulf, crossed if at all only with the greatest difficulty, between themselves and fools, between the righteous and the wicked, and perhaps between world-order and chaos. They thus had their own realms of sacred and profane. They possessed a distinctive value-system which revalued the life and behavior of outsiders to such a degree that we regard it as an in-group morality, though by no means closed to the world. Finally, there are indications of a specifically scribal ethical code probably associated with their employment as administrators and officials in governmental chancelleries and offices as well as the court.[93]

Kovacs's dissertation is a further development of these ideas, focusing on the sentences in Prov 15:28–22:16.[94] He uses phenomenological sociology to detect the ways in which the wise formally structure their world and find it

---

90. Ibid., 179.
91. Ibid., 183.
92. Ibid., 184–86.
93. Ibid., 187.
94. Brian W. Kovacs, "Sociological-Structural Constraints upon Wisdom: The Spatial and Temporal Matrix of Proverbs 15:28–22:16" (Ph.D. diss., Vanderbilt University, 1978).

meaningful, and how this fits with their social location.[95] Kovacs analyzes the way the wise in Proverbs conceive of space and how this elicits the notion of demesne or social domain. Particular groups have their areas of control and boundaries in which they operate and often define themselves in terms of these areas of control.[96]

He first discusses the wise men's ethic of restraint and self-discipline (e.g., 17:27–28). The wise use this to neutralize the powers of the un-wise and those more powerful than themselves, for example, the king (16:14). The wise sense the power of knowledge. Kovacs points out that the bribe sayings (e.g., 19:6; 18:16) indicate that the wise of necessity sometimes have to use less-than-savory means to influence the rich and powerful. The sayings that extol the king (e.g., 20:26) show that the wise generally support the royal establishment in spite of its liabilities. But while the wise respect power, they value wisdom more highly (e.g., 21:22). Wealth and power are valued chiefly as means of security from the manipulations of others. Wealth is to be shared with the poor (e.g., 22:9), so the wise see themselves as distanced from both the rich and the poor. This Kovacs describes as noblesse oblige, but the wise go beyond this responsibility. One's disposition is more important than one's economic status (e.g., 19:1). The wise are not "mere custodians of the status quo" (e.g., 22:2). The proverbs against being surety for others and borrowing (e.g., 17:18; 20:16) show that the sages avoided being dependent on others. In other words, they protect their social space and avoid attempts by others to violate it or by their own to stray from it. Kovacs maintains that the wise define themselves by what they are, not by what they do, as do the powerful.

He then examines various social institutions to which the wise make reference. He shows how numerous proverbs (e.g., 17:17; 19:7) demonstrate that family (parents, siblings, and their own children) and friends were important to the wise and they formed a relatively closed group. The law court was apparently a place where they served (e.g., 18:17). They refer also to the cult (e.g., 21:27), the market (e.g., 20:10), the countryside (e.g., 22:8), the battlefield (e.g., 18:11), and the school (e.g., 17:16). Kovacs then concludes about the wise:

> When they look outside their realm, their language and imagery become stereo-typical, symbolic, and sometimes banal. Their attention seems to be focused on a fairly restricted sphere . . . much of the social life is missing, because it did not occupy the attention of the wise. . . . The life of the lower classes and the world outside the city . . . scarcely appears.[97]

---

95. The following is a summary of ch. 5 of his dissertation (pp. 317–515).
96. See Kovacs, "Sociological-Structural Constraints," 393.
97. Ibid., 392.

He points out that there is a significant aesthetic dimension to wisdom that makes it an elite demesne—many are excluded, such as the ignorant and the poor.[98] This elitism is built not on power but on character and insight.

Kovacs's analysis is extremely important, and it is unfortunate that it is rarely cited. He has essentially captured the worldview, ethos, and social psychology of the scribes schooled in the wisdom tradition. He has detected the sense of identity and camaraderie that the scribes/sages shared. The contours of the scribal worldview that Kovacs discovers fit well with what has already been discussed concerning scribes as retainers, and this will connect with their role as intellectuals, which will be discussed next. The authors and audience of Proverbs were not the most powerful or the wealthiest, but neither were they poor. They did not completely trust the governing elites or the masses. They felt superior to those above and below them. They recognized the power of knowledge and valued it above all else, as it was essential for their own group's viability and survival. They compensated for their lack of power by focusing on intelligence and character.

Kovacs's analysis, however, is faulty on a couple of points. First, it is doubtful that one can fully determine the sages' *Weltanschauung* solely from one mode of literature (wisdom literature). No mode or genre of literature represents a total worldview.[99] The many lacunae that Kovacs detects in the sapiential perspective are largely due to this fact. Yet Kovacs has probably captured the salient features.

Second, though Kovacs frequently emphasizes that the wise believed that wisdom was valuable intrinsically and not instrumentally, he is not skeptical about the veracity of this perspective. The sapiential view that wisdom is not an instrumental value is probably due to the Hebrew conception of wisdom as containing both a moral and an ethical dimension. Wisdom for the ancients was not simply about doing what is most beneficial but also about doing the right thing. Thus, it involved an uneasy combination of intelligence and morality. This combination points to the conflicted nature of the Hebrew notion of wisdom. Wisdom, thus, contains both instrumental (knowledge and intelligence) and intrinsic (ethics) features. This is the classic distinction between means and ends. Rhetorically, persons pretend that their values are based on ends and not means, which are seen as inferior.[100] But the reality is that an end can became a means and vice versa. There is then a pragmatic, earthy, and utilitarian charac-

---

98. Ibid., 436.

99. See Sneed, "'Wisdom Tradition,'" 59–60.

100. See Chaïm Perelman and L. Olbrechts-Tyteca, *The New Rhetoric: A Treatise on Argumentation* (trans. John Wilkinson and Purcell Weaver; paperback ed.; Notre Dame, Ind.: University of Notre Dame Press, 1971), 432–36.

ter to wisdom that has been noted by several scholars and cannot be denied.[101] For the sages, if wisdom did not produce beneficial effects for its adherents, it would not be wisdom, plain and simple. From a Weberian perspective, wisdom contains both value and instrumental rationality, a dialectic that cannot be transcended. The instrumental side of traditional wisdom is significant for understanding Qohelet's deconstruction of wisdom, as shall be seen.

Qohelet has essentially the same worldview that Kovacs discerns in the sages in Proverbs. Though Qohelet sees the liabilities of wisdom, he still views it as more valuable than power (7:19; 9:16) or wealth (implied in 9:15 and 10:20) or at least equal to it (7:11–12). Though wisdom is limited, it is superior to folly (7:4–6). Qohelet also shares an interest in literary aesthetics. Note the literary finesse of the poem in 3:1–8 and the frame narrator's compliment that "the Teacher sought to find pleasing words" (12:10).[102] As will be discussed next, Qohelet is an intellectual who is concerned with viewing the world as meaningful and understandable and with somehow resolving or treating its many contradictions. Of course, Qohelet certainly does not completely support the status quo, though he finds it tolerable. His many references to injustices done by the powerful (e.g., 10:5–7) demonstrate this.

But Qohelet does not completely share their worldview. There is less focus on character or piety in Qohelet (cf. "Do not be too righteous" [7:16]). This appears to be because Qohelet does not believe that God is that concerned about human character, piety, or integrity (9:2). As already discussed, Qohelet seems to believe that God is more concerned about a person fearing him, not in the sense of piety but closer to the literal sense of trembling and being cautious in one's behavior so that one does not somehow inadvertently offend him. In other words, Qohelet believes that God is more concerned about how one approaches him and respects him (5:1–7) than in how ethically he/she might live. The mortal sin for Qohelet's God is hubris, not immorality. To put it briefly here (and more fully later), Qohelet places a greater gulf between mortals and the Immortal than does traditional wisdom. Humans are viewed as essentially totally depraved (7:20, 28–29). Qohelet's God is much more transcendent and personally detached than the God of Proverbs: "God is in heaven and you are on earth" (5:2). This is reflected in Qohelet's exclusive use of Elohim ("God") rather than the holy name.

---

101. Blenkinsopp, *Wisdom and Law*, 26–27; idem, *Sage, Priest, Prophet*, 36; Crenshaw, *Old Testament Wisdom*, 19–20.

102. Johan Yeong-Sik Pahk understands the last phrase not as aesthetical but as epistemological and translates it as "the matters of matters" or less literally "the meaning of reality," but most scholars will not concur ("The Role and Significance of *DBRY ḤPṢ* [Qoh 12:10A] for Understanding Qohelet," in *Congress Volume: Leiden 2004* [ed. André Lemaire; VTSup 109; Leiden: Brill, 2006], 325–53, esp. 349).

The pragmatic self-interest side of wisdom is more accented in Qohelet than its altruistic "do the right thing" side. As far as Qohelet is concerned, if wisdom does not produce benefits for its adherent, then why be wise (2:15; 6:8)? Again, wisdom has its benefits, but the optimistic approach to traditional wisdom has been abandoned in Qohelet. There is a strong egoism in Qohelet that other scholars have detected and that has already been noted. But this egoism and utilitarianism in Qohelet were a part of traditional wisdom as well; it is just more prominent in Qohelet. Qohelet, thus, focuses on the intellectual side of the Hebrew notion of wisdom, while downplaying the moral side, because he sees little benefit in moral aspirations. The development of moral character, then, is not a primary concern of Qohelet.[103]

Finally, unlike the sages of Proverbs, there is no clear noblesse oblige in Qohelet. He does reference the tears of the oppressed in 4:1 but nowhere counsels charity to the poor. But even this passage seems to be intended more as part of the cumulative data of the injustices of the powerful than as a genuinely empathetic concern for the oppressed. Though Seow has argued that 11:1-2, which recommends casting bread upon water because it will return later, refers to charity, it more likely involves advising investment, perhaps in mercantile trade.[104] At any rate, even if charity is the intent, a heavy utilitarian bent is involved here. Instead of focusing on charity for the poor, Qohelet seems to be more preoccupied with injustices done to members of his own or higher class (e.g., 6:1-6).

QOHELET AS INTELLECTUAL

This discussion of the wisdom literature reflecting a status group ethic of scribes provides a nice segue to an examination of the significance of Qohelet as an intellectual. Gottwald provides little treatment of intellectuals—basically because Marxists do not know what to do with intellectuals. Marxists usually attempt to integrate intellectuals into class positions, but intellectuals can to a certain extent transcend their class location. Many Marxists recognize this inherent class ambivalence of intellectuals. Sometimes, in terms of class, intellectuals can function to a certain extent as "free-floaters." Though Gramsci views intellectuals as tethered to the world of economic production, he describes it as "not as direct."[105] Even Lenin realized that the proletariat

---

103. Contra William P. Brown, who places Qohelet within a trajectory of character formation that includes virtues and vices (*Character in Crisis: A Fresh Approach to the Wisdom Literature of the Old Testament* [Grand Rapids: Eerdmans, 1996], 134–50).

104. Seow, *Ecclesiastes*, 341–44; cf. Crenshaw, *Ecclesiastes*, 178–79; Fox, *Rereading of Ecclesiastes*, 311–314.

105. Gramsci, *Prison Notebooks*, 12. Berlinerblau uses Gramsci's notion of "tethered intellectual" to describe ancient Israelite scribes ("Uneven Triumphs," 108).

could not produce their own intellectuals, and so bourgeois intellectuals had to lead the way to the revolution. As has been noted, some Marxists even have tried to locate intellectuals "between" classes—they do not really belong to any social class![106] But this in itself admits the possibility that intellectuals can sometimes assume a trans-class character. They are part of a class, but they do things that benefit other classes besides their own. Thus, the Marxist obsession with social class does not adequately do justice to the intellectual. The social location of the intellectual is more complicated than that.

Usually, intellectuals arise from the more privileged classes, though some are recruited from the lower classes. They certainly reflect an elitist constitution. As Ahmad Sadri notes, intellectuals "depart from the quotidian reality of everyday life."[107] Their education and maintenance certainly require a high level of division of labor. Their necessary leisure time is possible only through the manual labor of lower classes, which allows them this privilege.

Weber provides a more sophisticated analysis of the role of intellectuals than do Marxists. He defines them as "those who usurp leadership in a *Kulturgemeinschaft* (that is, within a group of people who by virtue of their peculiarity have access to certain products that are considered 'culture goods')."[108]

---

106. E.g., E. O. Wright, "Intellectuals," 5–18. Often Marxists simply classify intellectuals as "petite bourgeoisie" (e.g., Nicos Poulantzas, "On Social Classes," *New Left Review* 78 [1973]: 38).

107. Ahmad Sadri, *Max Weber's Sociology of Intellectuals* (paperback ed.; New York: Oxford University Press, 1994), 115.

108. Weber, *Economy and Society*, 2:926; see Swedberg, *Max Weber Dictionary*, 127–28, s.v. "Intellectuals (*Intellektuelle*)." Many later sociologists have been influenced by this definition. Talcott Parsons, who is known as an important interpreter of Weber, also defines the intellectual as a "person who . . . is . . . expected . . . to put cultural considerations above social" ("'The Intellectual': A Social Role Category," in *On Intellectuals: Theoretical Studies; Case Studies* [ed. Philip Rieff; Garden City, N.Y.: Doubleday, 1969], 4). Similarly, intellectuals are "all of those who are considered proficient in and are actively engaged in the creation, distribution, and application of culture" (Seymour Martin Lipset and Richard B. Dobson, "The Intellectual as Critic and Rebel: With Special Reference to the United States and the Soviet Union," *Daedalus* 101, no. 3 [1972]: 137). Cf. others who view intellectuals as symbol specialists: Edward Shils, "Intellectuals," *International Encyclopedia of the Social Sciences* (ed. David L. Sills and Robert K. Merton; 19 vols.; New York: Macmillan and Free Press, 1968), 7:399; Charles Kadushin, *The American Intellectual Elite* (Boston: Little Brown, 1974), 4–7; Robert K. Merton, *Social Theory and Social Structure* (rev. and enl.ed.; Glencoe, Ill.: Free Press, 1957), 209; contra Lewis S. Feuer, who thinks that an identity as culture expert is too narrow for modern intellectuals and emphasizes more their educated, political, and alienated character ("What Is an Intellectual?" in *The Intelligentsia and the Intellectuals: Theory, Method and Case Study* [ed. Aleksander Gella; SABE Studies in International Sociology 5; Beverly Hills: SABE, 1976], 47–58). Eva Etzioni-Halevy emphasizes their pursuit of knowledge and ideas (*The Knowledge Elite and the Failure of Prophecy* [Controversies

This means that these producers of culture benefit not only themselves but all others who share in the culture. Connected with the notion of culture mainte-nance is another dimension of intellectualism that Weber discusses:

> The intellectual seeks in various ways . . . to endow his life with a pervasive meaning, and thus to find unity with himself, with his fellow men, and with the cosmos. It is the intellectual who conceives of the "world" as a problem of mean-ing. . . . The conflict of this requirement of meaningfulness with the empirical realities of the world and its institutions, and with the possibilities of conducting one's life in the empirical world, are responsible for the intellectual's characteristic flight from the world.[109]

The concern for a meaningful world connects intellectuals with their primary function in society: the rationalization of life and the world.[110] Intellectuals rationalize the world for their particular society; they make sense of it. This is especially true when it comes to religion. Sadri emphasizes this facet of Weber's understanding of intellectuals:

> Intellectuals . . . are the bearers of different levels and modes of rationality. The rationalization of the sphere of ideas occurs through intellectuals who have a stake in constructing ever more consistent images of the world. This general statement can be used as a guide to study the substantively diverse contents of various civilizations and the role intellectuals have played in creating and devel-oping the main thrust of ideas of that particular culture.[111]

The key word is consistency. Weber says, "Religious interpretations of the world and ethics of religions created by intellectuals and meant to be rational have been strongly exposed to the imperative of consistency."[112] Intellectuals are sensitive to consistency and strive to produce a world that is as rationally coherent as possible.

Weber emphasizes the importance of the religious intellectual's role in theodicy creation. One of the main functions of religious intellectuals is to produce and maintain theodicy strategies that make sense of evil in the world for the rest of society.[113] A major function of the book of Qohelet is to treat this problem, as will be shown.

---

in Sociology 18; London: G. Allen & Unwin, 1985], 9–16). Murray Hausknecht highlights the dissident character of modern intellectuals ("At First Glance: The Role of the Intellec-tual," *Dissent* 44, no. 2 [1986]: 131–32, 160).

109. Weber, *Economy and Society*, 1:506.
110. See Sadri, *Sociology of Intellectuals*, 14–15, 29, 58–68.
111. Ibid., 14.
112. Weber, "Religious Rejections," 324.
113. See Sadri, *Sociology of Intellectuals*, 65–68; Parsons, "Introduction," lvi–lviii.

Weber did not believe that intellectuals always produce ideas that are in their own best economic or even ideal interests.[114] In other words, they do not always propagate ideas that simply legitimize or reinforce their own class privileges. They can, to some extent, transcend their own social context. This conflicts with David Clines's observation that biblical authors would never produce anything against their own interests.[115] From a Weberian standpoint, intellectuals are more complicated than that.

However, in the case of Qohelet, it has been shown that economic interests are rather predominant. His comfortable retainer-class position shines through consistently in the book and largely explains his anti-utopian perspective and underscores his essentially nonsalvific religious constitution. But his employment of literary pessimism and skepticism, while reflecting aristocratic concerns, is better explained by his creative role as an intellectual, as shall be seen. He is also constrained by ideational factors, which will align this analysis more with Weber.

Finally, a word about Kovacs's analysis is in order. It should be pointed out that much of what he has said about scribes lacking substantive power in Israelite society is confirmed by many sociologists who describe modern intellectuals. Eva Etzioni-Halevy puts it well:

> Their position is special *in that they have much influence, but relatively little direct power over others.* Intellectuals are influential in the sense that they frequently succeed in convincing others of the validity and fruitfulness of the knowledge they provide. Also, they have an inordinate share in shaping the ideas that either legitimize or de-legitimize existing social and political structures. At the same time, intellectuals wield little direct power in the sense of being able to determine either the fate or the actions of large numbers of other people.[116]

In a similar way, as an intellectual, the scribe's power was his knowledge and skill in communication, whether verbally or literarily.[117] He counseled the truly powerful and the powerless and provided them both with necessary cultural products. He provided a worldview that made sense of life for both the powerful and the powerless. But these masters of culture were largely powerless from

---

114. See Sadri, *Sociology of Intellectuals*, 58–68.

115. Clines, *Interested Parties*, 38, 125–28.

116. Etzioni-Halevy, *Knowledge Elite*, 11. "In their own right, however, intellectuals, the more so the 'purer' in our sense of their cultural specialization, are necessarily not among the primary holders of political power or controllers of economic resources" (Parsons, "The Intellectual," 4); "Intellectuals and power are incompatible" (Peter Nettl, "Power and the Intellectuals," in *Power & Consciousness* [ed. Connor Cruise O'Brien and William Dean Vanech; London: University of London Press, 1969], 16).

117. See Person, "Scribe as Performer," 601–9.

a larger perspective: fundamental power resided with the governing elite. This is confirmed by the scribes' location as retainers, whose only power was as representatives of the governing class and was therefore conferred and residual.

CONCLUSION

The book of Qohelet does not contain any explicit historical allusions to its time and milieu. Of course, the references to oppression and corruption are certainly compatible with the Ptolemaic period, whether referring to the Ptolemaic officials or to the indigenous priestly aristocracy and tax-famers or both. This lack of historical particularities is typical of wisdom literature, which focuses on repeated patterns of behavior rather than individual events or actions.

The author of the book was a member neither of the governing class nor of the middle class; rather, he was part of the retainer class. This stratum would have formed the layer that served the governing class and provided a buffer between it and the masses, mediating each group's distinctive interests. The retainer class was not independent of the governing stratum and so should be considered the lower rung of the aristocracy rather than a true middle class, though one might possibly describe it as an upper middle class or layer. Qohelet's ambivalence about wealth and power is partially attributable to this social location. His class feels intellectually superior to the governing elite but does not consider itself among the truly poor.

Qohelet was a scribal scholar who wrote to young scribal apprentices. As a scribe, Qohelet was a member of a status group or guild. This group maintained its identity in terms of prestige or honor rather than solely in terms of economic standing. The members essentially shared the same lifestyle. They held an in-group ethic that disdained the ignorant and criticized the misuse of power by the wealthy and governing elite. Scribes served various necessary bureaucratic functions that aided both the governing elite and the masses and eased their conflicted relationship.

Scribes prided themselves on their knowledge and intellect, which reflects their category as intellectuals. As intellectuals they were masters and maintainers of culture. Religious intellectuals are especially necessary for systematizing and rationalizing religious beliefs and for creating the normative worldview of their respective societies, for providing the meaning of life for those societies. They are particularly important also for developing theodicy strategies. They could influence with adroit speech, sage advice, and literary products, but fundamental power did not reside with them.

5

Synchronic (Literary) Analysis
of the Book of Qohelet

A proper literary reading of Qohelet must first deal with the problem of how to translate the word הֶבֶל (*hebel*) in Qohelet and how this relates to the carpe diem ethic in the book. The frame narrator has supplied the reader with the leitmotif of the book: הֲבֵל הֲבָלִים הַכֹּל הָבֶל הֲבֵל ("Vanity of vanities; everything is vanity") (1:2; 12:8). In addition, הֶבֶל is used thirty-eight times in Qohelet, out of seventy-three in the entire Hebrew Bible, which reinforces this. אֱלֹהִים is used forty times in Qohelet, indicating that the relationship between the two is probably significant. Even a casual reading of the book will confirm the adequacy of this motto as a précis of Qohelet's message. It also points to the fact that Qohelet's ultimate message is not positive. The carpe diem ethic is a subordinate theme, though significant. Thus, one's translation and understanding of הֶבֶל will largely determine one's understanding of the book as a whole. This cannot be emphasized enough!

The Meaning of הֶבֶל in the Hebrew Bible

The lexicon of Brown, Driver, and Briggs (BDB) gives only two acceptations: literally "breath, vapour," then figuratively "vanity"; it also gives the following translation equivalents: "what is evanescent, unsubstantial, worthless."[1] Under "vanity," several examples are given, but these are not further categorized. Klaus Seybold's article in *TDOT* is, of course, much more comprehensive.[2] Because of the word's probable onomatopoeic origin, Seybold maintains that "*hebhel* consistently retains the meanings 'breath' and . . . 'vapor, mist, smoke.'"[3] But he adds that there is an inherent tendency for the word to take on an abstract connotation of transitoriness and fleetingness.[4] He adds that

---

1. BDB, 210–11.
2. K. Seybold, "הֶבֶל *hebhel*," *TDOT* 3:313–20.
3. Ibid., 314–15.
4. Daniel C. Fredericks argues that all the instances of הבל should be translated as "transience" in Ecclesiastes, but few commentators have followed this extreme position

onomatopoeic words are open to new meanings. Since *hebel* is one of several words meaning "vanity," it is used in condensed expressions, connoting emotion. He concludes that "the range of meaning of *hebhel* is open. It has a broad emotion-laden stratum with strong evocative possibilities, and it is especially suited therefore to be a keyword or catchword."

It is important to consider the paradigmatic relations of the term. According to Seybold, several terms and expressions appear in the semantic field of הֶבֶל: רִיק "empty" (Isa 30:7), תֹּהוּ "emptiness, nothing" (Isa 49:4), שֶׁקֶר "deceit, falsehood" (Jer 10:14; Zech 10:2; Prov 31:30), אָוֶן "deceit" or שָׁוְא "deceit, falsehood" (Zech 10:2), לֹא לְהוֹעִיל "to have no value, be good for nothing, be of no profit" (Isa 30:6; 57:12; Jer 16:19; cf. Lam 4:17), and in parallelism with רוּחַ "wind" (Isa 57:13; Jer 10:14; Qoh 1:14).[5]

Terms in opposition to הֶבֶל would include "riches" and "treasures" (things of value) (Isa 30:6). In Pss 39 and 62, God is contrasted with the הֶבֶל of humanity's existence. In Ps 62, God is described as a "rock," "deliverance," and "refuge" in contrast to humanity's הֶבֶל.

The term is used in particular ways in various sections of the Hebrew Bible. It is used in statements expressing worthlessness.[6] For example, the psalmist proclaims concerning mortals: "They are like a breath; their days are like a passing shadow" (Ps 144:4). The help of Egypt is useless (Isa 30:7), and so is a woman's beauty (Prov 31:30). Seybold notes that these are "things which in general are highly esteemed. The OT attacks them by breathing upon them the negating *hebhel* and thus emphatically rejecting them."

It is also used in laments:

Lord let me know my end,
and what is the measure of my days;
let me know how fleeting my life is.
You have made my days a few handbreaths,
and my lifetime is as nothing in your sight.
Surely everyone stands as a mere *breath*.
Surely everyone goes about like a shadow.
Surely for *nothing* they are in turmoil;
they heap up, and do not know who will gather.
....
You chastise mortals in punishment for sin,
consuming like a moth what is dear to them;
surely everyone is a mere *breath*. (Ps 39:4–6, 11)[7]

(*Coping with Transience: Ecclesiastes on Brevity in Life* [Biblical Seminar; Sheffield: JSOT Press, 1993]).

5. Seybold, "הֶבֶל *hebhel*," 314–15.

6. Ibid., 316.

7. See ibid., 317.

In the numerous laments he cites, Seybold notes that two items are described as הֶבֶל: humans and the days of their lives. Seybold concludes that in these laments, the context is very emotional but that "*hebhel* obviously had a liberating effect." In other words, הֶבֶל is used to help resolve the dissonance the psalmist feels in a state of oppression and distress. In Ps 39, the Psalmist does this by emphasizing to God that humans are too insignificant and puny for his continued punishment of their sins. This is essentially Job's response in 7:17–21.

Finally, before looking at its use in Qohelet, Seybold discusses the employment of הֶבֶל as a polemic against the worship of foreign gods or idols.[8] An example is Jer 10:14–15:

> Everyone is stupid and without knowledge;
> Goldsmiths are all put to shame by their idols; for their images are false,
> And there is no breath in them.
> They are *worthless*, a work of delusion;
> At the time of their punishment they shall perish.

Seybold points out that the word is used in this special sense in the Deuteronomistic polemic against foreign deities. For example, Deut 32:21 reads: "They made me jealous with what is no god, provoked me with their *idols*." It occurs with a group of Hebrew words for "idols" that essentially deny the idols' existence: שֶׁקֶר ("falsehood"), שָׁוְא ("emptiness, vanity"), אֱלִיל ("vanity, worthlessness"), and . . . לֹא אֵל or לֹא אֱלֹהִים, "no god."

THE MEANING OF הֶבֶל IN QOHELET

While Qohelet can use הֶבֶל in a conventional way, as in 11:10: "Youth and dark hair are vanity," meaning transient, he usually employs an idiosyncratic meaning. This is indicated by the frame-narrator's motto for the book "'Vanity of vanities' says Qohelet . . . 'all is vanity'" (1:2; 12:8). What is distinctive in usage here is that while other occurrences in the Hebrew Bible restrict its application to human existence, here everything is described as הֶבֶל. What could this possibly mean?

Again, Seybold's analysis is especially penetrating.[9] He notes the importance of the following words and phrases: רְעוּת רוּחַ or רַעְיוֹן רוּחַ "chasing after the wind" or "feeding on the wind" (1:14, 17), which point to its meaning as "vanity."[10] He also indicates that יִתְרוֹן ("profit, advantage, gain"), which is used

---

8. Ibid., 317.
9. See ibid., 318–20.
10. Ibid., 319. This is similar to the proverb about sowing the wind and reaping the

in antithesis to הֶבֶל, is significant for understanding it. It means "'that which counts or matters,' 'that which results or issues from all our work.' It forces upon *hebhel* the special sense of 'that which does not count or matter,' 'null,' 'vain,' 'that which yields no results.'"[11]

In addition, the parallel words צֵל "shadow" (6:12) and רוּח "wind" (5:15) further clarify the meaning of הֶבֶל, as well as חֳלִי "affliction" (6:2) and רָעָה "evil" (5:12). Antithetical terms include חֵלֶק "portion/lot" (2:10), טוֹב "good" (2:3), and יִתְר "profit, advantage" (6:11). Seybold concludes:

> The dominant use of *hebhel* in a nominal statement shows that for Qoheleth too the word serves the purpose of evaluation, or, more accurately, devaluation, with a critico-polemic intention. The total equalization of all earthly, human activity in 1:14 runs contrary to a sapiential value system; such a radical disqualification is directed against the norm of *yithron* thinking which underlies this system.[12]

Specific values and possessions that are devaluated include striving after wisdom (1:17; 2:15), laughter and pleasure (2:2), the life work of the wise (2:19, 21, 23, 26), energy expended by the skillful (4:4), wealth (4:8; 5:9), the career of the wise (4:16), zeal (6:9), criticism by the wise (7:6), decisions of the mighty (8:10), and confidence in the law of just retribution (8:14). All of these, Seybold notes, are

> particular ways and goals of life that wisdom holds in high esteem. Thus *hebhel* serves as "destructive judgment,"[13] a devaluation of the system of norms established by traditional wisdom, a polemic against its sensible value regulations, a defamation of the wisdom ideal of life. It proves to be an effective catchword to the extent that it extends those values into the grotesque.[14]

---

whirlwind, which symbolizes the results of wickedness (Hos 8:7; cf. Job 4:8; Ps 126:5–6; Prov 11:29; 22:8).

11. Seybold, "הֶבֶל *hebhel*," 319, citing Kurt Galling, *Der Prediger* in *Die fünf Megilloth* (Handbuch zum Alten Testament, 18; Tübingen: Mohr Siebeck, 1969), 79; cf. "*Nichtigkeit*," (Lauha, *Kohelet*, 18). John Jarick argues that artistic wordplay is involved in Qohelet's framing motto, which he renders "Everything is nothing!" with his noting that the *kap* and *bet* are very similar in appearance and, thus, interchangeable ("The Hebrew Book of Changes: Reflections on *Hakkōl Hebel* and *Lakkōl Zᵉmān* in Ecclesiastes," *JSOT* 90 [2000]: 79–83). Cf. Crüsemann's "everything is shit" for Qohelet's motto ("Unchangeable World," 57).

12. Seybold, "הֶבֶל *hebhel*," 319.

13. Ibid., 320, citing R. Albertz, *Theologisches Handwörterbuch zum Alten Testament* (ed. Ernst Jenni with Claus Westermann; 2 vols.; Munich: Kaiser, 1971, 1976), 1:467–69.

14. Though הבל has a negative connotation, translating it as "bad" (Rainer Albertz, "הֶבֶל *hebel* breath," *TLOT* 1:352) or "foul" (Miller, *Symbol and Rhetoric*, 95–97) is not justified. See D. M. Clemens, review of Miller, *Symbol and Rhetoric in Ecclesiastes*, *JNES* 66 (2007): 220.

Finally, Seybold resists any translations of "incomprehensible" or "unintelligible," which are based on the cult mysteries.[15]

Four aspects of Seybold's analysis of Qohelet's use of הֶבֶל need emphasizing. First, הֶבֶל is an emotive term. Second, it is a judgmental term, used to evaluate various human aspirations. Third, it is polemical and aimed specifically at critiquing traditional wisdom. Fourth, it never means "incomprehensible" or "unintelligible."

Regarding the latter, many recent scholars have favored a translation that denotes some sense of cognitive incongruity (irrational, senseless, meaningless, nonsense, etc.).[16] The most significant and popular of these suggestions is by Fox, who translates הֶבֶל as "absurd."[17] He points out that "the absurd is a disjunction between two phenomena that are thought to be linked by a bond of harmony or causality, or that *should* be so linked."[18] He draws on the existentialist Albert Camus to nuance its meaning in Qohelet.[19] He even attempts preemptively to counter accusations of anachronism by citing what he perceives are existential examples of absurdity from the ancient Near East (Egyptian prophetic laments: Nerferti, Khakheperre-Sonb, and Ipuwer).[20]

Fox attempts to prove that the word has this meaning by examining 8:14.[21] Here is his translation: "There is a *hebel* that happens on the earth: there are righteous people who receive what is appropriate to the deeds of

---

15. Seybold, "הֶבֶל *hebhel*," 318.

16. "Meaningless" (NIV); "incomprehensible" or "beyond mortal grasp" (Seow, *Ecclesiastes*, 102; idem, "Beyond Mortal Grasp: The Usage of *Hebel* in Ecclesiastes," *ABR* 48 [2000]: 1–16); "senseless" (Shields, *End of Wisdom*, 121); "enigmatic/mysterious" (Ogden, *Qoheleth*, 22; cf. idem, "'Vanity' It Certainly Is Not," *BT* 38 [1987]: 301–7; Bartholomew, *Ecclesiastes*, 104); "absurdity" (Crenshaw, *Ecclesiastes*, 57); "senseless" (Albertz, *TLOT* 1:352).

17. Fox, *Rereading of Ecclesiastes*, 30–33; originally, see idem, "The Meaning of *Hebel* for Qohelet," *JBL* 105 (1986): 409–27. Scholars who have accepted Fox's translation include Sibley Towner, "The Book of Ecclesiastes," *NIB* 5:279–80, 282–84; William H. U. Anderson, "The Semantic Implications of הבל and רעות רוח in the Hebrew Bible and for Qoheleth," *JNSL* 25, no. 2 (1999): 70–71. See the following for literary and philosophically oriented translations: "incongruence" or "ironic" (Good, *Irony*, 182; Polk, "Wisdom of Irony," 7–9); "inconstant" (R. Christopher Heard, "The Dao of Qoheleth: An Intertextual Reading of the *Daode Jing* and the Book of Ecclesiastes," *Jian Dao* 5 [1996]: 89); "contingency" (Martin Shuster, "Being as Breath, Vapor as Joy: Using Martin Heidegger to Re-Read the Book of Ecclesiastes," *JSOT* 33 [2008]: 229; cf. John E. McKenna, "The Concept of *Hebel* in the Book of Ecclesiastes," *SJT* 45 [1992]: 28).

18. Fox, *Rereading of Ecclesiastes*, 31.

19. Cf. Benjamin Lyle Berger, "Qohelet and the Exigencies of the Absurd," *BibInt* 9 (2001): 164–73.

20. Fox, *Rereading of Ecclesiastes*, 32–33.

21. Ibid., 30.

the wicked and there are wicked people who receive what is appropriate to the deeds of the righteous. I said that this too is *hebel*." He notes that the two *hebel* judgments frame a fact. He rejects the meaning of futility for לבֶהֶ here, explaining, "It is true that the deeds of the righteous may prove futile insofar as they aim at a reward, but the passage also describes the fate of the wicked, and their receiving what the righteous deserve does not imply any futility in *their* actions."²²

While Fox's explanation is certainly possible in view of the ambiguous nature of the pronouns and the indeterminate meaning of הֶבֶל, the problem with it is that Qohelet's observation here is not directed at the wicked but at the potentially *wise*, who might consider being righteous and anticipate only good results. Qohelet's observation then would serve to caution against such an expectation: there are no guarantees that piety will issue only in fortune. Thus, the translation of הֶבֶל here could be "futility" or something like "illusion," futile in the sense of relying on piety for beneficial results and illusory in the sense of piety's bogus promises. In both cases, human striving after virtue and the expectations associated with piety share qualities similar to idols: they promise much but deliver little and are only disappointing in the end.

This leads to another deficit of Fox's translation. He sees Qohelet's usage as polemical but not toward traditional wisdom. Fox states, "It is a caricature to depict 'traditional' wisdom as a monolithic body of orthodox doctrines against which a radical Qohelet is bravely rebelling. . . . He never sets himself against traditional wisdom, but simply folds traditional (which is to say, earlier) wisdom into his own teachings and moves in a direction of his own."²³

First of all, it should be pointed out that Fox here is rejecting a consensus that is old and venerable. Second, Fox seems to be presenting a false dichotomy: that if one is polemical, then one must totally reject the tradition one is attacking. This, of course, is not true. For example, Jacques Derrida, the father of deconstruction, is known for his polemic against Western philosophy, especially its metaphysical types. But he freely admits that his criticisms operate within the parameters of Western philosophy. While he polemically attacks it, he certainly does not dismiss it tout court.²⁴ Similarly, Qohelet can be polemical toward traditional wisdom and not reject it in toto. In fact, as

---

22. "Futility" is the translation used by JPS; cf. Crenshaw, *Ecclesiastes*, 57; Krüger, *Qoheleth*, 42–43.

23. Fox, *Rereading of Ecclesiastes*, 26.

24. See Jeff Collins and Bill Mayblin, *Introducing Derrida* (New York: Totem, 1997; repr., Cambridge: Icon, 2000), 48; Niall Lucy, *A Derrida Dictionary* (Malden, Mass.: Blackwell, 2004), 72, s.v. "Logocentricism"; John D. Caputo, *Deconstruction in a Nutshell* (New York: Fordham University Press, 1997), 49–70.

shall be seen, Qohelet uses traditional wisdom's own values and methodology to deconstruct it, which means he is about modifying traditional wisdom, not totally rejecting it.[25]

But if Fox does not see Qohelet attacking traditional wisdom, against what or whom does he see him arguing? It appears it is God. With Fox's translation of "absurdity" comes the concomitant notion of protest.[26] It also connects with his belief that Qohelet holds on to dissonance and never seeks to dissolve it. Fox states,

> Underlying Qohelet's *hebel*-judgments is the assumption that the system that relates deed to outcome *should* be rational. For Qohelet, this means that actions should reliably produce appropriate consequences. Qohelet stubbornly expects this to happen; see 3:17; 5:5; 7:17; 8:12b-13. He believes in the rule of divine justice. That is why he does not resign himself to injustice, but is continually shocked by it. It clashes with his belief that the world *must* work equitably.[27] Injustices are offensive to reason. And the individual absurdities are not mere anomalies. Their absurdity infects the entire system, making *everything* absurd.

He concludes, "'All is absurd' is ultimately a protest against God." Thus, instead of Qohelet being polemical toward traditional wisdom, Fox has redirected Qohelet's animus toward God himself.

Fox views the book as essentially schizophrenic, with Qohelet intending to describe and maintain the contradictory character of life: "I too take Qohelet's contradictions as the starting point of interpretation. My primary thesis is a simple one: The contradictions in the book of Qohelet are real and intended. We must interpret them, not eliminate them."[28] He points out that these contradictions are not so much Qohelet contradicting himself, as his observation of life's incongruities. "To him they seem to be *antinomies*, two equally valid but contradictory principles. He does not resolve these antinomies but only describes them." Qohelet's descriptions of these antinomies lead to the ultimate goal of the book: "Qohelet's persistent observation of contradictions is a powerful cohesive force, and an awareness of it brings into focus the book's

---

25. Heard uses the Chinese concept of Dao (guiding discourse) to interpret Qohelet; he argues that Qohelet's use of הבל implies a critique of the guiding discourses of Qohelet's time: sometimes they work, sometimes they do not ("*Dao* of Qoheleth," 65–93).

26. Fox, *Rereading of Ecclesiastes*, 49.

27. Bernon Lee's analysis of the proverb in 1:15 also reveals the standard of justice that Qohelet uses in assessment: "The implication in his evaluation of things being 'crooked' and deficient is that there exists an ideal state (real or conceptual) where these imbalances are addressed" ("A Specific Application of the Proverb in Ecclesiastes 1:15," *Journal of Hebrew Scriptures* 1, article 6 [1997]: 12, online at http://www.arts.ualberta.ca/JHS/Articles/article6.pdf [accessed April 6, 2011]).

28. Fox, *Rereading of Ecclesiastes*, 3.

central concern: the problem of the meaning of life. The book of Qohelet is about *meaning*: its loss and its (partial) recovery."

Qohelet may well believe that the world *should* operate according to traditional notions of divine justice. He would have certainly been born into this way of thinking. It was the worldview he inherited from his family and community and was probably reinforced in his schooling. It is also true that Qohelet gets frustrated about the instances of injustice ("I hated life" [2:17]) he observes and uses negative terms such as "evil" to describe some of them (e.g., 6:1), as has been seen. Fox is correct that Qohelet sees the world as largely absurd (irrational is a better word), but again that does not mean that הֶבֶל means "absurd."

Nor does it mean that Qohelet's eliciting of these examples is intended primarily as a protest. Protest is an appropriate word for Job in the dialogue and the laments of the Psalter. But in these cases, Job and the psalmists are attempting to motivate God to action. No such attempt is found in Qohelet. He has given up on God's deliverance of individuals or the nation. Qohelet has psychologically moved beyond protest to resignation and acceptance, and he wants his audience to do the same.

This correlates with de Jong's thesis that Qohelet's main message is *human limitation*.[29] All of his argumentation and advice are geared toward advancing that message. His concern is primarily anthropology, not theology.[30] A theology of Qohelet can be derived only artificially through inferences and indirect statements he makes. Qohelet's primary goal is to lower expectations about humanity and its abilities. God is brought into play only as references to him aid in lowering these expectations.

הֶבֶל is an important part of this rhetorical process. Therefore, instead of "absurd," הֶבֶל is better translated as "futility" or "illusion" and not in the sense of protest but resignation to the fact that life does not operate as one might expect or wish. Qohelet uses הֶבֶל to lower his reader's expectations, not to raise them, which would be the case if הֶבֶל means "absurd." Essentially, Qohelet is saying that the world is largely irrational, so deal with it! It is not going to change! This, of course, fits better with the pessimistic mood of the book than does "absurdity."

Qohelet indeed attempts to dissolve the dissonance of a world where expectations are not met. He does not simultaneously hold to God's justice and deny seeing it. Rather, as will be shown in the next chapters, he expands the notion of divine justice to include God's standards that are beyond the ken of mortals. This allows Qohelet to speak rightly of divine justice, while simul-

---

29. De Jong, "God in the Book," 166; cf. idem, "A Book on Labour: The Structuring Principles and the Main Theme of the Book of Qohelet," *JSOT* 54 (1992): 107–16.

30. See de Jong, "God in the Book," 161–64.

taneously not seeing it, as far as human standards are concerned. This strategy, indeed, dissolves or helps mitigate the effects of the theodicy problem.

While modern authors may revel in the maintenance of dissonance, Fox's insistence that Qohelet does this flies in the face of ancient religious literature. Religious literature does not usually accentuate the problem of evil; it attempts to resolve or mitigate it. If Fox is correct, Qohelet only exacerbates the problem; he does nothing to solve it. While this is possible for a religious document, it is unlikely.

But the most lethal problem with Fox's translation of הֶבֶל as "absurdity" is that it is found nowhere else in the Hebrew Bible.[31] Although this meaning is not impossible, it is unlikely. Stuart Weeks puts it this way:

> Although it does not fit all the uses without a certain amount of shoving and squeezing, Fox's interpretation is valuable and insightful. It faces the substantial objection, however, that *hebel* does not have this meaning elsewhere, and it is difficult to see either how 'breath' could have come to mean 'absurd', or how the original readers were supposed to deduce this meaning.[32]

Weeks rightly prefers the terms "illusory or deceptive." Similarly, Lohfink argues that, while Qohelet is certainly skeptical of human epistemological capacity, הֶבֶל is never used by him to express this.[33] For Qohelet, הֶבֶל "serves neither metaphysical nor cosmological expressions but rather only anthropological" (my translation).[34] He concludes, "When Qohelet speaks of הֶבֶל, then he speaks of actions, things, situations, results. He speaks of the objective world, not of the subject and his epistemological possibilities" (my translation).

Thus, it appears that the traditional translation of "vanity" by the KJV is not far off the mark.[35] The translation "meaningless" by the NIV is largely apologetic and reflects the standard evangelical interpretation that distinguishes between under and above the sun, with "under the sun" denoting the world of humanity, which is meaningless apart from God.[36] It reflects the typical

---

31. Seybold indicated this for the term "incomprehensible" ("הֶבֶל *hebhel*," 318).

32. Weeks, *Study of Wisdom Literature*, 81.

33. Norbert Lohfink, "Ist Kohelets הבל–Aussage erkenntnistheoretisch gemeint?" in *Qohelet in the Context of Wisdom* (ed. Anton Schoors; BETL 136; Leuven: Leuven University Press and Peeters, 1998), 41–59.

34. Ibid., 59.

35. Lauha prefers the German word (*Eitelkeit*) for "vanity" as the translation of הבל (*Kohelet*, 30).

36. E.g., Tremper Longman III maintains that Christians should look "above the sun" when interpreting Ecclesiastes ("Challenging the Idols of the Twenty-First Century: The Message of the Book of Ecclesiastes," *Stone Campbell Journal* 12 [2009]: 207–16).

medieval interpretation that understood Qohelet to be contemptuous toward the world in favor of monasticism.[37] This interpretation fails to acknowledge that Qohelet found aspects of God's activities (above the sun) problematic or oppressive (e.g., 1:13 ["unhappy business"]; 6:1) and not just activities below the sun, detached from God.

GOD AS PRIMARY ORIENTATION FOR QOHELET AND HIS AUDIENCE

Though הֶבֶל is used negatively to devalue the wisdom tradition, it has another, more positive function. The proper antonym of הֶבֶל is technically יִתְרוֹן, but אֱלֹהִים may in fact function in this way as well.[38] אֱלֹהִים and הֶבֶל each occur a total of thirty-eight times, if you discount the gloss in 12:13–14 (where אֱלֹהִים occurs an additional two times). Schoors notes that since אֱלֹהִים is one of the most frequently occurring words in Qohelet, it "shows that this philosophical preoccupation has a strong component of theodicy."[39] That in turn points to a positive function for God in Qohelet that Fox ignores.

This is not to suggest that Qohelet has an orthodox and largely positive and primarily benevolent understanding of God. However, Crenshaw and Fox go too far in the opposite direction. They view Qohelet's notion of God as having few redeeming features, and Crenshaw goes even further, describing his deity as almost demonic, as has been seen.[40] While Qohelet's conception of God is not very positive, neither is it entirely negative. Fox and Crenshaw are missing the comforting qualities that Qohelet's deity had for him. Though Qohelet cannot comprehend the actions of God, he seems to find some consolation in God's omnipotence and sovereignty. In fact, divine omnipotence and sovereignty serve to compensate for what Qohelet sees as liabilities in God's standards of judgment. Qohelet describes the possibility of the carpe diem ethic as a "gift" from God, even if he conceives of it as seemingly capricious. It is clear that Qohelet's ultimate point of reference for viewing the cosmos and humanity's place in it is God. Thus, God supplies an orienting function for Qohelet, even if he finds aspects of God's activities problematic. This orienting function of deities should not be taken lightly in assessing Qohelet's concep-

---

37. See Bartholomew, *Ecclesiastes*, 25–31.

38. I demonstrate how Qohelet's contrast of הבל with יתרון instead of the usual יתרון/חסרון ("debit") dichotomy serves to deconstruct traditional wisdom's reliance on profit ("Qoheleth as 'Deconstructionist,'" *OTE* 10 [1997]: 308–10).

39. Anton Schoors, "Words Typical of Qohelet," in *Qohelet in the Context of Wisdom* (ed. Anton Schoors; BETL 136; Leuven: Leuven University Press and Peeters, 1998), 39.

40. Fox, *Rereading of Ecclesiastes*, 137–38; Crenshaw, "Eternal Gospel," 43–44.

tion of God. Even demons, among polytheists, have a positive orienting function for them: they explain evil.

Nowhere does Qohelet use הֶבֶל to describe God or God's activities.[41] Instead, הֶבֶל is used to depict the futility of trying to circumvent these activities or counter them or to describe certain expectations connected with them, which end up being illusory. Or, in other words, God's activities may contribute to the futility of human aspirations or demonstrate the illusory character of certain assumptions. Even 6:1, which seems to direct the valuation of הֶבֶל at God's providing a person with wealth, possessions, and honor and yet not allowing the person to enjoy them is not describing God's activities. Rather הֶבֶל is directed at false assumptions about wealth (the illusion that they should be permanent) or at futile human attempts to preserve wealth once attained in view of God's sovereignty. Or as Marie Maussion suggests, this individual is a "sinner" (see 2:26) whose wealth is removed (by God?).[42] Qohelet restricts the judgment הֶבֶל to human strivings, aspirations, and assumptions, particularly those of traditional wisdom. Before God's sovereignty and determinism, human wishes and desires to accomplish great and enduring things and wisdom's notions about the way things should be are simply הֶבֶל.

GOD AND HUMANITY: THE GREAT DIVIDE

In many respects הֶבֶל is the antonym of אֱלֹהִים. Even Fox admits that God is not הֶבֶל![43] This demonstrates a certain positivity for the deity in Qohelet. It also leads to the observation that this dichotomization reflects another: humanity and its existence can be characterized essentially as הֶבֶל, in contrast to אֱלֹהִים, so the underlying dichotomy is really אלהים/אדם (humanity/God). Human activity is fleeting, and human life is transitory (1:4; 7:15; cf. youth in 11:9). What God does endures forever and cannot be changed. (3:14; cf. the earth in 1:4). Humans are weak and frail; they are but beasts (3:18).[44] But God is powerful and eternal (6:10). God is wise and omnipotent, but humanity is foolish and unable to attain true wisdom (8:17). Humans are wicked and morally culpable (7:20). However, God made them upright (7:29). All of this boils down to one basic message: God is everything, and humans are nothing, mere dust (cf. 3:21)! This is the message found often throughout the Hebrew Bible, espe-

---

41. See Zimmer, *Tod und Lebensglück*, 31.
42. Maussion, "Qohélet VI 1–2," 501–10, esp. 508.
43. Fox, *Rereading of Ecclesiastes*, 165.
44. Aron Pinker argues that the purpose of this verse is to demonstrate to humans not that they are but animals but that apart from God they become egocentric. But his lexical choices are dubious and his overall argument is largely apologetic; that is, God would never view humans as mere animals ("Qohelet 3,18—A Test?" *SJOT* 23 [2009]: 282–96).

cially in the psalms, e.g., Pss 8 and 39, and Job (ch. 7 and the theophany [chs. 38–41]).[45] Essentially, the book of Qohelet attempts to create a great divide between the human and the divine that cannot be breached or overcome.[46] Humanity is the opposite of God, and God is the opposite of humanity. Rainer Albertz's third category of sense for הֶבֶל in Qohelet as humanity's frailty vis-à-vis God's power supports this position.[47] Of course, this creates tension with the Priestly account, which describes humans as created in the image of God (Gen 1:26).

Here one sees the fundamental solution Qohelet offers to the problem of evil and irrationality in the world. Qohelet dissolves the problem by making the two spheres totally opposite and exclusive. God and humanity are so distinct that "never the twain shall meet." Thomas Bolin has most eloquently demonstrated this strategy, though without connecting it to the problem of evil.[48] His thesis involves using René Girard's notion of mimetic desire to explain Qohelet's counsel that humans resign themselves to not being God. Bolin's thesis fits with Weber's notion of the jealous deity. The envious deity is jealous lest human beings become like him, which would threaten his sovereignty (thus Gen 3:22). Weber contrasts older and younger conceptions of the deity: "In the primitive view, still influential in the Yahwistic collection, as in all old myths, God's resolutions are guided by selfish interests, above all God's jealousy against being threatened by *hybris*, the increasing wisdom and power of man. In the later revisions, however, benevolent charity for man is the decisive motive."[49] Humans aspire to be like the gods, and the gods are fearful that humans will overtake their prerogative and domain (cf. Gen 3; 11; cf. also Gen 6, where humans and angels have cohabited, and this endangers this boundary). One sees here the positive function of Qohelet within the negativity. Qohelet's pessimism and skepticism are geared to persuading the reader to abandon the quest for wisdom and self-reliance and to become like God. This explains why the book was preserved by Qohelet's disciples and later readers. It is essentially a theological solution, though clothed in melancholic garb. It represents a return to a more primitive conception of God, ensconced in early

---

45. Bruce Vawter shows how Ps 90 and the Wisdom of Solomon contain this great divide and the notion of God as *deus absconditus*, though more optimistically ("Postexilic Prayer and Hope," *CBQ* 37 [1975]: 460–70).

46. The same divide may be between humans (transitory) and nature (eternal) (1:4); John F. A. Sawyer argues that the poem in Eccl 12 is not an allegory but a parable that depicts the failure of human effort over against unchanging nature ("The Ruined House in Ecclesiastes 12: A Reconstruction of the Original Parable," *JBL* 94 [1975]: 519–31).

47. Albertz, *TLOT* 1:352.

48. Bolin, "Girard and Qoheleth," 245–59.

49. Weber, *Ancient Judaism*, 213.

Yahwism, and thus represents an "orthodox," not a heterodox, turn of sorts. Based on this conception, God's benevolence is overshadowed by his jealousy or zeal for his own dominion and prerogatives.

Over against הֶבֶל is Qohelet's carpe diem ethic. Though several scholars have maintained that Qohelet views also his carpe diem ethic as הֶבֶל, he appears to distinguish between differing types of joy or pleasure, some futile, others not.[50] One can still view Qohelet's carpe diem ethic as an ethic of resignation and yet not הֶבֶל, and this all has to do with expectations. In 2:1 Qohelet tests pleasure (שִׂמְחָה) and mirth (טוֹב) and finds them lacking (2:2). These kinds of pleasures seem to represent a total and wanton abandonment to pleasure without intellectual accompaniment, as in 2:3.[51] In 2:10–11, Qohelet seems to contradict himself:

> Whatever my eyes desired I did not keep from them; I kept my heart from no pleasure, for my heart found pleasure in all my toil, and this was my reward for all my toil. Then I considered all that my hands had done and the toil I had spent in doing it, and again, all was vanity and a chasing after wind, and there was nothing to be gained under the sun.

As Fox notes, this pleasure is spoiled by the effort necessary to attain it.[52] Or it could be, as Lauha remarks, that the joy in v. 10 is only a "fleeting amusement."[53] Or, as Robert Holmstedt has so fascinatingly demonstrated, the "heart" (לֵב) here does not represent Qohelet's opinion completely but is a conversation partner with which he sometimes disagrees.[54] Later, in 2:20, Qohelet tries "to convince his heart that his toil was *not* enjoyable."

But these pleasures are not the famous carpe diem ethic of Qohelet. Qohelet is not recommending this ethic in these passages; he is doing his testing and noting the results. Here is the first carpe diem ethic citation in Qohelet, which forms the conclusion to the Solomonic experiment:

> There is nothing better for mortals than to eat and drink, and find enjoyment in their toil. This also, I saw, is from the hand of God; for apart from him who can eat or who can have enjoyment? For to the one who pleases him God gives wisdom and knowledge and joy; but to the sinner he gives the work of gathering and

---

50. E.g., Crenshaw, *Old Testament Wisdom*, 144; idem, *Ecclesiastes*, 91; Fox, *Rereading Ecclesiastes*, 38, 121–31.

51. Lauha, *Kohelet*, 48.

52. Fox, *Rereading of Ecclesiastes*, 122.

53. Lauha, *Kohelet*, 52.

54. Robert D. Holmstedt, "אֲנִי וְלִבִּי The Syntactic Encoding of the Collaborative Nature of Qohelet's Experiment," *Journal of Hebrew Scriptures* 9, article 19 (2009): 1–27, online at http://www.arts.ualberta.ca/JHS/Articles/article_121.pdf (accessed January 13, 2011).

heaping, only to give to one who pleases God. This also is vanity and a chasing after wind. (2:24–26)

The last line does not refer to the carpe diem ethic just cited but is Qohelet's conclusion to the Solomonic experiment.[55] It does, however, subordinate the ethic to Qohelet's dominant pessimistic theme.

The carpe diem ethic, then, represents an antidote to הֶבֶל. It differs from the other pleasures in that it is not involved in the human striving for profit. As Lauha puts it, instead of the frantic search for profit that 2:10 involves, Qohelet's concluding ethic is a passive resignation to the ultimate futility of human striving.[56] One simply enjoys the moment, for there is no guarantee of the future. Similarly, Tilmann Zimmer argues that, since all of life is a breath of wind, then even joy is technically הֶבֶל.[57] But since the carpe diem ethic has no expectation of profit, it is unnecessary to describe it as הֶבֶל. Nevertheless, Zimmer's suggestion would still make the ethic constitute a type of solution to the problem of life's character as הֶבֶל. Thus, the carpe diem ethic is not futile for two reasons. First, it is a gift from God. Second, it involves a lowering of expectations and does not involve the strife and toil that accompany human agonistic aspirations. As Maussion puts it, it is enjoying the simple pleasures of life that God supplies:

> One can then posit a hypothesis that Qohelet seems to distinguish two sorts of joy: on the one hand, that procured by sumptuous pleasures where the person is the soul protagonist and God absent, such would be the aim of the Solomonic fiction placed at the beginning of his work, and on the other hand, that procured by the simple pleasures of life, which are gifts from God, and which Qohelet chants in seven refrains distributed all along his book. (my translation)[58]

Nothing could be further from futility or vanity than this! שִׂמְחָה, with lowered expectations, then, should be seen as another antonym of הֶבֶל and a close corollary of אֱלֹהִים.

QOHELET—NO MODERN EXISTENTIALIST!

Qohelet is no existentialist in the modern sense. Gordis, years before Fox, demonstrated that, while there is an affinity between Camus and Qohelet, Qohelet never goes so far as Camus in proclaiming the world to be absurd.[59]

---

55. See Crenshaw, *Ecclesiastes*, 91.
56. Lauha, *Kohelet*, 57.
57. Zimmer, *Tod und Lebensglück*, 95–96.
58. Maussion, "Qohélet VI 1–2," 507.
59. Gordis, *Koheleth*, 112–21; cf. Zimmer, *Tod und Lebensglück*, 27 n. 26, 32 n. 61.

In other words, it is a matter of degree. Qohelet does not push the absurdity issue to the degree that modern existentialists do. His problem concerns the overrationality of traditional wisdom. Although Qohelet may not fully discern the meaning of life, this does not equate with seeing the world as *totally* meaningless or absurd. Recently, the philosopher Martin Shuster has demonstrated that Qohelet is no proto-existentialist.[60] Similarly, historian Matthew Schwartz has also contrasted Camus and Qohelet and, while certainly finding an affinity, sees striking differences. Whereas in Camus' *The Myth of Sisyphus*, the tragic hero must accept that the world is totally absurd, "Koheleth's world is neither meaningless nor absurd, and man may work, learn and be happy."[61] One could say that Qohelet certainly has a crisis of meaning, but he does not leave it at that. He finds meaning in life, though he finds life often oppressive. Fox's description of Qohelet's partial recovery of meaning after its loss actually implies that Qohelet never really saw the world as fully absurd in the first place and demonstrates that Fox indeed does believe that Qohelet attempts to mitigate the dissonance of the problem of evil and absurdity in the world! Qohelet does not maintain the tension, and, thus, he is not in the same category as modern existentialists, who revel in it.[62]

Again, though Qohelet is not fully positive about God's activities in the world, God does provide him with meaning and orientation. The irrationality of this world "under the sun" indirectly implies the possibility of rationality beyond this world, à la God.[63] Even Fox admits this, though he discounts it as insignificant as a source of comfort for Qohelet.[64] The philosopher Karl Haden captures the sense here, though his particular wording is too positive:

> [F]or Qoheleth, meaning may be elusive and cause the feeling of *hebel*, but nevertheless, meaning exists because God exists. . . . There is a higher level of meaning, that is, there is a level of meaning known only to God. When God serves as the reference point—or hub of existence for the individual—one finds equanimity in the belief that although he does not have all the answers, God does. It is this aban-

---

60. Shuster, "Being as Breath," 219, 232. Similarly, Kenneth W. James does a good job showing the similarities and differences between existentialism and Qohelet ("Ecclesiastes: Precursor of Existentialists," *TBT* 22 [March 1984]: 85–90).

61. Matthew J. Schwartz, "Koheleth and Camus: Two Views of Achievement," *Judaism* 35 (1986): 30–31.

62. Fox, *Rereading of Ecclesiastes*, 3.

63. Contrarily, Diethelm Michel maintains that Qohelet never transcends "the limits of immanence" indicated by "under the sun." This means that God as creator is no source of comfort for Qohelet ("«Unter der Sonne»: Zur Immanenz bei Qohelet," in *Qohelet in the Context of Wisdom* [ed. Anton Schoors; BETL 136; Leuven: Leuven University Press and Peeters, 1998], 102, 111).

64. Fox, *Rereading of Ecclesiastes*, 35, 165.

donment, faith, that allows joy to radiate from the higher level into the mundane life of mortal man.[65]

Fox believes, like Crenshaw, that Qohelet finds little comfort in anything, with Fox maintaining that the book is a protest against God's injustices. As already indicated, it is difficult to believe this, for if that were Qohelet's message, the book would have never been canonized. Such a position would not have helped anyone in Qohelet's time adjust to difficult circumstances. Crenshaw and Fox have projected their own modern angst and existentialism respectively back onto Qohelet. They essentially view Qohelet as a transparently contemporary work that easily speaks to their own postmodern condition. But both fail to appreciate that Qohelet was a religious text and that such texts are about solutions and not about modern atheistic angst over the absurdity of the world. If interpretations of Qohelet such as those of Fox and Crenshaw had prevailed in ancient times, the book would probably not have been preserved, let alone become canonical—or even been utilized throughout the ages, as in the festival of Booths. In short, the interpretations by Fox and Crenshaw are ultimately and quintessentially anachronistic, though their intuition on Qohelet's heterodox proclivities is accurate.[66]

QOHELET'S RHETORIC

A rhetorical analysis of Qohelet will further confirm this particular literary reading of the book. It will also support the notion that Qohelet is a polemic against traditional wisdom. Douglas Miller is the only scholar who has treated the topic of the rhetorical dimension of the book.[67] Though Miller is reluctant to call Qohelet a pessimist (he prefers "realist"), his analysis is significant because he views Qohelet as a rhetorician.[68] Drawing on classical Greek rhetoric, Miller categorizes Qohelet as a deliberative type of rhetoric: "concerned with persuading an audience to action." It is not judicial ("defending or condemning a person or event"); neither is it epideictic ("strengthening adherence to some belief or value"). He argues that Qohelet's rhetorical strategy has three parts: ethos, destabilitization, and restabilization. Ethos refers to the credibility that an author has

---

65. N. Karl Haden, "Qoheleth and the Problem of Alienation," *Christian Scholars Review* 17 (1987): 66, n. 59.

66. W. H. U. Anderson and Shuster both admit that Fox's translation of "absurdity" for הבל is somewhat anachronistic (Anderson, "Implications of הבל," 70; Shuster, "Being as Breath," 232).

67. Miller, "Rhetoric of Ecclesiastes," 215–35; see also idem, "Qohelet's Symbolic Use of הבל," *JBL* 117 (1998): 437–54.

68. Miller, "Rhetoric of Ecclesiastes," 220–21.

with his audience. Miller rightly argues that Qohelet is very much concerned with gaining the respect of his audience and gaining its trust. Ethos involves three facets: "the speaker's competence, the speaker's status, and the speaker's moral *character* (especially his or her benevolence, perceived concern for the welfare of the audience)."[69] For example, Qohelet's competence is demonstrated by his manifold personal observations about life.

Miller also discusses the importance of pathos in Qohelet, which is the emotional element of his argument. His examples almost all involve Qohelet's use of הֶבֶל. He distinguishes between Qohelet's detached coldness and his passionate outbursts, which he sees as only representing pathos. He also discusses logos in Qohelet and notes, "The format of Ecclesiastes gives the appearance of a strong, inductive, and empirically logical argument."[70] But then he downplays both pathos and logos, preferring to see Qohelet's chief rhetorical strategy as ethos.

But what is most significant in Miller's analysis is his discussion of Qohelet's destabilization and restabilization of his audience's beliefs. Miller acknowledges his reliance on Leo Perdue for these concepts. Perdue, drawing primarily on Philip Wheelwright and Paul Ricoeur, discusses the metaphorical process whereby a metaphor first shocks the hearer and creates destabilization but then allows mimesis, where the new idea seems to fit or mimic reality, and then finally transformation and restabilization, allowing a different perception of reality to be constituted.[71] Miller defines destabilization as "a process of challenging and disorienting an audience through a variety of means which ultimately serve to call into question the values and priorities of that audience."[72]

Miller sees Qohelet's use of הֶבֶל as a primary agent of this destabilization. He notes that the audience would have sensed the absurdity in Qohelet's statement that "all is הֶבֶל." He argues that Qohelet's audience would have found the term itself confusing and disorienting. Drawing on Raymond Johnson's investigation of Qohelet's use of rhetorical questions, Miller sees this as another destabilizing strategy on the part of Qohelet.[73] These questions "create gaps, an anticipation of resolution which Qoheleth regularly denies. This delay not only engages the reader's attention but also requires that the reader engage the assumptions and values of the speaker for as long

---

69. Ibid., 224.
70. Ibid., 226.
71. Leo G. Perdue, *Wisdom in Revolt: Metaphorical Theology in the Book of Job* (JSOTSup 112; Bible and Literature 29; Sheffield: Almond, 1991), 22–27.
72. Miller, "Rhetoric of Ecclesiastes," 228.
73. Ibid., citing Raymond Johnson, "The Rhetorical Question as a Literary Device in Ecclesiastes" (Ph.D. diss., Southern Baptist Theological Seminary, 1986).

as it takes to reach the answer."[74] For example, the question in 1:3 ("What do people gain from all the toil at which they toil under the sun?") is not answered until 2:11 ("All was vanity and a chasing after the wind, and there was nothing to be gained under the sun"). Miller sees Qohelet's restabilization indicated in his more positive advice.[75] He shows how Qohelet does not totally debunk wisdom, work, and pleasure, as shown in the carpe diem ethic of 2:24–26.

Miller's discussion of destabilization and restabilization is entirely accurate, though his view of Qohelet is still a little too positive and pietistic. The following is an adaptation of Miller's thesis. הֶבֶל in Qohelet is the ultimate questioning of traditional values. It can mean essentially "worthlessness" or "uselessness." Qohelet is being largely iconoclastic, challenging and questioning the traditional values and norms of his society, and especially those of the wisdom tradition. Thus, the rhetorical strategy of Qohelet becomes clearer. He is intent on radically questioning the normative values of his day, though not totally debunking them. Thus, his mantra "all is vanity" is hyperbolic and rhetorical. It is meant to shock readers and radically disorient them.

But Qohelet does not leave the reader with this radical deconstruction of all values. He rebuilds a new orientation, a new set of values and norms. His deconstruction has a positive function: to demolish the old values and worldview and reconstruct new values and a worldview better adapted to reality. Wisdom is deconstructed as a source of guaranteed blessing in the future; however, it is superior to folly, as light is to darkness (2:13–14). In turn, Qohelet's carpe diem ethic is essentially the new value. It does not rely on long-term goals and objectives but attends to what is available in the present. It does not focus on intellectual or cognitive pleasures or on life and cosmic mastery. Rather it emphasizes simple bodily pleasures and relationships. The real significance of understanding the rhetorical character of the book is that Qohelet's pessimism is not simply the natural psychological disposition of the author but the employment of a rhetorical strategy intended to persuade an audience to accept new and different values and norms.

Miller's assessment of Qohelet's logos, detected mainly in his inductive, logical format, appears sound. Fox has even described Qohelet's reasoning as empirical and largely resonating with the modern style of rationality.[76] However, Crenshaw rightly qualifies this, showing how many elements of Qohelet's

---

74. Miller, "Rhetoric of Ecclesiastes," 229.
75. Ibid., 230–32.
76. Fox, Rereading of Ecclesiastes, 75–86.

thinking are idealistic and not reliant on empirical observation, such as his observations about God.[77]

But pathos appears to be more important to Qohelet than either ethos or logos. הֶבֶל is quintessentially a pathetic expression, and this is reinforced by the melancholic mood of the book. Though Qohelet marshals observation after observation and shows concern for what his audience thinks of him, ultimately he is interested in touching its heart, not its head, in touching the emotions, not the intellect. Qohelet's pessimistic pathos is a strong reinforcement of his logical argument that the world is largely irrational and also is part of his solution to this problem: one apathetically (which actually is an emotion) resigns oneself to such irrationality. Thus, Miller's prioritization of ethos over pathos and logos in Qohelet appears faulty. In order of importance, it is pathos, logos, and then ethos.

Perhaps this is overly semantic, but Qohelet's argument is essentially epideictic, not deliberative. Epideictic rhetoric concerns itself with changing or affirming values and norms and cultural assumptions, and how one lives one's life; it is not properly deliberative rhetoric, which is a call to action, particularly political action.[78] Epideictic rhetoric is about cultural values, whether questioning or affirming them. Epideictic arguments can provide the basis for deliberative ones, but in and of themselves they are not a call to action.

Wisdom literature, in general, is epideictic and is about praising or blaming the values of a society. Jewish wisdom literature is not rightly a call to specific action but a call to lifestyle and virtuous behavior. Epideictic rhetoric often emphasizes ethos, and this fits with Miller's analysis. Qohelet's carpe diem ethic and God-fearing motif are not calls to action but serve as ethical counsel. While Qohelet blames traditional wisdom for not fitting the reality of his day, he praises his own ethical alternative, the carpe diem ethic, as more appropriate for his time.

Classic examples of deliberative rhetoric in the Hebrew Bible are the laments in the Psalter (e.g., Pss 13; 22; and 54).[79] The lamenters attempt to persuade God to act on their behalf. They often appeal to their innocence and God's shame in not delivering them. Or they might offer sacrifices to God or praise God in return for a divine response to their crises. But, of course, Qohelet has given up appealing to God for redemption or expecting salvation in any significant form.

---

77. Crenshaw, "Qoheleth's Understanding," 212–13.

78. See Cynthia Miecznikowski Sheard, "The Public Value of Epideictic Rhetoric," *College English* 58 (1996): 765–94; Perelman and Olbrechts-Tyteca, *New Rhetoric*, 21, 47–54.

79. Davida Charney, "Rhetorical Exigencies in the Individual Psalms" (paper presented at the Southwest regional meeting of the SBL, Irving, Texas, March 14, 2010).

It is interesting that the frame narrator or epilogist recognized the rhetorical intent of Qohelet: "The Teacher sought to find pleasing words" (12:10a). The word for "pleasing" is חֵפֶץ. As Martin Shields points out, this can refer either to the aesthetics or to the content of his words.[80] Shields opts for the latter and argues that Qohelet never achieved his intended result; he never could issue any definitive conclusions about anything. But the former interpretation is more appropriate. The epilogist recognizes that Qohelet's words were aesthetically and artistically sophisticated. He understands their hyperbolic and rhetorical goals, their intended effect on the reader, which Qohelet had masterly crafted.

CONCLUSION

A broadly literary reading of Qohelet has been conducted that has involved lexical semantics, an ancient Near Eastern comparison, and rhetorical analysis. These have combined to demonstrate that the book of Qohelet is indeed a polemic against traditional wisdom, as has been traditionally assumed among scholars. Fox's recent attack on that position, though popular, cannot be substantiated. Qohelet was not bent primarily on attacking God. This means, of course, that הֶבֶל should not be translated as "absurd" or "incomprehensible" or "meaningless." There is no clear evidence for these translations in the biblical material. Rather, in Qohelet, "futility" and "illusion" (a few times as "transience" [e.g., 7:15]) or "worthlessness" seem the best options, and this fits in with the primary intent of the book: a polemic against traditional wisdom that advises the futility of human striving, effort, and toil, and particularly the effort of traditional wisdom to master the world. Rather, the world is largely irrational and incomprehensible, and הֶבֶל is used to lower expectations about attempting to strive against these human limitations and constraints. Though Qohelet believes that the world is in many ways irrational, he never specifically uses הֶבֶל in that sense. Rather it is used by him as a tool to devalue many of traditional wisdom's sacred cows and to lower expectations in his audience about the role and value of traditional wisdom. It has some value but is largely bankrupt.

Instead of striving, aspiring, and constantly looking toward the future, Qohelet advises acceptance, resignation, and a focus on the present. Qohelet's use of הֶבֶל essentially lowers expectations about humanity, God, and the world, and psychologically enables his audience to face the world without serious disappointment. The book reflects a degree of existential angst, but it is better to view it as primarily representing a positive and practical response to a world

---

80. Shields, *End of Wisdom*, 64–66.

that does not run according to the dictates of traditional wisdom. Certainly the book is about the loss of meaning in the world, but it is not about simply describing or bemoaning it. Qohelet seeks actually to mitigate the problem. He sees God as oppressive, but he also recognizes comforting aspects that provide him and his audience with an orientation toward life and the world. Qohelet resolves (or dissolves) the problem of theodicy by largely broadening the gap between mortals and the Immortal and advising his audience to keep this continually in view in daily living.

6

QOHELET, THE PROBLEM OF EVIL,
AND COGNITIVE DISSONANCE

Two concepts will be explored in this chapter. First, focus will be placed on Qohelet's treatment of the problem of evil from a comparative-religion perspective and how best to categorize his solution. This issue has already been touched in the previous two chapters but will be fleshed out more fully now. Second, an attempt will be made to show how Qohelet's solution fits with the theory of cognitive dissonance, a major theory of social psychology. In this way it will be possible to show the creativity and brilliance of Qohelet as an intellectual, whose job it is to produce theodicy strategies that help the social class to which he belongs and/or society as a whole deal with the perennial problem of evil.

The problem of evil has been a perennial and major issue for both religion and philosophy. It is, in fact, a major subfield of the philosophy of religion today. Traditionally explained, the problem of evil is created by three factors: God is omnibenevolent and omnipotent (and omniscient), yet evil (both natural and moral) exists. Theodicy, classically defined, then becomes the attempt to justify God's allowance of evil to exist in the world (*theos* + *dikē*).

Theodicy may be defined either narrowly or broadly.[1] It is usually defined narrowly when treating the three monotheistic religions (Judaism, Christianity, and Islam). Defined narrowly, only a theodicy that attempts to defend or justify the one God's benevolence and his power in view of the reality evil in the world would be considered a bona fide theodicy. For example, a strategy that attempts to deny the reality of evil, as the Church of Christ Scientists does, would not be considered a theodicy in the classical sense because it fails to directly defend God's benevolence and power. However, comparative religionists such as Weber define it more broadly to include any attempt to lessen the tension created by the trilemma. This latter way of viewing theodicy will be the one utilized in this chapter.

---

1. Ronald Green, "Theodicy," *ER* 14:431–32.

Qohelet does not use a classical theodicy to treat the problem of evil, which makes the book unusual in the Bible (Job's strategy is comparable). In other words, Qohelet uses a strategy that is common in nonmonotheistic religions. Thus, defining theodicy more broadly allows one better to see exactly Qohelet's particular strain of theodicy and how it functions to alleviate the tension created by the trilemma that forms the problem of theodicy. Defining theodicy more narrowly would essentially exclude the book of Qohelet from consideration and inherently skew the perception of the book's positive function in treating the problem of evil, which tends to radicalize the book. In fact, Fox speaks of theodicy not working for Qohelet, and similarly Pin'has Carny says of Qohelet, "And so it becomes impossible to him to open his mind to the idea of theodicy." Both view Qohelet as quite heterodox.[2] Similarly, Ronald Green will only speak of Qohelet dissolving the theodicy problem rather than actually solving it.[3] But is not dissolving the problem largely solving it?

Religions around the world have attempted to resolve the problem of evil by essentially exaggerating or downplaying one of the three components of the trilemma.[4] But, as Bryan Turner points out, any attempt at doing this necessarily and simultaneously makes problematic God's omnipotence or justice, against its best intentions. Thus, theodicy is never a totally satisfactory resolution intellectually.[5] In other words, in resolving the theodicy problem, there is always a tradeoff in terms of one or more of the components of the trilemma.

An example is provided by Weber, who views the doctrine of karma, a particular theodicy created by the intellectuals of Hinduism, as most supreme and a pure type.[6] All evil or fortune in this life is attributed to a former life. It is an almost irresistible dogma because of its explanatory power. The poor cannot blame the powerful for their misfortune, and the powerful and wealthy need feel no guilt for their privileged lifestyles. Everyone deserves whatever state one finds oneself in. The teaching both explains evil and simultaneously legitimizes the caste system. A more foolproof, invincible theodicy could not be found.

---

2. Fox, *Rereading of Ecclesiastes*, 66; Pin'has Carny, "Theodicy in the Book of Qohelet," in *Justice and Righteousness: Biblical Themes and Their Influence* (ed. Henning Graf Reventlow and Yair Hoffman; JSOTSup 137; Sheffield: JSOT Press, 1992), 80.

3. Green, "Theodicy," 435.

4. The secular world has also found the notion of theodicy useful. D. Christopher Kayes uses Weber's concept of theodicy to explain corrupt business practices ("Organizational Corruption as Theodicy," *Journal of Business Ethics* 67 [2006]: 51–62. DOI: 10.1007/s10551-006-9004-x).

5. B. Turner, *For Weber*, 149; cf. Colin Campbell, "Theodicy," *Encyclopedia of Religion and Society*, n.p., online at http://hirr.hartsem.edu/ency/Theodicy.htm (accessed March 3, 2008).

6. Weber, *Sociology of Religion*, 145–6.

But, as Weber notes, even the most rationally consistent theodicy does not provide complete satisfaction. In the case of karma, this is because in its particular solution, it eliminates the need for the deities because the karmic order ultimately does not depend on them.[7] More generally, as Talcott Parsons notes, "A fully closed, rational system would be devoid of meaning" because the non-rational aspects of life (emotions, desire, etc.) are what drive it.[8]

Another pure type of theodicy that Weber discusses is Calvin's doctrine of predestination, which essentially eliminates the problem of evil rationally through the notion of God's sovereign right to elect some to salvation and others to damnation.[9] In other words, God's standards of judgment are ultimately beyond mortal comprehension, and no human has the right to question God's actions. But this rationally consistent doctrine solves one problem, while creating another:

> Calvinistic piety offers one of the many examples in the history of religion in which *logical* and *psychological* consequences for practical religious *behavior* have been mediated from certain religious ideas. Viewed *logically*, fatalism would naturally follow . . . as a deduction, from the idea of predestination. However, as a consequence of the insertion of the idea of "conduct as testifying to one's belief," the *psychological effect* was exactly the opposite.[10]

In other words, it solves the problem of evil for Calvinists, but it simultaneously incites their desire to know if they, individually, are among the elect. The rational solution, therefore, produced an irrational problem (yearning for assurance). Ann Swidler notes the "enormous power" of this doctrine, but also points out its significant liability:

> This extremely rationalized solution to the problem of evil made Calvinism so brutal in its psychological implications that is was forced to invent the not quite logical doctrine of proof as the antidote to the totally rationalized doctrine of predestination. Calvinism exemplifies both the power of rationalized thought and the ability of pragmatic religious interests to alter the implications of ideas.[11]

Another example involves contrasting Judaism with the other monotheistic religions. The theodicy problem is most poignant for Judaism with its strong version of monotheism, since it cannot blame evil on another deity or

---

7. Ibid., 146–47.

8. Parsons, "Introduction," xvii.

9. See Weber, *Sociology of Religion*, 142–44.

10. Weber, *Protestant Ethic*, 337 n. 76.

11. Ann Swidler, "The Concept of Rationality in the Work of Max Weber," *Sociological Inquiry* 43 (1973): 37.

on the devil.[12] Blaming another deity for evil is classically known as dualism.[13] Examples include Zoroastrianism and Manichaeism with their spiritual god of goodness and light and an evil creator of matter associated with darkness. Both Christianity and Islam have a dualistic component with Satan or a devil, though their main theodicy is eschatological, in which a heaven and a hell in the next life help resolve the problem of injustice in this life. Dualism works because it shifts the blame for evil from God to a devil, but the downside is that it simultaneously undermines the omnipotence of God—God has a rival who cannot be fully controlled. Few religions employ only one theodicy strategy, and often these strategies are not logically compatible with each other.

THEODICY STRATEGIES IN THE HEBREW BIBLE

The main classical theodicy strategy in the Hebrew Bible is the free will of humans.[14] This is the notion that humans deserve their suffering or good fortune because they freely choose to do evil or good and suffer/benefit from the consequences.[15] Suffering caused by free will, whether to the victims or as

---

12. See Green, "Theodicy," 431; P. Berger, *Sacred Canopy*, 73; B. Turner, *For Weber*, 149. In contrast, Wolfram von Soden demonstrates that in the ancient Near East the questioning of God's righteousness did not occur among the more primitive clan-oriented polytheistic religions, for example, the Sumerians. It occurred later during the rise of the more developed, urban, and individualistic religions, such as the Old Babylonians and the Israelites ("Das Fragen nach der Gerechtigkeit Gottes im Alten Orient," *MDOG* 96 [1965]: 41–62).

13. See Weber, *Sociology of Religion*, 144; Green, "Theodicy," 431. In popular Buddhism, Mara (Evil) is like the devil, while in the official religion it is more abstract (Chandra Wikramagamage, "Mara as Evil in Buddhism," in *Evil and the Response of World Religion* [ed. William Cenkner; St. Paul, Minn.: Paragon House, 1997], 109–15). This is essentially the strategy of many African religions (good versus evil spirits/gods): see, in the previously cited volume edited by Cenkner, E. O. Oyelade, "Evil in Yoruba Religion and Culture," 157–69; and Wande Abimbola, "Gods Versus Anti-Gods: Conflict and Resolution in the Yoruban Cosmos," 170–79.

14. See Green, "Theodicy," 432–33.

15. A Jewish twist on this is the notion of an evil and a good tendency (יצר) created within humans which war against each other for mastery. See Johann Cook, "The Origin of the Tradition of the יצר הטוב and יצר הרע," *JSJ* 38 (2007): 80–91; Sheldon R. Isenberg, "From Myth to Psyche to Mystic Psychology: The Evolution of the Problem of Evil in Judaism," in *Evil and the Response of World Religion* (ed. William Cenkner; St. Paul, Minn.: Paragon House, 1997), 24–26. Islam utilizes a similar notion: see, in the previously cited volume, Muhammed Al-Ghazali, "The Problem of Evil: An Islamic Approach," 70–79. In contrast to Isenberg, Christoph Schulte sees no possibility in philosophy for a Jewish theodicy after the Holocaust. Literature seems to have replaced this function ("Jüdisch Theodizee? Überlegungen zum Theodizee—Problem bei Immanuel Kant, Hermann Cohen und Max Weber," *ZRGG* 49 [1997]: 158–59).

consequences to the instigator, is usually explained as necessary for free will to be possible. In other words, God must allow moral evil as a possibility in order for free will to exist. Thus, moral evil is something even God cannot prevent, if free will is to remain a real possibility.[16]

The doctrine of retribution in the wisdom tradition functions partly as a free will strategy. Here God is not to blame for misfortune; it is due to the victim's sinful life, which he/she chooses and has particular consequences, including punishment by God in this life. However, a weakness of this strategy is that it fails to explain adequately the effects of moral evil that often inflict innocent bystanders. Further, the free will theodicy has difficulty explaining natural evil that inflicts persons capriciously.[17] In the Hebrew Bible, the cascading effects of moral evil are dealt with by extending the punishment of moral evil to the fourth generation (Exod 20:5; Deut 5:9) and through the notion of corporate responsibility.[18] The Deuteronomist employs these strategies. For example, the exteme piety of King Josiah could not undo the sins of Manasseh, his grandfather (2 Kgs 23:25b–27), which inevitably brought the exile upon the Jews. The notion of corporate responsibility is demonstrated in the story of Achan, whose entire family and livestock are stoned because of his sin (Josh 7). However, the obvious unfairness of this is resolved later by limiting God's punishment to the evildoer himself/herself as seen in Jeremiah ("the children's teeth are set on edge" no more [31:29–30; cf. Ezek 18:1–4]) and the Chronicler, who blames Josiah for not listening to God's words to stop pursuing Neco (2 Chr 35:20–27). But this is simply a return to the situation that produced the modification in the first place.

The doctrine of retribution in its traditional formulation is almost completely rejected by some authors of the Hebrew Bible. The book of Job does two things to counter or modify the traditional doctrine of retribution.[19] First, it deflects the focus on theodicy to anthropodicy. In other words, it switches the

---

16. C. Stephen Layman argues that theism can explain moral evil as well or better than naturalism. Naturalism has difficulty explaining moral responsibility (free will) ("Moral Evil: The Comparative Response," *International Journal for Philosophy of Religion* 53 [2003]: 1–23).

17. Nick Trakakis argues that, while there exist legitimate theodicies for explaining moral evil, none exists for natural evil ("Is Theism Capable of Accounting for Any Natural Evil at All?" *International Journal for Philosophy of Religion* 57 [2005]: 35–66).

18. Jože Krašovec argues that the notion of collective retribution in the Hebrew Bible is rhetorical and simply indicates that children naturally suffer the consequences of their parents' sin, but his argument is largely apologetic ("Is There a Doctrine of 'Collective Retribution' in the Hebrew Bible?" *HUCA* 65 [1994]: 35–89).

19. See Mark Sneed, "Job," in *The Transforming Word: One-Volume Commentary on the Bible* (ed. Mark Hamilton; Abilene, Tex.: Abilene Christian University Press, 2009), 423–24.

question from why God allows evil in the world to the question of disinterested righteousness. This is the question asked by the Satan: "Does Job fear God for nothing?" (1:9). In other words, it refocuses the problem so that the contest between the Satan and God over Job's piety becomes primary, and, thus, the problem of evil recedes into the background. But this strategy is actually a type of theodicy: educative theodicy.[20] This is the basis for the famous theodicy that Irenaeus used and is known more popularly today as the soul-making theodicy.[21] Thus, in Job 11:4–20 Zophar maintains that suffering is educative, that it strengthens people and thickens their skin, so to speak, allowing them to be more resilient with future suffering and giving them a broader perspective on life.[22] The notion of testing is closely connected with this strategy. That Job was being tested by God to determine his degree of faithfulness helps mitigate the problem of theodicy because it actually deflects the problem from God to the sufferer and provides a positive explanation for suffering.

Second, the divine speeches (chs. 38–42) also shift the focus from the problem of evil to the reality of human fallibility. God essentially bullies Job and questions his competence to understand the world that he has created. God argues that the universe is theocentric, not anthropocentric. If Job could only comprehend God's view of the world and adopt his vision, then he would ultimately understand his own suffering and stop his protests. Job cowers in the end and confesses, "Therefore I have uttered what I did not understand, things too wonderful for me, which I did not know" (42:3).

Ronald Green argues that one could view Job in two ways.[23] More radically, "*Job* may be read as an abandonment of the very effort to comprehend God's justice, as an assertion that a creature cannot ask its maker to render account."

---

20. See Green, "Theodicy," 433. Von Soden points out that this particular theodicy is not found among the Babylonians ("Gerechtigkeit Gottes," 57).

21. The classic articulation of this theodicy is by John Hick, *Evil and the God of Love* (rev. ed.; San Francisco: Harper & Row, 1978). For a Jewish adoption of it, see David J. Goldberg, "Providence and the Problem of Evil in Jewish Thought," in *Evil and the Response of World Religion* (ed. William Cenkner; St. Paul, Minn.: Paragon House, 1997), 40–42. In the same volume, Paul Badham demonstrates that the soul-making theodicy is found in all religions ("Toward a Global Theodicy," 241–51), and Jane Mary Zwerner applies the soul-making theodicy to the cross ("The Discovery of Christian Meaning in Suffering: Transformation and Solidarity," 43–55).

22. Alternatively, on the suffering of nonhumans, the Priestly source indicates that evil arose from the violence in killing animals (Gene G. James, "The Priestly Conceptions of Evil in the Torah," in *Evil and the Response of World Religion* [ed. William Cenkner; St. Paul, Minn.: Paragon House, 1997], 3–15). In the same volume, M. Darrol Bryant discusses the suffering of the earth ("Ecological Evil and Interfaith Dialogue: Caring for the Earth," 210–22).

23. Green, "Theodicy," 435.

Green classifies this type of strategy as a denial of God's justice. Green points out that "very few religious traditions openly hold God to be evil."[24] He notes, "More common than an outright denial of the deity's justice, however, is the claim that God's justice is somehow qualitatively different from our ordinary human ideas of right and wrong. Words like *justice* or *goodness* when applied to God have no relation to their meaning when applied to human beings." Less radically, Job may be read as what Green calls "deferred theodicy."[25] Deferred theodicy invokes the notion of the mystery of suffering that will be understood someday in the future.[26] Often this strategy stresses the limitations of human comprehension and the distance between God and humans, but it never goes so far as to deny God's justice, whether openly or not. Like Job, Qohelet also seriously questions God's justice, but his strategy will be dealt with in detail later.

Another response to the problems with retributive theology in the Hebrew Bible is found in Second Isaiah.[27] The new theodicy involves the notion of a suffering servant, an innocent person who suffers vicariously for others (the Jews) (e.g., Isa 53:3–10). Green maintains that this notion involves a combination of free-will, educative, and communion theodicies. A communion theodicy tries to connect God closely with suffering, viewing God as actually suffering with the sufferer.[28] This helps mitigate the problem somewhat.

Finally, the book of Daniel represents what Green calls an "eschatological (or recompense) theodicy."[29] This strategy simply pushes the retributive schema beyond this life to an afterlife (Dan 12:2) where all wrongs can be righted. Eschatological theodicy essentially solved the problem of the traditional doctrine of retribution but was reluctantly accepted by the Jews because of their long-standing resistance to this idea.[30]

---

24. Ibid., 431.
25. Ibid., 435.
26. Ibid., 434.
27. Ibid., 435.
28. Ibid., 434. John B. Curtis argues that the author of the Elihu speeches was dependent on Deutero-Isaiah and cast Elihu mockingly in the role of the Servant ("Elihu and Deutero-Isaiah: A Study in Literary Dependence," *Proceedings, Eastern Great Lakes and Midwest Biblical Societies* 10 [1990]: 31–38).
29. Green, "Theodicy," 433–35. David A. Skelton argues that Ben Sira is largely an eschatological theodicy that places hope in the Aaronide priesthood instead of a Davidide ("Ben Sira's Imaginative Theodicy: Reflections on the Aaronide Priesthood under Gentile Rule," *ResQ* 51 [2009]: 1–12). If Skelton is correct, this would constitute probably the first time that the wisdom tradition began to embrace echatologocal solutions.
30. This occurred in the wisdom tradition with the Wisdom of Solomon; on this trajectory, see J. T. Sanders, "Wisdom, Theodicy, Death," 263–77. A. P. Hayman argues that the Wisdom of Solomon, with its dualism, represents the return to a more mythological view of

All religions utilize a combination of theodicy strategies, so it should be no surprise that Qohelet uses more than one. He partially accepts the free-will strategy. In 7: 29, Qohelet states, "God made humans upright, but they have sought out many schemes." Similarly, in 7:20 Qohelet states unequivocally that all have sinned. Thus, at least here Qohelet is blaming humans for their wicked behavior.

But Qohelet's favorite way of treating the problem of evil is to deny God's justice, though certainly not openly![31] The problem of theodicy arises several times in the book of Qohelet (3:16–17; 4:1; 5:8; 6:1–6; 7:15; 8:10, 14; 9:11; 10:5–7). In most of these instances, it perplexes Qohelet that the righteous and wise seem to fare badly, while the wicked live long and prosper. Qohelet resolves this problem by referring to God's eventual judgment (3:17; 5:1–7; 7:18; 8:12–13; 11:9) but implying simultaneously that God's standards of judgment are beyond human comprehension (2:26; 3:11; 7:14; 8:16–17; 9:1).

What is intriguing is the way Crenshaw and Fox interpret the apparent contradiction of Qohelet's references to divine judgment and his simultaneous observations of injustices in the world. On the one hand, Crenshaw believes that Qohelet essentially denies God's justice, while viewing the judicial references as anomalies in the book.[32] Fox, on the other hand, maintains that Qohelet indeed truly believes that God is just—thus the judicial references make sense—but also that the world is unjust.[33] Fox believes that Qohelet holds two propositions simultaneously without reducing the tension: God is just; God is apparently unjust—a schizophrenic interpretation, as already noted.

In reality, there is truth in both positions. Crenshaw places more weight on Qohelet's apparent denial of God's justice, Fox on Qohelet's acknowledgment of God's justice. Both positions must be brought together to create a more nuanced understanding. Both scholars are faulty in not detecting the creative way Qohelet attempts to resolve this issue. In other words, both oversimplify Qohelet's strategy, going in opposite directions. For example, in 3:16–17, Qohelet states, "Moreover I saw under the sun that in the place of

---

God than that in the earlier wisdom tradition ("The Survival of Mythology in the Wisdom of Solomon," *JSJ* 30 [1999]: 125–39).

31. See Green, "Theodicy," 435. Similarly, the Zohar (Kabbalah) combines evil with good in God (Isenberg, "Evil in Judaism," 26–31). In the Kabbalah "evil is treated as something positive" (Goldberg, "Problem of Evil," 36).

32. See Crenshaw, "Birth of Skepticism," 15; idem, *Ecclesiastes*, 23.

33. See Fox, *Rereading of Ecclesiastes*, 51–70.

justice, wickedness was there, and in the place of righteousness, wickedness was there as well. I said in my heart, God will judge the righteous and the wicked, for he has appointed a time for every matter, and for every work." Crenshaw says that the second half of this verse contradicts Qohelet's other statements about injustices, so he suggests it may be a later gloss.[34] Fox, to the contrary, believes that the entire verse is authentic. Focusing on the context, Fox believes that God will indeed judge and then speculates on what this might entail (death or something else).[35]

Fox's problem is that he never considers that Qohelet may be using the notion of judgment in a way different from that of traditional wisdom or normative Judaism. This conclusion is key for discerning Qohelet's solution to the problem of theodicy. Qohelet assumes that God judges but only according to his own standard. In other words, Qohelet merely states that God will judge the righteous and wicked but he does not provide the verdict. He keeps this open. Perhaps an ostensibly wicked person might not receive the severe punishment expected by most Jews. Or perhaps the righteous person might be found guilty. The JPS translation captures this idea: "I mused, 'God will doom both righteous and wicked.'" This strategy preserves God's sovereignty yet allows Qohelet to be honest about the many injustices in life. Qohelet is saying that the fates of humans seem fickle, but God will judge as he sees fit. It is not for mortals to question God's judgment. Like Fox's position, this preserves the verse's authenticity yet is true to Qohelet's dominant motif of injustice. There is thus no need to view Qohelet as schizophrenic. This approach demonstrates that Qohelet is indeed attempting to resolve the problem of theodicy. There is evil. God is omnipotent (and omniscient). But God is unjust (by human standards, but mortals cannot challenge his sovereignty). Or God is just but not by human standards. Thus, Crenshaw is correct that Qohelet is tackling the problem of evil by denying God's justice, essentially, though not directly, which is closer to Fox's position.

Thus, the component of the trilemma on which Qohelet fixates to resolve the tension created by the theodicy problem is God's benevolence. But he does it in such a way as to avoid *directly* implicating God in evil or malevolence. This is, in fact, ingenious, and credit goes to Qohelet's intellectual ability. Qohelet's strategy essentially dissolves the theodicy problem away. It disappears because Qohelet no longer has to defend God's justice since it cannot be comprehended. With the problem dissolved, Qohelet can go on to other things.

---

34. Crenshaw, *Ecclesiastes*, 102.
35. Fox, *Rereading of Ecclesiastes*, 214–15.

To develop further Qohelet's particular theodicy strategy, I will summarize here two of my articles that deal with the subject. In one of the articles, I show Qohelet both to deconstruct traditional wisdom and to be deconstructed himself.[36] Qohelet subversively deconstructs favorite dichotomies of traditional wisdom and Judaism: wisdom and folly, righteousness and wickedness, the good and the bad, the clean and the unclean, those who offer sacrifices and those who do not, the saint and the sinner, those who vow and those who do not (9:2). He shows that both categories of each dichotomy result in the same consequence—death—and, thus, the paired categories are blurred and begin to deconstruct.

But Qohelet also has a conservative side. There is one dichotomy that Qohelet never touches—it is too sacred: God-fearer/non–God-fearer. Qohelet takes an old dichotomy and revamps it, going back to its more primitive meaning of trembling before the deity. The God-fearer is shown to be most likely the one who pleases God (2:26). The term "God-fearer" overlaps the categories of both "righteous" and "wicked" but is neither. The God-fearer is cautious before the deity (5:1–7), avoids excess wickedness (7:17a), and avoids premature death (7:17b). The non–God-fearer, of course, is reckless and extreme and may die young (5:6; 7:17).

In other words, Qohelet has deconstructed the older dichotomies and created his own that he sees as more flexible, vaguer, and, thus, truer to reality. He is sensitive to the ultimately irrational ways of God and avoids attempting to manipulate the deity in any way. By this cautious, hubris-avoiding approach, the God-fearer will often succeed (7:18; 8:12b–13), though nothing is guaranteed.[37]

This article is important for understanding Qohelet's theodicy strategy because it demonstrates how Qohelet speaks of God's standard of judgment in a way never before encountered among the Jews and how his ethic is compatible with it. In the second article, I attempt to demonstrate that the notoriously difficult verses 8:12b–13 are authentic to Qohelet and do not contradict the following verse (v. 14). This approach is the opposite of the scholarly consensus.[38] Here is the unit, plus v. 14 (8:11–14):

---

36. Mark Sneed, "(Dis)closure in Qohelet: Qohelet Deconstructed," *JSOT* 27 (2002): 119–22.

37. Wayne A. Brindle ("Righteousness and Wickedness in 7:15–18," *AUSS* 23 [1985]: 256–57) speculates that the two items Qohelet says hold on to in v. 18 are "righteousness" and "wisdom," not "good" and "evil" (a golden mean [e.g., Gordis, *Koheleth*, 277]) or the two prohibitions (vv. 16–17) not to be too righteous/wise or wicked/foolish (e.g., Loader, *Polar Structures*, 48). Brindle's position ignores the symmetry of Qohelet's prohibitions that implies a means between the extremes, demonstrating Brindle's ulterior apologetic agenda.

38. Mark Sneed, "A Note on Qoh 8,12b–13," *Bib* 84 (2003): 412–16. The following commentators view the verses as a gloss: Crenshaw, *Ecclesiastes*, 48; Müller, "Theonome Skepsis," 16 n. 70; George Barton, *A Critical and Exegetical Commentary on the Book of*

Because sentence against an evil deed is not executed speedily, the human heart is fully set to do evil. Though sinners do evil a hundred times, and prolong their lives, *yet I know that it will be well with those who fear God, because they stand in fear before him, but it will not be well with the wicked, neither will they prolong their days like a shadow, because they do not stand in fear before God.* There is a vanity that takes place on earth, that there are righteous people who are treated according to the conduct of the wicked, and there are wicked people who are treated according to the conduct of the righteous. I said that this is vanity.

I argue that these verses do not contradict v. 14 because the latter treats only the categories of the righteous and wicked, whereas these verses only deal with God-fearers/non–God-fearers. In addition, these verses belong to the preceding unit that includes v. 11, which warns against supposing that delayed retribution means no retribution. Verses 14–15 are about predicting consequences and recommend enjoying the moment rather than trying to predict the future. Thus, there is no clash. I show that these two units demonstrate that Qohelet does not fully deny the doctrine of retribution, but he modifies and reformulates its traditional pattern.[39]

This article is significant for understanding Qohelet's theodicy strategy because it further reinforces the notion that God-fearing is part of Qohelet's preferred life strategy and further demonstrates how Qohelet uses traditional language in idiosyncratic ways. One simply needs to be attuned to the ambiguity of Qohelet's usage to see that he is viewing God's standard of judgment in a radically different way.

THE ASSETS AND LIABILITIES OF REDEFINING GOD'S STANDARD OF JUDGMENT

As has been said, any theodicy strategy will have to compromise one of the components of the trilemma, which will entail negative consequences. On

---

Ecclesiastes (ICC; 1908; repr., Edinburgh: T. & T. Clark, 1959), 154. Others see it as a contradiction or a traditional saying that the author then rejects or qualifies: J. A. Loader, *Ecclesiastes* (trans. J. Vriend; Text and Interpretation; Grand Rapids: Eerdmans, 1992), 101; Roland E. Murphy, *Ecclesiastes* (WBC 23a; Dallas: Word, 1992), 85; Diethelm Michel, *Qohelet* (EdF 258; Darmstadt: Wissenschaftliche Buchgesellschaft, 1988), 155–56; Panc Beentjes, "'Who Is like the Wise?' Some Notes on Qohelet 8,1–15," in *Qohelet in the Context of Wisdom* (ed. Anton Schoors; BETL 136; Leuven: Leuven University Press and Peeters, 1998), 313–14; Scott, *Proverbs. Ecclesiastes*, 242–43; Gianfranco Ravasi, *Qohelet* (La parola di Dio; Milan: Paoline, 1991), 272–73; Hans Wilhelm Hertzberg, *Der Prediger* (KAT 17/4; Gütersloh: Mohn, 1963), 30, 174; Longman, *Ecclesiastes*, 219–20; André Barucq, *Ecclésiaste. Qohéleth* (VS, Ancien Testament 3; Paris: Beauchesne, 1968), 152–53.

39. Thus, Loader is wrong when he surmises Qohelet's reaction to the doctrine: "This doctrine does not operate—that is no problem" ("Different Reactions," 47).

the positive side, Qohelet dissolves the theodicy problem because, with the acknowledgment that God is not so benevolent or that his justice cannot be comprehended, there is no need to further defend God's justice. Another positive benefit is that, by essentially denying God's justice, Qohelet can feel free to describe honestly the unjust situation of the world. Qohelet is very candid about the evil in the world, moral and natural. His dark and somber anecdotes are true to the painful reality of life and the world. Many have valued Qohelet's "realism" here.[40] This, of course, is in contrast to religions that have attempted to deny the reality of evil in the world, a type of dissolution of the problem.[41] Examples include the Church of Christ Scientists, who believe that physical illness is essentially an illusion and is caused by a wrong kind of thinking. Also, Hindus believe that once one takes the divine perspective, the reality of evil disappears.[42] Qohelet chooses to be brutally honest about the reality of evil. One could say that he might even exaggerate it, a point taken up in a later chapter.

There is a serious downside to this strategy, however. Denying or questioning God's justice or benevolence creates its own problems. Obviously, Qohelet's solution creates tension for normative Judaism. The rabbis recognized that Qohelet was clearly denying God's justice, which they could not countenance.[43] It helps that Qohelet does not directly accuse God of injustice, as does Job, but even with that, the capricious character of Qohelet's deity has been disturbing for ancient and modern Jews and Christians alike.

There is another tradeoff. Because Qohelet essentially views God as capricious and often rather malevolent (instead of omnibenevolent), even if Qohelet believes this is God's sovereign right, it affects Qohelet's view of God and the human capacity to have any meaningful relationship with him. Qohelet

---

40. E.g., Miller, "Rhetoric of Ecclesiastes," 220–21; Seow, *Ecclesiastes.*

41. See Green, "Theodicy," 431–32.

42. See Stephen Kaplan, "Three Levels of Evil in Advaita Vedanta and a Holographic Analogy," in *Evil and the Response of World Religion* (ed. William Cenkner; St. Paul, Minn.: Paragon House, 1997), 116–29; and, in the same volume, William Cenkner, "Hindu Understandings of Evil: From Tradition to Modern Thought," 130–41; Francis Xavier D'Sa, "A New Understanding of the Bhagaved Gita: Trinitarian Evil," 142–53. In Buddhism, on one level, evil is viewed as ignorance, but on another it is educative and necessary (Medagama Vajiragnena, "A Theoretical Explanation of Evil in Theravada Buddhism," in Cenkner, *Evil and the Response of World Religion*, 99–100).

43. See Isenberg, "Problem of Evil," 21–24; Ruth N. Sandberg, *Rabbinic Views of Qohelet* (Mellen Biblical Press 57; Lewiston, N.Y.: Mellen, 1999), 230. David Ray Griffin states personally that, for him as a Christian theologian, the goodness of God is not negotiable ("Divine Goodness and Demonic Evil," in *Evil and the Response of World Religion* [ed. William Cenkner; St. Paul, Minn.: Paragon House, 1997], 225–26).

appears to have no real personal relationship with God. Qohelet's God, by definition, cannot. He is essentially impersonal, detached, and distant, which is
the expected character of an amoral, capricious heavenly despot. God is more
a force than a person and takes on an abstract dimension. The more sovereign,
powerful, and yet capricious God is, the less Qohelet's deity is able to have any
meaningful relationship with mortals.

Similarly, there was negative reaction to Calvin's doctrine of predestination and its conceptualization of the deity. The doctrine had to be modified
because of its liabilities. Colin Campbell explains,

> Calvin's conception did not adequately incorporate all the critical characteristics
> of the divine; notably that it did not make sufficient allowance for God's good-
> ness. Consequently it remained open for the critics of Calvinism to argue, as
> indeed they did, that Calvin's theology was incomplete because it emphasized
> some of God's characteristics at the expense of others.[44]

This means that Qohelet's distant God is not the simple reflection of the
distant Ptolemaic king that Gottwald surmises but the result of Qohelet's creative strategy to resolve the theodicy problem by redefining God's justice.[45]
Thus, Gottwald's Marxism is vulgar in this case. Though Qohelet's conception
of God may have been influenced by the despotic character of the Ptolemaic
regime, it makes more sense to see his conception of the deity as primarily
and logically derived from his particularly creative theodicy strategy. It is simply the residual effect of his strategy. This conclusion would confirm Weber's
notion that ideas do have a somewhat independent force apart from economic
interests. Thus, Qohelet's conception of the deity is produced by economic and
ideal interests, not one or the other alone. It is the interaction between these
two realms that best explains the matrix of his conceptualization.

Because Qohelet essentially denies God's benevolence, he is forced to compensate by accentuating one or more of the other components of the trilemma.
Thus, he is pushed into accentuating God's sovereignty or omnipotence and
omniscience. In fact, God becomes so sovereign in Qohelet that there is little
place for human agency, except for accepting God's gift of the possibility of the
carpe diem ethic (this actually creates tension with Qohelet's allusion to the
free-will strategy mentioned above). Several scholars have noted the strong

---

44. Colin Campbell, "Weber, Rationalisation, and Religious Evolution in the Modern Era," in *Theorising Religion: Classical and Contemporary Debates* (ed. James A. Beckford
and John Walliss; Aldershot: Ashgate, 2006), 28.
45. Gottwald, *Socio-Literary Introduction*, 582.

thread of determinism in the book, and this is a necessary effect of magnifying God's sovereignty.[46]

The dissolution of the theodicy problem, the implicit denial of God's justice, is a common strategy among the world religions. It might also be represented by Job, though more likely Job is not really denying God's justice but merely pushing it forward to a future time when God's plans will be revealed and will then seem reasonable—the theodicy deferred.[47] Weber comes close to viewing Job more in the former light, seeing the book as representing the dissolution of the theodicy problem and emphasizing how God's standards are depicted as far beyond the ken of mortals.[48] Weber compares Job's strategy to Calvin's doctrine of predestination and even to the fatalism in Islam. Essentially, with this strategy, whatever happens is God's will, and no humans dare challenge it. God's sovereignty is elevated to such an extent that human agency and its significance are greatly mitigated. But with Job, Calvin, and Islam, the justice of God is still essentially preserved, at least ostensibly, and God retains his benevolent character to a large degree. Qohelet pushes farther and abandons these sentiments.[49]

THE SOCIAL LOCATION OF THEODICY

Though Qohelet's dissolution of the theodicy problem appears to be a highly creative and intellectual endeavor that attempts to mitigate the stress created by the reality of human and natural evil and a traditionally beneficent and omnipotent deity, it is intricately connected to social interests and interacts dynamically with them. It has already been shown that Qohelet's pessimistic solution to the problem is closely connected with his retainer-class location. But it is also connected with the oppression of the Jews by the Ptolemies, and so one must view his strategy as complicated, just as his social location is complicated.

Several scholars, including Weber, have emphasized that theodicy is always a social phenomenon and is closely connected to social class conflict. Though theodicy appears to be a purely intellectual and transcendent endeavor, it is

---

46. See esp. Rudman, *Determinism in Ecclesiastes*, 33–69.

47. Green, "Theodicy," 435.

48. Weber, *Sociology of Religion*, 112, 142–43.

49. Drawing on the theory of Kenneth Burke, Douglas G. Lawrie distinguishes between Qohelet and Job: Qohelet generalizes despair as the common lot of humanity and as part of the natural world, which serves to attenuate it to some extent, while the book of Job particularizes Job's suffering as unnatural and places God as his opponent. This sets up an agonistic struggle that involves the hope that change will occur ("The Dialectical Grammar of Job and Qoheleth: A Burkean Analysis," *Scriptura* 66 [1998]: 217–34).

heavily ensconced in social interests and forces. In fact, the theodicy strategy of the German philosopher Leibniz, who actually coined the term, heavily reflects societal interests. He argued that our world is the best possible world and that the irregularities in it are there inherently and necessarily. God could do no better than the world that exists. Bryan Turner points out that Leibniz's particular theodicy strategy actually served to legitimize the status quo. "The notion of the 'best of all possible worlds' 'apparently satisfied the Queen of Prussia. Her serfs continued to suffer the evil, while she continued to enjoy the good, and it was comforting to be assured by a great philosopher that this was just and right.'"[50]

From a sociological perspective, Weber sees two kinds of theodicy: the theodicy of fortune and that of misfortune.[51] Theodicy works in different ways for different strata, depending on their location. Those oppressed want to understand why God is allowing them to suffer in view of their superiors' apparent comfortable situation. Those in power are not content simply to have their wealth and privileges. They want to feel that they deserve such privileges, that they are superior to those who do not have these things, that is, anthropodicy.[52]

These theodicy types connect with Nietzsche's theorization about the birth of the concepts of good and evil.[53] Nietzsche essentially sees these concepts as constituting class ideology. Those with power describe their own lifestyle and advantages as noble, just, and good, and those they dominate as liars, thieves, and evil. Thus, the elite often believe that their advantages actually stem from

---

50. Turner, *For Weber*, 152, citing Bertrand Russell, *History of Western Philosophy* (London: G. Allen & Unwin, 1945), 613. Cf. Voltaire's *Candide*, a short novel that delightfully parodies Leibniz's theodicy and deconstructs the Optimist philosophy (*Candide or Optimism* [trans. Robert M. Adams; Norton Critical Editions; New York: Norton, 1966]). For an introduction to the novel, see Thomas Walsh, introduction to *Readings on Candide* (ed. Thomas Walsh; Literary Companion; San Diego: Greenhaven, 2001), 9–31. In this anthology, several scholars argue that Voltaire's novel, though it critiques optimism, never embraces pessimism but a sort of realism that acknowledges that all is not as it should be in the world: in *Readings on Candide,* see Virgil W. Topazio, "Voltaire's Attack on Optimism Has a Humanitarian Goal," 47–55, esp. 47; Hayda Mason, "Using Characters to Disprove Optimism," 39–46, esp. 35, 46; William F. Bottiglia, "A Garden of Hope," 81–87.

51. Weber, *Sociology of Religion*, 107; Swedberg, "Theodicy," 274; cf. P. Berger, *Sacred Canopy*, 59; see Walter Brueggemann, "Theodicy in a Social Dimension," *JSOT* 33 (1985): 6–7.

52. Robert Nozick represents a modern example of the theodicy of fortune. A champion of libertarianism, he argues that the amassing of wealth is not unjust if it violates no one else's rights (*Anarchy, State, and Utopia* [New York: Basic Books, 1972], esp. 160–64, 232–75).

53. Friedrich Nietzsche, *On the Genealogy of Morals* (trans. Horace B. Samuel; Barnes & Noble Library of Essential Reading; New York: Barnes & Noble, 2006), 5–9.

the gods and that they constitute their blessings on them. This rings true for the Hebrew Bible, where wealth and prosperity are certainly connected with righteousness and piety. Of course, Nietzsche argues that eventually the Jews and Christians, as they became subjugated to the empires, turned this conceptuality upside down, so that the good became the oppressed, the poor, and the bad became the oppressor, the aristocrats. This is his famous notion of *ressentiment*, that the poor resented their oppressors, so they turned them into the bad guys. Of course, Nietzsche sees this as a terrible turn, and he wants a return to the noble, Greco-Roman values. B. Turner aptly summarizes Nietzsche's thesis:

> What we conventionally regard as moral evil is in fact merely an account of the world from the point of view of the powerless. There is, in this sense, not one problem of theodicy, but two. Aristocratic conceptions of virtue and evil are totally incompatible with slave moralities. While Nietzsche does not explicitly state his argument in these terms, in practice, he implies that the theodicy of the poor acts simultaneously as a critique of power and as a compensation for their powerlessness.[54]

Weber actually adapts Nietzsche's conception of *ressentiment* in his notion of the Jews as pariah people.[55] He argues that the Jews after the exile were converted into an oppressed people, and, thus, into a religious and ethnic sect instead of being an independent nation as they had been before the exile. As subjugated people, they turned inward and defined themselves ethnically rather than politically. Their kosher dietary laws and notions of purity served essentially as defense mechanisms to retreat into themselves and preserve their identity over against the pagan world. They created suffering and eschatological theodicy strategies whereby they explained their oppression as due to their sins or a testing of their faith, and they yearned for Yahweh someday to deliver them from their oppressors and to vindicate them. Their oppressors, thus, were the evil and wicked ones. They were the righteous who held stubbornly to the hope of Yahweh's eventual vindication of them as his holy people.

Thus, Weber's notion of theodicy in general, and in particular with ancient Israel, is intricately connected with class interests. Turner aptly states this: "When Weber goes on to formulate the relationships between theodicies and class privileges, he comes very close to treating theodicy as the ideological expression of class interest."[56]

---

54. Turner, *For Weber*, 157.
55. Turner notes that both Nietzsche and Weber essentially reduce theodicy to class psychology (*For Weber*, 159).
56. Turner, *For Weber*, 149.

The deep social dimensions of theodicy are emphasized also by Brueggemann in connection with ancient Israel.[57] He essentially argues that while most Hebrew Bible scholars view theodicy as merely a theological and intellectual phenomenon, it is saturated with social concerns. He points out that the evil that is being explained in Hebrew Bible theodicies is actually social evil, fundamentally.[58] In his recapitulation of Peter Berger's notion of theodicy, he puts it this way, "To some extent theodicy, then, exists to rationalize and make things palatable."[59] Reflecting Robert Merton's analysis of anomie, he presents the main thesis of the article: "Every theodicy settlement (including its religious articulation) is in some sense the special pleading of a vested interest. . . . There is no theodicy that appeals to divine legitimacy that is not also an earthly arrangement to some extent contrived to serve special interests."[60]

Qohelet's theodicy strategy, though ostensibly radical, is just as conservative as that of traditional wisdom and ultimately serves to legitimize the status quo. While his references to an ethically neutral category of those who are "pleasing to him" (2:26) and those who are not seems to reflect a sensitivity to God's apparently incomprehensible standard of judgment, Qohelet's resolution of this problem serves to legitimize the current political arrangements. His solution basically says that the way things are is the way God wants them. Brueggemann says, "It is the case that the deed-consequence construct as a system of social rewards and punishments is not ordained in the cosmic ordering of things, but is a social construction to maintain certain disproportions."[61] When Qohelet reconfigures this doctrine, the result amounts to the same thing.

Qohelet actually represents a continuation of the "good"-equals-noble perspective of Nietzsche. According to Qohelet, the wealthy and blessed are still God's favorites, while the poor and disadvantaged must somehow be to blame. Though Qohelet bemoans the declassed nobleman of 6:1–2, no doubt he would have to conclude that that person must not have been one of God's favorites. If Lauha's interpretation of this passage is correct, then this text

---

57. Bruggemann, "Theodicy," 3–25.

58. Ibid., 5. For criticism of the social aspects of traditional theodicies, see Riffay Hassan, "Feminist Theology as a Means of Combating Injustice toward Women in Muslim Communities and Culture," in *Evil and the Response of World Religion* (ed. William Cenkner; St. Paul, Minn.: Paragon House, 1997), 80–95; and, in the same volume, Mary Ann Stenger, "The Ambiguity of the Symbol of the Cross: Legitimating and Overcoming Evil," 56–69; Peter C. Phan, "Prophecy and Contemplation: The Language of Liberation Theology against Evil," 183–98; and Anthony J. Guerra, "The Unification Understanding of the Problem of Evil," 199–209.

59. Brueggemann, "Theodicy," 6.

60. Ibid., 7.

61. Ibid., 8–9.

essentially legitimizes the Ptolemaic regime because it would be responsible for the nobleman being murdered and his property being given to a Greek official ("stranger").[62] Qohelet views the incident, though, as essentially an act of God. Thus, there is a tension in Qohelet when he laments the oppressive acts of the Ptolemies, yet ultimately he must see these as God's will, since the deity is in control of all events. Though he speaks of injustice in the land and judgment of righteous and wicked (3:16), this never leads to the positing of some eschatological kingdom of God where all injustices will be righted. The ambiguity essentially further legitimizes the status quo, even under the Ptolemies.

The ambivalent position of Qohelet can be explained only as due to his own complicated social location as teacher of governmental officials under foreign hegemony. Of course, Qohelet himself must be among those "who please him" because he apparently still has a job and enough privileges and comforts to issue his carpe diem ethic sincerely.[63] Certainly, he views himself as able to take advantage of the very carpe diem ethic he counsels or else become guilty of hypocrisy or bad faith. All of this is a result of Qohelet's own social position of being very close to power and privilege, though very aware of the oppression of his own people. But his closeness to power tips the scale on the side of valuing the preservation of the status quo, even if it is not ideal. Qohelet does not radically critique the status quo because he finds it worth preserving based on the advantages it brings him personally.

In comparison with Hinduism and karma, one can see that Qohelet's solution is constrained and weakened by the fact that the Jews of his time did not contemplate a belief, or a very developed belief, in life after death. This confined retribution to this life only, which made it more vulnerable to skepticism than the doctrine of karma.

Ironically Qohelet's theodicy strategy also serves to legitimize the Jew's colonialization by the Greeks. It must be God's will! So, Qohelet's resignation to the current inferior position of the Jews during the Ptolemaic period as part of God's inscrutable plans is not necessarily in his or his people's best interest. It removes the possibility of revolt or contestation. It only makes the Jews more pliable in the hands of the Ptolemies. It, in fact, ultimately serves their interests.

QOHELET'S NON-SALVIFIC RELIGIOUS PERSPECTIVE

Though Qohelet lived in postexilic times and, thus, according to Weber's general thesis, should exude resentment or a misfortune theodicy of the suffering that the Jews sustained, he does not. For example, consider 4:1: "Again

---

62. Lauha, "Verhältnis zur Geschichte," 400.
63. Contra Fox, *Rereading of Ecclesiastes*, 191.

I saw all the oppressions that are practiced under the sun. Look, the tears of the oppressed—with no one to comfort them! On the side of the oppressors there was power—with no one to comfort them." It is hard to imagine a Jew who could compose these words. The lack of any reference to God, who could redress this situation, is indeed shocking. Perhaps this is due to Qohelet's book belonging to the wisdom literature, which does not treat national issues. But even on the individual level, there really is nothing to be saved from in Qohelet. There is salvation of a sort with God's gift of the possibility of the carpe diem ethic. But it is a stretch to call this salvific. Rather, with Qohelet, one's main task is to learn to avoid angering or irritating the deity. Thus, one might call it a negative type of salvation: being cautious before the deity to avoid punishment. But one is largely on one's own for surviving the world.

Though Qohelet is polemical toward traditional wisdom, both share the same worldview, which one could label as scribal, politically conservative, and constituting a professional ethic. Because of this, the religious ethos expressed in the wisdom literature appears closer to Confucianism than to normative Judaism.[64] This is because Confucianism was originally a bureaucratic or administrative religion. In fact, Weber compares the scribes of Confucianism with those of the ancient Near East:

Confucianism is quite explicitly the ethic of a particular social class or, more correctly, a systematization of rules of etiquette appropriate to an elite class the members of which have undergone literary training. The situation was not different in the ancient Levant and Egypt, so far as is known. There the intellectualism of the scribes, insofar as it led to ethical and religious reflection, belonged entirely to the type of intellectualism that is sometimes apolitical and always aristocratic and anti-plebian.[65]

With Confucianism there is an emphasis on stability, loyalty, and an orderly cosmos. Honor is a key to understanding the guild and its religion. This is strikingly similar to the Israelite and ancient Near Eastern wisdom literatures. The main difference between Israelite wisdom and Confucianism is the ancestor worship or focus on familial piety. With the Jewish faith, allegiance to Yahweh eclipsed any reverence of parents or ancestors.

This may explain why wisdom literature is often connected with creation theology rather than with salvation history. With this view, wisdom's God is often depicted as a creator deity who maintains the cosmic order.[66] Wisdom, then, is represented as the attempt to align oneself with this order and achieve

---

64. For a good summary of Weber's discussion of Confucianism, see Bendix, *Max Weber*, 98–141; John Love, "Max Weber's Orient," in *The Cambridge Companion to Weber* (ed. Stephen Turner; Cambridge: Cambridge University Press, 2000), 173–79.

65. Weber, *Sociology of Religion*, 127.

66. E.g., Crenshaw, *Old Testament Wisdom*, 18–19.

success in daily life. Further, though it may seem that Qohelet does not ostensibly see an orderly cosmos, the idea is hidden under the façade of his skepticism about the doctrine of retribution *as traditionally conceived*. Though with Qohelet the doctrine has become ambiguous and steeped in mystery, it does imply a divine order behind it that humans cannot penetrate. Thus, Qohelet does ultimately still believe in an orderly cosmos, similarly to Confucianism and even to the concept of *maat* in Egyptian literature, though it may not be apparent.

Even with its emphasis on creation theology, traditional wisdom would certainly be compatible with a savior deity. The lack of references to salvation history in wisdom literature can be explained largely by the genre's focus on the individual's success. But Qohelet is another matter. His God is certainly a creator God and not a savior. Because God's standards of judgment are beyond the ken of mortals, they would apply to national affairs as well as individual ones. God might deliver a nation or not, but predicting it would be impossible. Thus, based on Qohelet's view of the deity, his religious views are not salvific in any real sense, and this makes his worldview closer to that of Confucianism than traditional wisdom is. Though Qohelet is a member of a subjugated, colonized nation and one would therefore expect him to adopt utopian or apocalyptic tendencies, as a member of the indigenous Jewish aristocracy he chooses to reject these possibilities and to adopt a theodicy strategy that transforms the typical savior deity into the creator God or Master of the Universe in order to adapt to the harsh realities.[67]

Qohelet's transformation of the Jewish deity into an essentially amoral despot is a strategy typical of intellectuals. It is one that few nonintellectuals or the masses would find comforting or helpful.[68] Again, this makes sense with Qohelet's intended audience: mature, elite, scribal apprentices who would find such a solution very helpful in their own future vocations as governmental officials who would be constantly exposed to oppressive measures by the Ptolemies against their own people. Qohelet's theodicy strategy would then have been to make these young scribes comfortable in their complicated roles as

---

67. The book of Job also represents this view of the deity, though God seems more personable in the epilogue. Mark Hamilton detects hints of salvific hope for the upper classes in Job, but this appears strained ("Elite Lives: Job 29–31 and Traditional Authority," *JSOT* 32 [2007]: 69, 87).

68. Crenshaw argues that Qohelet's skepticism is more at home among the masses than among the official religionists, but, as has been discussed already, he fails to recognize that Qohelet's skepticism is of a different nature than that of the masses and that Qohelet by definition operates within the official sphere. He reacts against it, while simultaneously being a part of it. Deviant masses are by definition outside it ("Popular Questioning," 380–95).

bureaucrats who found themselves working for the ultimate good of the Ptolemies, though providing services for their own people and being sympathetic to their plight. Often among the masses magic and personal gods are popular.[69] The lower classes have little interest in the rational theodicy strategies of intellectuals that involve a cosmic order or highly transcendent deity.[70] Moreover, Qohelet's lack of loving faith in his deity and his God's detached demeanor would not sit well with the masses. Qohelet's type of highly rational faith is an option primarily for intellectuals, not the people in general, particularly, the lower class.

Thus, in summary, Qohelet represents a rational, intellectual response to the problem of theodicy. He attempts to solve it by dissolving it, by being honest about God's lack of benevolence (and implicit justice). He is also very candid about evil and suffering in the world, even perhaps exaggerating it. He compensates for this by exaggerating God's omnipotence and omniscience, and this leads to an emphasis on God's sovereignty and a strong notion of divine determinism and fatalism with its concomitant lack of human freedom or the significance of human agency. Though Qohelet's dissolution represents a rational strategy to mitigate the tension of the theodicy problem, as shall been seen, his negative assessment of human wisdom and his carpe diem ethic actually represent a turn toward nonrationality (or irrationality) or anti-intellectualism.

QOHELET'S MITIGATION OF COGNITIVE DISSONANCE

The final section of this chapter will focus on how the social-psychological theory of cognitive dissonance is illuminative for understanding how the book of Qohelet functioned positively and creatively to help its audience deal with the troubling times of the Ptolemaic period. The notion of cognitive dissonance began with Leon Festinger in the 1950s.[71] Dissonance is an uncomfortable feeling caused by holding two contradictory ideas simultaneously. The "ideas" or "cognitions" may involve beliefs, attitudes, and/or behaviors. The theory of cognitive dissonance proposes that people will attempt to reduce this dissonance by either changing their attitudes, beliefs, and behaviors or by rationalizing them. The theory also stipulates that the more valued the cognition, the less likely will the person be to change it. In addition, the more closely one is connected to persons who believe the same cognition, the easier one can maintain the belief. This is because remaining within this network will aid in

---

69. See Weber, *Sociology of Religion*, 108–9.
70. Ibid., 103.
71. For a good introduction to this theory, see Carroll, *When Prophecy Failed*, 87–110; see also idem, "Dissonance Theory," 135–51.

preventing dissonant information from getting to the person and in persuading the person of the credibility of the belief. Cognitive dissonance theory is one of the most influential theories ever formulated in social psychology.

An example of cognitive dissonance would be a smoker who knows that smoking will eventually kill him. This dissonance can be reduced in a number of ways. He can deny that the medical facts about lung cancer are true. He can be further aided by studies done by the tobacco industry that counter much of the factual information that the medical association has promulgated. Of course, doing this would be difficult since in Western societies the medical facts have been circulated so widely and their validity is credibly presented. Another possibility is to quit smoking, actually to change the risky behavior one is engaged in. This is what most smokers eventually do. They change their behavior and, thus, remove the dissonance. Others who find quitting very difficult can rationalize or justify it. When asked why they do not quit, often smokers will rebut, "You gotta die of something." Of course, this is a true statement, but one can see how it is being used to mitigate the dissonance. This excuse essentially trivializes death and even human existence to some extent so that the smokers do not feel guilty essentially killing themselves prematurely. Others rationalize by saying that if they quit smoking, they would gain weight, which would also be harmful physically. But, again, one can see how they are trying to avoid the problem. Finally, some are honest about the harmful effects of smoking, but they rationalize and claim they are so addicted that they cannot quit. Or they say that they enjoy smoking so much that it is worth the risk.

Another facet of rationalizing smoking is that smokers often congregate with other smokers. This grouping of smokers helps them feel more comfortable about their habit and further reduces the dissonance they feel. For many smokers, smoking is such a significant part of their identity and offers such pleasure that they refuse to stop. They are then compelled to rationalize the dissonance they feel in knowing that they are driving themselves to an early grave.

The biblical scholar who has applied cognitive dissonance theory to the Hebrew Bible most successfully is the Irishman Robert Carroll. Carroll is a biblical sociologist who has used social theory in analyzing biblical texts and topics but has been more wary and cautious than most. He often charges other biblical sociologists with being anachronistic with their use of theory to interpret biblical phenomena.[72] Carroll is known for his work on sociologi-

---

72. See Robert P. Carroll, "Prophecy and Society," in *The World of Ancient Israel: Sociological, Anthropological and Political Perspectives. Essays by Members of the Society for Old Testament Study* (ed. Ronald E. Clements; paperback ed.; Cambridge: Cambridge University Press, 1991), 203–25.

cal approaches to prophecy. His *When Prophecy Failed* is one of the earliest and most successful attempts to apply social theory to the Hebrew Bible.[73] He specifically applies cognitive dissonance theory to failed prophecy in ancient Israel. According to Carroll, when prophets made predictions that failed to materialize, instead of the rejection of the prophecy, often it was hermeneutically explained away or reinterpreted so that the dissonance is reduced. Failed prophecy was a dominant concern in postexilic times, when the ascendency of Judah and its predicted prosperity never materialized.

A specific example is provided by Zechariah.[74] Both Haggai and Zechariah put their hopes in Zerubbabel becoming the new messianic king, purportedly a Davidide who would overthrow the world powers like the Persians and make Judah preeminent. Obviously, however, this failed to materialize. An example of how this was handled is found in Zech 6:11–14. Here two crowns are mentioned, which are to be placed on Joshua the high priest. Originally, Carroll hypothesizes, the two crowns were for both Zerubbabel and Joshua, but Zerubbabel's name has been removed because he failed to become the new founder of the Davidic dynasty.[75] This is a classic example of the reduction of cognitive dissonance. The prediction of Zerubbabel as the next messianic king is simply transferred to the high priest alone, and the dissonance is thereby largely avoided.

Carroll also reinterprets Paul Hanson's theory of the rise of apocalyptic. Hanson argues that early apocalyptic texts come from oppressed non-Zadokite priests who project a utopian worldview to transcend imaginatively their miserable situation.[76] According to Hanson, the failure of earlier prophecies of a period of peace and prosperity essentially is resolved by denying the failure and projecting the fulfillment farther into the future, thus delaying the problem. Carroll then argues, "*With its roots in prophecy, apocalyptic became the resolution of the dissonance caused by the lack of fulfillment of prophecy in the early post-exilic period*" (emphasis in original).[77]

Carroll's application of cognitive dissonance theory to biblical prophecy is significant and persuasive. The general theory and especially his integration of

---

73. Cyril S. Rodd praises Carroll's work more than the other sociological approaches he reviews, but ultimately he does not think that the sociological approach is legitimate for ancient texts since the theories cannot be tested ("On Applying a Sociological Theory to Biblical Studies," in *Social-Scientific Old Testament Criticism* [ed. David J. Chalcraft; Biblical Seminar 47; Sheffield: Sheffield Academic Press, 1997], 22–33, esp. 30–33; repr. from *JSOT* 19 [1981]: 95–106).

74. Carroll, *When Prophecy Failed*, 157–83.

75. Cf. Paul L. Redditt, "Zerubbabel, Joshua, and the Night Visions of Zechariah," *CBQ* 54 (1992): 257.

76. See Hanson, *Dawn of Apocalyptic*, 211–18, 282, 408–9.

77. Carroll, *When Prophecy Failed*, 205.

it with Hanson's theorization of early apocalyptic are especially significant for Qohelet. A few scholars have argued that Qohelet is anti-apocalyptic—or, perhaps better phrased, anti-eschatological—as has been seen. For Qohelet "there is nothing new under the sun," and that is a direct polemic against proto-apocalyptic Isaiah's references to a new thing God will be doing (43:19). This statement points to Qohelet's attempt to challenge the prevailing utopian means of dissolving the dissonance created by failed prophecy. Qohelet is essentially anti-utopian.[78]

It must be admitted, however, that eschatological prophecy is not the main polemic of Qohelet. Rather, as we have mentioned often, Qohelet's polemical aim is directed at the wisdom tradition. Yet the failures of the wisdom tradition are related to the failure of prophecy in postexilic times. The doctrine of retribution is essentially the eschatological principle applied to mundane affairs primarily in the present. In other words, the future retribution applied on a national level in eschatological prophecy is intricately related to the daily retribution applied to the individual in the wisdom tradition. The differences are the time element (primarily present versus future) and the scope (the individual versus the nation).

Thus, Qohelet's polemic is aimed not specifically at failed prophecy but at failed mundane retribution. As has been seen, the doctrine of retribution was the ancient principle of cause and effect. It was almost universally held in the ancient world and is even popular among religious adherents today. But it also reflects the essentially retributive character of the Jewish faith, especially after the exile, when the Jews became a pariah people, according to Weber, and came to see their deity in terms of his eventual retribution against those who oppressed them. The retributive dimension of the Jewish faith had become so paramount that questioning it was an absolute impossibility.

This reality is demonstrated by the skeptical tradition of the wisdom tradition. Both Job and Qohelet question the doctrine of retribution, but they actually never totally abandon it because this would be largely unthinkable. Job, as he debates his friends, certainly questions the doctrine and even goes so far as to question God's justice. But the doctrine is essentially modified and reformulated, not totally abandoned. In the epilogue, the doctrine of retribution is reinstated in that Job receives back essentially all he had lost when God allowed the Satan to take away his possessions and family. However, the doctrine is not the same; now the doctrine includes the notion that one's suffering may be simply a test or contest to see if one will remain faithful. If one

---

78. J. Gerald Janzen argues that Qohelet was a disillusioned eschatologist who had once swallowed apocalyptic scenarios "hook, line, and sinker" but found the oppressiveness of foreign rule too real to deny ("Qohelet on Life 'Under the Sun,'" *CBQ* 70 [2008]: 465–83, esp. 479–80).

perseveres and overcomes the challenge, one will be returned to one's previous status. Thus, the doctrine survives, but it is modified, expanded, and made more flexible.

The same occurs in Qohelet. When faced with the apparent failure of the doctrine to be actuated in real life, he does not resort to rejecting it, but instead modifies it, a type of rationalization like that of the smokers described above. When Qohelet broadens and makes ambiguous the notion of God's judgment, which we have discussed extensively, he is doing just that. God is still retributive, but he does it in his own way and by his own standards.

As already shown, Qohelet creates a new ethical category (God-fearing) that coincides with this broadening of God's justice. Thus, when Qohelet questions the doctrine of retribution, he is not completely rejecting it. Rather his skepticism serves to enable him to reformulate the doctrine so that whatever happens, the doctrine still holds true. In other words, he makes it so vague and flexible, that whatever happens, it is God's will and his justice.

This means that Qohelet's modification of the doctrine of retribution is a remarkable feat of mitigating cognitive dissonance. Its strength is that Qohelet can be honest about the fact that the traditional way the doctrine is formulated is not always actualized. But Qohelet's modification also preserves the doctrine in a new form and, thus, technically preserves God's "integrity" and "justice," though these concepts become heavily watered down. Thus, Qohelet can essentially "have his cake and eat it too." Qohelet's reduction of the dissonance is essentially fail-proof. No matter what happens and what God does (its corollary), it is still God working his retribution his own way.

Qohelet's mitigation is not applicable only to the present but to the future as well. This is not true for the attempts to rationalize failed prophecy by hermeneutically explaining it away. Often these interpretations simply postpone the problem into the future, and the problem will eventually need further postponement or rationalization. Qohelet's solution simply denies the relevance of the future. With Qohelet, there are no guarantees of God's redemption of his people, only the security in knowing God is in control and sovereign. The future is open, but no promises are guaranteed. Essentially, Qohelet's solution can never be falsified, unlike problematic prophecies. Even ambiguous prophecies must eventually "pay the piper," when even their vaguest statements fail to materialize. Qohelet, thus, represents the quintessential reduction of cognitive dissonance and demonstrates his intellectual creativity in dealing with stressful times for his guild and perhaps for some beyond it.

But as mentioned earlier, Qohelet's rational solution to the problem of dissonance associated with the doctrine of retribution may be close to perfect, but this perfection may point to its ultimate flaw because of the trade-off that it in fact questions God's justice, though not directly. Moreover, the impersonal

God that Qohelet portrays was unlikely to have been very appealing to most religious persons of his day.

Conclusion

Qohelet resolves the problem of theodicy by essentially dissolving it. Like Job, Qohelet portrays God's standards of judgment as beyond the ken of mortal comprehension. Who are mortals to question God's allowance of suffering if God is the sovereign of the universe? But this amounts to questioning God's omnibenevolence and, implicitly, divine justice, which results in Qohelet's conception of God becoming impersonal and capricious, which marks his solution as very intellectualistic. Qohelet's resolution provides not just a theodicy of misfortune to explain the oppression of his people but also of fortune, his own. The privileged strata need to see themselves as deserving of their advantages. This, of course, essentially legitimizes the status quo. The reality is that any theodicy strategy is complicit in social interests.

But Qohelet's resolution of the theodicy problem also relates to his reduction of cognitive dissonance felt by the failure of the doctrine of retribution actually to materialize during his time. Both the book of Job and the book of Qohelet modify the doctrine instead of completely rejecting it, since it is such a basic assumption of the ancient world. But Qohelet goes further than Job by not guaranteeing the eventual rewarding of pious behavior, which makes Qohelet's approach fail-proof and quite rationally consistent. Qohelet provides no certain promise of reward for any style of behavior. He does, however, provide wise counsel that may increase one's chances of good success, such as living cautiously (God-fearing), moderately, and enjoying the present instead of depending on long-term possibilities. But this strategy would not have been very appealing to the masses, who would have rejected his capricious deity. Thus, with every theodicy solution there is a trade-off.

7

QOHELET'S IRRATIONAL RESPONSE
TO THE (OVER-)RATIONALIZATION
OF TRADITIONAL WISDOM

In this chapter, I treat Qohelet's polemic against the wisdom tradition, especially his skepticism about the doctrine of retribution, from a sociological perspective. Weber's notion of rationalization and over-rationalization will be employed to explain Qohelet's endeavor. This approach will provide a "big picture" perspective that will enable the modern interpreter better to understand the nature of Qohelet's polemic and to connect it with modern developments. Thus it will provide a helpful hermeneutical perspective, as well as a sociological one.

The concept of rationalization is perhaps the most important one that Weber utilized in his analysis of societies and religions.[1] It is found as a constant thread throughout his works.[2] It can be defined as the process whereby reason and the intellect are increasingly brought to bear on a particular social facet such as economics, law, or religion. It is related to the notion of rationality, which is the human need for calculability, meaning, and order, a need that flies in the face of the essential irrationality of the world and its largely incalculable character.[3] It is opposed to irrationality or lack of reason, as expressed in heightened emotions or its supreme form: sexual drive. Weber constantly invokes this dichotomy to characterize the development of religions, law, poli-

---

1. For a succinct description of rationalization and irrationality, see Ann Swidler, foreword to Max Weber, *The Sociology of Religion* (trans. Ephraim Fischoff; paperback ed.; Boston: Beacon, 1991, xiv–xvii. On defining the irrational, see Swedberg, *Max Weber Dictionary*, 133, s.v. "Irrationality (*Irrationalität*)."

2. Hiroshi Orihara argues that Weber uses a four-stage rationalization grid of degrees of human social organization throughout the long compositional history of *Economy and Society*. This is in contrast to scholars that deny the grid to certain textual layers ("Max Weber's 'Four-Stage Rationalization-Scale of Social Action and Order' in the 'Categories' and Its Significance to the 'Old Manuscript' of His 'Economy and Society': A Positive Critique of Wolfgang Schluchter," *Max Weber Studies* 8 [2008]: 141–62).

3. See John Elster, "Rationality, Economy, and Society," in *The Cambridge Companion to Weber* (ed. Stephen Turner; Cambridge: Cambridge University Press, 2000), 21–41.

tics, and other social processes. But Weber does not value one more than the other. He sees assets and liabilities with both. Weber understood that humans are essentially a combination of both aspects: cognitive and emotive. Certain forms of rationality, in fact, often contain irrational features.[4] Among humans, an eternal struggle between the sides exists.

THE STRUGGLE BETWEEN THE RATIONAL AND THE IRRATIONAL

One can say that this dichotomization involves the struggle for dominance of the human higher-level brain function over the lower-level reptilian brain. A human devoid of either side would be rather boring. Most would admit that a rational life without passion and emotion or moral sensitivity would not be worth living. It is no wonder, then, that Spock (as well as Data later) in *Star Trek* could not have been an intriguing character as a pure Vulcan (or cybernaut).[5] His human mother provided him with struggles one finds very human and inspiring. But a passionate cave man would be no fun either, constantly resorting to violence to solve any problems. The irrational side needs the rational for control, discipline, and cooperation. But the rational needs the irrational for a meaningful and interesting existence where values come to the fore. Karl Mannheim notes that

> the irrational is not always harmful but that, on the contrary, it is among the most valuable powers in man's possession when it acts as a driving force towards rational and objective ends or when it creates cultural values through sublimation, or when, as pure élan, it heightens the joy of living without breaking up the social order by lack of planning.[6]

Societies are the same. They are neither totally rational nor irrational, but are a blend of both that involves a perpetual give-and-take and back-and-forth struggle between the two.

---

4. E.g., Simon Locke shows that conspiracy theories are actually a type of secular theodicy that blame culture. He argues that they are certainly rational because they are a form of moral and mundane reasoning but are simultaneously irrational for obvious reasons ("Conspiracy Culture, Blame Culture, and Rationalization," *Sociological Review* 57 [2009]: 567–85).

5. On the many cultural references to the classics (e.g., Shakespeare and the Bible) in the television series, see Larry Kreitzer, "The Cultural Veneer of Star Trek," *Journal of Popular Culture* 30, no. 2 (1996): 1–28.

6. Karl Mannheim, *Man and Society in an Age of Reconstruction: Studies in Modern Social Structure* (trans. Edward Shils; New York: Harcourt Brace, 1940), 62–63.

Not just humans and societies fall prey to this dilemma. The world as a whole and nature contain both rational and irrational elements, order and chaos, with the latter predominant. Life itself is largely irrational; it does not come with any instructions, and it has its share of pain and suffering. But among societies, the rational has usually maintained the upper hand, and in modern society, rationalization has attempted, in fact, to eliminate the irrational, but to no avail. One of the best summaries of this process and Weber's response to it is by Alan Sica:

> Modern societies are forever striving to order what in its "natural" state is less ordered or even randomly occurring. Where people once noisily milled about, now they are put in rows or ranks of quiet obedience; where fiscal accounting was done from memory and rough approximation, now it is taken to the hundredth of one percentage point, or beyond; where music was the work of a single minstrel inventing melodies and lyrics as he strolled, now it requires an orchestra that plays perfectly in unison from a printed score, willful deviation from which is a cardinal sin. Weber realized that the organization of thought and action into regimented forms had virtually replaced religion as the unquestioned, motivating creed across much of "advanced civilization." And while he recognized in these developments admirable achievements, particularly in the production of material goods, he saw as well those seedbeds of pathology that affected individuals as much as the societies in which they struggled, vainly he thought, to maintain their individuality and freedom.[7]

Thus, Weber definitely saw a dark side to the increasing rationalization in human history and especially in the West, what he refers to as the disenchantment of the world. While he certainly saw the positive effects of the development of science and technology, he also saw a darker side where traditional values and conceptions have become uprooted. Weber became very pessimistic about the prospects of humanity in such a world.

Sica provides an interesting example of this dilemma with the fast food king McDonald's, which represents the "rationalization of restaurant work to a previously unknown extreme."[8] Sica points out, "By using an array of robots, computers, and associated equipment, the restaurant can guarantee delivery of an order within ninety seconds at rush hour, or forty-five seconds at calmer moments, in those sixty-four experimental outlets where the tech-

---

7. Alan Sica, "Rationalization and Culture," in *The Cambridge Companion to Weber* (ed. Stephen Turner; Cambridge: Cambridge University Press, 2000), 42. Sica demonstrates how Weber was conflicted about the irrational side of humanity, both professionally and personally. He usually suppressed it, preferring to focus on human rationality (*Weber, Irrationality, and Social Order* [Berkeley: University of California Press, 1988]).

8. Sica, "Rationalization and Culture," 43, citing George Ritzer, "The McDonaldization of Society," *Journal of American Culture* 6 (1983): 100–107.

nology is in place."[9] Some view this "McDonaldization" "as a form of cultural fascism, which implants corrosive behavior and demand patterns, especially among children, that would be the envy of any authoritarian regime, e.g., 'The benign nature of capitalist production portrayed by McDonaldland and Ronald McDonald is a cover for a far more savage reality.'"[10]

In 2004, a documentary came out called *Super Size Me*, produced by Morgan Spurlock, who also played the starring role. He consumed McDonald's food three times a day for a month. He gained almost twenty-five pounds, increased his cholesterol level, and developed fat on his liver. It took fourteen months for him to lose all the weight he had gained. The point of the film is to demonstrate that McDonald's profits while contributing to the poor health of its customers. McDonald's has responded recently to critics of its poor quality of food by providing more healthful options, especially for children. Of course, when these items do not sell well (e.g., the Asian Chicken Salad), they usually are dropped from the menu. Hamburgers and fries remain a major percentage of their profit. Of course, McDonald's is only one restaurant among hundreds in the fast food industry in the United States and the world. This industry has as a whole been subjected to criticism and largely blamed for the increased obesity in the United States, especially among children. Yet the fast food industry is not solely responsible. Parents and the entire U.S. culture are also to blame, with their demand for convenience and instant gratification. But all of these factors are simply indicative of the continued rationalization of Western culture.

Another example is the fitness and sports industry, in which the ideal body is nothing like that of the athletes of the past.[11] These industries attempt "to produce a perfect specimen impossible to better." One thinks of the recent Olympics with such swimmers as Michael Phelps with his eight gold medals and Dara Torres, the forty-one-year-old female swimmer who competed in her fifth Olympic Games. Reports have detailed how extensive Torres's regimen of exercise, massage, and diet is. The number of supplements she takes daily is unbelievable. Of course, no average person could afford her training costs, so she is dependent on numerous sponsors. With her heavy use of supplements, she has to be very careful which ones have been placed on the officially banned list of substances.[12] More recently, one can recall the banning of the type of

---

9. Sica, "Rationalization and Culture," 44.

10. Ibid., citing Michael Raphael, "Professor Argues McDonald's Brainwashes Youth," Associated Press (August 1, 1997) from State College, Pennsylvania.

11. Sica, "Rationalization and Culture," 45–46.

12. See Amanda Schafter, "Dara Torres Demystified: Do the Swimmer's 'Secrets to Success' Hold Up?" *Slate* (July 16, 2008): n.p., online at http://www.slate.com/id/2195473/pagenum/all/#p2 (accessed January 28, 2011).

swimsuit that Phelps used when he won his record number of gold medals. This obsession with the perfect body and game has driven modern athletes to such extreme measures.[13]

THE PROCESS OF RATIONALIZATION

It would be helpful at this point to look at examples of the process of rationalization that Weber studied. One is the rationalization of law.[14] Weber believes that the earliest laws were created by law prophets. When village leaders could not decide a legal case, they would turn to law prophets, who would receive an oracle that would decide the case (e.g., Deborah [Judg 4:4–5]). The use of the ordeal is another very primitive form of judicial trial (e.g., the bitter-water ordeal for adultery [Num 5]) . Though moderns would consider such a strategy largely irrational and involving the element of luck, it was rational for traditional societies because it allowed them to make decisions that appeared free of bias and interest. In addition, their techniques had a ritualized element (formal rationality) and had to be carried out perfectly, or else there would be a mistrial.

The next stage of rationalization involved legal notables who would decide cases; they would eventually become permanent officials. But what is characteristic of both of these primitive forms is that neither type of legality is oriented toward rules or norms or bound by them. Both of these forms also involved primarily what Weber calls substantive justice in contrast to formal justice. Substantive justice is where the particular case is most important, and the jurists have to use their own sense of justice in making decisions.

The next stage is the imposition of laws by secular and theocratic authorities. Laws imposed by the king are a well-known phenomenon. Their implementation also involved substantive justice, which could be arbitrary, with grace or harshness applied at the whim of the arbiter. In the West, the church began separating secular from sacred law, another form of rationalization. In

---

13. Haley C. Schwarz, Richelle L. Gairrett, Mara S. Aruguete, and Elizabeth S. Gold studied the body images and eating habits of female college students and found that perfectionistic athletes who participated in judged sports had higher risk for eating disorders ("Eating Attitudes, Body Dissatisfaction, and Perfectionism in Female College Athletes," *North American Journal of Psychology* 7 [2005]: 345–52). Male bodybuilders have higher rates of eating disorders than other athletic and nonathletic males because of body dissatisfaction (Gary S. Goldfield, Arthur G. Blouin, and D. Blake Woodside, "Body Image, Binge Eating, and Bulimia Nervosa in Male Bodybuilders," *Canadian Journal of Psychiatry* 51 [2006]: 160–68).

14. See Harold J. Berman and Charles J. Reid Jr., "Max Weber as Legal Historian," in *The Cambridge Companion to Weber* (ed. Stephen Turner; Cambridge: Cambridge University Press, 2000), 223–39; Bendix, *Max Weber*, 385–416; B. Turner, *For Weber*, 318–51.

both of these cases, norms and customs technically become laws because they could be enforced by the use of force, that is, the police. The last stage is the most rationalized. It involves "the systematic elaboration of law and professionalized administration of justice by persons who have received their legal training in a learned and formally logical manner."[15] Here lawmaking can become quite abstract and formal, where laws represent rules to which lawyers and jurists are bound. The general and typical become more important than the particular, and so legal precedence becomes dominant in legal decision making. Thus, there is a tendency for lawyers and jurists to peg or categorize individual cases so that the broader legal norms apply and the case is solved.

Formal rationality promotes a greater sense of justice based on formal procedures that apply to all indiscriminately, and there is no heavy hand of a king or nobleman. However, it often fails because the particular and unique features of a situation are often ignored, and substantive justice therefore does not occur.[16] When the judge and lawyer argue about a case in terms of semantics and what precedent applies, questions of fairness and substantive justice obviously recede. It seems more an academic game than an attempt to provide justice. The lawyer and judge seem to be totally unconcerned about how their legal casuistries actually affect the plaintiff.

The rationalization of law also relates to the rationalization of authority or domination (legitimatization).[17] Early forms of authority, which continue in forms today, include charismatic authority, where one follows a leader who has special abilities (divine inspiration, skilled warrior or diplomat, etc.).[18] Exam-

---

15. Bendix, *Max Weber*, 391.

16. Isher-Paul Sahni argues that, though ostensibly it may appear that Weber preferred formal rationality and its exemplar in Continental law, he actually was more impressed with the creativity and leeway that English law (Common Law) allows its judges. Sahni demonstrates that Weber's legal analytic categories are still valid and illuminating for today's world ("Max Weber's Sociology of Law: Judge as Mediator," *Journal of Classical Sociology* 9 [2009]: 209–33. DOI: 10.1177/1468795X09102123). Robert M. Marsh demonstrates that Weber's characterization of Chinese law as formally irrational is only partly correct ("Weber's Misunderstanding of Traditional Chinese Law," *American Journal of Sociology* 106 [2000]: 281–302).

17. See Swedberg, *Max Weber Dictionary*, 64–66, s.v., "Domination (*Herrshaft*)"; Peter Lassman, "The Rule of Man over Man: Politics, Power and Legitimation," in *The Cambridge Companion to Weber* (ed. Stephen Turner; Cambridge: Cambridge University Press, 2000), 83–98; Bendix, *Max Weber*, 285–457.

18. See Max Weber, "The Sociology of Charismatic Authority," in *From Max Weber: Essays in Sociology* (trans. and ed. Hans H. Gerth and C. Wright Mills; paperback ed.; New York: Oxford University Press, 1958), 245–52; Swedberg, *Max Weber Dictionary*, 31–33, s.v., "Charisma (*Charisma*)."

ples would be prophets or warlords. This type of leadership is usually viewed as temporary, and there is no inheritance of the position. But charismatic authority can be routinized, usually by followers or disciples, and become institutionalized.[19]

Another, more primitive form is traditional authority. This is considered more stable than charismatic authority. Often charismatic authority develops into the traditional type. This is referred to as the routinization of authority. Examples would be elders of a village or kings. Authority is often hereditary here, and one can speak of monarchic dynasties, noblemen, or patriarchs. The authority of the king is considered legitimate because of his power and ability to maintain peace. There are laws and tradition that curtail the power of the king, but he can often install his own laws and resist traditional norms.

The last form of rationalization of authority is known as legal domination. This is where laws are actually binding on everyone indiscriminately, and the authority of a leader is not based on charisma or personal power or lineage but resides in the position itself. Thus, the notion of the office as powerful and not the person occupying it becomes sacrosanct.

With this form of domination, bureaucracies develop. Weber viewed this as a necessary development superior to the older forms of domination, but he is famous for his criticisms of this form.[20] Bureaucracies represent the age of the expert, where anyone can obtain a position with a degree and by passing an examination, not through one's lineage or favors. Thus, there can be a very democratic and egalitarian character to bureaucracies. The problem is that, if left unchecked, bureaucracies can become very powerful and imper-

---

19. S. N. Eisenstadt explains that, while charismatic authority can certainly have a destabilizing, destructive character, it is also necessary for the creation and maintenance of institutions (introduction to *Max Weber on Charisma and Institution Building: Selected Papers* [ed. S. N. Eisenstadt; Heritage of Sociology; Chicago: University of Chicago Press, 1968], ix–lvi). Pierluigi Piovanelli uses neo-Weberian theories, including New Leadership approaches, to nuance Jesus' charismatic authority so as to include his clear articulation of a vision and an ability to convince followers to invest themselves in it. He shifts the focus from Jesus' personal charismatic features to his attractiveness to followers ("Jesus' Charismatic Authority: On the Historical Applicability of a Sociological Model," *JAAR* 73 [2005]: 395–427). Similarly, Jonathan E. Brockopp, who nuances Weber, shows how the charisma of Muhammad is routinized to include not just marginalized individuals, such as Sufis, but also legal scholars. This is achieved by the composition of hagiographies about these scholars ("Theorizing Charismatic Authority in Early Islamic Law," *Comparative Islamic Studies* 1 [2005]: 129–58) .

20. See Swedberg, *Max Weber Dictionary*, 18–21, s.v. "Bureaucracy (*Bürokratie*)"; Weber, "Bureaucracy," in *From Max Weber: Essays in Sociology* (trans. and ed. Hans H. Gerth and C. Wright Mills; paperback ed.; New York: Oxford University Press, 1958), 196–244.

sonal. Bureaucracies can begin to serve their own interests and protect their own prerogatives and, in the end, become as despotic as the more primitive forms of authority. But in their attempt to eliminate every passion and emotion from decision making, bureaucracies can be quite efficient in what they do and can improve calculability because the same rules and laws apply to all people, whether powerful or not.

But this also means that bureaucracies tend to be cold in their treatment of citizens. Their high level of formal rationality means that citizens often perceive bureaucrats as obstacles to their own interests. They often are callous about unique circumstances in a particular case. Bureaucrats are by nature rule oriented. Many today complain about bureaucratic "red tape" and having to "jump through the hoops" to get benefits. Thus, citizens often perceive bureaucracies as actually inefficient. Most people do not realize that bureaucracies are intricately connected with the development of capitalism and democratic governments. Bureaucracies are essentially a necessary evil that replaces the earlier personal fiefdoms which ran the patrimonial monarchies. But Weber predicted that socialistic governments could also not avoid the development of bureaucracies, and of course he has been proven right. Again, all of this discussion is pertinent because it shows that rationalization always has positive and negative features.

THE RATIONALIZATION OF RELIGION

Rationalization has had perhaps the most devastating effects for religion and ethics. For modernists, rationalization refers to the increasing disenchantment or secularization of the world. In today's world, the safety, comfort, order, and meaning that religion used to supply no longer apply. This has thrown modern humanity into a state of frenzy, where people scramble to adjust to a life without religion that sometimes seems chaotic. Moderns are forced to create their own order, norms, and values. Modern ethics become relative and without mooring. The new "order" created by positivistic science is neither comfortable nor helpful. The postmodern movement is in many ways a negative reaction to this, just as nineteenth-century Romanticism was a response to an earlier world order.

It is ironic that the secularization and rationalization of the West gained critical mass with the Reformation. The break away from Roman Catholicism was the first step in this process. The questioning of the church's authority essentially opened Pandora's box and invigorated the process of religious and economic rationalization. Weber argues that Calvin's doctrine of predestination actually helped propel capitalism along a fast track.[21] The asceticism that

---

21. See Weber, "The Protestant Sects and the Spirit of Capitalism," in *From Max Weber: Essays in Sociology* (ed. and trans. Hans H. Gerth and C. Wright Mills; paperback

emerged from his doctrine, in which adherents sought out the "proof" of their election through good works, holy industriousness, and intense frugality, catapulted capitalism in a way never before seen. Thus, the calculating dimension of capitalism and the emphasis on saving and investments actually go back to religious roots. The "Protestant Work Ethic" was born, and capitalism began to flourish, and the "spirit of capitalism" propelled it. Ironically, this religious development ultimately led to further secularization of Western capitalist nations. The ingenuity and ascetic goal of "mastery of the world" by the early Protestants, in the end, undermined their own fervently religious faith. The calculating rational character of early capitalism eventually turns this rationalization against its own religious origins.

Rationalization also is intricately connected with the development of science and technology in the Western capitalistic milieu. Thus, ironically, secularism has religious roots. All of this is actually the normal evolution of the process of rationalization, but it has developed most rapidly and fully in the West. The distinctive economic and religious character of the Orient has slowed the process down, but it is inevitable.[22] The world is becoming increasingly secularized, though religion certainly has not been eliminated.[23] However, its significance has been mitigated.

---

ed.; New York: Oxford University Press, 1958), 302–22; Alastair Hamilton, "Max Weber's *Protestant Ethic and the Spirit of Capitalism*," in *The Cambridge Companion to Weber* (ed. Stephen Turner; Cambridge: Cambridge University Press, 2000), 151–71; Swedberg, *Max Weber Dictionary*, 213–15, s.v. *"The Protestant Ethic and the Spirit of Capitalism" (Die protestantische Ethik und der Geist des Kapitalismus;* various translations); Bendix, *Max Weber*, 49–82; Kalberg, "Introduction," 8–63. On the Protestant ethic debate, see Kalberg, "Introduction," 50–56. Colin Campbell argues that current sociologists are contradictory when they laud the book as a supreme example of sociology at work and yet never utilize its methodology ("Do Today's Sociologists Really Appreciate Weber's essay *The Protestant Ethic and the Spirit of Capitalism?*" *Sociological Review* 54 [2006]: 207–23). Matti Peltonen shows how sociologists have rejected Weber's thesis because of a crude oversimplification of it, while economic historians first rejected the actual thesis, then recently have generally accepted it ("The Weber Thesis and Economic Historians," *Max Weber Studies* 8 [2008]: 79–98). Hamilton, a historian, concludes that "there is not much in the various parts of Weber's thesis which stands up to examination" ("Weber's *Protestant Ethic*," 171).

22. See B. Turner, *For Weber*, 257–86; Love, "Weber's Orient," 172–99.

23. Christopher L. Walton argues that secularization does not mean the end of religion ("Is Disenchantment the End of Religion?" *Philocrites: Religion, Liberalism, and Culture* 2003, n.p., online at http://www.philocrites.com/essays/weber.html [accessed January 4, 2010]). Kayes in fact secularizes theodicy and shows its usefulness in analyzing explanations of business corruption ("Corruption as Theodicy," 51–62). David Morgan bemoans the inverse problem of theodicy, where religion and morality no longer aid in explaining pain and suffering ("Pain: The Unrelieved Condition of Modernity," *European Journal of Social Theory* 5 [2002]: 307–22). Goldstein combines elements from Weber's theory of the

Weber usually defines religion in contrast to magic in terms of rational-ization.[24] Here he refers primarily "to the systematization of ideas, particularly religious values and images of the world."[25] The systematization of ideas has many aspects. "It may simply mean ordering discrete elements to make them more precise and internally consistent, as in the rationalization of magical or ritual practices." Essentially religion is simply a rationalized form of magic. Magic involves techniques used by magicians that have power over spirits or deities. The demon or spirit is not perceived as rational or reasonable. It simply responds to the brute force of the magic. According to Weber, religion devel-ops when these entities that are subject to magic begin to take on the nature of human personalities, who are increasingly conceived of as reasonable, with wants and desires and are subject to influence but not mechanically. Thus, sac-rifices to deities involve a less magical element since they are perceived as gifts or even "food" for the gods so that they will be persuaded, not compelled, to return the favor with blessings to their worshipers. Prayers still contain a magical element, but again the deities are viewed as capable of persuasion, not of being forced.

But magic is not completely without rationality. It is simply an ancient principle of cause and effect, though the relationship between cause and effect seems arbitrary to moderns. As Weber notes:

> Religiously or magically motivated behavior is relatively rational behavior, espe-cially in its earliest manifestations. It follows rules of experience, though it is not necessarily action in accordance with a means-end schema. Rubbing will elicit sparks from pieces of wood, and in like fashion the simulative actions of a magi-cian will evoke rain from the heavens. The sparks resulting from twirling sticks

---

rationalization of Judaism and Ernst Bloch's Marxist theory of secularization to produce a dialectical theory of secularization that involves a tension between the sacred and profane that is not to be resolved ("Religious Rationalization," 115–51). Basit Bilal Koshul employs Weber's critique of science and rationalism to show that the Qur'anic affirmation of mate-rial reality is compatible with science ("Scriptural Reasoning and the Philosophy of Social Science," *Modern Theology* 22 [2006]: 483–501). Campbell qualifies Weber's somewhat linear view of rationalization, which ultimately leads to secularism and disenchantment, to a cyclical view. He argues that after Calvin, notions of God became less transcendent and more immanent as in Eastern religions—thus, not disenchanted ("Weber, Rationalisa-tion, and Religious Evoulution," 19–31). Simone Chambers argues that Jürgeb Habermas believes that post-metaphysical philosophy needs religious concepts and language to treat certain ethical and existential dilemmas properly ("How Religion Speaks to the Agnostic: Habermas on the Persistent Value of Religion," *Constellations* 14 [2007]: 210–23).

24. See Weber, *Sociology of Religion*, 1–31.
25. Swidler, "Concept of Rationality," 36.

are as much a "magical" effect as the rain evoked by the manipulations of the rainmaker.[26]

Magic is also an attempt to deal with the problem of fate and free will. It represents an attempt at human resistance to misfortune brought on by natural calamity. It gives humans the illusion that they have some control in their world, which is ever threatening and brutal. It provides humans with the comfort that they can do certain things that might bring them advantages that they would not otherwise have. This sense of control and mastery is important for the human psyche. But in terms of rationality, the difference between magic and religion is one of degree and not of kind.

Those who practice magic certainly view it as rational. Richard Kieckhefer argues that

> the people in medieval Europe who used the term "magic" thought of it as neither irrational nor nonrational but as essentially rational. To conceive of magic as rational was to believe, first of all, that it could actually work (that its efficacy was shown by evidence recognized within the culture as authentic) and, secondly, that its workings were governed by principles (of theology or of physics) that could be coherently articulated.[27]

One could refer to magic as a weak versus a strong sense of rationality, which would be found in modern science.[28] The difference between magical and more scientific thinking is simply that magical thinking is not introspective, whereas science is critical of its own beliefs.[29] Two scholars who studied scientifically oriented and superstitious persons in the Slovak countryside found that their differing explanations for mysterious phenomena (e.g., strange lights at night) were similar in one important respect: "Both serve the same aim: to understand the supernatural phenomenon as a whole, without any other questions and doubts."[30] In other words, magical and scientific thinking both attempt to explain the mysteries, but in a different way. Magic and superstition have certainly not disappeared from the modern Western world. The secular,

---

26. Weber, *Sociology of Religion*, 1.

27. Richard Kieckhefer, "The Specific Rationality of Medieval Magic," *American Historical Review* 99 (1994): 814.

28. I. C. Jarvie and Joseph Agassi, "The Problem of the Rationality of Magic," *British Journal of Sociology* 18 (1967): 55–56.

29. Jarvie and Agassi, "Rationality of Magic," 69, 70–71.

30. Tatiana Podolinská and Milan Kováč, "'Mythos' versus 'Logos': Strategies of Rationalization at the Boundaries of Two Worlds in the Conceptions of Supernatural Beings in Slovak Countryside," *Dialogue and Universalism* 12, nos. 8–10 (2002): 85–99, here 99.

disenchanted world has always had pockets of magic. Even the venerable Sir Isaac Newton was an alchemist.

Religion, however, tightens matters up more than does magic. Its attempts at mastering the world are more intense and systematic. Swidler, summarizing Weber's thoughts, describes this process:

> The more religious systems move beyond ritual and magic, the more is involved in rationalization. Systematic ordering starts to mean not only ordering discrete elements, but also integrating the elements by finding some more abstract principle which relates them. Finally, rationalization may mean extending a system of ideas, increasing the range of cases to which it applies.[31]

She notes that Weber viewed priests and prophets as major players in this process of systematization, which involves "an increase in the integration, consistency, and comprehensiveness of a set of religious ideas."[32]

Religious ideas become significant only when they are rationalized into a coherent picture of the world and humanity's relation to it. Weber expresses this in relation to the concept of redemption: "Yet redemption attained a specific significance only where it expressed a systematic and rationalized 'image of the world' and represented a stand in the face of the world. For the meaning as well as the intended and actual psychological quality of redemption has depended on such a world image and such a stand."[33] It is this integrated view of the world with which people experience reality and whereby their actions are influenced: "'From what' and 'for what' one wished to be redeemed and, let us not forget, 'could be' redeemed, depended upon one's image of the world."[34]

RATIONALIZATION AND CONSISTENCY

A big part of religious rationalization involves an increase in consistency of ideas. As has already been shown, this is especially a concern for intellectuals. It is essentially their passion and their job to make sure that the religions they serve are theoretically as consistent as possible. But again, as with resolving the theodicy problem, there is always a trade-off with consistency. Consistency of religious ideas provides greater legitimacy for a particular religious worldview and a satisfying sense of order and meaning in a cruelly chaotic and absurd world. However, there is a darker side to this achievement. As is often true

---

31. Swidler, "Concept of Rationality," 36.
32. Ibid.
33. Weber, "Social Psychology," 280.
34. Ibid.

in the world, the resolution of one problem leads to new ones. Swidler summarizes Weber, "As ideas increase in consistency, integration, and comprehension, they create new problems which demand resolution in their own terms."[35] Again, it has been noted how Calvin's doctrine of predestination solves one problem (theodicy) but creates another (knowing one's redemptive state). Terrence Tilley argues that all theodicies end up denying either the reality of evil or God's goodness.[36] He proposes that instead of creating theodicies, Christians should offer defenses of Christianity that do not explain the presence of evil but demonstrate that the Christian faith is at least plausible in the context of a world that contains evil and is also not incoherent.

Here is where magic becomes superior to religion. Magic never attempts to synthesize all of its notions into one meaningful image of the world. It is an ad hoc endeavor and attempts to treat life's difficulties piecemeal. As humans evolved, the need for integration and systematization increased. There was an ever-increasing need for calculation and for perceiving an underlying order in the cosmos that made it seems less chaotic and more benign.

But with this another trade-off emerges. Irrationality can never completely be removed from the world or human behavior. It is a necessary component. As Swidler notes, "It was the genius of Weber's sociology of ideas to show that rationality is at its basis irrational. . . . rationality, as Weber understands it, depends upon strong irrational motives, such as the Protestant doctrine of proof or the idea of the 'calling' in capitalism."[37]

> Bringing all action under control by conscious ideas requires active effort, and must be powered by concentrated emotional energy. It is this need for an irrational spur to rationality which gives the problem of rationality its particular poignancy. . . . There is always a sphere of social life which is non-rational, and it is on the preservation of this sphere that the rationality of the rest of the system depends.[38]

Thus, again, the perpetual dance of rationality/irrationality among humans and within the world is noticeable.

Sica points out that too much reason can actually lead to irrationality.[39] Barbarism in a society can actually be viewed as a producer of culture and civilization, while, conversely, too much reason can lead back to barbarism.[40]

---

35. Swidler, "Concept of Rationality," 37.
36. Terrence W. Tilley, "The Use and Abuse of Theodicy," *Hor* 11 (1984): 304–19; cf. idem, *The Evils of Theodicy* (1991; repr., Eugene, Ore.: Wipf & Stock, 2000).
37. Swidler, "Concept of Rationality," 41.
38. Ibid.
39. Sica, "Rationalization and Culture," 46–47.
40. Sica, "Rationalization and Culture," 46, citing Arnaldo Momigliano, "Gibbon

He notes that too much formal rationality can lead to substantive irrationality.[41] Sica also quotes a former graduate student who had studied modern bureaucracy and concluded, "I'm beginning to think that George Orwell was the greatest prophet who's ever lived."

Irrational (or Non-Rational) Reaction

Sica points out a typical response to the increasing rationalization in the world today. Often persons retreat from it and engage in chemical and electronic diversion.[42] Or films can symbolize the response. Sica provides the example of George Lucas's1973 movie *THX 1138*, a futuristic anti-romance of the dystopian genre, as a contemporary reaction to over-rationalization in today's society.[43] In it Robert Duvall portrays a renegade who resists his society's attempt to make passion and interpersonal attachment illegal. His deeper-than-allowed attachment to a computer-selected mate gets him into trouble, and the attempt to escape such controls leads to his demise. Sica includes the movies *Brazil*, *Kafka*, and the Mad Max series. Also included could be films such as *Avatar*, with its environmental message in the context of the rationalization of the fossil fuel industry, and, of course, the Terminator series, where deep-seated fear of robotics (scientific and technological rationalization) is expressed. The many horror and dystopian films that express an underlying fear of radiation (*Night of the Living Dead*, *Omega Man*, etc.) are further examples. Recent American political rhetoric includes a fear of bureaucratization in the health care and insurance industries.

Another response is found in the literature and rhetoric of evangelical and fundamentalist Christians. One could say that these conservative religious groups are attempting to re-enchant the world in the face of the threat of secularism and science. For example, creationism is an interesting strategy that attempts to use a scientific façade to legitimize a nonscientific explanation of the origin of the universe.[44] These groups feel threatened by the relativism

---

from an Italian Point of View," in *Edward Gibbon and the Decline and Fall of the Roman Empire* (ed. G. W. Bowersock, John Clive, and Stephen R. Graubard; Cambridge: Cambridge University Press, 1977), 78–79.

41. Sica, "Rationalization and Culture," 46, citing Karl Mannheim, *Man and Society in an Age of Reconstruction: Studies in Modern Social Structure* (London: Routledge & Kegan Paul, 1940), 39–75.

42. Sica, "Rationalization and Culture," 56–58.

43. Ibid., 43.

44. On the history and nature of creationism, see Arthur McCalla, "Creationism," *Religion Compass* 1 (2007): 547–60. DOI: 10.1111/j.1749-8171.2007.00034.x. On the debate about the "conflict thesis," whether science and religion are really incompatible, see Gregory W. Dawes, "Can a Darwinian Be a Christian?" *Religion Compass* 1 (2007): 711–24. DOI:

involved in secularization and yearn for absolute, unquestioned truths and a sense of meaning in the cosmos that science is unable to provide.

WEBER AND THE RATIONALIZATION OF YAHWISM

Weber was especially interested in Judaism because he saw it as critical for the eventual secularization of the Western world and the development of capitalism. Weber believed that the West manifests a much higher degree of rationalization, particularly economical, than the other parts of the world, for example, the Orient, which did display elements of rationalization but not to the degree of the West. Weber saw the explanation in the asceticism of Protestantism, which got its rational character from Judaism.

Weber believed that Judaism was at first more magically oriented and focused on the cult, like other ancient Near Eastern religions.[45] However, over time, the religion became increasingly rationalized.[46] This began with the prophets, who did not approach the Jewish religion in terms of cultic requirements or magic but emphasized keeping God's covenant and obeying his commandments. With the prophets, God began to be conceived of as more reasonable than the earliest view of God as a war deity, who angrily crushed his enemies and whose anger had to be placated. The war deity was vigilant and jealous lest mortals commit hubris. God began to be perceived as a benevolent and merciful deity who had entered into a covenant with the Israelite people exclusively. Yahweh had a deep and personal relationship with the people and demanded their loyalty. In other words, this new view of God constituted seeing God as like a human being, with tender emotions and fierce loyalty. Being faithful to this God meant a practical life of good citizenship and keeping God's commands. In return, God would bless the Israelites as a people and individually with prosperity and peace. Conversely, failure to remain faithful would result in punishments of devastation and calamities on a national and individual level.

Weber saw the levitical priests as also involved in the process of rationalization.[47] These priests had the task of determining what sin had been committed that brought about disease or misfortune. This meant implementing the prophetic message about ethics and commandment-keeping so that people

---

10.1111/j.1749-8171.2007.00050.x. For a creationist perspective, see Michael J. Behe, *Darwin's Black Box: The Biochemical Challenge to Evolution* (New York: Free Press, 1996).

45. Weber, *Ancient Judaism*, 90–193, 219–225. The best summary of *Ancient Judaism* is by Love ("Weber's *Ancient Judaism*").

46. See Weber, *Ancient Judaism*, 194–218, 223.

47. See ibid., 212–18, 222, 228–29, 235.

might be whole and secure. These priests were intricately involved in the production of the numerous laws in the Torah.

When disasters hit the nation, the prophets were the chief instigators of rationalization and explained destruction and exile as God's punishment for the nation's sinful behavior and unfaithfulness to God.[48] They also provided hope with their pushing of retribution against their enemies into the future. A theodicy of suffering developed, whereby the Jews were God's people who suffered for the cause of God, who would eventually redeem them. Their suffering then became an emblem of honor, a calling, and not a shameful punishment for their sin. Here Judaism transformed from a nation to a religious and ethnic sect of "pariah people" who were scattered throughout the world and suffered as a minority but stubbornly survived through many catastrophes.[49] Jews became subjugated people who yearned for their eventual redemption. Judaism transformed into a salvation religion, a religion of the oppressed who hoped for better times.

Weber believes that the prophets were not poor but neither were they among the powerful.[50] They are representative of plebeian intellectuality. The Deuteronomists, the Elohist, and the Yahwist were also in this stratum, whose members were not afraid to criticize the kings and their covenant disobedience.[51] The king and the aristocracy in Israel were never able to repress prophetic criticism completely, largely because Israel was so small in comparison with the other great powers like Egypt or Assyria. Moreover, many of the oracles of the prophets came true, and this further legitimized their status. This plebian intellectuality was the class that carried the day, and their vision of Yahwism became normative. The anti-plebian, scribal stratum, represented by the wisdom literature, did not prevail. The Pharisees, according to Weber, also plebian, and urban craftsmen, essentially carried the torch of the Jewish faith and continued the legacy of the prophets.[52] They continued the "pariah" character of Judaism, which was carried over into Christianity, which was heavily influenced by the Pharisaic tradition. The trajectory eventually led to Protestant asceticism in Calvinism, which spurred on the further development of capitalism and rationalization in the West. The "Protestant Work Ethic," with it frugality and emphasis on investments and savings propelled the West into a heavily rationalistic track.

Weber's emphasis on the greater rationalization in Judaism is used ultimately to explain why rationalization developed so much more fully in the

---

48. See ibid., 267–335.
49. See ibid., 336–82.
50. See ibid., 277–86.
51. Ibid., 205–18.
52. Ibid., 385–424.

West than in other regions.[53] Confucianism had rationalistic and capitalistic elements, but these never developed as in the West because of the familial piety and ancestor worship that were integral to Confucianism. Yahwism was vehemently opposed to this kind of piety.[54] Not the ancestors but Yahweh alone was worthy of worship! Another factor also contributed to the West's greater degree of rationalization. Confucianism was the religion of a patrimonial form of government that was very centrist in its rule and prevented the spread of capitalistic entrepreneurial enterprises. Medieval Christendom, however, was more feudal and less centrist, and this allowed more entrepreneurial activities, which provided a supportive soil for the growth of capitalism.

RATIONALIZATION IN THE WISDOM TRADITION

Rationalization did not occur in ancient Israel only in connection with the prophets and levitical priests. It also occurred in the wisdom literature, though probably not independently of the former process. This literature has a natural affinity with rationalization because it served essentially bureaucratic or scribal interests, as has been seen. It was aimed at training apprentice scribes to be loyal and efficient governmental officials. It also aimed at enabling them to be successful in attaining increasingly higher bureaucratic positions. In essence, the wisdom literature constituted a training manual for young scribes. Thus, the notion of calculability is crucial. The important question then becomes how should scribes behave in order that they might succeed in their governmental roles? In other words, how should they act in order that they might achieve their career goals?

---

53. For the best explanation of this process, see B. Turner, *For Weber*, 203–368; cf. Love, "Weber's Orient," 172–99; Bendix, *Max Weber*, 13–281. Schluchter demonstrates how for Weber the Hebrew Bible was the crucial turning point in cultural history for the Near East and the West ("Weber's Sociology of Religion," 33–56, here 45).

54. See Weber, *Ancient Judaism*, 139, 143. Barbalet explains how Weber is forced to characterize the Jews as pariah people to explain why they themselves did not function in the same way as Protestants in advancing capitalism ("Weber and Judaism," 51–67). James Mahon demonstrates that the Chinese preference for sons transforms from substantive (Confucian care of deceased parents' souls by the firstborn son) to formal rationality (sons are needed to care for aged parents) ("Weber's Protestant Ethic and the Chinese Preference for Sons: An Application of Western Sociology to Eastern Religions," *Max Weber Studies* 5 [2005]: 59–80). Drawing on the Darwinian notions of selection and adaptation, W. G. Runciman shows how Weber uses similar concepts and how they can be employed to strengthen his Protestant ethic thesis. According to Runciman, Chinese culture did not contain the necessary characteristics to propel capitalism ("Was Max Weber a Selectionist in Spite of Himself?" *Journal of Classical Sociology* 1 [2001]: 13–32).

There are two types of rationality involved here. The first is the rationality of action. The scribes learn behavior that is rationally oriented to fulfilling their goal of becoming successful in their vocation and their personal lives. The second type involved the rationalization of religious ideas. Here the doctrine of retribution comes into play. It systematizes the wisdom tradition and provides a causal explanation for the consequences of action, which is intricately related to the deity.

These two types of rationality are reflected in two broad types of wisdom, especially in Proverbs. The first is what can be called ad hoc wisdom. This is instruction on specific behavior appropriate in particular circumstances that should aid the scribe in furthering his career. For example, in Prov 23:1–3:

> When you sit down to eat with a ruler, observe carefully what is before you,
> and put a knife to your throat if you have a big appetite.
> Do not desire the ruler's delicacies, for they are deceptive food.

Advice is given for a scribe to maintain strict discipline around a superior. The scribe should never lose sight of the fact that he is before his superior while dining with him. Restraint and class consciousness are the key to succeeding in such a situation. One should maintain personal distance from the situation and an impersonal demeanor. The last phrase contains a hint of the superiority that the status group of the sages feels vis-à-vis the ruler's power and his undisciplined appetite, and so wisdom takes on the role of a lifestyle and begins to depart from its ad hoc character here. This passage is remarkably similar to Ptah-hotep's advice to scribal apprentices:

> If you serve a powerful patron,
> Take what your patron offers.
> Do not look about with envy,
> Do not always hope for more . . .
> Stand humbly until your patron speaks to you,
> Speak only when spoken to.
> Laugh when your patron laughs . . .
> When the powerful are at the table,
> They may seem to dispense favors as they see fit,
> Patrons may seem to bless only their clients,
> But their *ka*-souls are guided by the divine assembly,
> Therefore, do not complain about their choices. (120–42)[55]

It differs in that it is less cynical about the patron's intentions. But both of these passages demonstrate the importance of specific instruction in dealing with

---

55. Matthews and Benjamin, *Old Testament Parallels,* 284.

a concrete situation that would inevitably arise in the life of a typical scribe. Both passages are rationalistic in the sense that they calculate the most appropriate way to respond in this kind of situation so that this advice enables the scribe successfully to negotiate one of the many pitfalls that would arise in the course of his career.

The other type of wisdom is what can be called lifestyle wisdom. This is the notion that a particular style of life, and not just the application of ad hoc cunning to particular situations, enables the scribe to be successful. This entails the many instances where the righteous, the wise, and the industrious are pitted against the wicked, the fool, and the lazy. It involves the notion of biological, economic, and career success. But this lifestyle also involves the notion of honor or prestige and the status-group ethic of the Israelite sages. The sages see themselves furthering their own careers and securing the fortune of their families but also believe themselves to be "doing the right thing," to be living according to the dictates of Israelite society, within its norms, and becoming responsible citizens who were concerned about the poor and disadvantaged. Though there is certainly an elitism connected with this (the wise could not have enjoyed their wise lifestyle without the privileges they held), still they see themselves as not ultimately pursuing wealth and personal advantage but as embracing principles and norms they feel deeply about, as ultimately disillusioned as they might be about this. Sica points out that absolute values are technically irrational, so here one sees the typical combination of the rational and the irrational in human behavior.[56]

This form of wisdom is a type of rationalization in that it assumes that a certain lifestyle is more likely to be successful, especially for scribes. The dichotomies used (wisdom versus fool, righteous versus wicked, etc.), of course, are applicable beyond the scribal guild and ring true to reality and life in most situations. The dichotomies essentially represent conformity versus nonconformity or deviance. In general, conformists usually succeed better in society than nonconformists, who usually find themselves in trouble and thereby jeopardize their lives and fortune, depending on the severity of their noncompliance. Thus, it is generally true that in the ancient world and, particularly, in ancient Israel, the righteous do well. They live long and prosper, while it is also true that the wicked do not do well and do not live long. Thus, in terms of rationalization, even according to modern secular standards, this type of dichotomization appears credible and rational. Even in terms of piety or religious categorization, in ancient Israel, the Yahwist, being pious, clean, and a member of the official religious party, would normally fare better than the non-Yahwist or the syncretist. The Yahwistic purist would enjoy social

---

56. Sica, *Weber, Irrationality,* 161.

advantages because of his association with the party in power. In a society such as ancient Israel, the religious and pious person would normally succeed in life in contrast to the religious deviant. Further, as Durkheim has shown, religion has a tendency to curtail the innate selfish tendencies of humanity, to unite people and make them more altruistic and community oriented.[57] Being pious or righteous or wise, then, has a social and community dimension in that a person with these characteristics actually benefits not just him/herself, but the community as whole.

The notion of divine retribution, however, adds a dimension that moderns would consider irrational. Weber himself notes that rationalization is relative.[58] What is rational to one person or group is irrational to another. But from an ancient perspective, the notion that a person's righteousness and piety and the positive benefits it produces are, in fact, rewarded by the deity is completely rational. This is because religion functions to provide meaning for life and to integrate the cosmos into a coherent whole that is understandable. Thus, the rational element is there, though moderns would say that this belief is itself false, that the benefits received from piety have nothing to do with gods or deities. Rationalization does not have to be true to be functional. However, this form of false rationalization will eventually lead to problems when the falsity of the beliefs becomes evident.

Thus, lifestyle wisdom works on two connected levels. Conformists generally succeed in life in a particular community. Thus, conformity works and is true to life on a practical level. The other level is that the benefits accrued by conformity are attributed to a divine plan and order. This works on an intellectual level and provides a sense of order and meaning in an overwhelmingly violent and chaotic world. Both of these levels work as long as the benefits keep accruing. But when they do not, problems begin.

THE FEASIBILITY OF THE DOCTRINE OF RETRIBUTION

During the days of Israel's independence before the exile, the doctrine of retribution worked well for the scribes as they carried on their daily activities. In such a close, tight-knit nation, the doctrine would have generally functioned on a number of levels for this status group. First of all, it was pedagogically necessary. In order to motivate young apprentice scribes to study hard as they prepared for their professional life, scribal instruction needed to emphasize the benefits of the profession and lifestyle. Wisdom and righteousness and wealth and honor, thus, were intricately connected. Though wealth was not

---

57. See Émile Durkheim, *The Elementary Forms of Religious Life* (trans. Carol Cosman; Oxford World's Classics; Oxford: Oxford University Press, 2001).

58. See Weber, *Sociology of Religion*, 1–2.

the primary goal of the sages, it was highly valued and was a necessary incentive for the young apprentices to study hard and persevere. Thus, the doctrine of retribution provided a ready-made pedagogical tool.

Second, it legitimized their own privileged status as well-to-do retainers. This is Weber's notion of theodicy of fortune.[59] This status group would not be content simply to assume a theodicy of misfortune. It would not be enough merely to view the poor as deserving of their undesirable status. The wealthy needed to feel that they deserved their many advantages and privileges, that they had earned such blessing. It was simply reward for their good behavior.

Third, it made the world meaningful and pushed chaos to the edges of existence, containing it. It meant that there was a clear cause and effect in the world and that the world was indeed calculable. If the people lived a particular kind of life, they could be confident they would succeed and be prosperous. Chaos and unforeseen calamities, the unpredictable, were relegated to the background as an anomaly. The doctrine of retribution served to push the incalculable, the mysterious, chance, outside the normative parameters of the cosmos, which is what magic also attempts to do. Magic mitigates chance to some extent, just not as completely as religions usually do. Similarly, the doctrine of retribution connected mundane daily existence with the rhythm and order of the cosmos. Daily behavior and activities take on cosmic and divine significance. In this construal of the world, very little occurs for no reason; life makes sense. God is reasonable and so are his expectations. One simply must resign oneself to this cosmic pattern and live prosperously.

However, when Israel experienced the exile and began to be continuously subjugated to foreign empires, this nice and neat construal began to disintegrate. The relationship between righteousness/wisdom and wickedness/folly and the respective consequences of fortune/misfortune became more problematic. Certainly, for the sages, that pagan nations and empires seem to prosper would have been troubling. Further, the necessary compromises the Jewish elite would have made to be successful under these foreign powers also upset this neat system, as the books of Daniel (chs. 1–6) and Esther demonstrate. Now one found oneself in a situation where being righteous and pious, as traditionally understood, might, in fact, jeopardize one's governmental career.

Again, this fits with Weber's notion of the development of Israel into a "pariah" minority, which contrasts sharply with its days of glory under Solomon as an independent nation that received tribute from other neighboring

---

59. Kayes shows how companies use secular theodicies to reinforce existing social structures and power ("Corruption as Theodicy," 60). Morgan states concerning the management of pain today, "Assessments of risk, and subsequent attributions of liability and blame, now circulate as the surrogate forms of theodicy within the corporate institutions of the modern world" ("Condition of Modernity," 319).

nations. The psalms indicate this change, where the designation "the wicked" often refers to foreign oppressors. More and more, Israel begins to identify itself as the oppressed, a people yearning for a future day of retribution. The book of Job depicts how the political changes affected the wisdom tradition, which reflects Israel's upper-class perspective. Ultimately, the book of Job preserves the doctrine of retribution, but in a modified form, as has been seen. Qohelet does as well. Both strategies essentially support the status quo.

Life was tolerable enough for the sages. They did not personally or directly experience many of the sufferings of their people. The changes in society were more of an intellectual problem for them because the doctrine of retribution did not appear to function properly. Thus, their primary goal was to preserve this doctrine, though in a modified form. The doctrine of retribution, as traditionally formulated, worked during the earlier period of the monarchy but was challenged and needed modification under the periods of colonization and domination by foreign empires. Job and Qohelet represent a loosening up, an uncoupling of this doctrine from its over-rationalization, to make it more flexible, manageable, and functional under the new polity.

This means fundamentally that the doctrine of retribution was an essentially rational teaching during the preexilic period, even though faulty from the perspective of later generations and, of course, a modern perspective. It enabled the royal sages to approach the world in a rational and calculative way, and it provided a meaningful worldview that excluded the chaotic and disorderly as much as possible. However, when social conditions changed, and the social categorization of the doctrine did not match up with the expected life consequences, a crisis emerged. The doctrine became too rationalized for these new circumstances. Thus, after the exile it became or represented increasingly an over-rationalization of life. The idea that the doctrine became increasingly dogmatized is inaccurate; rather, the doctrine failed to explain reasonably the new realities of Jewish existence. This made it appear to be hyper-rationalized.

QOHELET'S IRRATIONAL RESPONSE
TO THE OVER-RATIONALIZATION OF THE WISDOM TRADITION

The effects of over-rationalization in the modern world and the often romantic and irrational responses to it, like flight into fantasy or even narcotics or the turn to fundamentalism, have been noted. Qohelet's carpe diem ethic is his solution to this problem. It is a fundamental turn from rationality toward the noncognitive, the emotional and physical pleasures and relationships.[60]

---

60. Vincent P. Branick argues that the pessimistic wisdom literature acknowledges the uncontrollable aspects of the future and, thus, focuses on the present. He believes that this perspective could help businesses that are so future-oriented and bent on success that

Qohelet finds the entire wisdom enterprise with its calculations and attempts to comprehend God's ways entirely frustrating: "For in much wisdom is much vexation, and those who increase knowledge increase sorrow" (1:18). In his royal testing of wisdom and folly, both are found wanting, and so his solution is to reject them both. The world is so irrational that there is nothing better than to eat, drink, and be merry—"hedonism" or physical satisfaction versus cognitive pleasure. Qohelet fundamentally distrusts human cognitive capacity. His carpe diem ethic is indeed a type of hedonism. It counsels the momentary, physical pleasures of life in contrast to constant striving for long-term goals—to achieve greatness and to master life and comprehend the cosmic pattern. It is certainly a restrained hedonism, for he cautions against a total abandonment to wanton pleasure (11:9). But it is a resignation to the harsh brutality and irrationality of life and represents an attempt to gain some pleasure in the veil of tears called life. Lang is correct: Qohelet's carpe diem ethic is his narcotic, his drug that enables him to endure the painful existence of life. It is a reaction to the over-rationalization of life represented by the wisdom tradition, an over-rationalization that became increasingly obvious in the corrupted world of the Ptolemaic period.[61]

Qohelet's carpe diem ethic represents an anti-ascetic or antinomian response. It is the opposite of world mastery.[62] It is an acceptance of the world as it is and making the most of it, which is similar to mysticism. There is no salvation element here, no escaping the world (world flight versus mastery) into another realm as in Buddhism; neither is there a resistance to the world by mastering it through harshness to the physical body and repressing desires. It is the acceptance of bodily pleasures and desires and abandonment of striving after illusory long-term goals and inane business pursuits. It is a quiet resignation that is realistic about life and its possibilities, and it attempts to capitalize on what pleasures make themselves available.

The rabbis were right to suspect the heterodoxy of this position, which they reinterpreted to mean study of Torah, as has already been shown. It flies in the face of the Jewish tendency to obsess about law-keeping and ritual. Weber speaks of the Jews having certain ascetic characteristics, but he never identified Judaism as ascetic as he did Calvinistic Protestantism.[63] One might

---

they become corrupt. If they could have a little more fun in their business endeavors, they might actually be more successful ("Wisdom, Pessimism, and 'Mirth': Reflections on the Contribution of Biblical Wisdom Literature to Business Ethics," *JRE* 34 [2006]: 69–87).

61. Étan Levine shows that in Qohelet the fool is humorous in his rigidity about and oversimplification of the complexities of life ("The Humor in Qohelet," *ZAW* 109 [1997]: 71–83).

62. See Weber, "Religious Rejections," 323–59.

63. See Weber, *Ancient Judaism*, 343–55, 400–404, 410.

call the Jews proto-ascetic.[64] Of course, the tradition of reading Ecclesiastes at the Feast of Booths or Tabernacles implies that the Jews accepted Qohelet's counsel of joy and indicates that they may have welcomed bodily pleasures more easily than did Christians. Jewish views of sexuality were not prudish compared to Christian standards. However, the Jewish fixation on the Torah and its implementation carried a certain ascetic character. Keeping the law became the badge of identity for the Jews and the test of their faithfulness.[65] It created a disciplined people that became the envy of the Gentiles, many of whom eventually became proselytes because they saw Judaism as a means to self-mastery.[66] Self-mastery is essentially mastery of the world.

Because the doctrine of retribution did not work as traditionally formulated, Qohelet did not see any value in emphasizing law-keeping positively. He did recognize the importance of law-keeping negatively, however. One should pay one's vows once made, but, of course, Qohelet's preferred advice is to not vow at all and so avoid the problem (5:2–5). One should certainly not indulge in blatant wickedness (7:16). Thus, Qohelet was not averse to law-keeping, just to investing one's future in it. Avoiding angering the deity was much more important to him (5:6). This means that recent commentators who have argued that the pious gloss of 12:13 to fear God and keep his commandments is not foreign to the rest of the book are far off the mark.[67] Fearing God is certainly a major motif of Qohelet, but he uses it in an unconventional way. However, the idea that this verse can represent a précis of Qohelet's dominant message is unwarranted.

---

64. Steven D. Fraade argues that ancient Judaism reflects an "ascetic tension" ("Ascetical Aspects of Ancient Judaism," in *Jewish Spirituality: From the Bible through the Middle Ages* [ed. Arthur Green; Encyclopedia of World Spirituality 13; New York: Crossroad, 1986], 253–88).

65. Herbert Basser argues that the Pharisaic fixation on the law was due to their reaction to the hellenized Sadducean priesthood that could no longer be trusted. The faithful Jews avoided philosophical speculation typical of Hellenistic Jews and focused on law and ethics ("The Development of the Pharisaic Idea of Law as a Sacred Cosmos," *JSJ* 16 [1985]: 108).

66. See Stanley K. Stowers, *A Rereading of Romans: Justice, Jews, and Gentiles* (New Haven: Yale University Press, 1997), 42–82.

67. Bartholomew, *Ecclesiastes*, 87–89; Krüger, *Qoheleth*, 213; cf. idem, "Die Rezeption der Tora im Buch Kohelet," in *Das Buch Kohelet: Studien zur Struktur, Geschichte, Rezeption und Theologie* (ed. Otto Kaiser; BZAW 254; Berlin: de Gruyter, 1997), 303–25. Perrin argues that 12:13–14 "represent not the denial of Qoheleth's musings, but the culmination of his extended philosophical experiment" ("Messianism," 52). He sees 12:9–14 as part of the frame narrator's attempt to legitimize Qohelet's words by incorporating messianic undertones (pp. 37–60).

It is also important to emphasize that Qohelet's conception of God is directly connected to his irrational reaction to the over-rationalization of the wisdom tradition. Qohelet, in fact, returns to an older, more primitive concept of God. His God is similar to the early angry, jealous war God who was primarily focused on divine honor, glory, and preeminence. This God seeks out any instances of human hubris (5:6). This God wants a great divide to exist between the divine and the human. This God wants a monopoly of power and wisdom/knowledge before humanity's weakness and folly. This God hardly has a benevolent side. Second Samuel 24 reveals this unsavory side of early depictions of Yahweh. God incites David to take the census but then surprisingly condemns him afterwards. In 1 Kgs 22 God sends a lying spirit to Ahab's prophets to entice him to battle, which ends in defeat. Isaiah 45:7 says that God creates both weal and woe. As Richard Nelson notes, "Until late in the Old Testament period, Israel was more concerned about boldly confessing God's unlimited power than carefully safeguarding God's goodness and virtue."[68]

However, Qohelet's God is even less benevolent than this portrayal in that the deity apparently has no covenantal relationship with the Jews, no elect and holy people. This God is merely the supreme sovereign of the cosmos and has little interest in humanity except to demonstrate to them how lacking and depraved they really are. Qohelet's notion of the deity is much closer to the magical than to the traditional conception of the divine in Judaism. However, Qohelet has no magical tricks with which to confound or manipulate the deity. In other words, Qohelet's notion of the deity is as irrational as the magical view, except without the magic. His rationality as an intellectual will not allow him to turn to the irrationality of magic as a solution. He will not commit intellectual suicide. He must content himself with the irrational pleasures of the carpe diem ethic. His response is an anti-intellectualism that does not reject intellect entirely. Throughout history, intellectuals are often instigators of anti-intellect. Though trained as a rabbi and a gifted writer, Paul decries human wisdom as the folly of God and vice versa (1 Cor 3).

Qohelet does not completely reject his rational capacities. Even in his experiment, his wisdom was with him (2:3). Though wisdom ultimately provides no profit in life, it is as superior to folly as light is to darkness (2:13–14). Qohelet's theodicy strategy of denying God's justice is a product of his rationality. Thus, his carpe diem ethic is an irrational response to the rationalization of the wisdom tradition, though guided by rationality. Perhaps nonrationality is a better term. This explains his development of the dichotomy between humans and the deity. Humans have no capacity to understand the ways of God. God

---

68. Richard D. Nelson, *The Historical Books* (IBT; Nashville: Abingdon, 1998), 49–50.

is the one with true wisdom and knowledge, and humans must resign themselves to being largely ignorant of his plans and purposes. God must, thus, remain quintessentially *deus absconditus*, the hidden deity.

Qohelet thus represents a return to a more primitive religious orientation that preserves the fundamental separation of mortality and divinity.[69] The book of Qohelet represents a religious reaction to a form of secularization that had begun to develop within the wisdom tradition that began increasingly to view God as predictable and even able to be manipulated. Qohelet attempts to counter this calculative relationship of humans to God. Thus, the irony is that, although Qohelet certainly has an affinity to modern secularity and sensibility, traditional wisdom is actually the more secular and heading in the direction of the disenchantment of the world that Weber emphasizes. In essence, Qohelet saves the wisdom tradition from itself as an over-rationalized phenomenon and movement.

Qohelet's reaction to the over-rationalization of the wisdom tradition is not identical with the modern reaction to today's secular world. He is reacting not merely to the dominance of rationality and calculability but rather also to the falsity of the rationalization, to the fact that the doctrine of retribution, as traditionally formulated, does not work. In the modern world, this falsity is rarely present. The problem today is simply the lack of sensitivity in rationalization to the irrational and emotional needs of humans.

CONCLUSION

Proverbs and the doctrine of retribution are forms of rationality that enabled young Jewish scribes to be successful in their careers and provided an intellectual framework that made the cosmos appear meaningful and orderly. The doctrine worked well as long as it was confined to serving the scribes under Solomon and the other Judean kings who were able to maintain the nation's independence. It served to legitimize their privileged status and provided them with a way to predict the consequences of actions and of particular lifestyles. However, after the exile, the doctrine became increasingly problematic for the sages. With Job and then Qohelet, it had to be reformulated. With both, the doctrine and the wisdom tradition as a whole appeared to be increasingly frustrating. To its over-rationalization and calculative character, Qohelet has an opposite reaction, embracing irrationality, not madness but a noncognitive, passive acceptance of life's fleeting pleasures that aid in surviving the chaotic

---

69. Hayman argues that with the Wisdom of Solomon the wisdom tradition has returned to the dualistic early mythological view of God and the world, which runs counter to the focus on rationality and logic that characterizes traditional wisdom ("Wisdom of Solomon," 125–39).

nature of life. Qohelet's book enabled young apprentice scribes to manage the oppressive and irrational character of their society. It helped them survive their tolerable conditions by redirecting them to the simple pleasures of life instead of holding materialistic goals or striving for the rational mastery of life.

Thus, in a way, Qohelet is more true to religious instincts than is traditional wisdom. He returns to a more primitive view of God, who is ultimately mysterious and beyond mortal grasp. Traditional wisdom, guilty of over-rationalization and life mastery in the time of Qohelet, finds itself actually on a trajectory toward the disenchantment or secularization of the world, which got its latest significant impetus from the "Protestant Work Ethic." Today one feels the full effect and consequences of the attempt for world and life mastery— rationalization and secularization to the nth degree! Thus, ironically, although the book of Qohelet certainly has a secular and contemporary feel to it, it ultimately represents the more fundamental religious impulse.

8

THE POSITIVE POWER OF QOHELET'S PESSIMISM

The purpose of this chapter is to demonstrate how being honest about Qohelet's pessimism or, more properly, his use of the pessimistic genre does not mean a negative verdict on the book's relevance either within the canon or for the world today.[1] In other words, this chapter will show that a respect for Qohelet's pessimism is certainly compatible with a positive assessment of the book's theological value and potential. Pessimism, certainly a negative emotion, does not necessarily detract from the book's positive function within the society for which it was created or for later religious communities. In this chapter, the psychology of pessimism as a mood and its rhetorical function as a genre will be the focus.[2]

Qohelet's pessimistic mood is a component of his irrational (or nonrational) strategy to counter traditional wisdom. Many scholars divide the wisdom literature up into optimistic and pessimistic wisdom.[3] They do this even for the Egyptian and Mesopotamian wisdom corpora. Some of these pessimistic examples have already been examined. Thus, one could argue that, in the other wisdom traditions, similar responses to over-rationalization may have been occurring. In this section pessimism will be presented as an intentional strategy on the part of Qohelet to counter the rationalistic character of traditional wisdom. It is not merely a passive response on his part due to the difficult circumstances in which he found himself, though this is a factor. It is a rhetorical response and largely proactive. By viewing pessimism this way, one can discern its positive function for Qohelet and his original audience.

In the United States today especially, one resists the notion that pessimism serves any positive good. For Americans optimism is a cherished, sacred value. Being optimistic, not giving up, and climbing the ladder of success function

---

1. For the classic argument that Qohelet is indeed a pessimist, see Forman, "Pessimism of Ecclesiastes," 336–43.

2. For an early study of the psychology of Qohelet's pessimism, from a psychoanalytical perspective, see Zimmermann, "Some Psychological Observations," 301–305.

3. E.g., Brannick, "Wisdom, Pessimism, and 'Mirth,'" 69–87; Scott, *Proverbs. Ecclesiastes*, xix.

as part of the pursuit of the American dream. They are part and parcel of the slogan "life, liberty, and the pursuit of happiness." But in the harsh and deadly world of the ancients, pessimism was an important coping mechanism for oppressed peoples. Also, being optimistic or pessimistic may be less a choice and more dependent on one's natural demeanor.[4] There seem to be a lot of organic pessimists in America.[5] Even age is a factor, with the elderly being more pessimistic and youth generally more optimistic.

Recently, several American psychologists have observed a form of pessimism that occurs even in the world of capitalist business.[6] It is known as defensive pessimism.[7] Some people are simply more prone to being pessimistic than optimistic and find it helpful in being successful in the business world.[8] For example, the psychologists found that optimists who are going to make a business presentation are often cocky, do not prepare enough, and are not attuned to their own weaknesses. When something goes wrong, they are not able to recover well. Defensive pessimists, however, will often mentally go over all the possible things that could go wrong while making their presentations. In other words, they lower their expectations about the future and themselves. They prepare for the worst, and when something goes wrong, they are able to recover and do well. In fact, these psychologists found that defensive pessimists were just as likely to succeed as optimists.

This shows that pessimism is a survival strategy that can deliver positive benefits. Pessimism has a distinct payoff, in other words. If it did not, it would not be adopted. Pessimism does not have to lead to depression or to the kind

---

4. See Julie K. Norem and Edward C. Chang, "The Positive Psychology of Negative Thinking," *Journal of Clinical Psychology* 58 (2002): 993–1001.

5. James A. Patterson points out that by the late 1960s evangelicals were becoming pessimistic about the revivalistic hopes of the postwar generation. In turn intellectual leaders like Francis Schaeffer, Carl Henry, and Charles Colson used pessimistic rhetoric to muster evangelicals to greater diligence in influencing American culture. Patterson does not see this as a good strategy ("Cultural Pessimism in Modern Evangelical Thought: Francis Schaeffer, Carl Henry, and Charles Colson," *JETS* 49 [2006]: 807–20).

6. Branick argues that the pessimistic wisdom literature could help business people become more ethical and healthy in their business practices ("Wisdom, Pessimism, and 'Mirth,'" 69–87).

7. Norem and Chang, "Negative Thinking," 996; cf. Caroline V. Clarke, "The Power of Negative Thinking," *Black Enterprise* (June 2002): 254; Barbara S. Held and Arthur C. Bohart, "Introduction: The (Overlooked) Virtues of 'Unvirtuous' Attitudes and Behavior: Reconsidering Negativity, Complaining, Pessimism, and 'False' Hope," *Journal of Clinical Psychology* 58 (2002): 961–64.

8. See esp. Julie Norem, *The Positive Power of Negative Thinking: Using Defensive Pessimism to Harness Anxiety and Perform at Your Peak* (paperback ed.; New York: Basic Books, 2002), 1–2, 81, 115–16, 127–28.

of retreating inactivity associated with melancholy. It is not always pathological and paralytic. It can actually help people cope effectively with the difficulties of life. This is what Qohelet's use of pessimism did for him and his original
audience.

Though Americans laud optimism as a supreme American virtue, it has its
liabilities. In view of the recent economic crisis in the United States and abroad
due chiefly to the overly optimistic business practices of the investment world,
the words of Julie Norem and Edward Chang from 2002 are eerily prophetic:

> Optimism and positive thinking can derail us if they lead us to ignore or dis-
> count important cues and warnings. . . . Much is made, for example, of the self-
> confidence, optimism, personal accomplishments, and resilience of American
> business leaders. When business practices fail, we are likely to attribute the soft
> landings (aided by "golden parachutes") of executives and their often spectacular
> comebacks to their positive attitudes. Much less often, however, do we tally up the
> costs to employees (and sometimes investors and clients) when overly optimistic
> expansions and acquisitions lead to bankruptcy and layoffs.[9]

Thus, especially in current times, it is mandatory that Americans not under-
value pessimism's positive possibilities!

As these psychologists have pointed out, pessimism can be a psychological strategy or approach for dealing with problems and stress. But it is also
properly a mood or emotion that is just as natural and healthy as anger, joy,
laughter, or envy, and that needs to be acknowledged by biblical scholars. Of
course, any emotion that is not curtailed or restrained can lead to unhealthy
results. Anger unchecked is a perfect example. Thus, unchecked pessimism
or melancholy can, of course, lead to depression and eventually suicide. But it
also can be harnessed for healthy results.

Qohelet's use of pessimism is a specific strategy to treat a world that
seemed largely irrational and unfair.[10] It is evident in the book that his mood
lowered his expectations about the world and those of his audience, and this
was healthy, as long as it did not lead to a largely inactive, passive kind of lifestyle. In spite of the American penchant for stubborn optimism and disdain
for pessimism, pessimism need not be considered maladaptive.

Of course, the living conditions in the United States today are not those of
the Jewish scribes in the Ptolemaic period. Constant dwelling on God's eventual salvation for his people would not have psychologically enabled Jewish
scribes to do their jobs and function effectively. One needs to keep in mind

---

9. Norem and Chang, "Negative Thinking," 998.

10. W. H. U. Anderson understands pessimism to be a largely passive attitudinal
response to an oppressive reality ("Genre Analysis of Qoheleth," 290–92). This chapter
views pessimism in a more active, voluntary sense.

that Qohelet and his audience did not live in a democracy. In Qohelet's day, individual freedom was quite limited. Qohelet and his young audience lived under the rule of an empire. Social change was possible but not nearly so as in Western culture today. Qohelet's pessimistic world enabled him and his young students to ease the psychological tension that they would have felt daily with their complicated social status.[11]

Though one could be sympathetic, Qohelet and his scribal social group would still be morally culpable if they did nothing to address the suffering of their poorer compatriots. If they found their social and economic situation tolerable and chose to do nothing about the situation of their poorer citizens, that is intolerable, even though one should have some degree of empathy with their complicated situation. Since these intellectuals found their own situation tolerable, they may have simply repressed their class guilt about their own more fortunate situation through the production of literature.[12] Literature such as Ecclesiastes could explain the Ptolemaic subjugation in such a way that both oppressor and oppressed could more manageably negotiate the experience and not consider the more threatening proposition of actually changing the society. As suggested by Jameson, literature serves to repress and cover over the social contradictions of society. Thus, instead of Qohelet and his scribal guild lifting up arms in support of their poorer brethren, through literature they could simply cause the whole terrible mess to disappear as part of God's ultimately mysterious plan. But it is still incumbent upon biblical scholars to try to understand how Qohelet's literary pessimism functioned for him and his audience.

GENERIC PESSIMISM

In the reference to literary pessimism, how Qohelet uses the mood of pessimism in his book is significant. This mood can actually create a distinct and functional genre, an established one in the ancient Near East, often referred to as pessimistic literature.[13] But one needs to define what a genre is to properly understand this phenomenon.

---

11. While Ardel B. Caneday acknowledges the enigmatic and disturbing character of the book, in the end he views Qohelet as a godly sage and no true pessimist ("Qoheleth: Enigmatic Pessimist or Godly Sage?" *Grace Theological Journal* 7 [1986]: 21–56).

12. On the production of literature as a social act, see Jameson, *Political Unconscious*, 1–102. On legitimization of class advantages, see Weber, *Sociology of Religion*, 107.

13. Karel van der Toorn shows how the ancient Near Eastern literary dialogue, often considered a type of pessimistic literature, is not meant primarily to deconstruct traditional tenets that have become problematic. Rather, these dialogues serve to offer new possibilities or compromises in difficult times ("The Ancient Near Eastern Literary Dialogue as a

A brief sketch of how genres produce meaning is in order.[14] Genres are not technically in texts or other media, but one can say that media share in them. Rather, it is better to speak of genres existing in the minds of author/senders and readers/receivers. Genres are necessary for the production of meaning. In fact, without genres, all forms of communication would come to a sudden halt. In acts of communication, people are constantly using genres, largely unconsciously. Genres are the grease that lubricates the wheels of communication. They provide clues/cues to the receivers on what to expect in subsequent communication. One can use and comprehend them so easily because since birth, a major part of socialization has involved their inculcation. Schools represent a significant contribution to this process, especially for literary genres.

Genres partake in an inherent tension between the universal and the particular. They constitute, on the one hand, the universal, and this is what builds expectations in the reader, which are known as conventions. This is done by consciously or unconsciously categorizing a text or medium as like other texts/media. On the other hand, the particular also has a part to play in this process. Every medium, while it draws on a genre or genres, in some way departs from it/them and forms the particular or the unique. Otherwise, all communication would be so generic that it would communicate only generalities. But if the departure from the universal is too great, then there is the risk of not communicating at all! So this tension is necessary and beneficial.

Genres produce worlds, but not what are properly called worldviews. Generic worlds are never complete.[15] Each genre reflects built-in assump-

---

Vehicle of Critical Reflection," in *Dispute Poems and Dialogues in the Ancient and Mediaeval Near East: Forms and Types of Literary Debates in Semitic and Related Literatures* [ed. G. J. Reinink and H. L. J. Vanstiphout; OLA 42; Leuven: Departement Oriëntalistiek, 1991], 59–75). After examining the semantic possibilities of הבל (including cognates) and רעות רוח in the Hebrew Bible and Qohelet, W. H. U. Anderson concludes that they "are of a *negative force* in Qoheleth." ("Semantic Implications," 71).

14. For introductions to genre criticism, see Frow, *Genre*; Alastair Fowler, *Kinds of Literature: An Introduction to the Theory of Genres and Modes* (Cambridge, Mass.: Harvard University Press, 1982); E. D. Hirsch Jr., *Validity in Interpretation* (New Haven: Yale University Press, 1967) 68–126; Garin Dowd, Lesley Stevenson, and Jeremy Strong, eds., *Genre Matters: Essays in Theory and Criticism* (Bristol: Intellect, 2006). For genre criticism applied to Hebrew Bible texts, see Sparks, *Ancient Texts*, 6–21; D. Brent Sandy and Ronald L. Giese Jr., eds., *Cracking Old Testament Codes: A Guide to Interpreting the Literary Genres of the Old Testament* (Nashville: Broadman & Holman, 1995); and Carol A. Newsom, "Spying Out the Land: A Report from Genology," in *Bakhtin and Genre Theory in Biblical Studies* (ed. Roland Boer; SemeiaSt 63; Atlanta: Society of Biblical Literature, 2007), 19–30.

15. Frow, *Genre*, 75–77, 85–87. Bakhtin scholars refer to literary genres conveying worldviews, but even they admit that these are not complete (Newsom, "Spying Out the Land," 30; Christine Mitchell, "*Eros*, and Biblical Genres," in *Bakhtin and Genre Theory in*

tions, values, and expectations that are different from those of other genres. Each genre creates its own particular, conventional world. As an example, the genre of horror films creates its own dark and scary world, where things "go bump in the night" and where special effects can be quite gory. Often the supernatural plays a significant role in such films, as in Gothic horrors but unlike sci-fi horrors. The latter is an example of the mixing of genres, which actually creates a new genre. The "Alien" series is a good example. It is certainly of the sci-fi genre, with spaceships and a projection into the future, but it is also a horror with the terrible monsters (aliens) that continually attempt to kill spaceship crews. The ability to mix genres creates interesting effects and shows the flexibility inherent in them, demonstrating how their "worlds" are not complete. Thus, a generic world is not the same thing as a worldview that a particular social group holds. Genres are simply not capable of carrying that much information; they are not comprehensive enough for that.

Genres are also intricately associated with social settings.[16] Genres have work to do, and they do it in certain kinds of settings, in recurring types of contexts and situations. They were created to provide strategic responses to these situations. Again, they are the lubrication of communication.

Not recognizing a genre can lead to misinterpretation. The receiver has to be attentive and sensitive to generic clues or risk failure to understand completely.

There are many ways to define a genre. It can be based on theme, structure, form, rhetoric, audience, and so on, in an assortment of combinations. With pessimistic literature, one can see that mood is the most significant factor in identifying this genre. Pessimistic literature was apparently used in a number of ways. The Admonitions of Ipuwer was used politically to discredit the former regime so that the current one would appear exemplary and profitable.[17] The dark world portrayed in the Admonitions contrasts with the positive and hopeful one represented by the contemporary Egyptian government. Here, essentially, pessimism is being used in the service of propaganda.

No doubt pessimistic literature often had a cathartic effect, much as did laments. The brutal honesty about the veil of tears that comprises life experiences is surely psychologically helpful, a way to vent and remove negative emotions, a means to prepare for eventual reconstruction and healing. One notes that Elisabeth Kübler-Ross's steps of depression and acceptance are crucial for facing the prospects of death.[18] Denial only exacerbates the problem. Facing

---

Biblical Studies [ed. Roland Boer; SemeiaSt 63; Atlanta: Society of Biblical Literature, 2007], 34).

16. See esp. Frow, *Genre*, 12–17.

17. Faulkner, "Introduction," 210.

18. See Elisabeth Kübler-Ross, *On Death and Dying: What the Dying Have to Teach Doctors, Nurses, Clergy, and Their Families* (paperback ed.; New York: Touchstone, 1997).

reality is an important component in any psychologically healthy adjustment. Even television's pop psychologist Dr. Phil preaches the importance of first *acknowledging* a problem before it can ever be resolved. Thus, ancient pessimistic literature probably had that kind of function: actually facing the frustrating and disappointing realities of life and the inevitability of death.[19]

It is important to point out that while in the modern world there is nothing identical to ancient pessimistic literature, there are certainly literary and cinematic genres, such as film noir, that are dark and melancholic. Of course, the genre of horror enables its viewers or readers to experience several negative emotions such as fear, anxiety, shock, repugnance, and even sometimes moments of hopelessness. Film critics speak of the cathartic effect these films have.[20] They also point to the safety of these films in that they allow the viewer to experience the intensity of these dark emotions in the safety of a theater. The adrenaline rush that occurs with viewing such dark films appears to be almost addictive because people keep going back to view them again and again. It may indicate the degree of boredom that modern life contains. Moderns are so sheltered from the dangers of the natural world in their urban cocoons that they need to attend movies to experience these dangerous events vicariously. The theme of death, which is so prominent in these movies, may reflect a fascination with death since in modern societies people are often sheltered from the reality of it.[21] Movies about vampires, in fact, may be a way for moderns to grapple with the primal fear of death. The living dead, then, are a way to deny the finality of death or work out anxiety about it.[22] Conversely, as Cosimo

---

19. Alison Lo argues that Qohelet's fascination with death serves to unite the book as a whole and is not morbid but ultimately the means to living more deeply ("Death in Qohelet," *JNES* 31 [2008]: 85–98). Similarly, Robert Davidson states, "That Koheleth is obsessed with a morbid interest in death, this, I think, is a wrong conclusion. He is not obsessed by death" ("The Exposition of the Old Testament: Koheleth as a Test Case," *ExpTim* 115, no. 1 [2003]: 6). Cf. Stefan Fischer, who shows that both the Egyptian Harper Songs and Qohelet share an ambivalent view of death wherein one lives more joyously in view of it, while doing this simultaneously enables one to forget about it ("Qohelet and 'Heretic' Harpers' Songs," *JSOT* 98 [2002]: 113).

20. Lena Vasileva demonstrates how Tim Burton's films depict a monstrous child, whom society wants to destroy, who uses creativity to redeem himself ("The Father, the Dark Child and the Mob That Kills Him: Tim Burton's Representation of the Creative Artist," in *Psyche and the Arts: Jungian Approaches to Music, Architecture, Literature, Film and Painting* [ed. Susan Rowland; London: Routledge, 2008], 87–95).

21. On the distinction between death-denying cultures like America and death-accepting ones like ancient Israel, see Lloyd R. Bailey, *Biblical Perspectives on Death* (OBT 5; Philadelphia: Fortress, 1979).

22. Angela Connolly argues that the monsters in horror films are ultimately about dealing with the problem of otherness (= monsters) within society ("Jung in the Twilight Zone: The Psychological Functions of the Horror Film," in *Psyche and the Arts: Jungian*

Urbano argues, modern horror films are a masochistic reenactment of the death wish; they elicit the pleasure of being passively out of control and, thus, annihilated.[23]

Even more comparable to ancient Near Eastern pessimistic literature are the noir movies that elicit dark emotions in viewers/readers. Film noir, named so by the French, who saw in such films a parallel with their pessimistic exis-tentialism, is characterized by somberness and cynical pessimism.[24] The pro-tagonist (often a private eye) is doomed to failure and then death (often via a femme fatale), to which he stoically resigns himself. Deep determinism over-shadows the movie with reciprocal fatalism in the characters. Film scholars point out that film noir (1945–55) represents a reaction to the postwar malaise and disenchantment.[25] Later noir movies (neo noir) include *Fargo* (a Coen brothers film; many of their films are in fact noir) or even the sci-fi cult thriller *Blade Runner* with Harrison Ford. Mark Bould states that "film noir continues to evoke the absurd and impenetrable world of late capitalism."[26] He sees the films providing a form of consolation: "They offer an image of the world that, however distorted, is familiar and comprehensible."[27] Noir films used to be called melodramas because of their play with extreme emotions, violence, and sex. Similar genres can be found in literature. The popularity of books and film that depend on eliciting negative emotions shows how fundamentally impor-tant these emotions are and that they cannot be ignored.

Even though in America pessimism and melancholy are eschewed as vices and are unacceptable as schemas for viewing the world, people still find a way to tap into the power of their negativity. The reality is that dark emotions like melancholy and a perspective like pessimism have important functions not only for individuals but for society as a whole, both in the past and today.

Thus, it is significant that Qohelet is consciously employing a recognizable genre of his day aimed at eliciting a particular mood in the reader for a par-ticular effect. Most scholars fail to recognize that Qohelet is even employing a genre. They simply conclude that he is a general pessimist. Recognizing the generic character of Qohelet's pessimism means a number of things. First of

Approaches to Music, Architecture, Literature, Film and Painting [ed. Susan Rowland; Lon-don: Routledge, 2008], 128–38).

23. See Cosimo Urbano, "Projections, Suspense, and Anxiety: The Modern Horror Film and Its Effects," *Psychoanalytic Review* 85 (1998): 889–908.

24. See Bruce Crowther, *Film Noir: Reflections in a Dark Mirror* (New York: Con-tinuum, 1989), 7–12.

25. See ibid., 9–12; Mark Bould, *Film Noir: From Berlin to Sin City* (Short Cuts; London: Wallflower, 2005), 49.

26. Bould, *Film Noir*, 114.

27. Ibid., 109.

all, Qohelet, by using this genre, is creating a world, not a complete worldview.[28] This is an important distinction. Qohelet's dark depiction of the world may not necessarily be his general view. Rather, the dark and dreary world he depicts is contrived for rhetorical effect. In other words, his pessimistic "world" might be confined to the particular problems the book addresses, such as the problem of theodicy. In the same way, the pessimistic worldview in the book of Lamentations might not be meant as a general way to view the world beyond the literary world of the text. The elicitation of the emotion is technically confined to the literary world that the text creates. Whether the emotion continues in the reader after reading the text is another matter.

Admittedly, Qohelet's work comes close to creating a complete worldview, but many elements are missing or neglected. Ninian Smart lists six dimensions of a worldview: experiential, mythic, doctrinal, ethical, ritual, and social.[29] As wisdom literature, the ethical dimension receives all the attention and, here, specifically it is directed at the individual, not the nation. Many components of the Jewish religion are hardly touched on in wisdom literature in general, and in Qohelet in particular. Things such as the patriarchs, the covenants, Israelite history, and the cult are rarely if ever mentioned. This does not mean that these matters were not important to the sages, contra the opinion of many wisdom literature experts.[30] Rather, it points to the necessary particular focus of genres and the limit of their purview and scope. The wisdom literature of the Hebrew Bible is essentially a torso without a head or extremities when it comes to worldview. Thus, Qohelet's dreary world is not properly a complete worldview but a particular strategy to treat particular problems. Of course, Qohelet may in fact have been a general pessimist, but one cannot draw that conclusion simply from his short twelve-chapter book, which focuses on individual ethics, particularly scribal.

Second, since Qohelet's melancholic world is generic, one should consider that it is not a true or complete reflection of the reality of his day. In other words, it has been contrived for rhetorical effect. It should be noted that all of Qohelet's anecdotes are negative. One would get the impression that nothing happens as expected in life, ever! Of course, this is not reality, as oppressive as it might be. Thus, Qohelet's consistent series of negative anecdotes is rhetorically pitched to persuade his audience that "everything is futile!" This hyper-

---

28. See Sneed, "'Wisdom Tradition,'" 50–71.

29. See Ninian Smart, *Worldviews: Crosscultural Explorations of Human Beliefs* (New York: Scribner's Sons, 1983). Susan Niditch applies Smart's paradigm to the Israelite worldview (*Ancient Israelite Religion* [New York: Oxford University Press, 1997], esp. 3–5).

30. E.g., Crenshaw, *Old Testament Wisdom*, 29.

bolic effect should be kept in mind while reading Qohelet; Qohelet's "reality" is in fact somewhat skewed.

The perception of Qohelet's use of rhetoric can be seen in his modification of the doctrine of retribution. In several places, Qohelet *seems* to deny the doctrine completely (3:16; 7:15; 8:14; cf. 9:11). But when the book is examined more closely, it appears that Qohelet denies the doctrine only as a regularly occurring phenomenon. In 7:15, Qohelet bluntly appears to deny the doctrine. But then in vv. 16–17, he does not counsel wickedness or folly, as might be expected if the doctrine were totally invalid for him. Rather, he counsels avoiding extremes. This shows that Qohelet does not completely negate the doctrine. In fact, he says that extreme wickedness is deadly (7:17). Further, immediately before 8:14 are vv. 11–13, which seem to be saying that there are delayed consequences to wickedness. Thus, one should not count on doing evil with impunity. Though it may appear otherwise, consequences will eventually come! Thus, once again Qohelet reveals that he never completely abandons the doctrine of retribution. As Fox has pointed out, Qohelet focuses only on the exceptions to the rule.[31] He modifies it, as has been demonstrated already. The apparent denial is for rhetorical effect.

The same degree of rhetoric is involved in Qohelet's eliciting the mood of pessimism in his book. Qohelet uses a pessimistic mood strategically to resolve particular social and religious problems. He employs melancholy rhetorically to solve a particular psychological and social tension in his readers. The rhetorical usage Qohelet makes of pessimism in generic form has never been recognized by Qohelet experts. Yet understanding this is critical for comprehending the purpose of the book. How Qohelet does so specifically will be investigated next.

LOWERING EXPECTATIONS IN QOHELET

The basic psychological function of pessimism is to lower expectations.[32] This destabilization of the audience's worldview is achieved by pessimism's lowering of various expectations of Qohelet's audience, and all of the expectations relate in one way or another to the wisdom tradition. Again, this involves the book's primary character as a polemic against the wisdom tradition.

---

31. Fox, *Rereading of Ecclesiastes*, 68.

32. Lena Lim studied Singapore undergrads and found that defensive pessimism is compatible with high achievers in that it lowers expectations to a more realistic degree and motivates them to prepare for possible obstacles. Defensive pessimism is distinct from typical pessimism, which is passive and contributes to failure ("A Two-Factor Model of Defensive Pessimism and Its Relations with Achievement Motives," *Journal of Psychology* 143 [2009]: 318–36).

Commendation of Wisdom

The most direct and devastating counter to the wisdom tradition is Qohelet's skepticism about human cognitive ability. Time and time again, Qohelet speaks of the severe limits placed on the human intellect by God (Eccl 3:11 has been cited numerous times). God has placed a consciousness of time in humans, but not the ability to master life by discerning the times. No one can know when a particular time will occur. Once a particular time begins to evolve, humans are powerless to resist it. Again, one sees a strong sense of divine determinism in Qohelet. It flies in the face of traditional wisdom, which is largely opportunistic, calculative, and reliant on human freedom. While Qohelet acknowledges the practical feasibility of opportunism in certain situations (8:5–6; 11:6), long-term opportunism or guaranteed opportunism is out of the question for him.[33] This inability to calculate beneficial results by acting at the right moment seriously undermines the goals of the wisdom tradition.[34]

The inability to predict the future is expressed again in 8:7: "Indeed, they do not know what it is to be, for who can tell them how it will be?" The last phrase is probably referring to the impotence of the wise to predict the future in regard to a king receiving his just deserts.[35] But the passage also admits that some knowledge is possible, which allows sages to avoid royal contempt (8:1b–6).[36] Compare 10:14: "No one knows what is to happen, and who can tell anyone what the future holds?" (cf. 3:22; 9:3). Of course, attempting to discern God's ways and plans is also largely eliminated: "Then I saw all the work of God, that no one can find out what is happening under the sun. However much they may toil in seeking, they will not find it out; even though those who are wise claim to know, they cannot find it out" (8:17). Compare: "In the day of prosperity be joyful, and in the day of adversity consider; God has made the one as well as the other, so that mortals may not find out anything that will come after them" (7:14). This means, of course, that the wise do not have the capacity or ability to advise others on how best to live their lives: "For who knows what is good for mortals while they live the few days of their vain life,

---

33. Jones's argument that 8:1–9 is about the liabilities of mantic wisdom fits this suspicion about long-term prediction ("Qohelet's Courtly Wisdom," 211–28).

34. Richard L. Schultz qualifies this inability by examining Qohelet' view of time (esp. 3:1–8) and finding that there is a degree of opportunism reflected in Qohelet that is constrained by God's ordering of the times ("A Sense of Timing: A Neglected Aspect of Qoheleth's Wisdom," in *Seeking Out the Wisdom of the Ancients* [ed. Ronald L. Troxel, Kelvin G. Friebel, and Dennis R. Marary; Winona Lake, Ind.: Eisenbrauns, 2005], 257–67).

35. See Jones, "Qohelet's Courtly Wisdom," 223–26.

36. Beentjes argues that 8:1b–5 is traditional material that Qohelet then critiques in vv. 6–9 ("Qohelet 8,1–15," 304–9), but Jones demonstrates effectively that vv. 2–5 are also part of Qohelet's counsel ("Qohelet's Courtly Wisdom," 219–23).

which they pass like a shadow? For who can tell them what will be after them under the sun?" (6:12).

The limitation of human cognition is matched by Qohelet's skepticism about the value of a wise lifestyle. Qohelet says, "Again I saw that under the sun the race is not to the swift, nor the battle to the strong, nor bread to the wise, nor riches to the intelligent, nor favor to the skillful; but time and chance happen to them all" (9:11). The last three categories, of course, are cognates for wisdom. Again, Qohelet's skepticism about the doctrine of retribution is relevant here. Thus, Qohelet's skepticism is not for skepticism's sake but has a positive function. It serves as his means for lowering expectations about the wisdom tradition. His skepticism undermines wisdom's legitimacy and value.

In this way, one sees the proper relationship between Qohelet's pessimism and skepticism. Qohelet's pessimism is primary; the skepticism is secondary and merely in service of the pessimism and reinforces his pessimistic conclusion that all is vanity. The skepticism deconstructs any lasting or absolute value of the wisdom tradition. The skepticism says, "Wisdom is useless." Thus, one can refer to Qohelet's skepticism as the handmaiden to his pessimism.

Again, however, Qohelet does not totally debunk the wise lifestyle. It is certainly superior to the foolish lifestyle. It has a relative value. It may prevent the early death that folly usually brings (7:17). But there are no guarantees. For Qohelet, what is superior to the wise lifestyle is God-fearing: cautious behavior before the deity that avoids unnecessarily offending him and knows that attempting to manipulate him is dangerous (5:1–7). Caution rather than wisdom as traditionally conceived is, thus, Qohelet's preference. The God-fearer will more likely succeed in life (7:18; 8:12b-13), though, again, there are no guarantees.

But the value of the wise life is also delivered a serious blow by death, another distinction of humans over against God. The traditional sages usually got around this by pointing to a type of immortality involving the perpetuation of a good name or reputation ("The memory of the righteous is a blessing, but the name of the wicked will rot" [Prov 10:7]) or remembrance by progeny. Of course, a good reputation was highly revered in traditional wisdom: "A good name is to be chosen rather than great riches, and favor is better than silver or gold" (Prov 22:1). But Qohelet, while seeing the relative superiority of wisdom to folly, says this,

Yet I perceived that the same fate befalls all of them.[37] Then I said to myself, "What happens to the fool will happen to me also; why then have I been so very

---

37. Gianto Austinus compares two wisdom texts from Emar with Qohelet and shows that both the Emar texts and Qohelet describe the immutability of divine destinies and find meaning in the joys of life ("Human Destiny in Emar and Qohelet," in *Qohelet in the*

wise?" And I said to myself that this also is a vanity. For there is no enduring remembrance of the wise or of fools, seeing that in the days to come all will have been long forgotten. How can the wise die just like fools? (2:14b–16)

Qohelet is saying that the reputation of the wise does not long survive their death.[38] Qohelet, thus, is deconstructing traditional wisdom's main source of immortality. Not only do the wise die, just like the foolish, but the memory of both soon evaporates (contra Sir 44–50). What lasting and enduring value, then, does wisdom have over folly? This is an effective critique of traditional wisdom. Qohelet's standard of evaluation is not inexplicable or unreasonable, contra Fox,[39] who fails to see the rhetorical effect of Qohelet's strategies. The rhetoric here is all geared toward deconstructing traditional wisdom—further proof that Qohelet is a polemical book.

But elsewhere Qohelet even deconstructs the value of prestige or reputation that supposedly accompanies the wise. The anecdote about the poor wise man who saves the city with his wisdom but is forgotten because of his low status (9:13–16) demonstrates that status does not necessarily accrue to being wise. Again, in 9:11, Qohelet notes that "favor" does not accrue to the skillful or wise (literally "those who know"). The word for favor here חֵן means prestige or honor in this context. In 7:1 Qohelet includes a proverb whose first couplet sounds like something out of the book of Proverbs, but then, in his usual way, Qohelet immediately deconstructs it: "A good name is better than precious ointment, and the *day of death, than the day of birth.*" This proverb is part of a segment where Qohelet emphasizes the importance of keeping death always in view as one journeys through life. The point is quite profound and fits with Qohelet's carpe diem ethic. Though ostensibly negative, it achieves a positive result. Always keeping death in mind prioritizes life and forces one to focus on what is really important, such as the simple pleasures life offers. How counterintuitive, but true! But, at any rate, the proverb of 7:1 serves to deconstruct traditional wisdom's focus on reputation, though that is not the primary point of the proverb.

All these instances reveal that in Qohelet's day, the honor and respect traditionally ascribed to scribes was not in evidence. It might have been that the Ptolemies viewed the Jewish scribes as rather barbaric and unrefined compared to their own bureaucrats. Or it could be that the Jewish masses were suspicious of these scribes' collaboration with the Ptolemaic regime. It probably

---

Context of Wisdom [ed. Anton Schoors; BETL 136; Leuven: Leuven University Press and Peeters, 1998], 473–79).

38. Peter Machinist demonstrates how Qohelet's use of מקרה is unique in the Hebrew Bible in that it refers exclusively to death and is the first sophisticated treatment of the problem of time ("Fate, *miqreh*, and Reason," 159–75).

39. See Fox, *Rereading of Ecclesiastes*, 138–39.

also reflects the reality that the pious and orthodox believers of Qohelet's day were increasingly ostracized by the Jewish elite and separated from substantive power, resulting in their loss of status. Thus, as Anton Schoors points out, the pious Torah adherents were becoming increasingly alienated and disenfranchised during the Ptolemaic period.[40]

But something deeper is going on here. In Proverbs, life and death take on metaphorical significance, with life signifying not just the delay of physical death but a way of life that involves prosperity, progeny, success, and honor.[41] It means conforming to societal norms and essentially upholding the moral order of society. Following the path of wisdom means engaging in right behavior and living a righteous life. It means being on God's side, being for the good of the community. It is the path of light and hope. It means being on the side of truth and justice. The path of folly, conversely, is the path to destruction, not just physically but also socially and religiously. It means straying from the norms of society and embracing deviance and selfishness. It represents a stand against the community. It is being on the side of darkness, chaos, and disorder. It represents apathy and despair.

Qohelet is also attempting to deconstruct this broader, metaphorical significance of wisdom. He is attempting to cast doubt on the validity of these aspirations connected to the path of wisdom. Thus, Qohelet is not merely saying that physical death mitigates the value of wisdom, but, metaphorically, he is saying the sapiential lifestyle is not "all it's cracked up to be." He is saying that its claims and promises cannot be substantiated, the payoff is not there. In his day, such an idealistic portrayal of the good life just did not fit reality. Thinking about life needed to change and adapt to the new circumstances.

OPTIMISTIC ANTHROPOLOGY

The emphasis on the limitation of human cognition and the liabilities of the sapiential lifestyle goes hand in hand with Qohelet's skepticism about human morality. Qohelet has a very low estimate of human moral capability. He has a pessimistic anthropology, something he shares with Paul.[42] In fact, in Rom

---

40. Schoors, "Changing Society," 68–87.

41. Cf. Derek Kidner, *Proverbs* (TOTC; Leicester: Inter-Varsity Press, 1964), 53–56; J. T. Sanders, "Wisdom, Theodicy, Death," 264.

42. On Paul, see Charles H. Talbert, *Romans* (Smyth & Helwys Bible Commentary; Macon, Ga.: Smyth & Helwys, 2002), 193–202. Steve Moyise argues that both Paul and Qohelet believe life is futile, though Paul's expectation of glorification mitigates this ("Is Life Futile? Paul and Ecclesiastes," *ExpTim* 108, no. 6 [1997]: 178–79). Jennifer L. Koosed and Robert P. Seesengood observe that the imputed authorship of both Qohelet and Hebrews served to ensure the canonicity of each and to soften the undesirable elements of each

3:10, Paul may be citing Eccl 7:20: "Surely there is no one on earth so righteous as to do good without ever sinning." Qohelet's exhortation in 7:16 not to be too righteous seems to constitute a recognition that human moral potential is limited. Similarly, in 5:6, Qohelet says that one should not say it was a mistake to make a vow you did not pay. It would be better to confess one's stupidity than try to rationalize one's actions or make excuses. That would do no good.

Further, in 7:28–29, Qohelet says, "One man among a thousand I found, but a woman among all these I have not found. See this alone I found, that God made human beings straightforward, but they have devised many schemes." Apparently, Qohelet is referring to morality, especially with the reference to the wickedness of women in general in v. 26 and the moral context assumed in v. 28. Qohelet appears to be saying that there are few moral humans in his day: only one man in a thousand, and no women, which indicates Qohelet's misogyny.[43] The Hebrew word for "straightforward" יָשָׁר in v. 29 can be translated "upright," indicating that God made humans originally as morally pure, but they have strayed from this state. This is the classic free-will theodicy that blames humans for moral evil in the world. יָשָׁר is the same word that is used in 3:11, which is usually translated as "appropriate," "beautiful" or "suitable."

In addition, Qohelet expresses himself regarding the depravity of the human heart: "Because sentence against an evil deed is not executed speedily, the human heart is fully set to do evil" (8:11). All of these coincide with Qohelet's observations about the typicality of injustice and corruption in the world and his counsel that one should not be amazed at it (3:16; 5:8; 8:10). Compare the following:

> All this I observed, applying my mind to all that is done under the sun, while one person exercises authority over another to the other's hurt. (8:9).

> Then I saw that all toil and all skill in work come from one person's envy of another (4:4).

Qohelet notes the hypocrisy of those who are quick to condemn their slaves for cursing them when, in fact, they know they have done the same thing (7:21). Finally, Qohelet refers to the tendency of fools to "not know how to keep from doing evil" when they attempt to offer acceptable sacrifices to God (5:1).

("Constructions and Collusions: The Making and Unmaking of Identity in Qoheleth and Hebrews," in *Hebrews: Contemporary Methods—New Insights* [ed. Gabriella Gelardini; Biblical Interpretation Series 75; Leiden: Brill, 2005], 265–80).

43. See Sneed, "Qohelet Deconstructed," 122–23; cf. Fox, *Rereading of Ecclesiastes*, 266–67.

Another related limitation that Qohelet acknowledges about humans is their impotence before God. Qohelet states, "Consider the work of God: who can make straight what he has made crooked?" (7:13). He says further, "Whatever has come to be has already been named, it is known what human beings are, and that they are not able to dispute with those who are stronger" (6:10b). Most scholars see the reference to the "stronger" as God.[44] Since life is unchangeable, it is pointless for humans to try to dispute with God. The emphasis on limited cognitive ability in humans, their lack of moral fortitude, and their impotence before God are again part of Qohelet's strategy to emphasize human finitude and distinction from God. Here, again, one sees the pitting of humanity as הֶבֶל over against a deity who is not limited.

CONCEPTION OF GOD

But Qohelet's polemic against traditional wisdom does not involve only lowering expectations about human potentiality and character. The polemic involves also countering traditional wisdom's conception of God as benevolent and maintaining covenant loyalty. As has already been mentioned, this strategy is in connection with Qohelet's attempts at dissolving the theodicy problem. Qohelet essentially views God (and the world) as unjust (or beyond the ken of human standards), but not in a protesting way, as seen in Job. Rather, Qohelet encourages his audience to resign itself to this fact of life. As already seen, Qohelet views God as rather oppressive in his treatment of humanity. Qohelet repeatedly refers to the "unhappy business" God has given to humanity as a whole or to specific individuals (1:13; 3:10; 4:8; 5:13; 8:16). God tests humanity to show them that they are like animals (3:18–21) and never reveals his ultimate plans to mortals "so that they may fear him" (3:11, 14). Qohelet also refers to what God does as "crooked" and unchangeable (1:15; 7:13–14). There is certainly a negative connotation here; but again, it is more resignation and less protestation.

Thus, the psychological effect of these depictions of God is that they lower expectations about the way God runs the world and may treat individuals. In other words, when it comes to God's ways with humans, one should not expect much. Certainly one should not anticipate necessarily benevolent or favorable treatment. Certainly one should not count on positive treatment simply for being righteous or pious! If one happens to receive blessings, this is because of God's idiosyncratic standard of judgment. One should respond by simply accepting this gift. God no longer seems to favor the Jews above other nations.

---

44. Crenshaw, *Ecclesiastes*, 130–31; Fox, *Rereading of Ecclesiastes*, 247–48.

The prosperity of the Ptolemies might have encouraged Qohelet even to contemplate them as God's favored! Qohelet frequently indicates with his anecdotes that things always happen in unexpected ways. Again, 6:1–2 is typical. God gives a man wealth, possessions, and honor—the standard items of blessing for a Jewish patriarch. But God does not allow him to enjoy these! One should remember that this incident may be the stereotypical strategy of a foreign despot who takes the opportunity to reward more loyal officials by giving them property confiscated from indigenous nobility, an observation offered by Lauha.[45] Thus, the effect of all these negative anecdotes is for Qohelet's reader to expect the unexpected, and, thus, psychologically one is prepared for anything and does not expect anything positive! This will certainly eliminate any tension between expectations and reality, but it has the nasty residual effect of making God appear arbitrary and less personable. Of course, with these anecdotes often involving the Ptolemies, this has the effect of legitimizing the status quo, as has been shown. Again, this viewpoint is expected with Qohelet's own privileged social location as a scribe. His position prevents him from becoming very critical of the status quo. He never contemplates overturning the sad state of affairs of his own people because of his own personal benefits. Thus, he simply resigns himself to the way things are. This removes any internal tension. Whatever happens is simply God's will; one must resign oneself to it and make the most of it.

The lowering of expectations about the world and God not only dissolves the theodicy problem but also helps assuage any class guilt Qohelet and his audience may have felt. Compared to Proverbs, there is very little concern for the oppressed in Qohelet, which is traditionally expressed in the form of noblesse oblige, as in advice about charity. As mentioned already, although Seow interprets 11:1 as advice to be charitable, most scholars agree that this passage is about diversifying investments, so that catastrophic loss might be prevented.[46] In 4:1 Qohelet does demonstrate empathy for the oppressed, but that is all it is: empathy. Never does he allow that empathy to propel him to advocate action that would help alleviate the suffering of the poor. As several scholars have noted, Qohelet's citation here is more a piece of evidence for his argumentation that the world is unjust than it is an emotional sentiment.[47]

In many ways Qohelet absolves himself and his audience from any responsibility toward the poor by shifting all of it to God. In other words, Qohelet mainly argues that if the world is unjust and oppressive, it is God's fault and not his or his audience's. Qohelet's exaggeration of God's sovereignty and the

---

45. Lauha, "Verhältnis zur Geschichte," 400–401. Maussion argues that this person must have been a "sinner," as in 2:26 ("Qohélet VI 1–2," 501–10).

46. Seow, *Ecclesiastes*, 341–44.

47. See Schoors, "Changing Society," 68; Hengel, *Judaism and Hellenism*, 1:117.

concomitant limitation of human freedom further serve to remove responsibility from his shoulders. Blaming God for life's troubles is a way for him and his readers to remain ignorant of their own complicity in this oppression. Qohelet never contemplates that his own privileged position and that of his readers could have been made possible only by the back-breaking work of the peasants around Jerusalem. His educational training and time for leisure allowed him to write his book, but it is all due to the work of these peasants. The indigenous Jewish scribes were a necessity for the Ptolemaic tax system to work. Records needed to be kept, documents needed to be written, and surveys needed to be done. But if all of this activity is considered simply to be part of God's mysterious plan, then Qohelet and his audience need not dwell on their own responsibility or culpability in the matter.

Of course, again, the options that Qohelet and the scribal guild had for promoting social justice were quite limited compared to today. But at least Qohelet could have commended charity. He could have been more critical of the Ptolemaic regime. In other words, he did not have to essentially legitimize the status quo. Qohelet, thus, reflects self-interest and a concern primarily for his guild and his colleagues. He is out for the benefit and survival of his own status group, and one can certainly understand that on one level, but must condemn it on another. Yet one does not know what Qohelet and his audience did for the poor in their actual personal lives.

COMMENDATION OF LABOR

Finally, Qohelet lowers expectations about human effort and striving, which also undermines traditional wisdom with its emphasis on industriousness, hard work, and its calculation of long-term benefits and goal-oriented perspective.[48] The wisdom tradition was geared toward maximizing the benefits and minimizing the liabilities of human behavior. De Jong has demonstrated that the book of Qohelet is essentially about labor.[49] The first rhetorical question of the book is significant and sets the tone for the rest of the book: "What do people gain from all of the toil at which they toil under the sun?" (1:3). Of course, as has been seen, a primary and favorite target Qohelet has in mind is intellectual labor or grasping, the need to master the cosmos. But Qohelet ingeniously keeps his aim broad, essentially undermining the entire human

---

48. William H. U. Anderson argues that Qohelet interacts with the account of the Fall in Gen 3 when he discusses the frustrations of labor ("The Curse of Work in Qoheleth: An Exposé of Genesis 3:17–19 in Ecclesiastes," *EvQ* 70 [1998]: 99–113). However, the basis for Qohelet's negative assessment of labor never appears to depend on the Genesis narrative; instead Qohelet provides personal observations and anecdotes.

49. De Jong, "Book on Labour," 107–16.

obsession with labor, acquisition, and accomplishments. Qohelet deconstructs human labor in four main ways.

First, he demonstrates that the effort itself is wearisome and unpleasant. Qohelet asks, "What do mortals get from all their toil and strain with which they toil under the sun? For all their days are full of pain, and their work is a vexation; even at night their minds do not rest. This is also a vanity" (2:23). In reference to intellectual labor, in becoming very wise, Qohelet describes the process as painful, "For in much wisdom is much vexation, and those who increase knowledge increase sorrow" (1:18). Concerning the acquisition of wealth, Qohelet states, "Sweet is the sleep of laborers, whether they eat little or much; but the surfeit of the rich will not let them sleep" (5:12). Qohelet sees the value in less effort, not more: "Better is a handful with quiet than two handfuls with toil, and a chasing after the wind" (4:6).[50]

Second, he demonstrates how once the goal is accomplished, it is not that valuable or satisfying. In other words, it was not worth all the effort; it is a disappointment. Concerning the goal of money, Qohelet says, "The lover of money will not be satisfied with money; nor the lover of wealth, with gain. This also is vanity" (5:10). Here the universal conclusion is invoked that wealth only increases one's appetite for more and does not diminish it. Near the end of his royal experiment, Qohelet admits that he got some joy out of all his effort (2:10), but ultimately it was disappointing. It was not worth the effort: "Then I considered all that my hands had done and the toil I had spent in doing it, and again, all was vanity and a chasing after the wind, and there was nothing to be gained under the sun" (2:11). All the effort and labor he had invested in his royal developments and acquisitions did not correlate with what little joy he got from them. It just did not add up. Thus, ultimately, no profit emerged; there were more expenditures than assets at the end of the day.

Again, Qohelet reckons wisdom as superior to folly, but in the end the liabilities outweigh the assets (2:12–17). Wisdom will not deliver the wise from death, nor will it necessarily prevent calamity and misfortune (7:14–15). Wisdom has serious liabilities. Its profitable character is, thus, seriously under-mined. Of course, profit and advantage are what wisdom is supposed to bring, its ultimate purpose. A wisdom that cannot bring advantage is not much use. Death ultimately cancels out any long-term prestige that wisdom might bring. Wisdom does not automatically bring prestige anyway, as has been seen (9:11,

---

50. Nili Wazana interprets the passage in which this verse occurs as a warning against the evil eye and, thus, as the promotion of social welfare. While her argument is enticing, it seems best to interpret the passage without this proposed background ("A Case of the Evil Eye: Qohelet 4:4–8," *JBL* 126 [2007]: 685–702).

13–18). Wanton pleasure is disappointing (2:1–2). It is fleeting and accomplishes nothing. Piety and righteousness do not do much either (7:15; 9:2).[51]

Third, Qohelet often demonstrates that the goal is unattainable in the first place. In 7:23–24, he attempts to become truly wise but concludes that this is impossible, "It was far from me. That which is, is far off, and deep, very deep; who can find it out?" He attempted to find wisdom and "the sum of things" (v. 26). He concludes, "See, this is what I found, says the Teacher, adding one thing to another to find the sum, which my mind has sought repeatedly, but I have not found" (v. 27–28). This is equivalent to Qohelet's proverb that "What is crooked cannot be made straight, and what is lacking cannot be counted" (1:15), when he tried to comprehend the deeds done under the sun.

Fourth, even if the goal is attained or goods acquired and valued, one often has no control over the outcome or cannot even enjoy it or have the power to dispense it. Or there is no one to share it with! In the royal experiment he complains about the toil itself, since the benefits eventually go to someone else: "I hated all my toil in which I had toiled under the sun, seeing that I must leave it to those who come after me" (2:18). He bemoans the irony that what has been acquired by wisdom might ultimately go to a fool and be enjoyed by him (v. 19)! As already mentioned in 6:1–2, a person is given "wealth, possessions, and honor," but God does not allow him to enjoy these! Qohelet also bemoans the loner: "Again, I saw vanity under the sun: the case of solitary individuals, without sons or brothers; yet there is no end to all their toil, and their eyes are never satisfied with riches. 'For whom am I toiling,' they ask, 'and depriving myself of pleasure?' This also is vanity and an unhappy business" (4:8).

Thus, Qohelet ingeniously deconstructs human effort and toil from nearly any angle.[52] Again, it is not that Qohelet has standards that are too high when he begins his deconstruction, contra Fox. Rather, in order to deliver a lethal blow to the wisdom tradition, which, of course, Fox erroneously denies, Qohelet must undercut the tradition at its base and fundamentally. Fox does not discern the rhetorical genius of Qohelet. Qohelet is intent on leaving no leg standing in the wisdom tradition. Then he can come back and speak of rela-

---

51. Again, Brindle's interpretation of 7:15–18 ignores one side of the equation: wickedness and folly, which Qohelet admonishes one not to indulge in to excess, just as he did for righteousness and wisdom ("Righteousness and Wickedness," 243–57). There is a mean between extremes here that Brindle apologetically avoids.

52. Another more positive interpretation of Qohelet's valuation of work is represented by William P. Brown, "'Whatever Your Hand Finds to Do': Qoheleth's Work Ethic," *Int* 55 (2001): 271–84. But Brown's argument that Qohelet finds joy in toil itself and not from its products strikes one as elitist (pp. 278–81). He also attempts to democratize Qohelet's carpe diem ethic, which distorts its nature (p. 281). As a whole, Brown's argument is apologetic and an attempt to put a positive spin on Qohelet's genuine pessimism.

tive goods and pleasures. All of this is part and parcel of his pessimistic strategy of lower expectations about the wisdom tradition and life in general. This will prevent disappointment but will also allow one to appreciate those simple pleasures and goods in life that do come one's way.

Qohelet's questioning of traditional values of his time, including the emphasis on human productivity and striving, should be seen in a largely positive and not a negative way. Qohelet enabled his original audience to see that the typical values scribes held during the earlier monarchic period were not as desirable or even as achievable in their current context. Access and enjoyment of prestige, power, and wealth were no longer restricted to those who were pious and wise according to traditional Jewish definitions. Now these scarce commodities were open to all lifestyles, including even the wicked. Essentially those who were closest to the Ptolemaic political system and who played by its rules were most likely to succeed in Qohelet's days, not those who adhered most closely to the Torah.[53]

Thus, Qohelet does a service for his audience by questioning most of the traditional values of olden times, and he brings Judaism into a new era where new values were needed and new strategies developed. Instead of exclusive emphasis on religious piety, wisdom, and industriousness, which are possible only with social stability and predictability, Qohelet emphasizes the precariousness of his culture and society. Caution, fatalism, resignation, enjoyment of the present, and moderation are the new virtues and strategic outlooks that are more likely to succeed. Thus, Qohelet's pessimism is the general "worldview" that will most likely enable Qohelet and his colleagues to be successful in the world of the Ptolemies.

The best way to see the positive function of Qohelet's pessimism for his own day is actually to contemplate how his pessimism could function hermeneutically in today's world. Qohelet's carpe diem ethic is the key. It represents an abandonment of calculating long-term goals and pleasures. In the rat race many find themselves in today, Qohelet's ethic provides a powerful message. While most moderns will never abandon long-term goals and aspiring to be successful, Qohelet's ethic calls on them to question focusing entirely on these efforts. It enables them to stand back from the race and re-prioritize their lives. While moderns aspire to their dreams and goals, there is also a place "to stop and smell the roses," to enjoy the simple pleasures of life. Life should not be totally consumed with striving and fighting but should also involve moments of resignation and contemplation. The carpe diem ethic assumes that there are no guarantees in life, so the enjoyment of the present is a necessity. If one overlooks the temporary pleasures that become available while pursuing long-

---

53. Schoors, "Changing Society," 68–87.

term dreams, there is something wrong. It shows that it is not always the ends but the means that provide the most pleasure. As one pursues long-term goals, will the ultimate achievement of them provide the most satisfaction? As they say, "Life is a journey." It is not the end of the road that is most significant but the relishing of the journey. As the character played by Robin Williams in *The Dead Poets Society*, advised his young students, "Suck the marrow out of life." This scene should be considered in its context of a prep-school for ambitious young elites. It does not deny the aspirations, but it does mitigate them with the counsel to enjoy oneself along the path to success.

Qohelet's pessimism also enables one to see the importance of companionship (4:8–12) and family (9:7–9) vis-à-vis career and colleagues. There is much more to life than career and professional ambition. Qohelet enables one to see that, though the world is largely filled with injustice and evil, there is good in it too. When the positive aspects of life become available, one should seize them as a gift from God (2:24–26). In other words, one has a God-given responsibility to take advantage of them (9:7).

Conclusion

Qohelet's pessimism and skepticism should not be viewed simply as aspects of his personal idiosyncratic demeanor or even as pathological. For his times, they represent survival strategies for a group of scribes attempting to be as successful as possible in their guild. This strategy reflects the status group's privileged social location, which was complicated by the nation's subjugation to the Ptolemaic regime. Qohelet's pessimistic worldview should not be viewed as solely a passive stance toward the troubling world in which he lived. Rather, it should be seen as a proactive response to the declassed status in which his peers and the nation found themselves. Before such a power, resistance was futile. Attempting to be successful as scribes by relying on traditional values and goals and following the traditional pious lifestyle of his day was largely ineffective and dangerous. Rather, Qohelet espouses a novel approach that was truer to the new circumstances in which he and his audience found themselves.

As has been seen, Qohelet's skepticism is secondary to his primary, pessimistic rhetorical strategy to deconstruct the path of traditional wisdom. It serves to deconstruct it by questioning the feasibility of both its values and its methodology. Deconstructing the doctrine of retribution as traditionally formulated, that is, the fundamental rationality of the tradition, is a major accomplishment of Qohelet's skepticism.

Qohelet's pessimism and skepticism both should be viewed as a reaction to the over-rationality of the wisdom tradition. This was created not by a dogmatization of the tradition but by the fact that in Qohelet's day, under the domination of a foreign empire, its rationality and calculation were no longer applicable or a good fit with reality. Qohelet's response is essentially irrational, a turning from cognition and intellectuality to the irrational, in the sense of the enjoyment of physical (carpe diem ethic), not intellectual, pleasures. In fact intellect produces pain. This irrational response is indicated also in Qohelet's conception of the deity, the *deus absconditus*, the hidden God, whose rationality is not accessible to mortals. This, of course, is compatible with his theodicy dissolution strategy of creating a vast gulf between humanity and the deity.

Qohelet's ethic is hermeneutically valuable for moderns today, whether theologically or not. Therefore, ultimately Qohelet's pessimism should be viewed positively and functionally and not negatively or pathologically as most scholars have done. Though not pathological, Qohelet's pessimism does suffer from elitism, with its concomitant legitimization of the status quo.

9

THE SOCIOLOGY OF THE BOOK
OF QOHELET'S CANONICITY

In this chapter, the issue of the canonicity of Qohelet will be examined from a sociological perspective. Specifically, if Qohelet was so heterodox, why was the book allowed to maintain a canonical status or even admitted? This will be answered in several ways. First, it will be shown that Qohelet was not as heterodox as some have maintained. Actually, he represents a return to a more primitive form of the Israelite religion and faith. He utilizes minor elements of traditional wisdom to construct his theological position, which means that he simply reconfigures traditional wisdom. Second, it will be demonstrated that Qohelet was canonized ultimately because of the inherent ambiguity of the book, misperceptions about it, and its underlying religious value. Third, the process of the book's canonization will be considered from a social science perspective, particularly Weberian.

THE DEGREE OF QOHELET'S HETERODOXY

SOCIAL CLASS AND HETERODOXY

It is important to note at the outset that Qohelet is classified as heterodox only on the basis of the standards of Pharisaic/rabbinic Judaism, which became normative after the destruction of Jerusalem.[1] From a Weberian perspective, Qohelet's essentially nonsalvific religious orientation and solution to the theodicy problem mean that his perspective does not fall neatly within the purview of the Jewish faith as a salvation religion. The Jews developed into a pariah people, a minority ethnic religion that yearned for apocalyptic resolution of their deprived social standing. In addition, Qohelet's dissolution of the theod-

---

1. For Weber's discussion of the postexilic sects and the formation of Judaism, see *Ancient Judaism*, 385–424; Love, "Weber's *Ancient* Judaism," 200–220. For a good summation of the theology of rabbinic Judaism, see E. P. Sanders, *Paul and Palestinian Judaism: A Comparison of Patterns of Religion* (paperback ed.; Philadelphia: Fortress, 1977).

icy problem through the questioning of God's justice would also place him in the heterodox category. God's justice became an important component of normative Judaism. Further, Qohelet's intellectual faith, which did not include the possibility of a personal relationship with God, does not fit normative Judaism. Love of God and faithful trust in God became essentials of normative Judaism. After examining the rabbinic discussion of Qohelet, Ruth Sandberg concludes:

> The rabbis cannot agree with Qohelet's view of a remote and unknowable deity at work in the universe, whose actions and reactions are not possible to predict or understand. Rabbinic Judaism insists upon believing that God is loving, merciful and just. . . . The rabbis cannot accept Qohelet's pessimistic generalizations about the permanent state of human injustice and the mystery of unmerited suffering. Qohelet Rabbah insists that all human wrongs will be judged and punished by God in the end, and all underserved suffering will be replaced with eternal joy.[2]

Sheldon Isenberg also emphasizes the rabbis' rationalistic view of retribution:

> Reward and punishment, in this life or the next, constitute the cornerstone of the rabbinic moral-legal calculus. Their sense of the rational, consistent ordering of a just reality required that punishments and rewards follow human actions regularly. . . . For the rabbis nothing that happens to a person or the people can truly be evil. It all must fit within the calculus. Suffering was punishment or test or would be balanced out in the world to come.[3]

Finally, Qohelet's irrational and anti-ascetic approach to the world and concomitant reduction in emphasis on Torah keeping place him beyond the bounds of normative Judaism. Torah keeping became the litmus test of orthodoxy in later Judaism. Thus, the answer to the question whether Qohelet is orthodox or heterodox is clear as far as Pharisaic/rabbinic Judaism is concerned: he is heterodox.

But determining Qohelet's orthodoxy before this period is more complicated, because in the earlier developmental stage of Israelite and Jewish religion there was far more heterogeneity than after Pharisaic/rabbinical dominance arose.[4] This is due chiefly to the fact that no one body of religious specialists controlled the process of religious document production and preservation.

---

2. Sandberg, *Rabbinic Views*, 230.

3. Isenberg, "Evil in Judaism," 22–23.

4. Steve Mason argues that Josephus was right about Pharisaic dominance among the Jews and that Jesus' charge of hypocrisy against them is authentic ("Pharisaic Dominance before 70 CE and the Gospel's Hypocrisy Charge [Matt 23:2–3]," *HTR* 83 [1990]: 363–81). Herbert Basser argues that the Pharisees made Torah observance central because of the Hellenistic tendencies of the Sadducees, though allowing theosophic speculation about it ("Pharisaic Idea of Law," 108).

Kings, priests, prophets, and scribes, with their differing emphases and per-spectives, were all part of this process. In comparison with Egypt and Mesopo-tamia, with their highly centralized governments and bureaucratic efficiency, Israel was a small nation whose religious production was less controlled by those in charge. As Hans Gerth and Don Martindale note:

> In none of the great river civilizations were religious institutions able to oppose the princes, kings, and scribes. The emergence of independent religious leaders like the Israelite prophets was blocked, religious and political authority was com-bined and religious leaders like the Brahmins in India and priesthoods of Baby-lon and Egypt and the Confucian literati in China came to serve state power.[5]

In Egypt and Mesopotamia, prophets who opposed the king could be repressed effectively. But in ancient Israel, the populist element was more pervasive and significant. The power of the king in ancient Israel was not absolute, and he could not afford to ignore or completely repress the critiques of the prophets (e.g., Saul could not ignore Samuel [1 Sam 15]; Ahab and Jezebel were unable to kill Elijah [1 Kgs 17–22]).

This brings up again Weber's detection of a dual social class representa-tion in the Hebrew Bible, which has already been discussed.[6] His conclusion is based on literature that is either pro-monarchic or anti-monarchic or, at least, in many ways critical of the monarchy. He sees an upper-class and pro-monarchic element reflected in the wisdom literature, including the Song of Songs. He even explicitly categorizes Job as a product of the upper class, and he describes the wisdom tradition as "anti-plebian" and associated with the monarchy. Weber also sees as significant that this literature is associated with Solomon. Against this strand, he sees other material that is definitely plebian.[7] He includes in this category what is called today the Deuteronomistic History, the prophets, and the Psalter and notes that the history is generally critical of the monarchy and that limits are placed on the power of the king. In fact, the king is even subject to the Deuteronomistic code! Weber does acknowledge that this historian, though, had to have access to the secular court records in order to write his history. Of course, this simultaneously points to the pres-

---

5. See Gerth and Martindale, Preface, *Ancient Judaism*, xix; Weber, *Ancient Judaism*, 195–97, 207–09.

6. Weber, *Ancient Judaism*, 112, 127, 194–218.

7. Weber also finds the origins of Christianity in the lower middle or bourgeois classes, not the lower class (*Sociology of Religion*, 73, 95). For a discussion of Weber's contri-bution to New Testament studies, see Walter F. Taylor Jr., "Sociological Exegesis: Introduc-tion to a New Way to Study the Bible: Part I: History and Theory," *Trinity Seminary Review* 11, no. 2 (1989): 102–4.

ence of a scribal system that was not anti-monarchic and that produced court records that were largely propagandistic for the kings.[8]

Weber's notion of the presence of a double strand of social-class interests in the Hebrew Bible is highly significant, even if one does not agree completely with his view of this history. Earlier his view was tempered, and it was concluded that the Deuteronomistic History was only ambivalent about the monarchy rather than truly anti-monarchic. The scribes who composed the history were, thus, more sympathetic to the plight of the poor than the scribes who composed the wisdom literature. The complicated relationship of the scribes as members of the retainer class allowed them the possibility of either turning more toward the masses below them or toward their masters above. The scribes who composed the Deuteronomistic History did the former, while the scribes who composed the wisdom literature did the latter.

What is significant is that this ability to criticize the monarchy in an official history means that the monarchy was never dominant in an absolute sense. That in turn is what fortunately allowed the Hebrew Bible to reflect both upper- and lower-class interests, both within the scribal matrix, which creates tension, of course. As a result, there is no consistent monolithic theology in the Hebrew Bible because it amounts to the combination of two different social-class perspectives. Theological tension, within limits of course, not homogeneity, then characterizes the Hebrew Bible because of this social complexity. Thus, in other words, for the Hebrew Bible as it stands, heterodoxy is in the eye of the beholder's social status.

In the Hebrew Bible, Qohelet's theology of resignation to the status quo is certainly compatible with the upper-class strand in it and is thus technically orthodox, since no single social class dominated the production and collecting of religious literature in ancient Israel. Aspects of Qohelet's theology, of course, resonate with the earliest layer of Israelite religion, which would have represented a more egalitarian tribal society. As has already been mentioned, Weber theorized that the early Yahweh was a war deity of nomads who was avenging and wrathful against any who broke his covenant. The early Yahweh was transcendent: "He was . . . a 'god from afar,' holding sway from his remote mountain seat near heaven and on occasion personally intervening in the course of events. From the beginning, this 'distance' gave him a special majesty."[9] Of course, Qohelet retains this distance in the sense of personal relationship and the great gap between mortals and the Immortal. As Crenshaw notes, Qohelet viewed world events essentially as God-determined.[10]

---

8. Jamieson-Drake argues that there is no evidence for such a system until the eighth century, but this is mainly an argument from silence (*Scribes and Schools*).

9. Weber, *Ancient Judaism*, 124.

10. Crenshaw, *Old Testament Wisdom*, 137.

God's wrath was revealed especially in his being a god of natural calamities.[11] He was a deity of salvation and promise, however, and his covenant with the tribal league was paramount. Qohelet forgoes these tendencies but preserves the wrathful avenging side, and he, of course, sees God as a universal deity, a later development among the Jews.[12] This frightful side of God, Weber notes, remained present with the prophets, though mingled with the merciful: "He is unscrupulous also in cunning and fraud. But one can never be certain not to provoke his wrath through some unwitting oversight. Nor can one be sure of not being suddenly pounced upon unexpectedly and unasked, or threatened with destruction by a divine noumenon from among his spirits."[13] Qohelet preserves especially the jealousy of this God who punishes human hubris.[14]

Also, according to Weber, the early Yahweh is not bound to any eternal law or world order: "God's ordainments come from his hand and are as such changeable. . . . He was not a god—note this—who esteemed an eternally valid ethic or could himself be ethically judged."[15] This last notion emerged only gradually as a product of intellectual rationalization. Vestiges of the old and early idea are represented in Job. Weber says,

> When Job requests God to answer for the unjust order of man's condition and when God makes his appearance in the storm, he argues with not a single word the wisdom of his order of human relations, as, for instance, the Confucian would presuppose. Instead Yahwe exclusively argues his sovereign might and greatness in the events of nature.[16]

This emphasis on God's sovereign right to change his mind and his laws and not be judged by mortals is completely compatible with Qohelet's perspective.

QOHELET'S REFORMULATION OF THE WISDOM TRADITION

Qohelet's orthodoxy in pre-Pharisaic/rabbinic Judaism can be seen in how he reshapes the wisdom tradition. As has been seen, in the book of Proverbs, it is evident that the emphasis is on the predictability of God's retributive system. The doctrine of retribution undergirds the majority of the aphorisms and is the basis for the portrayal of Woman Wisdom and Folly in chs. 1–9.[17] Life

---

11. See Weber, *Ancient Judaism*, 124–38.
12. See ibid., 123.
13. Ibid., 128.
14. See ibid., 198.
15. Ibid., 136.
16. Ibid., 133.
17. Claudia Camp shows how the conservatism of the portrayal of both women in Prov 1–9 can be hermeneutically undermined by aligning with the Strange Woman

is largely calculable in Proverbs, and one's lifestyle and path can essentially guarantee one's fortune.

Of course, the sages were aware that there were always exceptions to the rule. As already noted, Raymond Van Leeuwen has largely demonstrated that Proverbs was not dogmatic, that it reflects the realization that there were exceptions to the general rule of retribution.[18] He points out proverbs that reflect the problem of the righteous poor and the wicked rich (e.g., 11:16; 13:23, 28:15–16).[19] He even shows that the early sages projected future retribution in this life for such situations (e.g., 10:30; 24:20).[20] This is all fine and good and shows the inadequacy of the label "dogmatic," but by and large the world of Proverbs is rationalistic and calculable. Unexpected catastrophe and mishaps form only a small part of this world of the sages. The concept of rationalization is more appropriate for describing this process than dogmatism. The projected future retribution is, in fact, simply an aspect of rationalization, a way of making the notion of retribution more flexible and feasible. But all of these qualifications of retribution in Proverbs do not serve to undermine the system; rather, they reinforce the notion of retribution and make it stronger than ever.

Van Leeuwen's use of the term "contradiction" is unfortunate. These qualifications of retribution are quite compatible with it and with the reality at the time when the bulk of Proverbs was composed (the monarchic period). They make the system even more rational. Van Leeuwen fails to realize that the general rule of retribution functions to make the entire system meaningful as a whole, and without this notion the whole system falls. He also fails to express that the notion of divine retribution was an ancient causal perspective that represents the attempt to mitigate and repress the chaotic and accidental in the world. Again, it is important to note the patent falsity of this principle according to modern standards. Whether dogmatic or not, the system is an ancient attempt to make sense of the irrationality of life. Redeeming it from dogmatism does not save it from its ultimately false premise. Van Leeuwen's

---

("Woman Wisdom and the Strange Woman: Where Is Power to Be Found?" in *Power, Powerlessness, and the Divine: New Inquiries in Bible and Theology* [ed. Cynthia L. Rigby; Studies in Theological Education; Atlanta: Scholars Press, 1997], 209–39); cf. Mark Sneed, "'White Trash Wisdom': Proverbs 9 Deconstructed," *Journal of Hebrew Studies* 7, article 5 (2007): 1–10, online at http://www.arts.ualberta.ca/JHS/Articles/article_66.pdf (accessed April 24, 2011); Carol A. Newsom, "Woman and the Discourse of Partriarchal Wisdom: A Study of Proverbs 1–9," in *Gender and Difference in Ancient Israel* (ed. Peggy L. Day; Minneapolis: Fortress, 1989), 142–60.

18. Van Leeuwen, "Wealth and Poverty," 25–36. Loader in fact shows that there indeed was a doctrine of retribution in ancient Israel, though not in a mechanical sense ("Different Reactions," 43–44).

19. Van Leeuwen, "Wealth and Poverty," 30.

20. Ibid., 33–34.

detection of the qualifications of the general retributive system in Proverbs represents merely minor patching up of the cracks. They do not undermine the system as a whole; rather they serve it. Again, all of this is what rationalization involves—a constant modification of the system that makes it more flexible and durable and preserves its rationality.

To be sure, the sages were not arrogant enough to discount completely the mysterious and irrational aspects of the cosmos. They could not thoroughly integrate every aspect of reality into their scheme of rationality. They were especially interested in paradoxes. An example is Prov 11:22: "Like a gold ring in a pig's snout is a beautiful woman without good sense." In modern Western cultural caricatures, beauty and intelligence are not viewed as compatible (dumb blonde jokes), but this was not so with the ancients. Beauty and intelligence went hand in hand. It should be noted that Daniel and his three friends are superior to their Babylonian competitors both intellectually and physically ("young men without physical defect and handsome" [1:4]). Thus, the sages were fascinated with what they perceived as incongruities, such as a beautiful woman who is particularly foolish. The two just did not go together in their view.

Another example is 11:24: "Some give freely, yet grow all the richer; others withhold what is due, and only suffer want." Here the sages are amazed that one who is not stingy with his wealth often becomes even wealthier, while tightwads fall into poverty. Again, the sages were amazed at incongruities. A final example is 13:24: "Those who spare the rod hate their children, but those who love them are diligent to discipline them." Here the sages ponder the paradox that one who actually loves his/her child will inflict physical pain on the child, while the one who refrains from physical discipline actually does not care for the child. The paradox is that parents who love their children often must do what their children find unpleasant for their own good.[21]

But beyond paradoxes, the sages also recognized the limitations of human reasoning and attributed ultimate wisdom to God. This recognition is reflected in the motto of the book of Proverbs: "The fear of the Lord is the beginning of knowledge" (1:7a). This verse essentially asserts that wisdom has its origin in God and that all wisdom can come only from a proper pious relationship with the deity. Ronald Clark notes that the young addressees of Proverbs

---

21. Paul D. Wegner examines the passages in Proverbs about discipline and concludes that a full range of disciplinary measures are mentioned with corporal punishment and death as last resorts. He argues that restrained corporal punishment has not shown to be psychologically and physically harmful to children ("Discipline in the Book of Proverbs: 'To Spank or Not to Spank?'" *JETS* 48 [2005]: 715–32).

were challenged to grow in knowledge, possess insight, listen, and exhibit discipline. Yet the youths were also expected to begin with the fear of Yahweh, which the teacher claimed was the foundation for all Israelite wisdom. The school context seems to suggest that the values of Israelite schools were not only academic but also spiritual and moral, seeking to train youth to uphold the righteousness and justice of Yahweh as well as the community of Israel.[22]

There are in fact several places in Proverbs where "fear of the Lord" seems to be largely equated with wisdom and enjoys the same benefits:

The fear of the Lord is a fountain of life, so that one may avoid the snares of death. (14:27)
The reward for humility and fear of the Lord is riches and honor and life. (22:4)
By loyalty and faithfulness iniquity is atoned for, and by the fear of the Lord one avoids evil. (16:6)

The notion that God is the source of all wisdom is also common. In 2:6, one finds: "For the Lord gives wisdom; from his mouth come knowledge and understanding." The following proverbs should be noted:

The human mind plans the way, but the Lord directs the steps. (16:9)
There is a way that seems right to a person, but its end is the way to death. (14:12)
No wisdom, no understanding, no counsel, can avail against the Lord. The horse is made ready for the day of battle, but the victory belongs to the Lord. (21:30–31)
All our steps are ordered by the Lord; how then can we understand our own ways? (20:24)

Recognition of this principle leads to warnings against human hubris: "Trust in the Lord with all your heart, and do not rely on your own insight. In all your ways acknowledge him, and he will make straight your paths. Do not be wise in your own eyes; fear the Lord, and turn away from evil" (Prov 3:5–7; cf. 26:12). Humility thus becomes the fundamental virtue.[23]

Yet simultaneously the sages assume that wisdom can be had by hard work and study. The father says,

---

22. Clark, "School *Sitz im Leben*," 168.

23. J. Edward Owens compares the hithpael of חכם, put into the mouth of Pharaoh in Exod 1:10, with Qohelet's usage in 7:16 and several instances in Ben Sira to contrast the positivity of self-actualized wisdom in the latter, when accompanied with humility, with its negativity in the former ("'Come, Let Us Be Wise': Qoheleth and Ben Sira on True Wisdom, with an Ear to Pharaoh's Folly," in *Intertextual Studies in Ben Sira and Tobit* [ed. Jeremy Corley and Vincent Skemp; CBQMS 38; Washington, D.C.: Catholic Biblical Association of America, 2005], 227–40).

My child, if you accept my words and treasure up my commandments within you, making your ear attentive to wisdom and inclining your heart to understanding; if you indeed cry out for insight, and raise your voice for understanding; if you seek it like silver, and search for it as for hidden treasures—then you will understand the fear of the Lord and find the knowledge of God. (Prov 2:1–5)

Thus, one sees a fundamental tension: wisdom comes from actively seeking it and simultaneously passively receiving it from God, who is the source of wisdom. This tension is fundamentally between human and divine wisdom, and it is never resolved.

But there also is an acknowledgment that one can know God: "The fear of the Lord is the beginning of wisdom, and the knowledge of the Holy One is insight" (Prov 9:10; 2:5). Though there was certainly mystery to God, the sages in Proverbs believed that one could fundamentally know God, and this knowing ultimately is achieved through fearing the deity. That fits with Judaism's rationalization in general, where God is viewed as rational, reasonable, and fundamentally understandable.

However, this mysterious side to life and God is actually another facet of rationalization. The sages simply compensated for this troubling aspect of reality by integrating it into the sphere of divine mystery. Thus, its irrationality is only apparent. A full disclosure of God's purposes would reveal it. It is safe to say that the mysterious side of life has been pushed to the margins of the sages' worldview. The fundamentally religious perspective of the wise had to be preserved. God could never become totally calculable or understood in a completely rational way because this would bring the divine and the mortal dimensions too close. But it can be said legitimately that the sages in Proverbs do not see a very great gulf between God and humanity. They have largely closed this gap, though it faintly remains.

What Qohelet does is focus on the mysterious side and also on fearing God. He blows up the mysterious and irrational side of the cosmos and God while reducing the rational side. Although fearing God in Proverbs leads to knowing God, for Qohelet this is not possible. To the contrary, Qohelet concludes that fearing God means recognizing the great gulf between humans and God. Fearing God literally means trembling before this deity, who is essentially unknowable and unpredictable and avoiding the divine wrath against unwise actions. Qohelet does not believe that humans can know God. He never speaks of this. Qohelet essentially severs traditional wisdom's equating fearing God with knowing God. Qohelet's God remains the *deus absconditus* par excellence! Qohelet's God is the ultimate Unknowable!

In this way, Qohelet reveals his conservative side. He takes the very religious, pious, and humble side of traditional wisdom and makes it the centerpiece. He makes the mantra to not be wise in your own eyes in Proverbs the fundamental tenet of his theology, pushing it much further to the forefront. Human hubris becomes the primary sin in Qohelet, not the violation of a command. For Qohelet the ultimate sin is for one to think that he/she can know God (this is similar to Job)! Thus, one could argue that Qohelet's theology is even more religious and pious than that of Proverbs! Qohelet's perspective is, then, quintessentially religious. In terms of spectrum, Qohelet represents a turn to the religious, toward the re-enchantment of the world, while traditional wisdom leads ultimately toward the disenchantment of the world, a decidedly secular turn and path, where human rationality becomes increasingly dominant.[24] Qohelet revolts against that trajectory. Thus, contra Gordis, from this perspective, Qohelet is not the most modern book in the Bible.[25] It is the most ancient and primitive. It represents essentially a return to the magical and irrational perspective on the world, but without the magic.

Qohelet is orthodox also in his attempt to preserve the doctrine of retribution, though in modified form. Here he at least gives lip service to the retributive character of the Jewish faith. God is "just," at least, according to his own standards and regularly "judges" the actions of humanity. But the practical effect, of course, is that retribution plays no significant part in Qohelet's ethical advice because determining the standards of that retribution are beyond mortals. Rather, caution and the enjoyment of the moment become primary for Qohelet, though keeping the rudiments of the Torah are important as well (5:1–7).

Of course, Qohelet is orthodox in his refusal to countenance the notion of life after death, a mainstay of Judaism until the influence of Hellenism. Jack T. Sanders shows how the wisdom tradition, like the other Jewish traditions, was resistant to the idea of retribution in the next life. Within the wisdom tradition, this was not embraced until the time of the Wisdom of Solomon.[26]

ANTECEDENTS OF QOHELET'S CARPE DIEM ETHIC

Qohelet's carpe diem ethic also has deep Israelite roots. One could argue that the Israelite faith before the advent of Pharisaic/rabbinic teaching was not

---

24. Weber shows how the quintessentially religious doctrine of predestination in Calvinism is ultimately responsible for the secular world we now inhabit (*Protestant Ethic*); see Kalberg, Introduction, *Protestant Ethic*, 8–63. David Zaret rebuts Malcolm MacKinnon's claim that Weber misrepresented Calvinism among the Puritans; Zaret shows how MacKinnon is distortive in his selection of sources ("Calvin, Covenant Theology, and the Weber Thesis," *British Journal of Sociology* 43 [1992]: 369–91).

25. Gordis, *Koheleth*, x.

26. Sanders, "Wisdom, Theodicy, Death," 263–77.

as rationalistic or as proto-ascetic.[27] The Israelites believed in the enjoyment of physical and bodily pleasures. Sexual pleasures were appreciated; there were no vows of chastity. As a matter of fact, the priests were expected to marry. Even the divinely commanded celibacy of Jeremiah (Jer 16:1–2) gets corrected in legend with his having a daughter and her being impregnated with his semen while being in the same pool of water that he had been; she conceives Ben Sira ("Alphabet of Ben Sira").[28] Exposure of genitals was, of course, forbidden, and there seems to have been some degree of prudishness regarding this, which increased in Pharisaic/rabbinic times (a man was not allowed even to touch the penis while urinating). This may be indicated also in the Hebrew Bible by the reluctance to use the names of the genitals and substituting euphemisms ("feet" and "hand").[29] But, on the whole, sexuality was viewed in a positive way.

While drunkenness was condemned (Prov 20:1), wine was considered a gift from God (Ps 104:15; Judg 9:13). Feasting was a regular part of the Jewish culture and calendar. Wedding festivals lasted for weeks, and the normal round of seasonal feasts was also lengthy. The supreme evidence of the compatibility of Qohelet's carpe diem ethic and Jewish ethics is found in the practice of reading the book during the feast of Booths or Succoth. This is an agricultural feast celebrated at the harvest, when much food and drink and company were available. While many Jews have queried the appropriateness of reading such a dark book before the celebration of such a joyous festival—there have been several reasons given that are not totally satisfactory (e.g., Qohelet writes in the autumn of his life as Succoth is celebrated in the fall)—surely the carpe diem ethic peppered throughout the book serves to legitimize the joyous occasion. The message, thus, is the universal "Eat, drink, and be merry for tomorrow we die!" (Luke 12:19). In Jesus' day, a tendency toward asceticism in Judaism had developed, which is evident in that he and his disciples are condemned for being wine bibbers and gluttons

---

27. On its nonascetic character, see Weber, *Ancient Judaism*, 401–4; idem, *Sociology of Religion*, 246–47, 256. Fraade finds an ascetic tension in ancient Judaism ("Ascetical Aspects," 253–88).

28. David Stern argues that this work is the earliest example of Jewish scatology and involves spoofing rabbinic hagiography and simultaneously making fun of Jewish elementary teachers, from whom the rabbis attempted to distance themselves ("The *Alphabet of Ben Sira* and the Early History of Parody in Jewish Literature," in *The Idea of Biblical Interpretation* [ed. Hindy Najman and Judith H. Newman; JSJSup 83; Atlanta: Society of Biblical Literature, 2004], 423–48).

29. On this euphemistic tendency from a social-science perspective, see John H. Elliot, "Deuteronomy—Shameful Encroachment on Shameful Part: Deuteronomy 25:11–12 and Biblical Euphemism," in *Ancient Israel: The Old Testament in Its Social Context* (ed. Philip F. Esler; Minneapolis: Fortress, 2006), 161–76.

(Matt 11:19). This indicates that Jesus was no ascetic. To a certain extent Paul turned things in the other direction for early Christianity (1 Cor 7), as he had ascetic tendencies.[30]

Qohelet's Canonization as a Misperception

The Significance of Mistaken Authorship

Though Qohelet originally intended his scribal audience to pick up on his adoption of the Solomonic persona (a literary device), this turns into a literalism with the rabbinic discussion of the character of the book. The rabbis believed that Solomon wrote the book in his old age. They believed that, before he wrote it, he had repented of his apostasy, which is recounted in the book of Kings (1 Kgs 11), though they were still suspicious of its content:

> Just as his father had all his iniquities forgiven, as it says, *The Lord hath put away thy sin, thou shalt not die* (II Sam. XII, 13), so with him too; and more still, there rested on him the holy spirit, and he composed three books, Proverbs, Ecclesiastes, and The Song of Songs. . . . He lived three lives. R. Judan and R. Hunia explained this differently. R. Judan said: He was a king, then a subject, then a king again; he was wise, then foolish, then wise again; he was rich, then poor, then rich again. On what does he base this view? [Because Solomon said], *All things have I seen in the days of my vanity* (Eccl. VII, 15). A man does not call to mind his sufferings save when he is at ease again. (*Song Rab.* 1:1)

This goes along with the view that he wrote the book in his old age:

> R. Hiyya the Great taught: Only in the period of his old age did the holy spirit rest upon Solomon, and he composed three books—Proverbs, Ecclesiastes, and The Song of Songs. . . . R. Jonathan argues from the way of the world. When a man is young he composes songs. When he grows older he makes sententious remarks; when he becomes an old man he speaks of the vanity of things. (*Song Rab.* 1:1)

Marc Hirshman argues that the earliest rabbis included the book as Scripture not because of Solomonic authorship—on account of his lapse in faith at the end—but because the book treats the existential theme of death.[31] But he

---

30. On the asceticism of Paul from a Marxist perspective, see Jorunn Økland, "Textual Reproduction as Surplus Value: Paul on Pleasing Christ and Spouses, in Light of Simone de Beauvoir," in *Marxist Feminist Criticism of the Bible* (ed. Roland Boer and Jorunn Økland; Bible in the Modern World 14; Sheffield: Sheffield Phoenix, 2008), 182–203.

31. Marc Hirshman, "Qohelet's Reception and Interpretation in Early Rabbinic Literature," in *Studies in Ancient Midrash* (ed. James L. Kugel; Cambridge, Mass.: Harvard University Center for Jewish Studies, 2001), 87–99.

cites only one Tannaitic rabbi, R. Shimon b. Menasiya, as evidence that the rabbis did not put stock in Solomonic authorship for the acceptance of the book. However, the above citations show a different perspective, though they are perhaps later: Solomon was inspired when he wrote Ecclesiastes. Hirshman fails to acknowledge the significance of the fame of Solomon's wisdom and, thus, his heroic stature, even if flawed, for the Jews. As Roland Murphy states, "It is significant that the principle of Solomonic authorship shaped Jewish interpretation of Ecclesiastes."[32] Moreover, it is also hard to believe that the rabbis ultimately accepted the book because of its focus on death.

The literalizing or historicizing of the Solomonic persona is due in large part to the radical metamorphosis of the sage's status from scribe to rabbi.[33] There is a shift from governmental officials and instructors, who as retainers catered to their superiors, to religious experts who appealed to the masses. Victor Tcherikover speaks of the shift of interpreters of the law from the priesthood, which had become upper class and detached from the people, to the scribes, to whom the people progressively turned for deeper and richer interpretation.[34] In reference to the context of Ben Sira (e.g., 39:4; 20:27), Claude Orrieux refers to a major shift among the scribes (or doctors), "when the doctors of the Law renounced their traditional vocation as counselors to the ('great') in order to make themselves masters and spokesmen for the simple faithful" (my translation).[35] The shift takes its most fundamental turn under Roman domination, when the scribes eventually became totally disenfranchised as governmental officials. Whether the rabbis were urban and petit bourgeois and held secular jobs in addition to their rabbinic functions or were landed, well-to-do rural farmers is debated.[36] However, no longer functioning within the professional scribal system, the rabbis failed to detect the ancient

---

32. Roland E. Murphy, "Qohelet Interpreted: The Bearing of the Past on the Present," *VT* 32 (1982): 335.

33. On the transition from scribes to Pharisees to rabbis, see Lawrence H. Schiffman, *Understanding Second Temple and Rabbinic Judaism* (ed. Jon Bloomberg and Samuel Kapustin; Jersey City, N.J.: Ktav, 2003), 157–58.

34. Tcherikover, "Hellenistic Palestine," 124–25.

35. Orrieux, "Les papyrus de Zénon," 329.

36. Schiffman maintains that they were of the middle and lower classes (*Rabbinic Judaism*, 156). Shaye J. D. Cohen argues that in the second century the rabbis were unsalaried wealthy men of the countryside ("The Rabbi in Second-Century Jewish Society," *CHJ* 3:922–77). It is interesting that Alexei M. Sivertsev argues that rabbinic Judaism did not really develop until the urbanization and hellenization of Jewish sectarianism, when there were disciple circles (focus on individual salvation) versus a home matrix, around the first century B.C.E. or C.E. (*Households, Sects, and the Origins of Rabbinic Judaism* [JSJSup 102; Leiden: Brill, 2005]). This conflicts with Cohen's rural matrix; it is interesting to note that Weber (*Sociology of Religion*, 73, 95) does not locate the bearers of early Christianity in the

Near Eastern and cosmopolitan ethos of a book like Qohelet and its use of sophisticated genres and literary devices, such as the Solomonic persona. The rabbis were concerned mainly with religious edification, not with entertainment or literary subtleties. They approached the book primarily as a confessional text and not as an advanced wisdom treatise that catered to scribal and professional interests. Their concern was piety, not professional survival.

Thus, more than any other thing, the belief in Solomonic authorship of the book in rabbinic times is what clinched its canonicity.[37] As Gordis says,

> Nonetheless, the intention of the author aside, there was sufficient basis for the growth of a tradition of Solomonic authorship. Undoubtedly, this attitude was the prime factor for the admission of Koheleth to the Biblical canon and its retention there, for Rabbinic sources indicate how many and how strong were the reservations as to its sacred character.[38]

Thus, fortunately for modern believers, and ironically, the mistaken belief in Solomonic authorship preserved the book's inclusion in the canon and prevented the most conservative rabbis from excluding the book.

Once the book was canonized, however, the belief in Solomonic authorship could not save it from exclusion in the sense of being confined to the *genizah*, or storeroom. Thus, a debate ensued and centered on whether Qohelet "renders the hands unclean," an idiomatic expression indicating its status as inspired.

> According to the School of Shammai the book of Ecclesiastes does not render the hands unclean. And the School of Hillel says: it renders the hands unclean. (*m. ʿEd.* 5:3)

> The Sages wished to hide the Book of Ecclesiastes, because its words are self-contradictory; yet why did they not hide it? Because its beginning is religious teaching and its end is religious teaching. (*b. Šabb.* 30b)

> The following objection was raised: 'R. Meir says that [the scroll of] Koheleth does not render the hands unclean, and that about the Song of Songs there is a difference and opinion. R. Jose says that the Song of Song renders the hands unclean, and about Koheleth there is a difference of opinion. R. Simeon says that Koheleth is one of those matters in regard to which Beth Shammai were more stringent and Beth Hillel more lenient.' . . . It has been taught: R. Simeon b. Mena-

---

lowest class as do many New Testament scholars. On the significance of this, see Taylor, "Sociological Exegesis," 104.

37. Cf. Salters, "Qoheleth and the Canon," 340; Sandberg, *Rabbinic Views*, 18–19.

38. Gordis, *Koheleth*, 41.

sia said: Koheleth does not the render the hands unclean because it contains only the wisdom of Solomon. They said to him, Was this then all that he composed? Is it not stated elsewhere, *And he spoke three thousand words?* and it further says, *Add thou not unto his words?* Why this further quotation?—In case you might object that he composed very much, and what it pleased him to write he wrote and what it did not please him he did not write. There it says, *Add thou not to his words. (b. Meg.* 7a)

Here one sees that Rabbi Simeon is countered first by pointing out that Solomon wrote many other words that were never included in the canon, yet Qohelet was. Second, it is noted that it was not up to Solomon to choose which of his literary creations were inspired. Only those canonized were inspired.[39] For those who accepted the book, what was needed was to interpret it properly:

At first they maintained that Proverbs, the Song of Songs, and Qohelet should be suppressed, for they maintained that they are mere proverbs and not part of the sacred Writings. They therefore went and suppressed them. Then the men of the Great Assembly came along and spelled out their meaning. . . . So it is said, . . . *Come, let us drown ourselves in pleasure, let us spend a whole night of love; for the man of the house is away . . ."* (Prov 7:7–20). And it is written in the Song of Songs, *Come, my beloved, let us go out into the fields. . . . There I will give you my love* (Song of Songs 7:12–13). And it is written in Qohelet, *. . . Let your heart and your eyes show you the way . . .* (Qoh. 11:9) . . . One must conclude that . . . they spelled out [the correct meaning of the books]. (*'Avot R. Natan* A 1:4)

The citation of these three verses was intended to show that, if improperly interpreted, they could be made to teach heterodoxy. Sandberg provides the rabbinic logic here in this section:

Proverbs could easily be misread as advocating adultery. Song of Songs could be misunderstood as endorsing free sexual expression without the sanctification of marriage. Qohelet could be mistakenly viewed as advocating following one's heart and doing whatever one wishes, which contradicts the teachings of the Torah. Proper and necessary interpretation is the only antidote to the dangerous misreading of difficult but sacred sources.[40]

Thus, the more conservative rabbis were suspicious of the book's character, deeming it merely the human wisdom of Solomon, while the more liberal sages believed the book was worthy for public use because they believed that it

---

39. Sandberg, *Rabbinic Views*, 22–23.
40. Ibid., 23–24.

began and ended religiously and that it only appeared to be heretical; it simply needed to be properly interpreted.[41]

THE SIGNIFICANCE OF THE GLOSS
AND THE BOOK'S AMBIGUITY

It is with the more liberal position, however, that one begins to see two secondary factors that ensured the book's preservation. The first is the pious gloss in 12:13: "The end of the matter; all has been heard. Fear God, and keep his commandments; for that is the whole duty of everyone."[42] The larger gloss includes v. 14 and should be distinguished from the frame narrative (1:1–2 [or 1:1–11] and 12:9–12). The above reference to "religious teaching" must certainly apply to this gloss. The gloss is so fortunate because it serves to provide the book with a more orthodox appearance. It would not have stood out as a gloss to the later rabbis because it can be interpreted, with a little ingenuity, as compatible with the body of the book. Fearing God, of course, is a significant motif in the book, though, as has been indicated, it has its own idiosyncratic meaning. Commandment keeping, while not an emphasis in the body of the book, is certainly not in any direct way countered. Indirectly, it is countered in 11:9b ("Follow the inclination of your heart and the desire of your eyes"), and some rabbis thought this verse might be conducive to licentiousness (*Qoh. Rab.* 11:9). Ben Sira, of course, is famous for uniting God-fearing with commandment keeping: "Nothing is better than the fear of the Lord, and nothing sweeter than to heed the commandments of the Lord" (23:27).[43] But, as a whole, the body of the book presents no strong opposition to the gloss. Its ostensible form

---

41. Contrary to popular opinion, throughout her book, Sandberg shows that the rabbis actually avoided allegorical interpretation of Qohelet as much as possible (*Rabbinic Views*). For the comparable history of interpretation of the book by early Christians, see Sven Holm-Nielsen, "On the Interpretation of Qoheleth in Early Christianity," *VT* 24 (1974): 168–77.

42. Claude Cox speaks of Torah first embracing the historical materials and then later the wisdom and liturgical traditions of Israel as means of instruction. He supplies a practical paraphrase of this verse: "Thus it is that, while as human beings we may not have the answers to the really big, existential questions, we are not to throw up our hands in despair. No, we can still keep the commands as our duty and, at the same time, as our way to wisdom" ("When Torah Embraced Wisdom and Song: Job 28:28, Ecclesiastes 12:13, and Psalm 1:2," *ResQ* 49 [2007]: 65–74, esp. 71).

43. Jack T. Sanders demonstrates that Ben Sira and other late wisdom texts such as those from Qumran and Baruch assimilate aspects of the Torah of Moses without violating the central features of the wisdom tradition ("When Sacred Canopies Collide: The Reception of the Torah of Moses in the Wisdom Literature of the Second-Temple Period," *JSJ* 32 [2001]: 121–36).

as part of the conclusion to the book further increases its hermeneutical significance for the book as a whole. Of course, here one has another example of misperception that helped preserve the book because the gloss was thought to be from the hand of Qohelet.

The pious ending strangely gets reapplied to the beginning of the book by the rabbis. The "religious teaching" at the beginning apparently refers to 1:3. One might not think that this verse could be interpreted in such a pious way. In fact, it was suspect because the rabbis thought that the vanity of toil might apply to the study of Torah. This verse and 11:9 are the two primary verses that troubled the ancient rabbis.[44] Interestingly, as Fox notes, these two verses are not perceived as the most radical by modern scholars.[45] The rabbis, represented by the school of R. Yannai, got around this problem by focusing on the phrase "under the sun." The school interpreted this to refer to mundane activities, while excluding matters "before the sun" because it was believed that the Torah was created before the sun was:

> The Sages wished to hide the Book of Ecclesiastes, because its words are self-contradictory; yet why did they not hide it? Because its beginning is religious teaching, and its end is religious teaching. Its beginning is religious teaching, as it is written, *What profit hath man of all his labour wherein he laboureth under the sun?* And the school of R. Jannai commented: Under the sun he has none, but he has it [profit] before the sun. The end thereof is religious teaching, as it is written, *Let us hear the conclusion of the matter, fear God, and keep his commandments.* (*b. Šabb.* 30b).

Here is a similar explanation from the Midrash:

> The Sages sought to suppress the Book of Koheleth because they discovered therein words which savour of heresy. They declared: Behold all the wisdom of Solomon which he aims at teaching [in this Book] is, What profit hath man of all his labour? It is possible that the words may also be applied to man's labour in the Torah! On reconsidering the matter they declared: He did not say 'Of all labour' but Of all *his* labour—In his labour one should not labour, but one should toil in the labour of the Torah! (*Qoh. Rab.* 1:3)

Thus, now, the beginning and ending of the book could both be perceived as orthodox expressions of Torah piety. These bookends could then enable the more heterodox body of the book to withstand almost any onslaught; it might

---

44. Dominic Rudman connects 1:3 with 7:1–4, where Qohelet recommends sorrow instead of laughter. He shows that the verse is not universal but applies only to the wise who have embraced sorrow and ironically are then enabled to drive out sorrow and enjoy life ("The Anatomy of the Wise Man," in *Qohelet in the Context of Wisdom* [ed. Anton Schoors; BETL 136; Leuven: Leuven University Press and Peeters, 1998], 470).

45. Fox, *Rereading of Ecclesiastes*, 2.

make it more tolerable. As everyone knows, the way a book begins and ends is decisive for interpretation. As Fox notes,

> This frame provided sufficient buffer for the book's internal inconsistencies and other doctrinal difficulties. This is a surprising liberal hermeneutic. Qohelet-Solomon—writing in the Holy Spirit, and not just in his own wisdom—was allowed to explore dangerous territory, provided that he began and ended in profession of faith and obedience.[46]

The gloss was probably primary for convincing these early rabbinic interpreters that Qohelet was orthodox. From this basis and assumption, the rabbis simply attempted to harmonize all the problematic features of the body of the work. Their interpretation of 1:3 is a supreme example of their hermeneutical ingenuity once they were convinced of the book's orthodoxy.

Still there is more to it. There is another feature of the book, which, like the gloss, secondarily served to preserve the book's sacred character: its ambiguity. Many scholars have referred to Qohelet's ambiguity in language, style, and content.[47] It is the book's ambiguity that has allowed it to be interpreted in such diametrically opposite ways throughout the centuries. As has been mentioned, on the one hand, many modern scholars view the book as being as close to atheism as was possible in the ancient world. This view sees the book as radically heterodox. On the other hand, the pietistic approach is represented by Franz Delitzsch, who described the book as "The Song of the Fear of God."[48] Most recently, Craig Bartholomew views the book as consistently orthodox.[49]

The possibility of such divergent ways of interpreting the book can be explained only by the book's inherent ambiguity, notwithstanding the significant role of the interpreter's own biases. It has already been explored how Qohelet typically uses the terminology and conceptions of his day but in an idiosyncratic way. For example, his use of God-fearing and his conception of divine judgment are unconventional. With the latter, he even preserves the notion of retribution but in a new way. This does not, of course, mean that Qohelet deliberately meant to be ambiguous. It was simply that he had to use the terminology of his day to express himself. Thus, there are two misperceptions that ultimately served to preserve the book: Solomonic authorship and

---

46. Fox, *Rereading of Ecclesiastes*, 2.

47. E.g., Rick W. Byargeon, "The Significance of Ambiguity in Ecclesiastes 2,24–26," in *Qohelet in the Context of Wisdom* (ed. Anton Schoors; BETL 136; Leuven: Leuven University Press and Peeters, 1998), 367–72; B. Berger, "Exigencies of the Absurd," 141–79, esp. 161.

48. Delitzsch, "Ecclesiastes," 183.

49. Bartholomew, *Ecclesiastes*; see Mark Sneed, review of Craig G. Bartholomew, *Ecclesiastes, CBQ* 72 (2010): 559–60.

the belief in the authenticity of the gloss. These combined with the ambiguity saved the book from the *genizah*.

THE GLOSSATOR'S PERCEPTION OF QOHELET'S RELIGIOUS VALUE

The question arises why the glossator merely added his interpolation instead of simply discarding the book as whole. This is difficult to answer and, of course, speculative. By the time the glossator received the book, it had probably attained some degree of authority. The upper-(or retainer-)class scribes had preserved the book because it spoke to their pressing needs. It should be emphasized that neither Qohelet nor his frame narrator ever imagined that the book would someday become sacred Scripture. As already indicated, it was produced primarily for advanced students, and as wisdom literature it served essentially as a training manual for scribes. It was not written with a general audience or with a rabbinate in mind. By the time the Pharisaic glossator received it, it was part of the received tradition that the priests and scribes had preserved. Just being included in this collection gave the book credibility and status. This in itself would have discouraged the glossator from simply discarding the book.

But aside from this consideration, the glossator most likely perceived the fundamentally religious tenor of the book and its importance for Judaism.[50] Qohelet's emphasis on the sovereignty of God and his separation of the mortal and divine would have struck a chord during the glossator's time. These two themes were important for the Jews during the Seleucid rule, Maccabean revolt, Hasmonean dynasty, and beyond. The book of Daniel, written during the middle of the second century, emphasizes the sovereignty of God and the great gulf between humanity and God. It would differ from Qohelet only in its emphasis on Jewish piety and kosher sensitivities in chs. 1–6, a form of proto-asceticism. The sovereignty of God depicted in chs. 7–12 is also quite compatible with Qohelet's theology. Further, in the Dead Sea Scrolls hymns, there is evidence of the great chasm between mortals and God:

---

50. Martin A. Shields maintains that the frame narrator included Qohelet's words to discredit the wisdom tradition completely (*End of Wisdom*, 6). Shields sees the narrator as sympathetic to Qohelet's critique of wisdom but ultimately rejecting his solution to the problem. Shields's thesis is interesting and correct in perceiving the heterodoxy of Qohelet's words. But it ultimately fails in being too clever. However, the scathing review by Harold C. Washington fails to acknowledge the heterodoxy of Qohelet (review of Martin A. Shields, *The End of Wisdom*, RBL [2009]: n.p., online at http://www.bookreviews.org/pdf/5240_5519.pdf [accessed April 24, 2011]). On the trend of Qohelet scholars to focus on the frame narrative for discerning the book's theological significance, see Craig G. Bartholomew, "*Qoheleth* in the Canon?! Current Trends in the Interpretation of Ecclesiastes," *Themelios* 24, no. 3 (1999): 4–20.

But what is flesh (to be worthy) of this?
What is a creature of clay
for such great marvels to be done,
whereas he is iniquity from the womb
and in guilty unfaithfulness until his old age?
Righteousness, I know, is not of man,
nor is perfection of way of the son of man:
to the Most High God belong all righteous deeds.
The way of man is not established
except by the spirit which God created for him
to make perfect a way for the children of men,
that all his creatures might know
the might of his power,
and the abundance of his mercies
towards all the sons of His grace. (1QH 4:29–33)

Note the hint of predestination in the last lines. Also compare the following:

Who can endure Thy glory,
and what is the son of man
in the midst of Thy wonderful deeds?
What shall one born of woman
be accounted before Thee?
Kneaded from the dust,
his abode is the nourishment of worms. (1QS 11:20–21)[51]

The motif of fearing God in Qohelet would also have pleased the glossator. This would fit the emphasis on Jewish piety at the time when Hellenism was threatening to extinguish Jewish identity. Ben Sira, of course, as part of the wisdom tradition, touts God-fearing as the supreme virtue (e.g., 1:11–13). The mystery of God emphasized in Qohelet would also have suited the glossator.

The glossator no doubt would have been open also to the anti-intellectualism in Qohelet, in his rejection or severe qualification of human wisdom and knowledge.[52] This concern is reflected also in the epilogist's or frame narrator's words of 12:12: "Of anything beyond these, my child, beware. Of making many books there is no end, and much study is a weariness of the flesh." "These" most likely refers to the canonical wisdom literature. Bartholomew rightly notes that this verse may point to a polemic against Greek wisdom and philosophy.[53] Again, this is similar to Paul's anti-intellectualism in 1 Cor 3, where

---

51. Both cited in E. P. Sanders, *Paul and Palestinian Judaism*, 288–89; see also the general discussion (pp. 287–98, 305–12, and 327–28).

52. Sandberg points to two themes that the rabbis appreciated in Qohelet: God-fearing and God being beyond human comprehension (*Rabbinic Views*, 226).

53. Bartholomew, *Ecclesiastes*, 369.

he criticizes human wisdom. Of course, intensive study of the Torah was permissible and encouraged in rabbinic Judaism. But this was the only acceptable form of Jewish intellectualism, and it was very practically oriented.[54] Ben Sira's argument that wisdom is found among the Jews only in the form of the Torah is compatible with this sentiment (15:1; 24:8). Though de Jong's argument that Qohelet's main polemic is against Greek philosophy and wisdom is faulty, his thesis shows how the epilogist and glossator could reinterpret Qohelet's words in that direction.[55] Note the following remark by the rabbis concerning the words of Torah:

> "Recite them, . . . Treat them as the main thing and not as something peripheral [to your interests]. Your give and take should only have to do with [Torah teachings]. Do not mix other things—such as thus-and-so—with them. Might you say, "Now that I have learned the wisdom of Israel, I shall go and study the wisdom of the nations"? Scripture states, "To walk in them" (Lev. 18:4)—and not to exempt one from studying them. (*Sifre Deut.* 34 to Deut 6:7).

Apart from Qohelet's carpe diem ethic and cavalier attitude toward Torah keeping, the glossator would have seen much in Qohelet as beneficial. Qohelet's emphasis on the Immortal/mortal divide, God's sovereignty (and the predestination of the carpe diem ethic), God-fearing, and anti-intellectualism would all have served to entice the glossator to look favorably upon Qohelet.

He then did something ingenious. He co-opted Qohelet's version of God-fearing and connected this with his own emphasis on commandment keeping! This hermeneutical tour de force put a more positive spin on the book, giving it greater value for the glossator's own time and broadening its appeal. Thus, a document originally intended for bureaucratic scribes for career success in the guild was converted into a general treatise that served the interests of the glossator and his community. The glossator was probably onto the heterodoxy (from his perspective) of Qohelet, but he saw the benefits as outweighing the deficits. This coupled with its already authorized status enabled the glossator to continue the preservation of the book, along with his tweaking in the process. After the time of the glossator, when Pharisaic Judaism and the rabbinate were dominant, it was too late to discard the book. It did not end up in the *genizah* only because of misperceptions about it and the hermeneutical ingenuity of the glossator, coupled with its inherent ambiguity.

---

54. Weber, *Ancient Judaism*, 414–15.
55. De Jong, "Ambitious Spirit," 85–96.

Conclusion

The book is not really the most modern or "secular" book in the Hebrew Bible, contra Gordis. It represents a return to an older, more religious perspective that is closer to magic than the rationalized form of religion that Judaism was becoming. In this sense, Qohelet is not on the road to secularism, ironically, but in resistance to this process of disenchantment of the world. Qohelet's irrational response is to the over-rationalization of his day represented by the inherited wisdom tradition not being functional during the Ptolemaic period and perhaps the growing tendency toward asceticism and Torah piety that was becoming increasingly popular in his day. Qohelet represents a return to the more mysterious warrior deity of the early tribal league of Israel (with modification), but without the redemptive element, compatible with his upper-(retainer-)class status. His deity is a return to the wrathful and jealous deity that emerges from time to time throughout the Hebrew Bible: a deity who quickly punishes instances of human hubris. Qohelet represents a fundamental turn toward the religious perspective where God is god and humanity is humanity, and "never the twain shall meet." God, here, is essentially the ultimate Other of humanity. Though Qohelet views his deity as oppressive, there are comforting aspects in this Wholly Other, who is both sovereign Creator and maintainer of the cosmos.

Qohelet does not abandon the wisdom tradition but reconfigures it, emphasizing some aspects while suppressing others. Although he never completely abandons rationality (he does see some value in wisdom), he seriously deconstructs it and lowers expectations about it. Instead, he emphasizes the mysterious and paradoxical side of the cosmos, an important component in traditional wisdom as represented in Proverbs but forming only a marginal aspect. He never speaks of knowing God, as Proverbs is so fond of doing. He seriously questions the doctrine of retribution as traditionally formulated. He preserves the notion of retribution but mystifies it and relegates its "rationality" to the sovereignty of God, whose ways are ultimately unknowable. Thus, Qohelet's God is *deus absconditus*, and only God attains absolute wisdom and knowledge. Humans are relegated to a minimal echo of this capacity.

Modern believers are fortunate that an interpolator added his pious gloss in 12:13. Without this, the book may never have survived the canonical process. They are also fortunate that the sages who inherited this book, which was originally preserved by scribal circles, lacked professional scribal training, which prevented them from discerning the Solomonic literary device of the first two chapters. Because of this, the book's perceived Solomonic authorship and the hermeneutical reconfiguration of the book provided by the gloss helped ensure the book's eventual canonization. Further, the book's inherent ambiguity as well as the interpretive ingenuity of the rabbis both contributed to the book's survival and prevented its being deposited in the *genizah* and its exclusion from popular view. The glossator intuitively perceived its essentially religious tone and value, which outweighed its anti-ascetic tendencies. This enabled the book eventually to become part of the celebratory tradition, read at Succoth. Its perspective allowed the Jews to discard their somewhat ascetic lifestyles for a few days and enjoy food, fellowship, and drink much as Mardi Gras does for many Roman Catholics in New Orleans just prior to the beginning of Lent.

CONCLUSION

Qohelet's pessimism and skepticism are real and not to be explained away. The important question, then, is how the mood and cognitive disposition were used by the author to persuade his audience to adopt a particular perspective. The pessimism, which is the key element for identifying the genre of the book, serves to lower expectations of the audience about human wisdom, God, and human effort/morality. The lowering of expectations was necessary for mitigating the dissonance that had been created by the optimism of traditional wisdom and Judaism and the oppressed condition of the Jews under Ptolemaic hegemony. God appeared to have deserted his people. The skepticism serves as a handmaiden to the pessimism in that it helps further undermine the value of traditional wisdom, which is the main target of Qohelet's polemic. The lowering of expectations also enabled Qohelet, the scholar, and his young scribal audience better to handle the theodicy problem, and it assuaged any class guilt they might have felt in that they themselves enjoyed comfortable lives while their poorer compatriots suffered terribly. Thus, it helped the members of the scribal guild to feel better both about their vocational collaboration with the Ptolemies and about the dominated status of their people.

Therefore, Qohelet's pessimism is not simply a passive reflection of his particular social location. Rather, it is a voluntary and reactionary coping strategy. Qohelet's conception of God is not simply a vulgar reflection or homology of the despotic Ptolemaic king. Qohelet's conceptualization of the deity is a creative component of his theodicy strategy. In a world where God's standard of judgment seems capricious, resolving the theodicy problem by questioning God's justice or reconfiguring it to be beyond mortal comprehension was a logical and available solution that was not formulated from economic interests alone. Furthermore, Qohelet is constrained ideationally in that he cannot blame a devil or demon for the injustices in the world (dualism) because Jewish monotheism was stronger and purer in his time. In addition, he was constrained by the Jewish resistance to the notion of life after death, which would have provided a solution to the theodicy problem that he and his audience faced. Qohelet's solution is similar to Job's, though different. Both employ the notion of *deus absconditus*, but Job preserves the personable aspects of the deity, while Qohelet relinquishes these. Therefore, the creativity of two upper-class intellectuals who chose different solutions to the same problem demonstrates the legitimacy of Weber's more nuanced theorization about the relation between ideas and economic interests over against Marxist theory.

However, economic constraints have certainly influenced Qohelet. That his solution to the problem of evil is nonsalvific certainly has an affinity with his privileged status. He found the status quo at least tolerable. He has not suffered personally enough yet to project a future radical utopian dissolution of current conditions, as did his later scribal confrere who wrote Dan 7–12. Qohelet's theodicy solution, of course, is also very intellectual and would not have been popular among the masses, who typically favor saviors and deliverers. Thus, Qohelet's dark world and his particular theodicy solution are not merely the result of either solely economic or ideal interests. He was constrained by both, but, within their parameters, he hammered out his own particular path within Judaism, though it resonates with other solutions found among the other religions. This more complicated understanding of the dialectic between economic and ideal interests appears to fit reality better than the Marxist paradigm is willing to admit. A Weberian approach seems to fit the data better, at least as far as Qohelet is concerned.

Qohelet's conception of the deity and his view that the greatest sin is human hubris actually represent a return of sorts to an early form of Yahwism, when the God of the tribes was not perceived to be as rational as he became in later Judaism. The "big picture" approach that is available when adopting a Weberian perspective allows a more illuminative perspective. Qohelet's lowering of expectations and undermining of the wisdom tradition through skepticism represents a regression from the trajectory of increasing rationalization of Judaism in general and the wisdom tradition in particular. The process of rationalization became especially problematic during the Ptolemaic period. Qohelet represents an anti-intellectual resistance to this process. He essentially retreats from the arrogant attempt at cognitive mastery of the cosmos and turns toward acknowledgment of the ultimate impotence of human capacity vis-à-vis the sovereign deity. While he never completely rejects human wisdom, he seriously disqualifies it. Thus, Qohelet represents a significant reflex in the development of Judaism that warns of the dangers inherent in the process of rationalization within any religious tradition. Though rationalization certainly provides benefits to its practioners, there are always residual harmful effects. Rationalization is especially dangerous to religions. Early on it can serve as a handmaiden to them, organizing them, synthesizing them, and making them more rational. But it eventually threatens them because the inevitable consequence is increasing secularization.

Thus, Qohelet's irrational response to the over-rationalization of traditional wisdom is no different than that of the Romantics who reacted to the rationalization of Neo-Classicism and the dire effects of the Industrial Revolution. Qohelet's carpe diem ethic is essentially a rejection of the negative effects of this process in Judaism and, especially, in the wisdom tradition. It is a rejection of all the strategic calculation of traditional wisdom and its attempts at cosmic mastery, which failed to yield benefits or fit reality during the Ptolemaic period. The "big picture" approach that emerges allows one to see Qohelet for what he really is. Instead of being the most modern or "secular" author of the Hebrew Bible or the most radical, he is the most quintessentially religious. He represents the basic and primordial religious impulse, which is irrational and magical, that explains the world more in terms of enchantment, not rationality. Qohelet represents a return to a less rationalistic form of Yahwism, where God is no longer so predictable or reasonable but acts in mysterious and incomprehensible ways—a genuine *deus absconditus*. The more God was perceived as rational, as Judaism developed, the more human and less divine God became. Qohelet returns traditional wisdom to a vision of the deity as a more Wholly (or Holy) *Other*! He returns Judaism to its roots, when God and mortals were clearly distinguished and where a great gulf prevented one from crossing over to the other. This is fundamentally what enabled the book to become canonized, along with its anti-intellectual character. It is ironic that the trajectory of rationalization begun in Judaism later influenced Calvinism, which, in turn, provided the ideological support for economic rationalization, capitalism, which, in turn, led to our modern, secular world, where religion has been forced to take a back seat to the dominance of science and technology. Surprisingly, it turns out that Qohelet is not part of that trajectory. Thus, the book's importance for Judaism and Christianity (and even Islam) needs to be reevaluated. Though the book is technically heterodox within normative Judaism, it may hold the key to understanding what is primarily and fundamentally the latter's religious core and essence.

BIBLIOGRAPHY

Aberle, David. "A Note on Relative Deprivation Theory as Applied to Millenarian and Other Cult Movements." Pages 537–41 in *Reader in Comparative Religion: An Anthropological Approach*. Edited by William A. Lessa and Evon Z. Vogt. 2nd ed. New York: Harper & Row, 1965.

Abimbola, Wande. "Gods Versus Anti-Gods: Conflict and Resolution in the Yoruban Cosmos." Pages 170–79 in *Evil and the Response of World Religion*. Edited by William Cenkner. St. Paul, Minn.: Paragon House, 1997.

Aichele, George, et al. *The Postmodern Bible: The Bible and Culture Collective*. New Haven: Yale University Press, 1995.

Al-Ghazali, Muhammed. "The Problem of Evil: An Islamic Approach." Pages 70–79 in *Evil and the Response of World Religion*. Edited by William Cenkner. St. Paul, Minn.: Paragon House, 1997.

Alster, Bendt. *Wisdom of Ancient Sumer*. Bethesda, Md.: CDL, 2005.

Alter, Robert. *The Art of Biblical Poetry*. New York: Basic Books, 1985.

Anderson, Bernhard W. *Contours of Old Testament Theology*. Minneapolis: Fortress, 1999.

Anderson, William H. U. "The Curse of Work in Qoheleth: An Exposé of Genesis 3:17–19 in Ecclesiastes." *Evangelical Quarterly* 70 (1998): 99–113.

———. "Ironic Correlations and Scepticism in the Joy Statements of Qoheleth?" *Scandinavian Journal of the Old Testament* 14 (2000): 68–100.

———. "Philosophical Considerations in a Genre Analysis of Qoheleth." *Vetus Testamentum* 48 (1998): 289–300.

———. "The Semantic Implications of הבל and רעות רוח in the Hebrew Bible and for Qoheleth." *Journal of Northwest Semitic Languages* 25, no. 2 (1999): 59–73.

———. "What Is Scepticism and Can It be Found in the Hebrew Bible?" *Scandinavian Journal of the Old Testament* 13 (1999): 225–57.

Applebaum, Shimon. "Josephus and the Economic Causes of the Jewish War." Pages 237–64 in *Josephus, the Bible, and History*. Edited by Louis H. Feldman and Gohei Hata. Detroit: Wayne State University Press, 1989.

Athenaeus. *The Learned Banqueters*. Translated by S. Douglas Olson. 7 vols. Loeb Classical Library. Cambridge, Mass.: Harvard University Press, 2006–11.

Austinus, Gianto. "Human Destiny in Emar and Qohelet." Pages 473–79 in *Qohelet in the Context of Wisdom*. Edited by Anton Schoors. Bibliotheca ephemeridum theologicarum lovaniensium 136. Leuven: Leuven University Press and Peeters, 1998.

Badham, Paul. "Toward a Global Theodicy." Pages 241–51 in *Evil and the Response of World Religion*. Edited by William Cenkner. St. Paul, Minn.: Paragon House, 1997.

Bagnall, Roger S. *The Administration of the Ptolemaic Possessions outside Egypt.* Columbia Studies in the Classical Tradition 4. Leiden: Brill, 1976.

Bailey, Lloyd R. *Biblical Perspectives on Death.* Overtures to Biblical Theology 5. Philadelphia: Fortress, 1979.

Barbalet, Jack. "Max Weber and Judaism: An Insight into the Methodology of *The Protestant Ethic and the Spirit of Capitalism.*" *Max Weber Studies* 6 (2006): 51–67.

Barnes, Jonathan. "L'Ecclésiaste et le scepticisme grec." *Revue de théologie et de philosophie* 131 (1999): 103–14.

Bartholomew, Craig G. *Ecclesiastes.* Baker Commentary on the Old Testament. Grand Rapids: Baker, 2009.

———. "*Qoheleth* in the Canon?! Current Trends in the Interpretation of Ecclesiastes." *Themelios* 24, no. 3 (1999): 4–20.

Barton, George. *A Critical and Exegetical Commentary on the Book of Ecclesiastes.* International Critical Commentary. 1908. Repr., Edinburgh: T&T Clark, 1959.

Barucq, André. *Ecclésiaste. Qohéleth: Traduction et commentaire.* Verbum Salutis: Ancien Testament 3. Paris: Beauchesne, 1968.

Basser, Herbert. "The Development of the Pharisaic Idea of Law as a Sacred Cosmos." *Journal for the Study of Judaism* 16 (1985): 104–16.

Beentjes, Panc. "'Who is like the Wise?' Some Notes on Qohelet 8,1–15." Pages 303–315 in *Qohelet in the Context of Wisdom.* Edited by Anton Schoors. Bibliotheca ephemeridum theologicarum lovaniensium 136. Leuven: Leuven University Press and Peeters, 1998.

Behe, Michael J. *Darwin's Black Box: The Biochemical Challenge to Evolution.* New York: Free Press, 1996.

Bendix, Reinhard. *Max Weber: An Intellectual Portrait.* Paperback ed. Berkeley: University of California Press, 1977.

Ben Zvi, Ehud, ed. *Utopia and Dystopia in Prophetic Literature.* Publications of the Finnish Exegetical Society 92. Göttingen: Vandenhoeck & Ruprecht, 2006.

Bergen, Wesley J. "The Prophetic Alternative: Elisha and the Israelite Monarchy." Pages 127–37 in *Elijah and Elisha in Socioliterary Perspective.* Edited by Robert B. Coote. Semeia Studies. Atlanta: Scholars Press, 1992.

Berger, Benjamin Lyle. "Qohelet and the Exigencies of the Absurd." *Biblical Interpretation* 9 (2001): 164–73.

Berger, Peter L. "Charisma and Religious Innovation: The Social Location of the Prophets." *American Sociological Review* 28 (1963): 940–50.

————. *The Sacred Canopy: Elements of a Sociological Theory of Religion*. Paperback ed. New York: Anchor, 1969.

Berger, Peter L., and Thomas Luckmann. *The Social Construction of Reality: A Treatise in the Sociology of Knowledge*. Garden City, N.Y.: Doubleday Anchor, 1967.

Berlinerblau, Jacques. *Heresy in the University: The Black Athena Controversy and the Responsibilities of American Intellectuals*. New Brunswick, N.J.: Rutgers University Press, 1999.

————. "The 'Popular Religion' Paradigm in Old Testament Research: A Sociological Critique." *Journal for the Study of the Old Testament* 60 (1993): 3–26.

————. "The Present Crisis and Uneven Triumphs of Biblical Sociology: Responses to N. K. Gottwald, S. Mandell, P. Davies, M. Sneed, R. Simkins and N. Lemche." Pages 99–120 in *Concepts of Class in Ancient Israel*. Edited by Mark Sneed. South Florida Studies in the History of Judaism: The Hebrew Scriptures and Their World 201. Atlanta: Scholars Press, 1999.

————. *The Vow and the 'Popular Religious Groups' of Ancient Israel: A Philological and Sociological Inquiry*. Journal for the Study of the Old Testament: Supplement Series 210. Sheffield: Sheffield Academic Press, 1996.

Berman, Harold J., and Charles J. Reid Jr. "Max Weber as Legal Historian." Pages 223–39 in *The Cambridge Companion to Weber*. Edited by Stephen Turner. Cambridge: Cambridge University Press, 2000.

Bickerman, Elias. *Four Strange Books of the Bible: Jonah, Daniel, Koheleth, Esther*. New York: Schocken, 1967.

————. *The Jews in the Greek Age*. Cambridge, Mass.: Harvard University Press, 1988.

Billows, Richard A. *Antigonos the One-Eyed and the Creation of the Hellenistic State*. Paperback ed. Hellenistic Culture and Society. Berkeley: University of California Press, 1997.

Blenkinsopp, Joseph. "Ecclesiastes 3.1–15: Another Interpretation." *Journal for the Study of the Old Testament* 66 (1995): 55–64.

————. *Sage, Priest, Prophet: Religious and Intellectual Leadership in Ancient Israel*. Library of Ancient Israel. Louisville: Westminster John Knox, 1995.

————. *Wisdom and Law in the Old Testament: The Ordering of Life in Israel and Early Judaism*. Oxford Bible. Oxford: Oxford University Press, 1983.

Boer, Roland. "Jameson." Pages 138–43 in *Handbook of Postmodern Biblical Interpretation*. Edited by A. K. M. Adam. St. Louis: Chalice, 2000.

————. *Jameson and Jeroboam*. Semeia Studies. Atlanta: Scholars Press, 1996.

————. *Marxist Criticism of the Bible*. London: T&T Clark, 2003.

————. "Twenty-Five Years of Marxist Biblical Criticism." *Currents in Biblical Research* 5 (2007): 298–321.

Boer, Roland, and Jorunn Økland, eds. *Marxist Feminist Criticism of the Bible*. The Bible in the Modern World 14. Sheffield: Sheffield Phoenix, 2008.

Bolin, Thomas. "Rivalry and Resignation: Girard and Qoheleth on the Divine–Human Relationship." *Biblica* 86 (2005): 245–59.

Bosworth, A. B. *The Legacy of Alexander: Politics, Warfare, and Propaganda under the Successors.* Oxford: Oxford University Press, 2008.

Botterweck, G. J., and H. Ringgren, eds. *Theological Dictionary of the Old Testament.* Translated by J. T. Willis, G. W. Bromiley, and D. E. Green. 14 vols. Grand Rapids: Eerdmans, 1974–.

Bottiglia, William F. "A Garden of Hope." Pages 81–87 in *Readings on Candide.* Edited by Thomas Walsh. Literary Companion. San Diego: Greenhaven, 2001.

Bould, Mark. *Film Noir: From Berlin to Sin City.* Short Cuts. London: Wallflower, 2005.

Branick, Vincent P. "Wisdom, Pessimism, and 'Mirth': Reflections on the Contribution of Biblical Wisdom Literature to Business Ethics." *Journal of Religious Ethics* 34 (2006): 69–87.

Braun, Rainer. *Kohelet und die frühhellenistische Popularphilosophie.* Beihefte zur Zeitschrift für die alttestamentliche Wissenschaft 130. Berlin: de Gruyter, 1973.

Breasted, James Henry. *Development of Religion and Thought in Ancient Egypt.* 1912. Paperback ed. Philadelphia: University of Pennsylvania, 1972.

Brindle, Wayne A. "Righteousness and Wickedness in 7:15–18." *Andrews University Seminary Studies* 23 (1985): 243–57.

Brockopp, Jonathan E. "Theorizing Charismatic Authority in Early Islamic Law." *Comparative Islamic Studies* 1 (2005): 129–58.

Brown, Francis, S. R. Driver, and Charles A. Briggs. *A Hebrew and English Lexicon of the Old Testament.* Oxford: Clarendon, 1907.

Brown, William P. *Character in Crisis: A Fresh Approach to the Wisdom Literature of the Old Testament.* Grand Rapids: Eerdmans, 1996.

———. *Ecclesiastes.* Interpreting Biblical Texts. Louisville: Westminster John Knox, 2000.

———. "'Whatever Your Hand Finds to Do': Qoheleth's Work Ethic." *Interpretation* 55 (2001): 271–84.

Brueggemann, Walter A. *The Prophetic Imagination.* 2nd ed. Minneapolis: Fortress, 2001.

———. "The Social Significance of Solomon as a Patron of Wisdom." Pages 117–32 in *The Sage in Israel and the Ancient Near East.* Edited by John G. Gammie and Leo G. Perdue. Winona Lake, Ind.: Eisenbrauns, 1990.

———. "Theodicy in a Social Dimension." *Journal for the Study of the Old Testament* 33 (1985): 3–25.

———. "The Tribes of Yahweh: An Essay Review." *Journal of the American Academy of Religion* 48 (1980): 441–51.

Bryant, M. Darrol. "Ecological Evil and Interfaith Dialogue: Caring for the Earth." Pages 210–22 in *Evil and the Response of World Religion.* Edited by William Cenkner. St. Paul, Minn.: Paragon House, 1997.

Buccellati, Giorgio. "Wisdom and Not: The Case of Mesopotamia." *Journal of the American Oriental Society* 101 (1981): 35–47.

Buchanan, Ian. *Fredric Jameson. Live Theory*. London: Continuum, 2006.

Burkes, Shannon. *Death in Qoheleth and Egyptian Biographies of the Late Period*. Society of Biblical Literature Dissertation Series 170. Atlanta: Scholars Press, 1999.

Byargeon, Rick W. "The Significance of Ambiguity in Ecclesiastes 2,24–26." Pages 367–72 in *Qohelet in the Context of Wisdom*. Edited by Anton Schoors. Bibliotheca ephemeridum theologicarum lovaniensium 136. Leuven: Leuven University Press and Peeters, 1998.

Camp, Claudia. "Woman Wisdom and the Strange Woman: Where Is Power to Be Found?" Pages 209–39 in *Power, Powerlessness, and the Divine: New Inquiries in Bible and Theology*. Edited by Cynthia L. Rigby. Studies in Theological Education. Atlanta: Scholars Press, 1997.

Campbell, Colin. "Do Today's Sociologists Really Appreciate Weber's Essay *The Protestant Ethic and the Spirit of Capitalism?*" *Sociological Review* 54 (2006): 207–23.

———. "Theodicy." *Encyclopedia of Religion and Society*. No pages. Online at http://hirr.hartsem.edu/ency/Theodicy.htm (accessed March 3, 2008).

———. "Weber, Rationalisation, and Religious Evolution in the Modern Era." Pages 19–31 in *Theorising Religion: Classical and Contemporary Debates*. Edited by James A. Beckford and John Walliss. Aldershot: Ashgate, 2006.

Caneday, Ardel B. "Qoheleth: Enigmatic Pessimist or Godly Sage?" *Grace Theological Journal* 7 (1986): 21–56.

Caputo, John D. *Deconstruction in a Nutshell*. New York: Fordham University Press, 1997.

Carny, Pin'has. "Theodicy in the Book of Qohelet." Pages 71–81 in *Justice and Righteousness: Biblical Themes and Their Influence*. Edited by Henning Graf Reventlow and Yair Hoffman. Journal for the Study of the Old Testament: Supplement Series 137. Sheffield: JSOT Press, 1992.

Carr, David M. "Wisdom and Apocalpticism: Different Types of Educational/ Enculturational Literature." Paper presented at the annual meeting of the Society of Biblical Literature, San Antonio, Texas, November 21, 2004.

———. *Writing on the Tablet of the Heart: Origins of Scripture and Literature*. Oxford: Oxford University Press, 2005.

Carroll, Robert P. "Ancient Israelite Prophecy and Dissonance Theory." *Numen* 24 (1977): 135–51.

———. "Prophecy and Society." Pages 203–25 in *The World of Ancient Israel: Sociological, Anthropological and Political Perspectives. Essays by Members of the Society for Old Testament Study*. Edited by Ronald E. Clements. Paperback ed. Cambridge: Cambridge University Press, 1991.

———. *When Prophecy Failed: Reactions and Responses to Failure in the Old Testament Prophetic Traditions*. London: SCM, 1979.

Cenkner, William. "Hindu Understandings of Evil: From Tradition to Modern Thought." Pages 130–41 in *Evil and the Response of World Religion*. Edited by William Cenkner. St. Paul, Minn.: Paragon House, 1997.

Chambers, Simone. "How Religion Speaks to the Agnostic: Habermas on the Persistent Value of Religion." *Constellations* 14 (2007): 210–23.

Chaney, Marvin L. "Debt Easement in Israelite History and Tradition." Pages 127–39 in *The Bible and the Politics of Exegesis*. Edited by David Jobling, Peggy L. Day, and Gerald T. Sheppard. Cleveland: Pilgrim, 1991.

Charney, Davida. "Rhetorical Exigencies in the Individual Psalms." Paper presented at the Southwest regional meeting of the Society of Biblical Literature, Irving, Texas, March 14, 2010.

Childs, Brevard. *Introduction to the Old Testament as Scripture*. Philadelphia: Fortress, 1979.

Christian, Mark A. "Priestly Power That Empowers: Michel Foucault, Middle-Tier Levites, and the Sociology of 'Popular Religious Groups' in Israel." *Journal of Hebrew Studies* 9, Article 1 (2009): 1–81. Online at http://www.arts.ualberta.ca/JHS/Articles/article_103.pdf (accessed March 18, 2009).

Christianson, Eric S. *A Time to Tell: Narrative Strategies in Ecclesiastes*. Journal for the Study of the Old Testament: Supplement Series 280. Sheffield: Sheffield Academic Press, 1998.

Clark, Ronald R., Jr. "Schools, Scholars, and Students: The Wisdom School *Sitz im Leben* and Proverbs." *Restoration Quarterly* 47 (2005): 161–77.

Clarke, Caroline V. "The Power of Negative Thinking." *Black Enterprise* (June 2002): 254–55.

Clemens, D. M. Review of Douglas B. Miller, *Symbol and Rhetoric in Ecclesiastes: The Place of* Hebel *in Qohelet's Work* (Academia Biblica 2; Atlanta: Society of Biblical Literature, 2002). *Journal of Near Eastern Studies* 66 (2007): 216–21.

Clements, Ronald E. "Max Weber, Charisma and Biblical Prophecy." Pages 89–108 in *Prophecy and Prophets: The Diversity of Contemporary Issues in Scholarship*. Edited by Yehoshua Gitay. Semeia Studies. Atlanta: Scholars Press, 1997.

Clifford, Richard J. "Introduction to the Wisdom Literature." Pages 1–16 in vol. 5 of *The New Interpreter's Bible*. Edited by Leander Keck et al. 12 vols. Nashville: Abingdon, 1997.

———. *The Wisdom Literature*. Interpreting Biblical Texts. Nashville: Abingdon, 1998.

Clines, David J. A. *Interested Parties: The Ideology of Writers and Readers of the Hebrew Bible*. Journal for the Study of the Old Testament: Supplement Series 205: Gender, Culture, Theory 1. Sheffield: Sheffield Academic Press, 1995.

Cohen, Shaye J. D. "The Rabbi in Second-Century Jewish Society." Pp. 922–77 in vol. 3 of *Cambridge History of Judaism*. Edited by W. D. Davies and Louis Finkelstein. Cambridge: Cambridge University Press, 1984–.

Collins, Jeff, and Bill Mayblin. *Introducing Derrida.* New York: Totem, 1997. Repr., Cambridge: Icon, 2000.

Collins, John J. *The Apocalyptic Imagination: An Introduction to Jewish Apocalyptic Literature.* 2nd ed. Biblical Resource Series. Grand Rapids: Eerdmans, 1998.

———. "Cult and Culture: The Limits of Hellenization in Judea." Pages 38–61 in *Hellenism in the Land of Israel.* Edited by John J. Collins and Gregory E. Sterling. Christianity and Judaism in Antiquity 13. Notre Dame, Ind.: University of Notre Dame Press, 2001.

———. Preface to *Hellenism in the Land of Israel.* Edited by John J. Collins and Gregory E. Sterling. Christianity and Judaism in Antiquity 13. Notre Dame, Ind.: University of Notre Dame Press, 2001.

Connolly, Angela. "Jung in the Twilight Zone: The Psychological Functions of the Horror Film." Pages 128–38 in *Psyche and the Arts: Jungian Approaches to Music, Architecture, Literature, Film and Painting.* Edited by Susan Rowland. London: Routledge, 2008.

Cook, Johann. "The Origin of the Tradition of the יצר הטוב and יצר הרע." *Journal for the Study of Judaism* 38 (2007): 80–91.

Cook, Stephen L. *The Apocalyptic Literature.* Interpreting Biblical Texts. Nashville: Abingdon, 2003.

———. "The Lineage Roots of Hosea's Yahwism." *Semeia* 87 (1999): 145–61.

———. *Prophecy & Apocalypticism: The Postexilic Social Setting.* Minneapolis: Fortress, 1995.

Coote, Robert B., and Keith W. Whitelam. "The Emergence of Israel: Social Transformation and State Formation Following the Decline in Late Bronze Age Trade." *Semeia* 37 (1986): 107–47.

Cox, Claude. "When Torah Embraced Wisdom and Song: Job 28:28, Ecclesiastes 12:13, and Psalm 1:2." *Restoration Quarterly* 49 (2007): 65–74.

Crenshaw, James L. "The Birth of Skepticism in Ancient Israel." Pages 1–19 in *The Divine Helmsman: Studies in God's Control of Human Events.* Edited by James L. Crenshaw and Samuel Sandmel. New York: Ktav, 1980.

———. *Ecclesiastes.* Old Testament Library. Philadelphia: Westminster, 1987.

———. "The Eternal Gospel (Eccl. 3:11)." Pages 23–55 in *Essays in Old Testament Ethics.* Edited by James L. Crenshaw and John T. Willis. New York: Ktav, 1974.

———. Foreword to *Studies in Ancient Israelite Wisdom.* Edited by James L. Crenshaw. Library of Biblical Studies. New York: Ktav, 1976.

———. "Odd Book In: Ecclesiastes." *Bible Review* 6, no. 5 (1990): 28–33.

———. *Old Testament Wisdom: An Introduction.* Atlanta: John Knox, 1981.

———. "Popular Questioning of the Justice of God in Ancient Israel." *Zeitschrift für die alttestamentliche Wissenschaft* 82 (1970): 380–95.

———. "Qoheleth's Understanding of Intellectual Inquiry." Pages 205–24 in *Qohelet in the Context of Wisdom.* Edited by Anton Schoors. Bibliotheca ephemeridum theologicarum lovaniensium 136. Leuven: Leuven University Press and Peeters, 1998.

———. "Unresolved Issues in Wisdom Literature." Pages 215–27 in *An Introduction to Wisdom Literature and the Psalms*. Edited by H. W. Ballard Jr. and W. D. Tucker Jr. Macon, Ga.: Mercer University Press, 2000.

Cross, Frank Moore. *Canaanite Myth and Hebrew Epic: Essays in the History of the Religion of Israel*. 1973. Paperback ed. Cambridge, Mass.: Harvard University Press, 1997.

Crowther, Bruce. *Film Noir: Reflections in a Dark Mirror*. New York: Continuum, 1989.

Crüsemann, Frank. "Hiob und Kohelet: Ein Beitrag zum Verständis des Hiobbuches." Pages 373–93 in *Werden und Wirken des Alten Testaments: Festschrift für Claus Westermann*. Edited by Rainer Albertz, H. P. Müller, H. W. Wolff, and W. Zimmerli. Göttingen: Vandenhoeck & Ruprecht, 1980.

———. *The Torah: Theology and Social History of Old Testament Law*. Translated by Allan W. Mahnke. Minneapolis: Fortress, 1996.

———. "The Unchangeable World: The 'Crisis of Wisdom' in Koheleth." Pages 57–77 in *God of the Lowly: Socio-Historical Interpretations of the Bible*. Edited by Willy Schottroff and Wolfgang Stegemann. Translated by M. J. O'Connell. Maryknoll, N.Y.: Orbis, 1984.

Curtis, John B. "Elihu and Deutero-Isaiah: A Study in Literary Dependence." *Proceedings, Eastern Great Lakes and Midwest Biblical Societies* 10 (1990): 31–38.

Danby, Herbert, trans. *The Mishnah*. Oxford: Oxford University Press, 1933.

Davidson, Robert. "The Exposition of the Old Testament: Koheleth as a Test Case." *Expository Times* 115, no. 1 (2003): 1–7.

Dawes, Gregory W. "Can a Darwinian Be a Christian?" *Religion Compass* 1 (2007): 711–24. DOI: 10.111/j.1749-8171.2007.00050.x.

Delitzsch, Franz. "Commentary on the Song of Songs and Ecclesiastes." Pages 1–442 in *Commentary on the Old Testament in Ten Volumes*. Edited by C. F. Keil and F. Delitzsch. Translated by M. G. Easton. Grand Rapids: Eerdmans, 1950.

Derks, Hans. "Nomads, Jews, and Pariahs: Max Weber and Anti-Judaism." *The European Legacy* 4, no. 4 (1999): 24–48.

Diodorus Siculus. *The Library of History*. Translated by C. H. Oldfather et al. 12 vols. Loeb Classical Library. Cambridge, Mass.: Harvard University Press, 1935–67.

Doran, Robert. "Parties and Politics in Pre-Hasmonean Jerusalem: A Closer Look at 2 Macc 3:11." *SBL 1982 Seminar Papers*, 105–11.

Dowd, Garin, Lesley Stevenson, and Jeremy Strong, eds. *Genre Matters: Essays in Theory and Criticism*. Bristol: Intellect, 2006.

Dowling, William C. *Jameson, Althusser, Marx: An Introduction to the Political Unconscious*. Ithaca, N.Y.: Cornell University Press, 1984.

D'Sa, Francis Xavier. "A New Understanding of the Bhagaved Gita: Trinitarian Evil." Pages 142–53 in *Evil and the Response of World Religion*. Edited by William Cenkner. St. Paul, Minn.: Paragon House, 1997.

Durkheim, Émile. *The Elementary Forms of Religious Life*. Translated by Carol Cosman. Oxford World's Classics. Oxford: Oxford University Press, 2001.

———.*Suicide: A Study in Sociology*. Translated by John A. Spaulding and George Simpson. Paperback ed. New York: Free Press, 1966.

Dutcher-Walls, Patricia. "The Social Location of the Deuteronomists: A Sociological Study of Factional Politics in Late Pre-Exilic Judah." *Journal for the Study of the Old Testament* 52 (1991): 77–94.

Eagleton, Terry. *Ideology: An Introduction*. London: Verso, 1991.

———.*Marxism and Literary Criticism*. Berkeley: University of California Press, 1976.

Eddy, Samuel K. *The King Is Dead: Studies in the Near Eastern Resistance to Hellenism 334–31 B.C.* Lincoln: University of Nebraska Press, 1961.

Eisenstadt, Shmuel N. Introduction to *Max Weber on Charisma and Institution Building: Selected Papers*. Edited by S. N. Eisenstadt. Heritage of Sociology. Chicago: University of Chicago Press, 1968.

Elliot, John H. "Deuteronomy—Shameful Encroachment on Shameful Part: Deuteronomy 25:11–12 and Biblical Euphemism." Pages 161–76 in *Ancient Israel: The Old Testament in Its Social Context*. Edited by Philip F. Esler. Minneapolis: Fortress, 2006.

Elster, John. "Rationality, Economy, and Society." Pages 21–41 in *The Cambridge Companion to Weber*. Edited by Stephen Turner. Cambridge: Cambridge University Press, 2000.

Epstein, Isidore, ed. *The Babylonian Talmud*. 18 vols. London: Soncino, 1935–48.

Eshel, Esther. "The Onomasticon of Mareshah in the Persian and Hellenistic Periods." Pages 145–56 in *Judah and the Judeans in the Fourth Century B.C.E.* Edited by Oded Lipschits, Gary N. Knoppers, and Rainer Albertz. Winona Lake, Ind.: Eisenbrauns, 2007.

Eshel, Hanan. "The Governors of Samaria in the Fifth and Fourth Centuries B.C.E." Pages 223–34 in *Judah and the Judeans in the Fourth Century B.C.E.* Edited by Oded Lipschits, Gary N. Knoppers, and Rainer Albertz. Winona Lake, Ind.: Eisenbrauns, 2007.

Etzioni-Halevy, Eva. *The Knowledge Elite and the Failure of Prophecy*. Controversies in Sociology 18. London: G. Allen & Unwin, 1985.

Faulkner, R. O. Introduction to "The Admonitions of an Egyptian Sage." Pages 210–11 in *The Literature of Ancient Egypt: An Anthology of Stories, Instructions, Stelae, Autobiographies, and Poetry*. Edited by William Kelly Simpson. New Haven: Yale University Press, 1972.

Feldman, Louis H. *Studies in Hellenistic Judaism*. Arbeiten zur Geschichte des antiken Judentums und des Urchristentums 30. Leiden: Brill, 1996.

Feuer, Lewis S. "What Is an Intellectual?" Pages 47–58 in *The Intelligentsia and the Intellectuals: Theory, Method and Case Study*. Edited by Aleksander Gella. SABE Studies in International Sociology 5. Beverly Hills: SABE, 1976.

Fischer, Stefan. "Qohelet and 'Heretic' Harpers' Songs." *Journal for the Study of the Old Testament* 98 (2002): 105–21.

Fishbane, Michael. *Biblical Interpretation in Ancient Israel*. Oxford: Clarendon, 1988.

Fontana, Benedetto. *Hegemony & Power: On the Relation between Gramsci and Machiavelli*. Minneapolis: University of Minnesota Press, 1993.

Forman, Charles F. "The Pessimism of Ecclesiastes." *Journal of Semitic Studies* 3 (1958): 336–43.

Foucault, Michel. *Power/Knowledge: Selected Interviews & Other Writings 1971–1977*. Edited by Colin Gordon. Translated by Colin Gordon, Leo Marshall, John Mepham, and Kate Soper. New York: Pantheon, 1980.

Fowler, Alastair. *Kinds of Literature: An Introduction to the Theory of Genres and Modes*. Cambridge, Mass.: Harvard University Press, 1982.

Fox, Michael V. "Frame-Narrative and Composition in the Book of Qohelet." *Hebrew Union College Annual* 48 (1977): 83–106.

———. "The Meaning of *Hebel* for Qohelet." *Journal of Biblical Literature* 105 (1986): 409–27.

———. "The Social Location of the Book of Proverbs." Pages 227–39 in *Texts, Temples, and Traditions*. Edited by Michael V. Fox, Victor Avigdor Hurowitz, Avi Hurvitz, Michael L. Klein, Baruch J. Schwartz, and Nili Shupak. Winona Lake, Ind.: Eisenbrauns, 1996.

———. *A Time to Tear Down & A Time to Build Up: A Rereading of Ecclesiastes*. Grand Rapids: Eerdmans, 1999.

———. "What Happens in Qohelet 4:13–16." *Journal of Hebrew Scriptures* 1, article 4 (1996–1997): No pages. Online at http://www.arts.ualberta.ca/JHS/Articles/article4.pdf (accessed April 20, 2011).

———. "Wisdom in Qoheleth." Pages 115–31 in *In Search of Wisdom*. Edited by Leo G. Perdue, Bernard Brandon Scott, and William Johnston Wiseman. Louisville: Westminster John Knox, 1993.

Fraade, Steven D. "Ascetical Aspects of Ancient Judaism." Pages 253–88 in *Jewish Spirituality: From the Bible through the Middle Ages*. Edited by Arthur Green. Encyclopedia of World Spirituality 13. New York: Crossroad, 1986.

Fredericks, Daniel C. *Coping with Transience: Ecclesiastes on Brevity in Life*. Biblical Seminar. Sheffield: JSOT Press, 1993.

Frick, Frank S. "*Cui Bono?*—History in the Service of Political Nationalism: The Deuteronomistic History as Political Propaganda." *Semeia* 66 (1994): 79–92.

———. "Sociological Criticism and Its Relation to Political and Social Hermeneutics: With a Special Look at Biblical Hermeneutics in South African Liberation Theology." Pages 225–38 in *The Bible and the Politics of Exegesis*. Edited by David Jobling, Peggy L. Day, and Gerald T. Sheppard. Cleveland: Pilgrim, 1991.

Frow, John. *Genre*. New Critical Idiom. London: Routledge, 2005.

Galling, K. "Kohelet-Studien." *Zeitschrift für die alttestamentliche Wissenschaft* 50 (1932): 276–99.

Gardiner, Alan Henderson. *The Admonitions of an Egyptian Sage from a Hieratic Papyrus in Leiden, Pap. Leiden 344 Recto*. 1909. Repr., Hildesheim: Georg Olms, 1969.

Gardner, Gregg. "Jewish Leadership and Hellenistic Civic Benefaction in the Second Century B.C.E." *Journal of Biblical Literature* 126 (2007): 327–43.

Gera, Dov. "On the Credibility of the History of the Tobiads (Josephus, *Antiquities*, 12, 156–222, 228–236)." Pages 21–38 in *Greece and Rome in Eretz Israel: Collected Essays*. Edited by A. Kasher, U. Rappaport, and G. Fuks. Jerusalem: Yad Izhak Ben-Zvi/Israel Exploration Society, 1999.

Gerbrandt, Gerald Eddie. *Kingship According to the Deuteronomistic History*. Society of Biblical Literature Dissertation Series 87. Atlanta: Scholars Press, 1986.

Gerth, Hans H., and Don Martindale. Preface to Max Weber, *Ancient Judaism*. Translated and edited by Hans H. Gerth and Don Martindale. Paperback ed. New York: Free Press.

Gerth, Hans H., and C. Wright Mills. Introduction to *From Max Weber: Essays in Sociology*, 3–74. Translated and edited by Hans H. Gerth and C. Wright Mills. Paperback ed. New York: Oxford University Press, 1958.

Gese, Hartmut. "Die Krisis der Weisheit bei Kohelet." Pages 139–51 in *Les sagesses du Proche-Orient ancien*. Bibliothèque des centres d'études supérieures spécialisés. Paris: Presses Universitaires de France, 1963.

Giddens, Anthony. *Capitalism & Modern Social Theory: An Analysis of the Writings of Marx, Durkheim and Max Weber*. Cambridge: Cambridge University Press, 1971.

Goldberg, David J. "Providence and the Problem of Evil in Jewish Thought." Pages 32–42 in *Evil and the Response of World Religion*. Edited by William Cenkner. St. Paul, Minn.: Paragon House, 1997.

Goldfield, Gary S., Arthur G. Blouin, and D. Blake Woodside. "Body Image, Binge Eating, and Bulimia Nervosa in Male Bodybuilders." *Canadian Journal of Psychiatry* 51 (2006): 160–68.

Goldstein, Jonathan A. "The Tales of the Tobiads." Pages 85–123 in *Christianity, Judaism and Other Greco-Roman Cults: Studies for Morton Smith at Sixty*, vol. 3, *Judaism before 70*. Edited by Jacob Neusner. Studies in Judaism in Late Antiquity 12. Leiden: Brill, 1975. Repr., Eugene, Ore.: Wipf & Stock, n.d.

Goldstein, Warren S. "The Dialectics of Religious Rationalization and Secularization: Max Weber and Ernst Bloch." *Critical Sociology* 31 (2005): 115–51.

Good, Edwin M. *Irony in the Old Testament*. Philadelphia: Westminster, 1965.

Gordis, Robert. *Koheleth—The Man and His World: A Study of Ecclesiastes*. 3rd ed. New York: Schocken, 1968.

———. "The Social Background of Wisdom Literature." Pages 160–97 in *Poets,*

Prophets, and Sages: Essays in Biblical Interpretation. Edited by Robert Gordis. Bloomington: Indiana University Press, 1971. Repr. from *Hebrew Union College Annual* 18 (1943–44): 77–118.

Gottwald, Norman K. "Domain Assumptions and Societal Models in the Study of Pre-Monarchic Israel." Pages 170–81 in *Community, Identity, and Ideology: Social Science Approaches to the Hebrew Bible.* Edited by Charles E. Carter and Carol L. Meyers. Winona Lake, Ind.: Eisenbrauns, 1999. Repr. from *Congress Volume: Edinburgh, 1974.* Supplements to Vetus Testamentum 28. Leiden: Brill, 1976.

―――. "The Expropriated and the Expropriators in Nehemiah 5." Pages 1–19 in *Concepts of Class in Ancient Israel.* Edited by Mark Sneed. South Florida Studies in the History of Judaism: The Hebrew Scriptures and Their World 201. Atlanta: Scholars Press, 1999.

―――. *The Hebrew Bible: A Socio-Literary Introduction.* Philadelphia: Fortress, 1985.

―――. "Social Class as an Analytic and Hermeneutical Category in Biblical Studies." *Journal of Biblical Literature* 112 (1993): 3–22.

―――. "Sociology (Ancient Israel)." Pages 79–89 in vol. 6 of *The Anchor Bible Dictionary.* Edited by David Noel Freedman. 6 vols. New York: Doubleday, 1992.

Gramsci, Antonio. *Selections from the Prison Notes.* Edited and translated by Quintin Hoare and Geoffrey Nowell Smith. Paperback ed. New York: International Publishers, 2003.

Granger, John D. *Alexander the Great Failure.* London: Hambledon Continuum, 2007.

Green, Ronald. "Theodicy." Pages 430–41 in vol. 14 of *The Encyclopedia of Religion.* Edited by M. Eliade. 16 vols. New York: Macmillan, 1987.

Greenspoon, Leonard J. "Between Alexandria and Antioch: Jews and Judaism in the Hellenistic Period." Pages 421–65 in *The Oxford History of the Biblical World.* Edited by Michael D. Coogan. New York: Oxford University Press, 1998.

Griffin, David Ray. "Divine Goodness and Demonic Evil." Pages 223–40 in *Evil and the Response of World Religion.* Edited by William Cenkner. St. Paul, Minn.: Paragon House, 1997.

Guerra, Anthony J. "The Unification Understanding of the Problem of Evil." Pages 199–209 in *Evil and the Response of World Religion.* Edited by William Cenkner. St. Paul, Minn.: Paragon House, 1997.

Hadas, Moses. *Aristeas to Philocrates (Letter of Aristeas).* Edited and translated by M. Hadas. Dropsie College Edition: Jewish Apocryphal Literature. New York: Harper & Brothers, 1951.

―――. Introduction to *Aristeas to Philocrates (Letter of Aristeas).*

Haden, N. Karl. "Qoheleth and the Problem of Alienation." *Christian Scholars Review* 17 (1987): 52–66.

Hallo, William W., and William Kelly Simpson. *The Ancient Near East: A History.* New York: Harcourt Brace Jovanovich, 1971.

Hamilton, Alastair. "Max Weber's *Protestant Ethic and the Spirit of Capitalism.*" Pages 151–71 in *The Cambridge Companion to Weber.* Edited by Stephen Turner. Cambridge: Cambridge University Press, 2000.

Hamilton, Mark. "Elite Lives: Job 29–31 and Traditional Authority." *Journal for the Study of the Old Testament* 32 (2007): 69–89.

Hanson, Paul D. *The Dawn of Apocalyptic.* Philadelphia: Fortress, 1975.

Harrison, C. Robert. "Hellenization in Syria-Palestine: The Case of Judea in the Third Century BCE." *Biblical Archaeologist* 57 (1994): 98–108.

———. "Qoheleth among the Sociologists." *Biblical Interpretation* 5 (1997): 160–80.

———. "Qoheleth in Social-Historical Perspective." Ph.D. diss., Duke University, 1991.

Hassan, Riffay. "Feminist Theology as a Means of Combating Injustice toward Women in Muslim Communities and Culture." Pages 80–95 in *Evil and the Response of World Religion.* Edited by William Cenkner. St. Paul, Minn.: Paragon House, 1997.

Hatton, Peter T. H. *Contradiction in the Book of Proverbs: The Deep Waters of Counsel.* Society for Old Testament Studies Monograph Series. Aldershot: Ashgate, 2008.

Hausknecht, Murray. "At First Glance: The Role of the Intellectual." *Dissent* 44, no. 2 (1986): 131–32, 160.

Hayman, A. P. "The Survival of Mythology in the Wisdom of Solomon." *Journal for the Study of Judaism* 30 (1999): 125–39.

Heard, R. Christopher. "The Dao of Qoheleth: An Intertextual Reading of the *Daode Jing* and the Book of Ecclesiastes." *Jian Dao* 5 (1996): 65–93.

Heinen, H. "The Syrian-Egyptian Wars and Asia Minor." Pages 412–45 in *The Cambridge Ancient History,* vol. 7, part 1, *The Hellenistic World.* Edited by F. W. Walbank et al. 2nd ed. Cambridge: Cambridge University Press, 1984.

Held, Barbara S., and Arthur C. Bohart. "Introduction: The (Overlooked) Virtues of 'Unvirtuous' Attitudes and Behavior: Reconsidering Negativity, Complaining, Pessimism, and 'False' Hope." *Journal of Clinical Psychology* 58 (2002): 961–64.

Hengel, Martin. *Judaism and Hellenism: Studies in Their Encounter in Palestine during the Early Hellenistic Period.* Translated by John Bowden. 2 vols. Philadelphia: Fortress, 1974. Repr., Eugene, Ore.: Wipf & Stock, 2003.

———. "Judaism and Hellenism Revisited." Pages 6–37 in *Hellenism in the Land of Israel.* Edited by John J. Collins and Gregory E. Sterling. Christianity and Judaism in Antiquity 13. Notre Dame, Ind.: University of Notre Dame Press, 2001.

Hertzberg, Hans Wilhelm. *Der Prediger.* Kommentar zum Alten Testament 17/4. Gütersloh: Mohn, 1963.

Hick, John. *Evil and the God of Love.* Rev. ed. San Francisco: Harper & Row, 1978.

Hirsch, E. D., Jr. *Validity in Interpretation*. New Haven: Yale University Press, 1967.

Hirshman, Marc. "Qohelet's Reception and Interpretation in Early Rabbinic Literature." Pages 87–99 in *Studies in Ancient Midrash*. Edited by James L. Kugel. Cambridge, Mass.: Harvard University Center for Jewish Studies, 2001.

Holm-Nielsen, Sven. "On the Interpretation of Qoheleth in Early Christianity." *Vetus Testamentum* 24 (1974): 168–77.

Holmstedt, Robert D. "אֲנִי וְלִבִּי: The Syntactic Encoding of the Collaborative Nature of Qohelet's Experiment." *Journal of Hebrew Scriptures* 9, article 19 (2009): 1–27. Online at http://www.arts.ualberta.ca/JHS/Articles/article_121.pdf (accessed January 13, 2011).

Horkheimer, Max. "Montaigne and the Function of Skepticism." Pages 266–77 in *Between Philosophy and Social Science: Selected Early Writings*. Translated by G. Frederick Hunter, Matthew S. Kramer, and John Torpey. Cambridge, Mass.: MIT Press, 1993. Repr. from *Zeitschrift für Sozialforschung* 7 (1938).

Horsley, Richard A. "High Priests and the Politics of Roman Palestine." *Journal for the Study of Judaism* 17 (1986): 23–55.

Hunter, G. Frederick. Introduction to Max Horkheimer, *Between Philosophy and Social Science: Selected Early Writings*. Translated by G. Frederick Hunter, Matthew S. Kramer, and John Torpey. Cambridge, Mass.: MIT Press, 1993.

Isenberg, Sheldon R. "From Myth to Psyche to Mystic Psychology: The Evolution of the Problem of Evil in Judaism." Pages 16–31 in *Evil and the Response of World Religion*. Edited by William Cenkner. St. Paul, Minn.: Paragon House, 1997.

James, Gene G. "The Priestly Conceptions of Evil in the Torah." Pages 3–15 in *Evil and the Response of World Religion*. Edited by William Cenkner. St. Paul, Minn.: Paragon House, 1997.

James, Kenneth W. "Ecclesiastes: Precursor of Existentialists." *The Bible Today* 22 (March 1984): 85–90.

Jameson, Fredric. *The Political Unconscious: Narrative as a Socially Symbolic Act*. Ithaca, N.Y.: Cornell University Press, 1981.

Jamieson-Drake, David. *Scribes and Schools in Monarchic Judah: A Socio-Archaeological Approach*. Journal for the Study of the Old Testament: Supplement Series 109. Sheffield: Almond, 1991.

Janzen, J. Gerald. "Qohelet on Life 'Under the Sun.'" *Catholic Biblical Quarterly* 70 (2008): 465–83.

Jarick, John. "The Hebrew Book of Changes: Reflections on *Hakkōl Hebel* and *Lakkōl Zᵉmān* in Ecclesiastes." *Journal for the Study of the Old Testament* 90 (2000): 79–83.

Jarvie, I. C., and Joseph Agassi. "The Problem of the Rationality of Magic." *British Journal of Sociology* 18 (1967): 55–74.

Jenni, E., ed. *Theological Lexicon of the Old Testament.* Translated by M. E. Biddle. 3 vols. Peabody, Mass.: Hendrickson, 1997.

Jobling, David. "Deconstruction and the Political Analysis of Biblical Texts: A Jamesonian Reading of Psalm 72." *Semeia* 59 (1992): 95–127.

———. "Feminism and 'Mode of Production' in Ancient Israel." Pages 239–51 in *The Bible and the Politics of Exegesis.* Edited by David Jobling, Peggy L. Day, and Gerald T. Sheppard. Cleveland: Pilgrim, 1991.

Johnson, Raymond. "The Rhetorical Question as a Literary Device in Ecclesiastes." Ph.D. diss., Southern Baptist Theological Seminary, 1986.

Joll, James. *Antonio Gramsci.* Modern Masters. New York: Viking, 1977.

Jones, Scott C. "Qohelet's Courtly Wisdom: Ecclesiastes 8:1–9." *Catholic Biblical Quarterly* 68 (2006): 211–28.

Jong, Stephan de. "A Book on Labour: The Structuring Principles and the Main Theme of the Book of Qohelet." *Journal for the Study of the Old Testament* 54 (1992): 107–16.

———. "God in the Book of Qohelet: A Reappraisal of Qohelet's Place in Old Testament Theology." *Vetus Testamentum* 47 (1997): 154–67.

———. "Qohelet and the Ambitious Spirit of the Ptolemaic Period." *Journal for the Study of the Old Testament* 61 (1994): 85–96.

Josephus. Translated by H. St. J. Thacheray et al. 10 vols. Loeb Classical Library. Cambridge, Mass.: Harvard University Press, 1926–65.

Kadushin, Charles. *The American Intellectual Elite.* Boston: Little, Brown, 1974.

Kalberg, Stephen. Introduction to Max Weber, *The Protestant Ethic and the Spirit of Capitalism: The Revised 1920 Edition.* Oxford: Oxford University Press, 2011.

———. "Weber's Critique of Recent Comparative-Historical Sociology and a Reconstruction of His Analysis of Confucianism in China." *Current Perspectives in Social Theory* 19 (1999): 207–46.

Kaplan, Stephen. "Three Levels of Evil in Advaita Vedanta and a Holograhic Analogy." Pages 116–29 in *Evil and the Response of World Religion.* Edited by William Cenkner. St. Paul, Minn.: Paragon House, 1997.

Kaufmann, Wanda Ostrowska. *The Anthropology of Wisdom Literature.* Westport, Conn.: Bergin & Garvey, 1996.

Kayes, D. Christopher. "Organizational Corruption as Theodicy." *Journal of Business Ethics* 67 (2006): 51–62. DOI: 10.1007/s10551-006-9004-x.

Kemp, Barry J. "Old Kingdom, Middle Kingdom and Second Intermediate Period *c.* 2686–1552 BC." Pages 71–182 in B. G. Trigger, B. J. Kemp, D. O'Connor, and A. B. Lloyd, *Ancient Egypt: A Social History.* Cambridge: Cambridge University Press, 1983.

Kidner, Derek. *Proverbs.* Tyndale Old Testament Commentaries. Leicester: Inter-Varsity Press, 1964.

Kieckhefer, Richard. "The Specific Rationality of Medieval Magic." *American Historical Review* 99 (1994): 813–36.

Kim, Uriah Y. *Decolonizing Josiah: Toward a Postcolonial Reading of the Deuter-onomistic History*. Sheffield: Sheffield Phoenix, 2005.

Kippenberg, Hans G. *Religion und Klassenbildung in antiken Judäa: Eine reli-gionssoziologische Studie zum Verhältnis von Tradition und gesellschaftlicher Entwicklung*. Studien zur Umwelt des Neuen Testaments 14. Göttingen: Vandenhoeck & Ruprecht, 1978.

Kloner, Amos, and Ian Stern. "Idumea in the Late Persian Period (Fourth Century B.C.E.)." Pages 139–44 in *Judah and the Judeans in the Fourth Century B.C.E.* Edited by Oded Lipschits, Gary N. Knoppers, and Rainer Albertz. Winona Lake, Ind.: Eisenbrauns, 2007.

Klopfenstein, Martin A. "Die Skepsis des Kohelet." *Theologische Zeitschrift* 28 (1972): 97–109.

Knobel, Peter S., trans. *The Targum of Qohelet*. Aramaic Bible 15. Collegeville, Minn.: Michael Glazier, 1991.

Knoppers, Gary N. "Nehemiah and Sanballat: The Enemy Without or Within?" Pages 305–31 in *Judah and the Judeans in the Fourth Century B.C.E.* Edited by Oded Lipschits, Gary N. Knoppers, and Rainer Albertz. Winona Lake, Ind.: Eisenbrauns, 2007.

Koch, Klaus. "Is There a Doctrine of Retribution in the Old Testament?" Pages 57–87 in *Theodicy in the Old Testament*. Edited by James L. Crenshaw. Issues in Religion and Theology 4. Philadelphia: Fortress, 1983.

Koosed, Jennifer L., and Robert P. Seesengood. "Constructions and Collusions: The Making and Unmaking of Identity in Qoheleth and Hebrews." Pages 265–80 in *Hebrews: Contemporary Methods— New Insights*. Edited by Gabri-ella Gelardini. Biblical Interpretation Series 75. Leiden: Brill, 2005.

Koshul, Basit Bilal. "Scriptural Reasoning and the Philosophy of Social Science." *Modern Theology* 22 (2006): 483–501.

Kovacs, Brian W. "Is There a Class-Ethic in Proverbs?" Pages 173–89 in *Essays in Old Testament Ethics*. Edited by James L. Crenshaw and John T. Willis. New York: Ktav, 1974.

———. "Sociological-Structural Constraints upon Wisdom: The Spatial and Temporal Matrix of Proverbs 15:28–22:16." Ph.D. diss., Vanderbilt University, 1978.

Krašovec, Jože. "Is There a Doctrine of 'Collective Retribution' in the Hebrew Bible?" *Hebrew Union College Annual* 65 (1994): 35–89.

Kreitzer, Larry. "The Cultural Veneer of Star Trek." *Journal of Popular Culture* 30, no. 2 (1996): 1–28.

Krüger, Thomas. "Dekonstruktion und Rekonstruktion prophetischer Eschatolo-gie im Qohelet-Buch." Pages 107–29 in *"Jedes Ding hat seine Zeit . . .": Studien zur israelitischen und altorientalischen Weisheit*. Edited by Anja A. Diesel, Reinhard G. Lehmann, Eckart Otto, and Andreas Wagner. Beihefte zur Zeitschrift für die alttestamentliche Wissenschaft 241. Berlin: de Gruyter, 1996.

————.*Qoheleth: A Commentary.* Translated by O. C. Dean Jr. Hermeneia. Minneapolis: Fortress, 2004.

————. "Die Rezeption der Tora im Buch Kohelet." Pages 303–25 in *Das Buch Kohelet: Studien zur Struktur, Geschichte, Rezeption und Theologie.* Edited by Otto Kaiser. Beihefte zur Zeitschrift für die alttestamentliche Wissenschaft 254. Berlin: de Gruyter, 1997.

Kübler-Ross, Elisabeth. *On Death and Dying: What the Dying Have to Teach Doctors, Nurses, Clergy, and Their Families.* Paperback ed. New York: Touchstone, 1997.

Lang, Bernhard. "Ist der Mensch hilflos? Das biblische Buch Kohelet, neu und kritisch gelesen." *Theologische Quartalschrift* 159 (1979): 109–24.

————. "The Social Organization of Peasant Poverty in Biblical Israel." Pages 83–99 in *Anthropological Approaches to the Old Testament.* Edited by Bernhard Lang. Issues in Religion and Theology 8. Philadelphia: Fortress; London: SPCK, 1985.

Lassman, Peter. "The Rule of Man over Man: Politics, Power and Legitimation." Pages 83–98 in *The Cambridge Companion to Weber.* Edited by Stephen Turner. Cambridge: Cambridge University Press, 2000.

Lauha, Aarre. *Kohelet.* Biblischer Kommentar, Altes Testament 19. Neukirchen-Vluyn: Neukirchener Verlag, 1978.

————. "Kohelets Verhältnis zur Geschichte." Pages 393–401 in *Die Botschaft und die Boten: Festschrift für Hans Walter Wolff zum 70. Geburtstag.* Edited by Jörg Jeremias and Lothar Perlit. Neukirchen-Vluyn: Neukirchener Verlag, 1981.

————. "Die Krise des religiösen Glaubens bei Kohelet." Pages 183–91 in *Wisdom in Israel and in the Ancient Near East.* Edited by M. Noth and D. Winton Thomas. Supplements to Vetus Testamentum 3. Leiden: Brill, 1955.

Lawrie, Douglas G. "The Dialectical Grammar of Job and Qoheleth: A Burkean Analysis." *Scriptura* 66 (1998): 217–34.

Layman, C. Stephen. "Moral Evil: The Comparative Response." *International Journal for Philosophy of Religion* 53 (2003): 1–23.

Lee, Bernon. "A Specific Application of the Proverb in Ecclesiastes 1:15." *Journal of Hebrew Scriptures* 1, article 6 (1997): 1–19. Online at http://www.arts.ualberta.ca/JHS/Articles/article6.pdf (accessed April 6, 2011).

Lemaire, André. "Administration in Fourth-Century B.C.E Judah in Light of Epigraphy and Numismatics." Pages 53–74 in *Judah and the Judeans in the Fourth Century B.C.E.* Edited by Oded Lipschits, Gary N. Knoppers, and Rauber Albertz. Winona Lake, Ind.: Eisenbrauns, 2007.

Lenski, Gerhard E. *Power and Privilege: A Theory of Social Stratification.* New York: McGraw-Hill, 1966. Repr., Chapel Hill: University of North Carolina Press, 1984.

Leuchter, Mark. "Zadokites, Deuteronomists, and the Exilic Debate over Scribal Authority." *Journal of Hebrew Studies* 7, Article 10 (2007): 5–18. Online at http://www.arts.ualberta.ca/JHS/Articles/article_71.pdf (accessed March 18, 2009).

Levine, Étan. "The Humor in Qohelet." *Zeitschrift für die alttestamentliche Wissenschaft* 109 (1997): 71–83.

Levine, Lee I. *Judaism and Hellenism in Antiquity: Conflict or Confluence?* Seattle: University of Washington Press, 1998. Repr., Peabody, Mass.: Hendrickson, 1999.

Lichtheim, Miriam. *Ancient Egyptian Literature: A Book of Readings.* 3 vols. Berkeley: University of California Press, 1971–80.

Liddell, H. G., R. Scott, and H. S. Jones, *A Greek-English Lexicon.* 9th ed. Oxford: Clarendon, 1996.

Lim, Lena. "A Two-Factor Model of Defensive Pessimism and Its Relations with Achievement Motives." *Journal of Psychology* 143 (2009): 318–36.

Lipschits, Oded, and Oren Tal. "The Settlement Archaeology of the Province of Judah: A Case Study." Pages 33–52 in *Judah and the Judeans in the Fourth Century B.C.E.* Edited by Oded Lipschits, Gary N. Knoppers, and Rainer Albertz. Winona Lake, Ind.: Eisenbrauns, 2007.

Lipschits, Oded, and David Vanderhooft. "Yehud Stamp Impressions in the Fourth Century B.C.E.: A Time of Administrative Consolidation?" Pages 75–94 in *Judah and the Judeans in the Fourth Century B.C.E.* Edited by Oded Lipschits, Gary N. Knoppers, and Rainer Albertz. Winona Lake, Ind.: Eisenbrauns, 2007.

Lipset, Seymour Martin, and Richard B. Dobson. "The Intellectual as Critic and Rebel: With Special Reference to the United States and the Soviet Union." *Daedalus* 101, no. 3 (1972): 137–98.

Lloyd. Alan B. "The Ptolemaic Period (332–30 BC)." Pages 388–413 in *The Oxford History of Ancient Egypt.* Edited by Ian Shaw. Paperback and new ed. Oxford: Oxford University Press, 2003.

Lo, Alison. "Death in Qohelet." *Journal of Near Eastern Studies* 31 (2008): 85–98.

Loader, James A. "Different Reactions of Job and Qoheleth to the Doctrine of Retribution." Pages 43–48 in *Studies in Wisdom Literature.* Edited by W. C. van Wyk. Old Testament Studies: OTWSA 15, 16. Hercules, South Africa: N. H. W. Press, 1981.

———.*Ecclesiastes.* Translated by J. Vriend. Text and Interpretation. Grand Rapids: Eerdmans, 1992.

———.*Polar Structures in the Book of Qohelet.* Beihefte zur Zeitschrift für die alttestamentliche Wissenschaft 152. Berlin: de Gruyter, 1979.

Locke, Simon. "Conspiracy Culture, Blame Culture, and Rationalization." *Sociological Review* 57 (2009): 567–85.

Lohfink, Norbert. "Ist Kohelets הבל–Aussage erkenntnistheoretisch gemeint?" Pages 41–59 in *Qohelet in the Context of Wisdom.* Edited by Anton Schoors. Bibliotheca ephemeridum theologicarum lovaniensium 136. Leuven: Leuven University Press and Peeters, 1998.

———.*Qoheleth.* Translated by Sean McEvenue. Continental Commentaries. Minneapolis: Fortress, 2003.

Long, Burke O. "The Social World of Ancient Israel." *Interpretation* 36 (1982): 243–55.

Longman, Tremper, III. *The Book of Ecclesiastes.* New International Commentary on the Old Testament. Grand Rapids: Eerdmans, 1998.

———. "Challenging the Idols of the Twenty-First Century: The Message of the Book of Ecclesiastes." *Stone Campbell Journal* 12 (2009): 207–16.

Love, John. "Max Weber's *Ancient Judaism.*" Pages 200–220 in *The Cambridge Companion to Weber.* Edited by Stephen Turner. Cambridge: Cambridge University Press, 2000.

———. "Max Weber's Orient." Pages 172–99 in *The Cambridge Companion to Weber.* Edited by Stephen Turner. Cambridge: Cambridge University Press, 2000.

Lucy, Niall. *A Derrida Dictionary.* Malden, Mass.: Blackwell, 2004.

Luria, S. "Die Ersten werden die Letzen sein (Zur 'sozialen Revolution' im Altertum)." *Klio* n.F. 4 (1929): 1–27.

MacDonald, Duncan Black. *The Hebrew Literary Genius: An Interpretation Being an Introduction to the Reading of the Old Testament.* Princeton: Princeton University Press, 1933.

Machinist, Peter. "Fate, *miqreh*, and Reason: Some Reflections on Qohelet and Biblical Thought." Pages 159–75 in *Solving Riddles and Untying Knots: Biblical, Epigraphic, and Semitic Studies in Honor of Jonas C. Greenfield.* Edited by Ziony Zevit, Seymour Gitin, and Michael Sokoloff. Winona Lake, Ind.: Eisenbrauns, 1995.

McCalla, Arthur. "Creationism." *Religion Compass* 1 (2007): 547–60. DOI: 10.1111/j.1749-8171.2007.00034.x.

McKenna, John E. "The Concept of *Hebel* in the Book of Ecclesiastes." *Scottish Journal of Theology* 45 (1992): 19–28.

McKenzie, John L. "Reflections on Wisdom." *Journal of Biblical Literature* 86 (1967): 1–9.

Mader, Gottfried. *Josephus and the Politics of Historiography: Apologetic and Impression Management in the Bellum Judaicum.* Mnemosyne: Supplementum 205. Leiden: Brill, 2000.

Mahon, James. "Weber's Protestant Ethic and the Chinese Preference for Sons: An Application of Western Sociology to Eastern Religions." *Max Weber Studies* 5 (2005): 59–80.

Malamat, Abraham. "Charismatic Leadership in the Book of Judges." Pages 293–310 in *Community, Identity, and Ideology: Social Science Approaches to the Hebrew Bible.* Edited by Charles E. Carter and Carol L. Meyers. Winona Lake, Ind.: Eisenbrauns, 1999. Repr., pages 152–68 in *Magnalia Dei— The Mighty Acts of God: Essays on the Bible and Archaeology in Memory of*

G. Ernst Wright. Edited by F. M. Cross, W. E. Lemke, and P. D. Miller. New York: Doubleday, 1976

Mannheim, Karl. *Ideology and Utopia: An Introduction to the Sociology of Knowledge.* New York: Harcourt Brace, n.d.

———. *Man and Society in an Age of Reconstruction: Studies in Modern Social Structure.* Translated by Edward Shils. New York: Harcourt Brace, 1940.

Marsh, Robert M. "Weber's Misunderstanding of Traditional Chinese Law." *American Journal of Sociology* 106 (2000): 281–302.

Marx, Karl, and Frederick [Friedrich] Engels. *The German Ideology.* 1845. Repr., New York: International Publishers, 1970.

Mason, Hayda. "Using Characters to Disprove Optimism." Pages 39–46 in *Readings on Candide.* Edited by Thomas Walsh. Literary Companion. San Diego: Greenhaven, 2001.

Mason, Steve. "Pharisaic Dominance before 70 CE and the Gospel's Hypocrisy Charge (Matt 23:2–3)." *Harvard Theological Review* 83 (1990): 363–81.

Matthews, Victor. "Traversing the Social Landscape: The Value of the Social Science Approach to the Bible." Pages 214–36 in *Theology and the Social Sciences.* Edited by Michael Horace Barnes. Annual Publication of the College Theology Society 46. Maryknoll, N.Y.: Orbis, 2000.

Matthews, Victor, and Don C. Benjamin. *Old Testament Parallels.* 3rd ed. New York: Paulist Press, 2006.

Maussion, Marie. "Qohélet VI 1–2: 'Dieu ne permet pas . . .'" *Vetus Testamentum* 55 (2005): 501–10.

Mayes, A. D. H. "Idealism and Materialism in Weber and Gottwald." Pages 258–72 in *Community, Identity, and Ideology: Social Science Approaches to the Hebrew Bible.* Edited by Charles E. Carter and Carol L. Meyers. Winona Lake, Ind.: Eisenbrauns, 1999. Repr. from *Proceedings of the Irish Biblical Association* 11 (1988): 44–58.

———. *Judges.* Old Testament Guides. Sheffield: JSOT Press, 1985. Repr., Sheffield: Sheffield Academic Press, 1995.

———. *The Old Testament in Sociological Perspective.* London: Marshall Pickering, 1989.

———. "Sociology and the Old Testament." Pages 39–63 in *The World of Ancient Israel: Sociological, Anthropological and Political Perspectives. Essays by Members of the Society for Old Testament Study.* Edited by Ronald E. Clements. Paperback ed.; Cambridge: Cambridge University Press, 1991.

Mendenhall, George E. "The Hebrew Conquest of Palestine." Pages 152–69 in *Community, Identity, and Ideology: Social Science Approaches to the Hebrew Bible.* Edited by Charles E. Carter and Carol L. Meyers. Winona Lake, Ind.: Eisenbrauns, 1999. Repr. from *Biblical Archaeologist* (1962): 66–87.

Merton, Robert K. *Social Theory and Social Structure.* Rev. and enlarged ed. Glencoe, Ill.: Free Press, 1957.

Michel, Diethelm. *Qohelet.* Erträge der Forschung 258. Darmstadt: Wissenschaftliche Buchgesellschaft, 1988.

———. "'Unter der Sonne': Zur Immanenz bei Qohelet." Pages 93–111 in *Qohelet in the Context of Wisdom.* Edited by Anton Schoors. Bibliotheca ephemeridum theologicarum lovaniensium 136. Leuven: Leuven University Press and Peeters, 1998.

Miller, Douglas B. "Qohelet's Symbolic Use of הבל." *Journal of Biblical Literature* 117 (1998): 437–54.

———. *Symbol and Rhetoric in Ecclesiastes: The Place of* Hebel *in Qohelet's Work.* Academia Biblica 2. Atlanta: Society of Biblical Literature, 2002.

———. "What the Preacher Forgot: The Rhetoric of Ecclesiastes." *Catholic Biblical Quarterly* 62 (2000): 215–35.

Mitchell, Christine. "Power, *Eros,* and Biblical Genres." Pages 31–42 in *Bakhtin and Genre Theory in Biblical Studies.* Edited by Roland Boer. Semeia Studies 63. Atlanta: Society of Biblical Literature, 2007.

Morgan, David. "Pain: The Unrelieved Condition of Modernity." *European Journal of Social Theory* 5 (2002): 307–22.

Mosala, Itumeleng J. "Social Scientific Approaches to the Bible: One Step Forward, Two Steps Back." *Journal of Theology for Southern Africa* 55 (1986): 15–30.

Moyise, Steve. "Is Life Futile? Paul and Ecclesiastes." *Expository Times* 108, no. 6 (1997): 178–79.

Müller, Hans-Peter. "Neige der althebräischen 'Weisheit': Zum Denken Qohäläts." *Zeitschrift für die alttestamentliche Wissenschaft* 90 (1978): 238–63.

———. "Theonome Skepsis und Lebensfreude—Zu Koh 1:12–3:15." *Biblische Zeitschrift* n.F 30 (1986): 1–19.

———. "Der unheimliche Gast: Zum Denken Kohelets." *Zeitschrift für Theologie und Kirche* 84 (1987): 440–64.

Murphy, Roland E. *Ecclesiastes.* Word Biblical Commentary 23a. Dallas: Word, 1992.

———. "The 'Pensée' of Coheleth." *Catholic Biblical Quarterly* 17 (1955): 304–14.

———. "Qohelet Interpreted: The Bearing of the Past on the Present." *Vetus Testamentum* 32 (1982): 331–37.

Nelson, Richard D. *The Historical Books.* Interpreting Biblical Texts. Nashville: Abingdon, 1998.

Nettl, Peter. "Power and the Intellectuals." Pages 15–32 in *Power & Consciousness.* Edited by Connor Cruise O'Brien and William Dean Vanech. London: University of London Press, 1969.

Neusner, Jacob, trans. *The Fathers According to Rabbi Nathan: An Analytical Translation and Explanation.* Brown Judaic Studies 114. Atlanta: Scholars Press, 1986.

———, trans. *Sifre to Deuteronomy: An Analytical Translation.* Edited by Jacob Neusner et al. 2 vols. Brown Judaic Studies 98. Atlanta: Scholars Press, 1987.

Newsom, Carol A. "Job and Ecclesiastes." Pages 177–94 in *Old Testament Inter-*

pretation: Past, Present, and Future. Edited by James L. Mays, David L. Petersen, and Kent H. Richards. Nashville: Abingdon, 1995.

———. "Knowing and Doing: The Social Symbolics of Knowledge at Qumran." *Semeia* 59 (1992): 139–53.

———. "Spying Out the Land: A Report from Genology." Pages 19–30 in *Bakhtin and Genre Theory in Biblical Studies.* Edited by Roland Boer. Semeia Studies 63. Atlanta: Society of Biblical Literature, 2007.

———. "Woman and the Discourse of Partriarchal Wisdom: A Study of Proverbs 1–9." Pages 142–60 in *Gender and Difference in Ancient Israel.* Edited by Peggy L. Day. Minneapolis: Fortress, 1989.

Niditch, Susan. *Ancient Israelite Religion.* New York: Oxford University Press, 1997.

———. "Father-Son Folktale Patterns and Tyrant Typologies in Josephus' Ant. 12:160–222." *Journal of Jewish Studies* 32 (1981): 47–55.

Nietzsche, Friedrich. *On the Genealogy of Morals.* Translated by Horace B. Samuel. Barnes & Noble Library of Essential Reading. New York: Barnes & Noble, 2006.

Nisbet, Robert. *The Social Bond: An Introduction to the Study of Society.* New York: Knopf, 1970.

Norem, Julie K. *The Positive Power of Negative Thinking: Using Defensive Pessimism to Harness Anxiety and Perform at Your Peak.* Paperback ed. New York: Basic Books, 2002.

Norem, Julie K., and Edward C. Chang. "The Positive Psychology of Negative Thinking." *Journal of Clinical Psychology* 58 (2002): 993–1001.

Nozick, Robert. *Anarchy, State, and Utopia.* New York: Basic Books, 1972.

Ogden, Graham. "Historical Allusion in Qoheleth IV 13–16?" *Vetus Testamentum* 30 (1980): 309–315.

———. *Qoheleth.* Readings. Sheffield: JSOT Press, 1987.

———. "'Vanity' It Certainly Is Not." *The Bible Translatory* 38 (1987): 301–7.

Økland, Jorunn. "Textual Reproduction as Surplus Value: Paul on Pleasing Christ and Spouses, in Light of Simone de Beauvoir." Pages 182–203 in *Marxist Feminist Criticism of the Bible.* Edited by Roland Boer and Jorunn Økland. Bible in the Modern World 14. Sheffield: Sheffield Phoenix, 2008.

Ollenburger, Ben C., and Elmer A. Martens, and Gerhard F. Hasel, eds. *The Flowering of Old Testament Theology: A Reader in Twentieth-Century Old Testament Theology, 1930–1990.* Sources for Biblical and Theological Study 1. Winona Lake, Ind.: Eisenbrauns, 1992.

Oppenheim, A. Leo "The Intellectual in Mesopotamian Society." *Daedalus* 104 (1975): 37–46.

Orihara, Hiroshi. "Max Weber's 'Four-Stage Rationalization-Scale of Social Action and Order' in the 'Categories' and Its Significance to the 'Old Manuscript' of His 'Economy and Society': A Positive Critique of Wolfgang Schluchter." *Max Weber Studies* 8 (2008): 141–62.

Orrieux, Claude. "Les papyrus de Zénon et la préhistoire du mouvement maccabéen." Pages 321–33 in *Hellenica et Judaica*. Edited by A. Caquot, M.
Hadas-Lebel, and J. Riaud. Leuven: Peeters, 1986.

Overholt, Thomas W. "Prophecy: The Problem of Cross-Cultural Comparison." Pages 423–47 in *Community, Identity, and Ideology: Social Science
Approaches to the Hebrew Bible*. Edited by Charles E. Carter and Carol L.
Meyers. Winona Lake, Ind. Eisenbrauns, 1999. Repr. from *Semeia* 21 (1982):
55–78.

Owens, J. Edward. "'Come, Let Us Be Wise': Qoheleth and Ben Sira on True Wisdom, with an Ear to Pharaoh's Folly." Pages 227–40 in *Intertextual Studies
in Ben Sira and Tobit*. Edited by Jeremy Corley and Vincent Skemp. Catholic Biblical Quarterly Monograph Series 38. Washington: Catholic Biblical
Association of America, 2005.

Oyelade, E. O. "Evil in Yoruba Religion and Culture." Pages 157–69 in *Evil and
the Response of World Religion*. Edited by William Cenkner. St. Paul, Minn.:
Paragon House, 1997.

Pahk, Johan Yeong-Sik. "The Role and Significance of DBRY ḤPṢ [Qoh 12:10A]
for Understanding Qohelet." Pages 325–53 in *Congress Volume: Leiden 2004*.
Edited byAndré Lemaire. Supplements to Vetus Testamentum 109. Leiden:
Brill, 2006.

Parsons, Talcott. "'The Intellectual': A Social Role Category." Pages 3–24 in *On
Intellectuals: Theoretical Studies; Case Studies*. Edited by Philip Rieff. Garden
City, N.Y.: Doubleday, 1969.

———. Introduction to Max Weber, *Sociology of Religion*.

Patterson, James A. "Cultural Pessimism in Modern Evangelical Thought: Francis Schaeffer, Carl Henry, and Charles Colson." *Journal of the Evangelical
Theological Society* 49 (2006): 807–20.

Peck, Russell. "Ecclesiastes as a Pivotal Biblical and Literary Text." *Association of
Departments of English Bulletin* 81 (1985): 43–48.

Pedersen, Johannes. "Scepticisme israélite." *Revue d'histoire et de philosophie
religieuses* 10 (1930): 317–70.

Peltonen, Matti. "The Weber Thesis and Economic Historians." *Max Weber Studies* 8 (2008): 79–98.

Penchansky, David. *The Betrayal of God: Ideological Conflict in Job*. Louisville:
Westminster John Knox, 1990.

Perdue, Leo G. *The Sword and the Stylus: An Introduction to Wisdom in the Age of
Empires*. Grand Rapids: Eerdmans, 2008.

———. *Wisdom in Revolt: Metaphorical Theology in the Book of Job*. Journal for
the Study of the Old Testament: Supplement Series 112: Bible and Literature
29. Sheffield: Almond, 1991.

Perelman, Chaïm, and L. Olbrechts-Tyteca. *The New Rhetoric: A Treatise on
Argumentation*. Translated by John Wilkinson and Purcell Weaver. Paperback ed. Notre Dame, Ind.: University of Notre Dame Press, 1971.

Perrin, Nicholas. "Messianism in the Narrative Frame of Ecclesiastes?" *Revue biblique* 108 (2001): 37–60.

Person, Raymond F. "The Ancient Israelite Scribe as Performer." *Journal of Biblical Literature* 117 (1998): 601–9.

Petersen, David L. "The Nature of Prophetic Literature." Pages 23–40 in *Prophecy and Prophets: The Diversity of Contemporary Issues in Scholarship*. Edited by Yehoshua Gitay. Semeia Studies. Atlanta: Scholars Press, 1997.

Pfeiffer, Robert H. "The Peculiar Skepticism of Ecclesiastes." *Journal of Biblical Literature* 53 (1934): 100–109.

Phan, Peter C. "Prophecy and Contemplation: The Language of Liberation Theology against Evil." Pages 183–98 in *Evil and the Response of World Religion*. Edited by William Cenkner. St. Paul, Minn.: Paragon House, 1997.

Pinker, Aron. "The Doings of the Wicked in Qohelet 8:10." *Journal of Hebrew Studies* 8, article 6 (2008): 1–22. Online at http://www.arts.ualberta.ca/JHS/Articles/article_83.pdf (accessed April 20, 2011).

———. "Qohelet 2,12b." *Biblische Zeitschrift* 53 (2009): 94–105.

———. "Qohelet 3,18—A Test?" *Scandinavian Journal of the Old Testament* 23 (2009): 282–96.

———. "Qohelet 4,13–16." *Scandinavian Journal of the Old Testament* 22 (2008): 176–94.

Piovanelli, Pierluigi. "Jesus' Charismatic Authority: On the Historical Applicability of a Sociological Model." *Journal of the American Academy of Religion* 73 (2005): 395–427.

Pippin, Tina. "Eros and the End: Reading for Gender in the Apocalypse of John." *Semeia* 59 (1992): 193–210.

Pleins, J. David. "Poverty in the Social World of the Wise." *Journal for the Study of the Old Testament* 37 (1987): 61–78.

Podolinská, Tatiana, and Milan Kováč. "'Mythos' versus 'Logos': Strategies of Rationalization at the Boundaries of Two Worlds in the Conceptions of Supernatural Beings in Slovak Countryside." *Dialogue and Universalism* 12, nos. 8–10 (2002): 85–99.

Polk, Timothy. "The Wisdom of Irony: A Study of *Hebel* and Its Relation to Joy and the Fear of God in Ecclesiastes." *Studia Biblica et Theologica* 6 (1976): 3–17.

Poulantzas, Nicos. "On Social Classes." *New Left Review* 78 (1973): 27–54.

Priest, John F. "Humanism, Skepticism, and Pessimism in Israel." *Journal of the American Academy of Religion* 36 (1968): 311–26.

Pritchard, James B., ed. *Ancient Near Eastern Texts Relating to the Old Testament*. 3rd ed. Princeton: Princeton University Press, 1969.

Rad, Gerhard von. *Old Testament Theology*. Translated by D. M. G. Stalker. 2 vols. New York: Harper & Row, 1962.

———. *Wisdom in Israel*. Translated by James D. Martin. London: SCM, 1972. Repr., Nashville: Abingdon, 1988.

Ranston, Harry. *Ecclesiastes and the Early Greek Wisdom Literature*. London: Epworth, 1925.

Ravasi, Gianfranco. *Qohelet*. La parola di Dio. 2nd ed. Milan: Paoline, 1991.

Redditt, Paul L. *Daniel*. New Century Bible. Sheffield: Sheffield Academic Press, 1999.

———. "Zerubbabel, Joshua, and the Night Visions of Zechariah." *Catholic Biblical Quarterly* 54 (1992): 249–59.

Reden, Sitta von. *Money in Ptolemaic Egypt: From the Macedonian Conquest to the End of the Third Century* BC. Paperback ed. Cambridge: Cambridge University Press, 2010.

Rentería, Tamis Hoover. "The Elijah/Elisha Stories: A Socio-Cultural Analysis of Prophets and People in Ninth-Century B.C.E. Israel." Pages 75–126 in *Elijah and Elisha in Socioliterary Perspective*. Edited by Robert B. Coote. Semeia Studies. Atlanta: Scholars Press, 1992.

Roberts, Adam. *Fredric Jameson*. Routledge Critical Thinkers. London: Routledge, 2000.

Rodd, Cyril S. "On Applying a Sociological Theory to Biblical Studies." Pages 22–33 in *Social-Scientific Old Testament Criticism*. Edited by David J. Chalcraft. Biblical Seminar 47. Sheffield: Sheffield Academic Press, 1997. Repr. from *Journal for the Study of the Old Testament* 19 (1981): 95–106.

Rogerson, J. W. *Anthropology and the Old Testament*. 1978. Repr., Biblical Seminar. Sheffield: JSOT Press, 1984.

———. "The Potential of the Negative: Approaching the Old Testament through the Work of Adorno." Pages 24–47 in *Rethinking Contexts, Rereading Texts: Contributions of the Social Sciences to Biblical Interpretation*. Edited by M. Daniel Carroll R. Journal for the Study of the Old Testament: Supplement Series 299. Sheffield: Sheffield Academic Press, 2000.

Römer, Thomas. *The So-Called Deuteronomistic History: A Sociological, Historical and Literary Introduction*. Paperback ed. London: T&T Clark, 2007.

Rose, Martin. "De la 'crise de la sagesse' à la 'sagesse de la crise.'" *Revue de théologie et de philosophie* 131 (1999): 115–34.

Rosenberg, Stephen G. "Qasr al-Abd: A Mausoleum of the Tobiad Family?" *Bulletin of the Anglo-Israel Archeological Society* 19–20 (2001–2): 157–75.

Rostovtzeff, M. *The Social and Economic History of the Hellenistic World*. 3 vols. Oxford: Clarendon, 1941.

Rudman, Dominic. "The Anatomy of the Wise Man." Pages 465–71 in *Qohelet in the Context of Wisdom*. Edited by Anton Schoors. Bibliotheca ephemeridum theologicarum lovaniensium 136. Leuven: Leuven University Press and Peeters, 1998.

———. *Determinism in the Book of Ecclesiastes*. Journal for the Study of the Old Testament: Supplement Series 316. Sheffield: Sheffield Academic Press, 2001.

———. "A Note on the Dating of Ecclesiastes." *Catholic Biblical Quarterly* 61 (1999): 47–52.

——. Review of Stephen L. Cook, *Prophecy & Apocalypticism: The Postexilic Social Setting* (Minneapolis: Fortress, 1995). *Biblical Interpretation* 7 (1999): 454–55.

Runciman, W. G. "Was Max Weber a Selectionist in Spite of Himself?" *Journal of Classical Sociology* 1 (2001): 13–32.

Sadri, Ahmad. *Max Weber's Sociology of Intellectuals.* Paperback ed. New York: Oxford University Press, 1994.

Sahni, Isher-Paul. "Max Weber's Sociology of Law: Judge as Mediator." *Journal of Classical Sociology* 9 (2009): 209–33. DOI: 10.1177/1468795X09102123.

Saldarini, Anthony J. "Scribes." Pages 1012–16 in vol. 5 of *The Anchor Bible Dictionary.* Edited by David Noel Freedman. 6 vols. New York: Doubleday, 1992.

Salters, Robert B. "Qoheleth and the Canon." *Expository Times* 86 (1975): 339–42.

Sandberg, Ruth N. *Rabbinic Views of Qohelet.* Mellen Biblical Press 57. Lewiston, N.Y.: Mellen, 1999.

Sanders, E. P. *Paul and Palestinian Judaism: A Comparison of Patterns of Religion.* Paperback ed. Philadelphia: Fortress, 1977.

Sanders, Jack T. "When Sacred Canopies Collide: The Reception of the Torah of Moses in the Wisdom Literature of the Second-Temple Period." *Journal for the Study of Judaism* 32 (2001): 121–36.

——. "Wisdom, Theodicy, Death, and the Evolution of Intellectual Traditions." *Journal for the Study of Judaism* 36 (2005): 263–77.

Sandy, D. Brent, and Ronald L. Giese Jr., eds. *Cracking Old Testament Codes: A Guide to Interpreting the Literary Genres of the Old Testament.* Nashville: Broadman & Holman, 1995.

Sasson, Ann Showstack. *Gramsci's Politics.* 2nd ed. Minneapolis: University of Minnesota Press, 1987.

Sawyer, John F. A. "The Ruined House in Ecclesiastes 12: A Reconstruction of the Original Parable." *Journal of Biblical Literature* 94 (1975): 519–31.

Schäfer, Peter. "The Hellenistic and Maccabaean Periods." Pages 539–604 in *Israelite and Judean History.* Edited by John H. Hayes and J. Maxwell Miller. Old Testament Library. Philadelphia: Westminster, 1977.

——. *The History of the Jews in the Greco-Roman World.* London: Taylor & Francis, 2003.

Schafter, Amanda. "Dara Torres Demystified: Do the Swimmer's 'Secrets to Success' Hold Up?" *Slate* (July 16, 2008). N.p. Online at http://www.slate.com/id/2195473/pagenum/all/#p2 (accessed January 28, 2011).

Schams, Christine. *Jewish Scribes in the Second Temple Period.* Journal for the Study of the Old Testament: Supplement Series 291. Sheffield: Sheffield Academic Press, 1998.

Schiffman, Lawrence H. *Understanding Second Temple and Rabbinic Judaism.* Edited by Jon Bloomberg and Samuel Kapustin. Jersey City, N.J.: Ktav, 2003.

Schluchter, Wolfgang. "The Approach of Max Weber's Sociology of Religion as

Exemplified in His Study of Ancient Judaism." *Archive de sciences sociales des religions* 127 (2004): 33–56.

Schmid, Hans Heinrich. *Wesen und Geschichte der Weisheit: Eine Untersuchung zur altorientalischen und israelitischen Weisheitsliteratur.* Beihefte zur Zeitschrift für die alttestamentliche Wissenschaft 101. Berlin: de Gruyter, 1966.

Schoors, Anton. Introduction to *Qohelet in the Context of Wisdom.* Edited by Anton Schoors. Bibliotheca ephemeridum theologicarum lovaniensium 136. Leuven: Leuven University Press and Peeters, 1998.

———. "Qoheleth: A Book in a Changing Society." *Old Testament Essays* 9 (1996): 68–87.

———, ed. *Qohelet in the Context of Wisdom.* Bibliotheca ephemeridum theologicarum lovaniensium 136. Leuven: Leuven University Press and Peeters, 1998.

———. "Words Typical of Qohelet." Pages 17–39 in *Qohelet in the Context of Wisdom.* Edited by Anton Schoors. Bibliotheca ephemeridum theologicarum lovaniensium 136. Leuven: Leuven University Press and Peeters, 1998.

Schraub, J. Jonathan. "For the Sin We Have Committed by Theological Rationalizations: Rescuing Job from Normative Religion." *Soundings* 86, no. 3–4 (Fall–Winter 2003): 431–62.

Schulte, Christoph. "Jüdisch Theodizee? Überlegungen zum Theodizee—Problem bei Immanuel Kant, Hermann Cohen und Max Weber." *Zeitschrift für Religions- und Geistesgeschichte* 49 (1997): 135–59.

Schultz, Richard L. "A Sense of Timing: A Neglected Aspect of Qoheleth's Wisdom." Pages 257–67 in *Seeking Out the Wisdom of the Ancients.* Edited by Ronald L. Troxel, Kelvin G. Friebel, and Dennis R. Marary. Winona Lake, Ind.: Eisenbrauns, 2005.

Schwarz, Haley C., Richelle L. Gairrett, Mara S. Aruguete, and Elizabeth S. Gold. "Eating Attitudes, Body Dissatisfaction, and Perfectionism in Female College Athletes." *North American Journal of Psychology* 7 (2005): 345–52.

Schwartz, Matthew J. "Koheleth and Camus: Two Views of Achievement." *Judaism* 35 (1986): 29–34.

Schwienhorst-Schönberger, L. "Via media: Koh 7, 15–18 und die griechisch-hellenistische Philosophie." Pages 181–203 in *Qohelet in the Context of Wisdom.* Edited by Anton Schoors. Bibliotheca ephemeridum theologicarum lovaniensium 136. Leuven: Leuven University Press and Peeters, 1998.

Scott, R. B. Y. *Proverbs. Ecclesiastes: Introduction, Translation, and Notes.* Anchor Bible 18. Garden City, N.Y.: Doubleday, 1965.

Scroggs, Robin. "The Sociological Interpretation of the New Testament: The Present State of Research." *New Testament Studies* 26 (1980): 164–79.

Seibert, Eric A. *Subversive Scribes and the Solomonic Narrative: A Rereading of 1 Kings 1–11.* Library of Hebrew Bible/Old Testament Studies 436. New York: T&T Clark, 2006

Seow, Choon- Leong. "Beyond Mortal Grasp: The Usage of *Hebel* in Ecclesiastes." *Australian Biblical Review* 48 (2000): 1–16.

———. *Ecclesiastes: A New Translation with Introduction and Commentary.* Anchor Bible 18C. New York: Doubleday, 1997.

———. "Linguistic Evidence and the Dating of Qohelet." *Journal of Biblical Literature* 115 (1996): 643–66.

———. "The Socioeconomic Context of 'The Preacher's' Hermeneutic." *Princeton Seminary Bulletin* 17 (1996): 168–95.

———. "Theology When Everything Is Out of Control." *Interpretation* 55 (2001): 237–49.

Sheard, Cynthia Miecznikowski. "The Public Value of Epideictic Rhetoric." *College English* 58 (1996): 765–94.

Shields, Martin A. *The End of Wisdom: A Reappraisal of the Historical and Canonical Function of Ecclesiastes.* Winona Lake, Ind.: Eisenbrauns, 2006.

Shils, Edward. "Intellectuals." Pages 399–414 in vol. 7 of *International Encyclopedia of the Social Sciences.* Edited by David L. Sills and Robert K. Merton. 19 vols. New York: Macmillan and Free Press, 1968.

Shmueli, Efraim. "The Novelties of the Bible and the Problem of Theodicy in Max Weber's *Ancient Judaism.*" *Jewish Quarterly Review* 60 (1969): 172–82.

Shuster, Martin. "Being as Breath, Vapor as Joy: Using Martin Heidegger to Re-Read the Book of Ecclesiastes." *Journal for the Study of the Old Testament* 33 (2008): 219–44.

Sica, Alan. "Rationalization and Culture." Pages 42–58 in *The Cambridge Companion to Weber.* Edited by Stephen Turner. Cambridge: Cambridge University Press, 2000.

———. *Weber, Irrationality, and Social Order.* Berkeley: University of California Press, 1988.

Simkins, Ronald. "Patronage and the Political Economy of Monarchic Israel." *Semeia* 87 (1999): 123–44.

Simon, Maurice, trans. *Midrash Rabbah.* Edited by H. Freedman.10 vols. 3rd ed. London: Soncino, 1983.

Sivertsev, Alexei M. *Households, Sects, and the Origins of Rabbinic Judaism.* Journal for the Study of Judaism Supplement 102. Leiden: Brill, 2005.

Skelton, David A. "Ben Sira's Imaginative Theodicy: Reflections on the Aaronide Priesthood under Gentile Rule." *Restoration Quarterly* 51 (2009): 1–12.

Smart, Ninian. *Worldviews: Crosscultural Explorations of Human Beliefs.* New York: Scribner's Sons, 1983.

Sneed, Mark. "The Class Culture of Proverbs: Eliminating Stereotypes." *Scandinavian Journal of the Old Testament* 10 (1996): 296–308.

———. "(Dis)closure in Qohelet: Qohelet Deconstructed." *Journal for the Study of the Old Testament* 27 (2002): 119–22.

———. "Is the 'Wisdom Tradition' a Tradition?" *Catholic Biblical Quarterly* 73 (2011): 50–71.

———. "Job." Pages 423–44 in *The Transforming Word: One-Volume Commentary on the Bible*. Edited by Mark Hamilton. Abilene, Tex.: Abilene Christian University Press, 2009.

———. "A Middle Class in Ancient Israel?" Pages 53–69 in *Concepts of Class in Ancient Israel*. Edited by Mark Sneed. South Florida Studies in the History of Judaism: The Hebrew Scriptures and Their World 201. Atlanta: Scholars Press, 1999.

———. "A Note on Qoh 8,12b–13." *Biblica* 84 (2003): 412–16.

———. "Qohelet and His 'Vulgar' Critics: A Jamesonian Reading." *Bible and Critical Theory* 1, no. 1 (2004): 1–11. http://www.relegere.org/index.php/bct/article/viewfile/17/5.

———. "Qoheleth as 'Deconstructionist.'" *Old Testament Essays* 10 (1997): 308–10.

———. Review of Craig G. Bartholomew, *Ecclesiastes* (Baker Commentary on the Old Testament; Grand Rapids: Baker, 2009). *Catholic Biblical Quarterly* 72 (2010): 559–60.

———. Review of Dominic Rudman, *Determinism in the Book of Ecclesiastes* (Journal for the Study of the Old Testament: Supplement Series 316. Sheffield: Sheffield Academic Press, 2001). *Journal of Biblical Literature* 121 (2002): 549–51.

———. "The Social Location of Qoheleth." *Hebrew Studies* 39 (1998): 41–51.

———. "The Social Location of Qoheleth's Thought: Anomie and Alienation in Ptolemaic Jerusalem." Ph.D. diss., Drew University, 1990.

———. "Social Scientific Approach to the Hebrew Bible." *Religion Compass* 2 (2008): 287–300. DOI: 10.1111/j.1749-8171.2008.00072.x.

———. "'White Trash Wisdom': Proverbs 9 Deconstructed," *Journal of Hebrew Studies* 7, article 5 (2007): 1–10. Online at http://www.arts.ualberta.ca/JHS/Articles/article_66.pdf (accessed April 24, 2011).

Soares-Prabhu, George M. "Class in the Bible: The Biblical Poor a Social Class?" Pages 147–71 in *Voices from the Margin: Interpreting the Bible in the Third World*. Edited by R. S. Sugirtharajah. Maryknoll, N.Y.: Orbis, 1991.

Soden, Wolfram von. "Das Fragen nach der Gerechtigkeit Gottes im Alten Orient." *Mitteilungen der Deutschen Orient-Gesellschaft* 96 (1965): 41–62.

Sparks, Kenton L. *Ancient Texts for the Study of the Hebrew Bible: A Guide to the Background Literature*. Peabody, Mass.: Hendrickson, 2005.

Stager, Lawrence E. "The Archaeology of the Family in Ancient Israel." *Bulletin of the American Schools of Oriental Research* 260 (1985): 1–35.

Steinberg, Naomi. "The Deuteronomic Law Code and Politics of State Centralization." Pages 161–70 in *The Bible and the Politics of Exegesis*. Edited by David Jobling, Peggy L. Day, and Gerald T. Sheppard. Cleveland: Pilgrim, 1991.

Stenger, Mary Ann. "The Ambiguity of the Symbol of the Cross: Legitimating and Overcoming Evil." Pages 56–69 in *Evil and the Response of World Religion*. Edited by William Cenkner. St. Paul, Minn.: Paragon House, 1997.

Stern, David. "The *Alphabet of Ben Sira* and the Early History of Parody in Jewish Literature." Pages 423–48 in *The Idea of Biblical Interpretation*. Edited by Hindy Najman and Judith H. Newman. Journal for the Study of Judaism Supplement 83. Atlanta: Society of Biblical Literature, 2004.

Stern, Ephraim. "Between Persia and Greece: Trade, Administration and Warfare in the Persian and Hellenistic Periods (539–63 BCE)." Pages 432–45 in *The Archaeology of Society in the Holy Land*. Edited by Thomas E. Levy. New York: Facts on File, 1995.

Stern, Menahem. "Aspects of Jewish Society: The Priesthood and Other Classes." Pages 561–630 in *The Jewish People in the First Century: Historical Geography, Political History, Social, Cultural and Religious Life and Institutions*. Edited by S. Safrai and M. Stern. Compendium rerum iudaicarum ad Novum Testamentum 1/2. Assen: Van Gorcum, 1976.

Stowers, Stanley K. *A Rereading of Romans: Justice, Jews, and Gentiles*. New Haven: Yale University Press, 1997.

Stratton, Beverly J. "Ideology." Pages 120–27 in *Postmodern Biblical Interpretation*. Edited by A. K. M. Adam. St. Louis: Chalice, 2000.

Sugirtharajah, R. S. *Postcolonial Criticism and Biblical Interpretation*. Oxford: Oxford University Press, 2002.

Swedberg, Richard. *The Max Weber Dictionary: Key Words and Central Concepts*. Stanford: Stanford Social Sciences, 2005.

Sweeney, Marvin A. "The Critique of Solomon in the Josianic Edition of the Deuteronomistic History." *Journal of Biblical Literature* 114 (1995): 607–22.

Swidler, Ann. "The Concept of Rationality in the Work of Max Weber." *Sociological Inquiry* 43 (1973): 35–42.

———. Foreword to Max Weber, *The Sociology of Religion*. Translated by Ephraim Fischoff. Paperback ed. Boston: Beacon, 1991.

Takahashi, Yuko. "A Study on Max Weber's *Ancient Judaism*: Theoretical Framework and Methodology." *Max Weber Studies* 7 (2008): 213–29.

Talbert, Charles H. *Romans*. Smyth & Helwys Bible Commentary. Macon, Ga.: Smyth & Helwys, 2002.

Talstra, Eep. "Second Isaiah and Qohelet: Could One Get Them on Speaking Terms?" Pages 225–36 in *The New Things: Eschatology in Old Testament Prophecy*. Edited by F. Postma, K. Spronk, and E. Talstra. Amsterdamse Cahiers voor Exegese en bijbelse Theologie Supplement 3. Maastricht: Shaker, 2002.

Tamez, Elsa. *When the Horizons Close: Rereading Ecclesiastes*. Translated by Margaret Wilde. Maryknoll, N.Y.: Orbis, 2000.

Taylor, Walter F., Jr. "Sociological Exegesis: Introduction to a New Way to Study the Bible: Part I: History and Theory." *Trinity Seminary Review* 11, no. 2 (1989): 99–110.

Tcherikover, Victor A., ed. *Corpus papyrum judaicarum*. 3 vols. Cambridge, Mass.: Harvard University Press, 1971–80.

———. "Hellenistic Palestine." Pages 53–144 in *The Hellenistic Age*. Edited by Abraham Schalit. World History of the Jewish People 7. New Brunswick, N.J.: Rutgers University Press, 1972.

Thompson, Dorothy. "The Infrastructure of Splendour: Census and Taxes in Ptolemaic Egypt." Pages 242–57 in *Hellenistic Constructs: Essays in Culture, History, and Historiography*. Edited by Paul Cartledge, Peter Garnsey, and Erich Gruen. Hellenistic Culture and Society 26. Berkeley: University of California Press, 1997.

Tilley, Terrence W. *The Evils of Theodicy*. 1991. Repr., Eugene, Ore.: Wipf & Stock, 2000.

———. "The Use and Abuse of Theodicy." *Horizons* 11 (1984): 304–19.

Toorn, Karel van der. "The Ancient Near Eastern Literary Dialogue as a Vehicle of Critical Reflection." Pages 59–75 in *Dispute Poems and Dialogues in the Ancient and Mediaeval Near East: Forms and Types of Literary Debates in Semitic and Related Literatures*. Edited by G. J. Reinink and H. L. J. Vanstiphout. Orientalia lovaniensia analecta 42. Leuven: Departement Oriëntalistiek, 1991.

———. "Did Ecclesiastes Copy Gilgamesh?" *Bible Review* 16, no. 1 (Feb 2000): 23–30, 50.

———. "Echoes of Gilgamesh in the Book of Qohelet? A Reassessment of the Intellectual Sources of Qohelet." Pages 503–514 in *Veenhof Anniversary Volume: Studies Presented to Klaas R. Veenhof on the Occasion of His Sixty-fifth Birthday*. Edited by W. H. van Soldt et al. Uitgaven van het Nederlands Historisch-Archaeologisch Instituut te Istanbul 89. Leiden: Nederlands Instituut voor het Nabije Oosten, 2001.

———. *Scribal Culture and the Making of the Hebrew Bible*. Cambridge, Mass.: Harvard University Press, 2007.

Topazio, Virgil W. "Voltaire's Attack on Optimism Has a Humanitarian Goal." Pages 47–55 in *Readings on Candide*. Edited by Thomas Walsh. Literary Companion. San Diego: Greenhaven, 2001.

Towner, Sibley. "The Book of Ecclesiastes: Introduction, Commentary, and Reflections." Pages 267–360 in *Introduction to Wisdom Literature; Proverbs; Ecclesiastes; Song Songs; Book of Wisdom; Sirach*. Vol. 5 of *The New Interpreter's Bible*. Edited by Leander E. Keck. Nashville: Abingdon, 2001.

Trakakis, Nick. "Is Theism Capable of Accounting for any Natural Evil at All?" *International Journal for Philosophy of Religion* 57 (2005): 35–66.

Turner, Bryan S. *For Weber: Essays on the Sociology of Fate*. Boston: Routledge & Kegan Paul, 1981.

Turner, Eric G. "Ptolemaic Egypt." Pages 118–74 in *The Cambridge Ancient History*, vol. 7, part 1, *The Hellenistic World*. Edited by F. W. Walbank et al. 2nd ed. Cambridge: Cambridge University Press, 1984.

Turner, Stephen, ed. *The Cambridge Companion to Weber*. Cambridge: Cambridge University Press, 2000.

Urbano, Cosimo. "Projections, Suspense, and Anxiety: The Modern Horror Film and its Effects." *Psychoanalytic Review* 85 (1998): 889–908.

Vajiragnena, Medagama. "A Theoretical Explanation of Evil in Theravada Buddhism." Pages 99–109 in *Evil and the Response of World Religion*. Edited by William Cenkner. St. Paul, Minn.: Paragon House, 1997.

Vander Zanden, James W. *Sociology: The Core*. New York: McGraw-Hill, 1990.

Van Leeuwen, Raymond C. "Wealth and Poverty: System and Contradiction in Proverbs." *Hebrew Studies* 33 (1992): 25–36.

Vasileva, Lena. "The Father, the Dark Child and the Mob that Kills Him: Tim Burton's Representation of the Creative Artist." Pages 87–95 in *Psyche and the Arts: Jungian Approaches to Music, Architecture, Literature, Film and Painting*. Edited by Susan Rowland. London: Routledge, 2008.

Vawter, Bruce. "Postexilic Prayer and Hope." *Catholic Biblical Quarterly* 37 (1975): 460–70.

Visicato, Giuseppe. *The Power and the Writing: The Early Scribes of Mesopotamia*. Bethesda, Md.: CDL, 2000.

Voltaire. *Candide or Optimism*. Translated by Robert M. Adams. Norton Critical Editions. New York: Norton, 1966.

Walbank, F. W. "Monarchies and Monarchic Ideas." Pages 62–100 in *The Cambridge Ancient History*, vol. 7, part 1, *The Hellenistic World*. Edited by F. W. Walbank et al. 2nd ed. Cambridge: Cambridge University Press, 1984.

Walsh, Thomas. Introduction to *Readings on Candide*. Edited by Thomas Walsh. Literary Companion. San Diego: Greenhaven, 2001.

———, ed. *Readings on Candide*. Literary Companion. San Diego: Greenhaven, 2001.

Walton, Christopher L. "Is Disenchantment the End of Religion?" *Philocrites: Religion, Liberalism, and Culture* 2003. No pages. Online at http://www.philocrites.com/essays/weber.html (accessed January 4, 2010).

Warrior, Robert Allen. "A Native American Perspective: Canaanites, Cowboys, and Indians." Pages 400–405 in *Biblical Studies Alternatively: An Introductory Reader*. Edited by Susanne Scholz. Upper Saddle River, N.J.: Prentice Hall, 2003. Repr. from *Christianity & Crisis* 49 (Sept 1989): 261–65.

Washington, Harold C. Review of Martin A. Shields, *The End of Wisdom: A Reappraisal of the Historical and Canonical Function of Ecclesiastes* (Winona Lake, Ind.: Eisenbrauns, 2006). *Review of Biblical Literature* (2009). No pages. Online at http://www.bookreviews.org/pdf/5240_5519.pdf (accessed April 24, 2011).

Wazana, Nili. "A Case of the Evil Eye: Qohelet 4:4–8." *Journal of Biblical Literature* 126 (2007): 685–702.

Weber, Max. *Ancient Judaism*. Translated and edited by Hans H. Gerth and Don Martindale. Paperback ed. New York: Free Press, 1976.

———. "Bureaucracy." Pages 196–244 in *From Max Weber: Essays in Sociology*. Edited by Hans H. Gerth and C. Wright Mills. Paperback ed. New York: Oxford University Press, 1958.

———. *Economy and Society: An Outline of Interpretive Sociology.* Edited by Guenther Roth and Claus Wittich. Translated by Ephraim Fischoff et al. 2 vols. Paperback ed. New York: Bedminster, 1968. Repr., Berkeley: University of California Press, 1978.

———. *The Protestant Ethic and the Spirit of Capitalism: The Revised 1920 Edition.* Translated by Stephen Kalberg. Oxford: Oxford University Press, 2011.

———. "The Protestant Sects and the Spirit of Capitalism." Pages 302–22 in *From Max Weber: Essays in Sociology.* Edited by Hans H. Gerth and C. Wright Mills. Paperback ed. New York: Oxford University Press, 1958.

———. "Religious Rejections of the World and Their Directions." Pages 323–59 in *From Max Weber: Essays in Sociology.* Edited by Hans H. Gerth and C. Wright Mills. Paperback ed. New York: Oxford University Press, 1958.

———. "The Social Psychology of the World Religions." Pages 267–301 in *From Max Weber: Essays in Sociology.* Edited by Hans H. Gerth and C. Wright Mills. Paperback ed. New York: Oxford University Press, 1958.

———. "The Sociology of Charismatic Authority." Pages 245–52 in *From Max Weber: Essays in Sociology.* Edited by Hans H. Gerth and C. Wright Mills. Paperback ed. New York: Oxford University Press, 1958.

———. *The Sociology of Religion.* Translated by Ephraim Fischoff. Paperback ed. Boston: Beacon, 1991.

Weeks, Stuart. *Instruction and Imagery in Proverbs 1–9.* Oxford: Oxford University Press, 2007.

———. *An Introduction to the Study of Wisdom Literature.* T&T Clark Approaches to Biblical Studies. London: T&T Clark, 2010.

Weinfeld, Moshe. "Deuteronomy—The Present State of Inquiry." *Journal of Biblical Literature* 86 (1967): 249–62.

Weisman, Ze'ev. "Elements of Political Satire in Koheleth 4,13–16; 9,13–16." *Zeitschrift für die alttestamentliche Wissenschaft* 111 (1999): 547–60.

Weißflog, Kay. "Worum geht es in Kohelet 8,10?" *Biblische Notizen* 131 (2006): 39–45.

Whitley, Charles F. "Koheleth and Ugaritic Parallels." *Ugarit-Forschungen* 11 (1979): 810–24.

Whybray, R. N. *Ecclesiastes.* New Century Bible. Grand Rapids: Eerdmans, 1989.

———. *The Intellectual Tradition in the Old Testament.* Beihefte zur Zeitschrift für die alttestamentliche Wissenschaft 135. Berlin: de Gruyter, 1974.

———. "Qoheleth, Preacher of Joy." *Journal for the Study of the Old Testament* 23 (1982): 87–98.

———. "Qoheleth as a Theologian." Pages 239–65 in *Qohelet in the Context of Wisdom.* Edited by Anton Schoors. Bibliotheca ephemeridum theologicarum lovaniensium 136. Leuven: Leuven University Press and Peeters, 1998.

Wiesehöfer, Josef. "The Achaemenid Empire in the Fourth Century B.C.E.: A Period of Decline?" Pages 11–30 in *Judah and the Judeans in the Fourth Century B.C.E.* Edited by Oded Lipschits, Gary N. Knoppers, and Rainer Albertz. Winona Lake, Ind.: Eisenbrauns, 2007.

Wikramagamage, Chandra. "Mara as Evil in Buddhism." Pages 109–1115 in *Evil and the Response of World Religion*. Edited by William Cenkner. St. Paul, Minn.: Paragon House, 1997.

Will, Édouard. "The Succession to Alexander." Pages 23–61 in *The Cambridge Ancient History*, vol. 7, part 1, *The Hellenistic World*. Edited by F. W. Walbank et al. 2nd ed. Cambridge: Cambridge University Press, 1984.

Williams, Raymond. *Marxism and Literature*. Paperback ed. Marxist Introductions. Oxford: Oxford University Press, 1977.

Williams, Ronald J. "The Sage in Egyptian Literature." Pages 19–30 in *The Sage in Israel and the Ancient Near East*. Edited by John G. Gammie and Leo G. Perdue. Winona Lake, Ind.: Eisenbrauns, 1990.

Willis, Timothy M. "The Nature of Jephthah's Authority." *Catholic Biblical Quarterly* 59 (1997): 33–44.

Wilson, John A. Introduction to "The Admonitions of Ipu-Wer." Page 441 in *Ancient Near Eastern Texts Relating to the Old Testament*. Edited by James B. Pritchard. 3rd ed. Princeton: Princeton University Press, 1969.

———. Introduction to "A Dispute Over Suicide." Page 405 in *Ancient Near Eastern Texts Relating to the Old Testament*. Edited by James B. Pritchard. 3rd ed. Princeton: Princeton University Press, 1969.

———.Introduction to "A Song of the Harper." Page 467 in *Ancient Near Eastern Texts Relating to the Old Testament*. Edited by James B. Pritchard. 3rd ed. Princeton: Princeton University Press, 1969.

Wirth, Louis. Preface to Karl Mannheim, *Ideology and Utopia: An Introduction to the Sociology of Knowledge* (New York: Harcourt Brace, n.d.).

Wölfel, Eberhard. *Luther und die Skepsis: Eine Studie zur Kohelet-Exegeses Luthers*. Forschungen zur Geschichte und Lehre des Protestantismus 10/2. Munich: Kaiser, 1958.

Wright, Benjamin G., III. Review of Leo G. Perdue, *The Sword and the Stylus: An Introduction to Wisdom in the Age of Empires* (Grand Rapids: Eerdmans, 2008). *Review of Biblical Literature* 06/2009. No pages. Online at http://www.bookreviews.org/pdf/6647_7205.pdf (accessed June 16, 2009).

Wright, Erik Olin. "Class Boundaries in Advanced Capitalist Societies." *New Left Review* 98 (1976): 3–41.

———. "Intellectuals and the Working Class." *Insurgent Sociologist* 8 (1978): 5–18.

Yee, Gale. "Gender, Class, and the Social-Scientific Study of Genesis 2–3." *Semeia* 87 (1999): 177–92.

———. "Ideological Criticism: Judges 17–21 and the Dismembered Body." Pages 146–70 in *Judges and Method: New Approaches in Biblical Studies*. Edited by Gale Yee. Minneapolis: Fortress, 1995.

Yitzhak, Magen. "The Dating of the First Phase of the Samaritan Temple on Mount Gerizim in Light of the Archaeological Evidence." Pages 157–211 in *Judah and the Judeans in the Fourth Century* B.C.E. Edited by Oded Lipschits,

Gary N. Knoppers, and Rainer Albertz. Winona Lake, Ind.: Eisenbrauns, 2007.

Zaret, David. "Calvin, Covenant Theology, and the Weber Thesis." *British Journal of Sociology* 43 (1992): 369–91.

Zimmer, Tilmann. *Zwischen Tod und Lebensglück: Eine Untersuchung zur Anthropologie Kohelets*. Beihefte zur Zeitschrift für die alttestamentliche Wissenschaft 286. Berlin: de Gruyter, 1999.

Zimmerli, Walther. "The Place and Limit of the [*sic*] Wisdom in the Framework of the Old Testament Theology." *Scottish Journal of Theology* 17 (1964): 146–58.

Zimmermann, Frank. "The Book of Ecclesiastes in the Light of Some Psychoanalytic Observations." *American Imago* 5 (1948): 301–5.

———. *The Inner World of Qoheleth: With Translation and Commentary*. New York: Ktav, 1973.

Zwerner, Jane Mary. "The Discovery of Christian Meaning in Suffering: Transformation and Solidarity." Pages 43–55 in *Evil and the Response of World Religion*. Edited by William Cenkner. St. Paul, Minn.: Paragon House, 1997.

INDEX OF ANCIENT SOURCES

Hebrew Bible

Genesis
1:1 30
1:14–19 30
1:26 166
2–3 81
2:24 72
3 166
3:17–19 248 n. 48
3:22 166
6 166
11 166
49:14–15 116

Exodus
1:10 262 n. 23
20:5 181

Numbers
5 207

Deuteronomy
5:9 181
17:14–20 135–36
19–25 137 n. 53
32:21 157

Joshua
7 181

Judges
4–5 24
4:4–5 207
9:13 265
10–12 24

1 Samuel
8–12 135

15 257
15:22 1

2 Samuel
8:15–18 114
24 227

1 Kings
1–11 134
4:23 127
4:26 127
8:63 127
10:5 127
10:26–29 127
11 266
11–14 135 n. 45
11:3 127
17–20 257
21 129
22 227

2 Kings
22 114
23:25–27 181

1 Chronicles
27:32 114

2 Chronicles
35:20–27 181

Ezra
2:59–60 107
7:6 114
7:10 114
7:21–24 110
7:24 110

Nehemiah
4:3 107

Nehemiah (*continued*)

5	107, 118
8	114

Job

1:9	182
3	9
4:8	158 n. 10
7	166
7:6–10	8
7:11	1
7:17–21	157
11:4–2	182
14:1–7	8
17:13–16	8
20	5
21	5
28	7
29–31	196 n. 67
38–41	1, 166
38–42	182
40:35	5
42:3	182
42:6	6

Psalms

8	6, 166
13	173
22	173
39	156–57, 166
39:4–6	156
39:11	156
54	173
62	156
90	7, 166 n. 45
104:15	265
126:5–6	158 n. 10
144:4	156

Proverbs

1–9	143, 259, 259 n. 17
1:5	144
1:7	261
2:1–5	263
2:5	263
3:5–7	262
9:10	263
10:7	242

10:30	260
11:16	260
11:22	260
11:24	261
11:29	158 n. 10
13:23	260
13:24	261
14:12	262
14:27	262
15:23	146
15:28–22:16	146
16:6	262
16:9	262
16:14	147
16:20–30	146
17:2	145–46
17:16	147
17:17	147
17:18	147
17:27–28	147
18:11	147
18:16	147
18:17	147
19:1	147
19:6	147
19:17	147
20:1	265
20:10	147
20:16	147
20:24	262
20:26	147
21:22	147
21:27	147
21:30–31	262
22:1	242
22:2	147
22:4	262
22:8	147, 158 n. 10
22:9	147
22:16	18
23:1–3	220
24:20	18, 260
26:12	262
28:15–16	260
28:20	18
29:19	145
30:1–4	7

30:4	6	3:2	8
31:30	156	3:10	6, 246
		3:11	2–3, 64, 184, 241, 246
Ecclesiastes		3:12–13	2
1:1–2	4 n.17, 9, 270	3:13	64
1:1–11	4 n. 17, 270	3:14	62, 165, 246
1:2	7, 155, 157, 158 n. 11	3:16	5, 64, 128, 140, 194,
1:3	172, 248, 271–72, 271		240, 245
	n. 44	3:16–17	184–85
1:4	165, 166 n. 46	3:17	4, 64, 161, 184
1:9	142	3:18	6, 50, 165, 165 n. 44
1:12–2:12	139	3:18–21	8, 246
1:12–2:26	127–28	3:21	131, 142, 165
1:13	6, 50, 164, 246	3:22	2, 241
1:14	156–58	4:1	50, 64, 128, 138–40,
1:15	63, 161 n. 27, 246, 250		184, 194–95, 247
1:17	157–58	4:1–2	63
1:18	225, 249	4:1–2	68
2:1	167	4:2–3	8
2:1–2	250	4:4	139, 158, 245
2:2	158, 167	4:4–8	249, n. 50
2:3	158, 167, 227	4:6	249, 249 n. 50
2:4–8	68	4:8	158, 246, 250
2:10	158, 168, 249	4:8–12	252
2:10–11	167	4:13–16	128, 128 n. 13, 140
2:11	7, 172, 249	4:16	158
2:12	127 n. 11	5:1	245
2:12–17	249	5:1–2	1
2:13–14	172, 227	5:1–7	149, 184, 186, 242,
2:14–15	73		264
2:14–16	8, 242–43	5:2	149
2:15	150, 158	5:2–5	226
2:15–16	6, 7	5:5	161
2:17	7, 162	5:6	62, 186, 226–27, 245
2:18	250	5:7	128, 140
2:18–23	139	5:8	184, 245
2:19	158, 250	5:8–9	140
2:20	167	5:9	140, 140 n. 68, 158
2:21	158	5:10	143, 249
2:22–23	6	5:10–12	139
2:23	139, 158, 249	5:10–17	48
2:24	2	5:11	57, 139–40
2:24–26	167–68, 172, 252	5:12	68, 138, 158, 249
2:26	4, 129, 158, 165, 184,	5:13	139, 246
	186, 193, 247 n. 45	5:15	158
3:1–2	4	5:18–20	2
3:1–8	241 n. 34	5:19	60

Ecclesiastes (*continued*)

5:19–20	64
6:1	162, 164–65
6:1–2	2, 60, 193, 247, 250
6:1–3	129
6:1–6	139, 150, 184
6:2	158
6:3	139
6:7	139
6:8	150
6:9	158
6:10	165, 246
6:11	158
6:12	158, 241–42
7:1	243
7:1–4	8, 271 n. 44
7:4–6	149
7:6	158
7:7	140
7:11–12	149
7:12	138
7:13	246
7:13–14	246
7:14	50, 60, 184, 241
7:14–15	249
7:15	5, 33, 128, 165, 174, 184, 240, 250
7:16	149, 226, 245, 262 n. 23
7:16–17	240
7:17	161, 186, 240, 242
7:15–18	43 n. 121, 62, 186 n. 37, 250 n. 51
7:18	62, 184, 186, 242
7:19	139–40, 149
7:20	149, 165, 184, 245
7:21	245
7:21–22	139
7:23–24	250
7:26	245, 250
7:26–28	143
7:27	4
7:27–28	250
7:28–29	149, 245
7:29	49, 165, 184, 245
8:1–6	241
8:1–9	129 n. 20, 241 n. 33

8:1–15	241 n. 36
8:2	139
8:2–4	129, 140
8:2–5	139–40, 143
8:3	75
8:5–6	241
8:7	241
8:9	245
8:10	5, 130, 130 n. 22, 139, 158, 184, 245
8:11	245
8:11–13	240
8:11–14	186–87
8:12	64
8:12–13	4, 49, 62, 161, 184, 186, 186 n. 38, 242
8:14	5, 33, 128, 158–59, 184, 186–87, 240
8:14–15	187
8:15	1–2
8:16	246
8:16–17	6, 184
8:17	165, 241
9	143
9:1	184
9:1–6	8
9:2	149, 186, 250
9:3	241
9:2–6	8
9:7	252
9:7–9	252
9:7–10	2
9:11	5, 64, 184, 240, 242–43, 249
9:11–12	73
9:12	63
9:13–16	74, 76, 138, 140, 243
9:13–18	250
9:14–16	130, 130 n. 24
9:15	149
9:16	149
10:1	140
10:4	140, 143
10:5–6	27, 138, 140
10:5–7	68, 130, 139, 149, 184
10:6–7	140
10:7	77

10:14	241	Ezekiel	
10:16–17	131	18:1–4	181
10:19	68, 139		
10:20	68, 75, 140, 149	Daniel	
11:1	247	1–6	223, 273
11:1–2	150	1:4	261
11:1–4	139	7–12	273, 280
11:6	241	12:2	142, 183
11:7–10	2		
11:9	4, 143, 165, 184, 225,	Hosea	
	270–71	6:6	1
11:10	143, 157	8:7	158 n. 10
12	52, 166 n. 46		
12:1	143	Micah	
12:5–7	8	6:6–8	1
12:8	7, 155, 157, 158 n. 11		
12:8–12	4, 9	Zechariah	
12:9	143–44	6:11–14	199
12:9–12	144, 270	10:2	156
12:9–14	226 n. 67		
12:10	149, 149 n. 102, 174	**Apocrypha**	
12:11	142 n. 72		
12:12	143, 274	1 Maccabees	
12:13	4, 226, 270, 276	14:25–29	122
12:13–14	4, 9, 164, 226 n. 67		
12:14	142 n. 72	2 Maccabees	
		4	122
Isaiah			
30:6	156	Sirach	
30:7	156	1:11–13	274
40–55	142 n. 71	7:15	116
42:9	142	15:1	275
43:19	200	20:27	267
45:7	227	23:27	270
49:4	156	24:8	275
53:3–10	183	38–39	113
57:12	156	38:24	114
57:13	156	38:33	120
		38:34–39:6	115
Jeremiah		39:4	107, 267
10:14	156	44–50	243
10:14–15	157	50:1–7	103–4
16:1–2	265	50:1–24	41
16:19	156		
31:29–30	181		
36:10	114	**Versions, Aramaic**	
Lamentations		Targum of the Writings	
4:17	156	Eccles 2:24	3, 3 n. 15

Ancient Near Eastern Literature

The Admonitions of Ipuwer   27, 32, 33, 44, 159, 236
The Babylonian Theodicy   45
The Ballade of Early Rulers   45
The Complaints of Khakheperre-sonb   33, 44, 159
The Counsels of Pessimism   45
Dialogue of Pessimism   45
A Dispute Over Suicide   28
The Eloquent Peasant   44
Enlil and Namzitarra   45
The Gilgamesh Epic   45
I Will Praise the Lord of Wisdom   45
The Instruction of Any   45
The Instruction of King Amenemhet I for His Son Sesostris I   44
Nothing Is of Value   45
The Prophecies of Nerferti   44, 159
The Instruction of Ptah–hotep
  120–42   220
Proverbs from Ugarit   45
A Song of the Harper   28–29, 32
The Sumerian Job   45
The Teaching of Khety   138
The Underworld Vision of Gilgameš, Enkidu, and the Netherworld   45

Papyri, Ostraca, Epigraphical Citations, etc.

Corpus papyrorum judaicarum
  2a   90
  4   108
  5   108
  6   94

Papyrus Rainer R
  12–22   119–20

Qumran

1QH
  4:29–33   274
1QS
  11:20–21   274

Hellenistic Jewish Literature

Josephus
Against Apion
  2.165   104
Jewish Antiquities
  11.326   98
  12.1   129
  12.133   90
  12.142   102, 110, 111
  12.142–44   94
  12.144   120
  12.145–46   104
  12.158   93, 95
  12.159   91
  12.160   109
  12.160–63   109
  12.161   93, 102, 103, 110
  12.164–79   109
  12.165   93
  12.175–77   95
  12.180–81   96, 109
  12.224   98

Letter of Aristeas
  12–16   100
  92–95   104
  96–99   103
  112–18   99–100

New Testament

Matthew
  11:19   266
  23:2–3   256 n. 4
Luke
  12:19   265
Romans
  3:10   244–45
1 Corinthians
  3   227, 274
  7   266

Classical Literature

Athenaeus
The Learned Banqueters
  5.203b   88
Diodorus Siculus
The Library of History
  40.3.5–6   102

Rabbinic Literature

Mishnah
m. ʿEd.
  5:3   4, 268

Tannaitic Midrash
Sifre Devarim
  34 to Deut 6:7   275
Avot de R. Natan A
  1:4   269

Babylonian Talmud
b. Meg.
  7a   268–69
b. Šabb.
  30b   4, 268, 271

Amoraic Midrash
Eccles. Rab.
  1:3   3, 271
  2:24   3
  11:9   270
Song Rab.
  1:1   266

Other

Alphabet of Ben Sira   265,
                          265 n. 28

Index of Modern Authors

Aberle, David   142 n. 71, 283
Abimbola, Wande   180 n. 13, 283
Aichele, George   61 n. 25, 283
Agassi, Joseph   213 nn. 28–29, 297
Albertz, Rainer   158 n. 14, 159 n. 16, 166, 166 n. 47
Al-Ghazali, Muhammed   180 n. 15, 283
Alster, Bendt   45, 45 n. 131, 283
Alter, Robert   61, 62 n. 26, 283
Anderson, Bernhard W.   10 n. 35, 283
Anderson, William H. U.   8 n. 29, 9 n. 32, 45, 45 n. 132, 46 n. 135, 159 n. 17, 170 n. 66, 233 n. 10, 235 n. 13, 248 n. 48, 283
Applebaum, Shimon   89, 89 n. 26, 106 n. 122, 127 n. 9, 283
Aruguete, Mara S.   207 n. 13, 309
Austinus, Gianto   242 n. 37, 283

Badham, Paul   182 n. 21, 284
Bagnall, Roger S.   31 n. 75, 90, 90 nn. 35–36, 91 nn. 38, 43–44, 93 n. 63, 284
Bailey, Lloyd R.   237 n. 21, 284
Barbalet, Jack   118 n. 187, 219 n. 54, 284
Barnes, Jonathan   46, 46 n. 135, 284
Bartholomew, Craig G.   29, 29 n. 65, 42, 42 n. 113, 46 n. 136, 53, 53 n. 166, 129 n. 19, 130 n. 25, 159 n. 16, 164 n. 37, 226 n. 67, 272, 272 n. 49, 273 n. 50, 274, 274 n. 53, 284, 311

Barton, George   186 n. 38, 284
Barucq, André   187 n. 38, 284
Basser, Herbert   226 n. 65, 256 n. 4, 284
Beentjes, Panc   187 n. 38, 241 n. 36, 284
Behe, Michael J.   217 n. 44, 284
Bendix, Reinhard   20 n. 29, 117 n. 185, 145 n. 85, 195 n. 64, 207 n. 14, 208 n. 15, 17, 211 n. 21, 219 n. 53, 284
Benjamin, Don C.   138 n. 60, 220 n. 55, 302
Ben Zvi, Ehud   69 n. 44, 284
Bergen, Wesley J.   135, 135 n. 46, 284
Berger, Benjamin Lyle   272 n. 47, 159 n. 19, 284
Berger, Peter L.   16 n. 16, 18, 23 n. 41, 25, 25 n. 50, 73, 74, 74 nn. 62–64, 180 n. 12, 191 n. 51, 193, 284–55
Berlinerblau, Jacques   16 n. 16, 22 n. 35, 79 n. 80, 136 n. 52, 150 n. 105, 285
Berman, Harold J.   207 n. 14, 285
Bickerman, Elias   1 n. 2, 2 n. 11, 31 n. 75, 34 n. 86, 89, 89 n. 27, 90, 90 nn. 31, 33–34, 91, 91 nn. 39, 45, 93, 93 n. 65, 107 nn. 128, 130, 110, 110 n. 144, 112, 113, 113 nn. 154–55, 114 n. 161, 115 n. 171, 116, 116 nn. 174, 176, 120, 120 nn. 196–97, 201, 121, 121 n. 204,

122 n. 212, 132, 132 n. 29, 285

Billows, Richard A.   86 n. 2, 87 n. 8, 285

Blenkinsopp, Joseph   3 n. 12, 125 n. 2, 126 n. 6, 135 n. 43, 149 n. 101, 285

Blouin, Arthur G.   207 n. 13, 293

Boer, Roland   22 n. 34, 55 n. 1, 60 n. 22, 61 n. 22, 64 n. 28, 67 n. 36, 135 n. 45, 266 n. 30, 285, 304

Bohart, Arthur C.   232 n. 7, 295

Bolin, Thomas   81, 81 n. 83, 82, 166 n. 48, 286

Bosworth, A. B.   87 nn. 8–10, 88 n. 16, 286

Botterweck, G. J.   xv, 286

Bottiglia, William F.   191 n. 50, 286

Bould, Mark   238, 238 nn. 25–27, 286

Branick, Vincent P.   224 n. 60, 232 n. 6, 286

Braun, Rainer   42, 42 n. 115, 286

Breasted, James H.   50, 50 n. 152, 286

Briggs, C. A.   xiii, 155 n. 1, 286

Brindle, Wayne A.   186 n. 37, 250 n. 51, 286

Brockopp, Jonathan E.   209 n. 19, 286

Brown, Francis   xiii, 155, 155 n. 1, 286

Brown, William P.   16 n. 15, 150 n. 103, 250 n. 52, 286

Brueggemann, Walter A.   22, 22 nn. 34, 36, 23, 37, 37 n. 94, 38, 38 n. 95, 72, 72 n. 59, 191 n. 51, 193, 193 n. 59, 286

Bryant, M. Darrol   182 n. 22, 286

Buccellati, Giorgio   47 n. 140, 287

Buchanan, Ian   60 n. 22, 287

Burkes, Shannon   8 n. 31, 79, 79 n. 81, 80, 80 n. 82, 287

Byargeon, Rick W.   272 n. 47, 287

Camp, Claudia   259 n. 17, 287

Campbell, Colin   187 n. 5, 189, 189 n. 44, 211 n. 21, 212 n. 23, 287

Caneday, Ardel B.   234 n. 11, 287

Caputo, John D.   160 n. 24, 287

Carny, Pin'has   178, 178 n. 2, 287

Carr, David M.   112 n. 153, 125 n. 3, 143 n. 78, 287

Carroll, Robert P.   19 n. 27, 30, 30 n. 71, 197 n. 71, 198, 198 n. 72, 199, 199 nn. 73–74, 77, 287

Cenkner, William   188 n. 42, 288

Chambers, Simone   212 n. 23, 288

Chaney, Marvin L.   22 n. 34, 288

Charney, Davida   173 n. 79, 288

Childs, Brevard   10 n. 36, 288

Christian, Mark A.   114, 114 n. 163, 288

Christianson, Eric S.   15, 15 n. 13, 288

Clark, Ronald R., Jr.   144 n. 80, 261, 262 n. 22, 288

Clarke, Caroline V.   232 n. 7, 288

Clemens, D. M.   158 n. 14, 288

Clements, Ronald E.   23 n. 40, 106 n 125, 288

Clifford, Richard J.   16, 16 n. 15, 125 n. 3, 288

Clines, David J. A.   60 n. 22, 138, 138 nn. 62–63, 153, 153 n. 115, 288

Cohen, Shaye J. D.   267 n. 36, 288

Collins, Jeff   160 n. 24, 289

Collins, John J.   36, 36 n. 92, 109, 109 n. 138, 122 nn. 211–212, 142 n. 71, 289

Connolly, Angela   237 n. 22, 298

Cook, Johann   180 n. 15, 289

Cook, Stephen L.   25, 25 n. 51, 36, 36 n. 91, 37, 37 n. 93, 44, 44 n. 124, 289

Coote, Robert B.   22 n. 34, 289

Cox, Claude   270 n. 42, 289

Crenshaw, James L.   1, 1 nn. 1–2, 3, 3 nn. 12–13, 4 n. 17, 5, 5 n. 20, 8, 8 n. 30, 9, 9 n. 33, 13, 13 n. 2, 14,

Crenshaw, James L. (*continued*)
14 n. 5, 30 n. 72, 35, 35
n. 89, 36, 38, 38 n. 99,
42, 42 n. 117, 45, 45
n. 133, 46, 46 n. 138,
51, 51 n. 157, 52, 60,
60 n. 18, 125 n. 2, 126
n. 6, 129 n. 19, 130
n. 23, 132, 132 n. 30,
143, 143 n. 76, 149
n. 101, 150 n. 104, 159
n. 104, 159 n. 16, 160
n. 22, 164, 164 n. 40,
167 n. 50, 168 n. 55,
170, 172, 173 n. 77,
184, 184 n. 32, 185,
185 n. 34, 186 n. 38,
195 n. 66, 196 n. 68,
239 n. 30, 246 n. 44,
258, 258 n. 10, 289–90
Cross, Frank Moore   135 n. 47, 290
Crowther, Bruce   238 n. 24, 290
Crüsemann, Frank   6 n. 22, 13 n. 1, 14
nn. 4, 6, 17 n. 19, 27
n. 54, 66, 70, 70 n. 51,
71, 71 nn. 53–56, 72,
73, 76 n. 67, 80, 96
n. 72, 74, 132, 132
n. 29, 135, 135 n. 43,
158 n. 11, 290

Curtis, John B.   183 n. 28, 290

Danby, Herbert   290
Davidson, Robert   237 n. 19, 290
Dawes, Gregory W.   216 n. 44, 290
Delitzsch, Franz   3 n. 14, 272, 272 n. 48,
290
Derks, Hans   118 n. 187, 290
Dobson, Richard B.   151 n. 108, 300
Doran, Robert   101 n. 103, 290
Dowd, Garin   235 n. 14, 290
Dowling, William C.   60 n. 22, 61
n. 23, 291
Driver, S. R.   xiii, 155, 155 n. 1, 286
D'Sa, Francis Xavier   188 n. 42,
291

Durkheim, Émile   21, 21 n. 30, 69, 69
n. 46, 70, 73–75, 75
nn. 65–66, 222, 222
n. 57, 291
Dutcher-Walls, Patricia   136 n. 51,
291

Eagleton, Terry   61 n. 24, 291
Eddy, Samuel K.   96 n. 72, 291
Eisenstadt, Shmuel N.   77, 209
n. 19, 291
Elliot, John H.   265 n. 29, 291
Elster, John   203 n. 3, 291
Engels, Frederick   16, 16 n. 17, 302
Epstein, Isidore   291
Eshel, Esther   97 n. 77, 291
Eshel, Hanan   102 n. 109, 291
Etzioni-Halevy, Eva   151 n. 108, 153, 153
n. 116, 291

Faulkner, R. O.   27 n. 56, 236 n. 17,
291
Feldman, Louis H.   101, 101 n. 99, 104,
292
Feuer, Lewis S.   151 n. 108, 292
Fischer, Stefan   237 n. 19, 292
Fishbane, Michael   144, 144 n. 79, 292
Fontana, Benedetto   67 n. 37, 292
Forman, Charles F.   8 n. 29, 44, 44
nn. 127–28, 50, 50
n. 153, 231 n. 1, 292
Foucault, Michel   16 n. 16, 292
Fowler, Alastair   235 n. 14, 292
Fox, Michael V.   4 n. 17, 13, 13 n. 3,
15, 16 n. 14, 43, 43
nn. 122–23, 46, 128
n. 13, 129 n. 19, 130
n. 25, 150 n. 104, 159–
60, 159 nn. 17–18,
20–21, 160 n. 23, 161
nn. 26, 28, 164 n. 40,
175 n. 43, 167–70, 167
nn. 50, 52, 169 nn. 62,
64, 170 n. 66, 172,
172 n. 76, 174, 178,
178 n. 2, 184–85, 194
n. 33, 185 n. 35, 194

n. 63, 240, 240 n. 31,
243, 243 n. 39, 245
n. 43, 246 n. 44, 250,
271–72, 271 n. 45, 272
n. 46, 292

Fraade, Steven D.   226 n. 64, 265 n. 27,
292

Fredericks, Daniel C.   155 n. 4,
292

Frick, Frank S.   22 n. 34, 137 n. 54,
292–93

Frow, John   126 n. 4, 235 nn. 14–
15, 236 n. 16, 292

Gairrett, Richelle L.   207 n. 13, 309
Galling, K.   39 n. 104, 293
Gardiner, Alan Henderson   27, 27 n. 55,
33, 33 n. 83, 293
Gardner, Gregg   122, 122 n. 216, 293
Gera, Dov   101 n. 103, 292
Gerbrandt, Gerald Eddie   135 n. 48,
136, 293
Gerth, Hans H.   20 n. 29, 117 n. 185,
118 n. 187, 257, 257
n. 5, 293
Gese, Helmut   6 n. 22, 15, 15 n. 9, 27
n. 54, 29, 29 n. 66, 51
n. 156, 293
Giddens, Anthony   21 n. 30, 69 n. 45, 293
Giese, Ronald L., Jr.   235 n. 14, 308
Gold, Elizabeth S.   207 n. 13, 309
Goldberg, David J.   182 n. 21, 184 n. 31,
293
Goldfield, Gary S.   207 n. 13, 293
Goldstein, Jonathan A.   95 nn. 70–
71, 97, 97 nn. 75, 79,
100, 10l nn. 100, 103,
293
Goldstein, Warren S.   20 n. 28,
118 n. 190, 211 n. 23,
293
Good, Edwin M.   9 n. 32, 159 n. 17, 293
Gordis, Robert   9 n. 32, 31 n. 73,
34–40, 34 nn. 85, 87,
36 n. 90, 132, 132
n. 29, 143, 143, n. 75,
168, 168 n. 59, 186

n. 37, 264, 264 n. 25,
268, 268 n. 38, 276,
294
Gottwald, Norman K.   22, 22
nn. 34–35, 24 n. 43,
30 n. 68, 59, 59 nn. 13,
17, 73, 88 n. 17, 90
n. 37, 94 n. 67, 95
n. 70, 96 nn. 72,
74, 101, 101 n. 196,
118 n. 189, 119, 119
n. 194, 132, 132 n. 29,
150, 189, 189 n. 45,
294
Gramsci, Antonio   67, 67 nn. 36–37,
87, 87 n. 7, 150, 150
n. 105, 294
Granger, John D.   85 n. 2, 294
Green, Ronald   177 n. 1, 178, 178
n. 3, 180 nn. 12–14,
182–83, 182 nn. 20,
23, 183 n. 29, 184
n. 31, 188 n. 41, 190
n. 47, 294
Greenspoon, Leonard J.   100 n. 96,
121 n. 203, 294
Griffin, David Ray.   188 n. 43, 294
Guerra, Anthony J.   193 n. 58, 294

Hadas, Moses   99 n. 93, 100, 100
nn. 94–95, 103–4,
294–295
Haden, N. Karl   169, 170 n. 65, 295
Hallo, William W.   27 n. 56, 31 n. 76, 295
Hamilton, Alastair   211 n. 21, 295
Hamilton, Mark   196 n. 67, 295
Hanson, Paul D.   36, 96 n. 72, 199–200,
199 n. 76, 295
Harrison, Robert   31, 31 n. 74, 38, 46, 46
n. 134, 73, 73 n. 61,
76, 76 nn. 67–69, 77
nn. 70–75, 78–79,
78 nn. 76–77, 115,
115 n. 172, 121,
121 nn. 205–7, 209,
132–33, 132 n. 30, 295
Hasel, Gerhard F.   9 n. 35, 304

Hassan, Riffay 193 n. 58, 295
Hatton, Peter T. H. 4 n. 18, 295
Hausknecht, Murray 152 n. 108, 295
Hayman, A. P. 183 n. 30, 228 n. 69, 295
Heard, R. Christopher 159 n. 17, 161 n. 25, 295
Heinen, H. 87 n. 11, 90 nn. 32, 34, 91 n. 45, 295
Held, Barbara S. 232 n. 7, 295
Hengel, Martin 6 n. 22, 39, 39 nn. 102–4, 42, 42 n. 116, 46 n. 136, 91 n. 39, 94 n. 66, 95 n. 70, 96 n. 72, 98 n. 80, 99 n. 89, 102 n. 110, 107 n. 126, 108, 108 n. 134, 110 n. 141, 132, 132 n. 29, 247 n. 47, 295
Hertzberg, Hans Wilhelm 187 n. 38, 296
Hick, John 182 n. 21, 296
Hirsch, E. D., Jr. 235 n. 14, 296
Hirshman, Marc 266–67, 266 n. 31, 296
Holm-Nielsen, Sven 270 n. 41, 296
Holmstedt, Robert D. 167, 167 n. 54, 296
Horkheimer, Max 55–58, 56 nn. 3, 5–7, 58 n. 11, 65, 296
Horsley, Richard A. 105, 106 n. 121, 296
Hunter, G. Frederick 58 n. 11, 296

Isenberg, Sheldon R. 180 n. 15, 184 n. 31, 188 n. 43, 256, 256 n. 3, 296

James, Gene G. 182 n. 22, 296
James, Kenneth W. 169 n. 60, 296
Jameson, Fredric 17, 17 n. 20, 60–61, 60 nn. 20–22, 61 n. 22, 63, 234, 234 n. 12, 296
Jamieson-Drake, David 144 n. 80, 258 n. 8, 296

Janzen, J. Gerald 200 n. 78, 296
Jarick, John 158 n. 11, 296
Jarvie, I. C. 213 nn. 28–29, 297
Jenni, E. xv, xvi, 297
Jobling, David 22 n. 34, 60 n. 22, 297
Johnson, Raymond 171, 171 n. 73, 297
Joll, James 67 n. 36, 297
Jones, H. S. xv, 93, 300
Jones, Scott C. 129 n. 20, 241 nn. 33, 35–36, 297
Jong, Stephan de 3 n. 14, 48, 48 n. 143, 127 n. 9, 162 nn. 29–30, 248, 248 n. 49, 275, 275 n. 55, 297

Kadushin, Charles 151 n. 108, 297
Kalberg, Stephen 79, 79 n. 79, 141 n. 70, 211 n. 21, 264 n. 24, 297
Kaplan, Stephen 188 n. 42, 297
Kaufmann, Wanda O. 127 n. 8, 297
Kayes, D. Christopher 178 n. 4, 211 n. 23, 223 n. 59, 297
Kemp, Barry J. 31 n. 76, 297
Kidner, Derek 244 n. 41, 297
Kieckhefer, Richard 213, 213 n. 27, 298
Kim, Uriah Y. 66 n. 34, 298
Kippenberg, Hans G. 70–71, 70 n. 52, 88 n. 17, 91 nn. 43–44, 92 nn. 49, 56, 93 n. 58, 94 n. 66, 96–97, 96 nn. 72–74, 102 n. 110, 109 n. 140, 110–11, 110 nn. 142–43, 111 n. 145, 120 n. 195, 298
Kloner, Amos 97 n. 77, 298
Klopfenstein, Martin A. 6 n. 22, 14, 14 n. 7, 298
Knobel, Peter S. 298
Knoppers, Gary N. 107 n. 131, 298
Koch, Klaus 4 n. 18, 298
Koosed, Jennifer L. 244 n. 42, 298
Koshul, Basit Bilal 212 n. 23, 298

Kováč, Milan 213 n. 30, 306
Kovacs, Brian W. 145–49, 145 nn. 87–
89, 146 nn. 90–94, 147
nn. 95–97, 153, 298
Krašovec, Jože 181 n. 18, 298
Kreitzer, Larry 204 n. 5, 298
Krüger, Thomas 16 n. 15, 38, 38
n. 97, 127 n. 9, 132,
132 n. 30, 142 n. 72,
160 n. 22, 226 n. 67,
298–99
Kübler-Ross, Elisabeth 236, 236
n. 18, 299

Lang, Bernhard 53–58, 53 nn. 162–65,
56 n. 2, 57 n. 10, 58
n. 12, 65–66, 72, 75,
118 n. 190, 120 n. 198,
132, 132 n. 29, 138,
138 n. 61, 225, 299
Lassman, Peter 208 n. 17, 299
Lauha, Aarre 2, 2 n. 9, 5 n. 21,
6 n. 22, 52–53, 52
n. 160, 127–31, 127
n. 10, 128 nn. 12, 14,
129 nn. 16, 18, 130
nn. 21, 23, 26, 131
n. 27, 139 n. 65, 140,
142 n. 72, 158 n. 11,
163 n. 35, 167–68, 167
nn. 51, 53, 168 n. 56,
193, 194 n. 62, 247,
247 n. 45, 299
Lawrie, Douglas G. 208 n. 17, 299
Layman, C. Stephen 181 n. 16,
299
Lee, Bernon 161 n. 27, 299
Lemaire, André 97 n. 78, 98 nn. 84–86,
102 n. 109, 116 n. 175,
299
Lenski, Gerhard E. 92 n. 50, 98 n. 88,
105 nn. 115, 117–20,
106, 106 nn. 122–24,
111, 111 nn. 146–50,
115 nn. 167–70, 116,
116 nn. 173, 178–79,
120 nn. 199–200, 137

n. 57, 138 nn. 58–59,
299
Leuchter, Mark 114 n. 165, 300
Levine, Étan 225 n. 61, 300
Levine, Lee I. 40 n. 107, 42, 43
n. 120, 47, 48 n. 142,
122 nn. 210, 213–14,
300
Lichtheim, Miriam xiii, 31–33, 32
nn. 77–78, 80–81, 300
Liddell, H. G. R. Scott xv, 93, 300
Lim, Lena 240 n. 32, 300
Lipschits, Oded 97 n. 77, 98 n. 83, 100
nn. 94, 97, 300
Lipset, Seymour Martin 151 n. 108,
300
Lloyd. Alan B. 86 n. 3, 88 nn. 13–15,
89 nn. 18–21, 102
n. 108, 300
Lo, Alison 237 n. 19, 300
Loader, James A. 2, 2 n. 10, 5, 5 n. 19,
51 n. 155, 186 n. 37,
187 nn. 38–39, 260
n. 18, 300
Locke, Simon 204 n. 4, 300
Lohfink, Norbert 16 n. 15, 40, 40 n. 105,
43 n. 119, 127 n. 9,
163, 163 nn. 33–34,
300–301
Long, Burke O. 24, 24 n. 48, 301
Longman, Tremper, III 15, 15 n. 12,
163 n. 36, 187 n. 38,
301
Love, John 117 n. 185, 118 n. 187,
195 n. 64, 211 n. 22,
217 n. 45, 219 n. 53,
255 n. 1, 301
Lucy, Niall 160 n. 24, 301
Luria, S. 33, 33 n. 82, 301

McCalla, Arthur 216 n. 44, 301
MacDonald, Duncan 2 n. 11, 301
Machinist, Peter 43, 43 n. 121, 47, 243
n. 38, 301
McKenna, John E. 159 n. 17, 301
McKenzie, John L. 125 n. 3, 301
Mader, Gottfried 100 n. 99, 301

Mahon, James 219 n. 54, 301
Malamat, Abraham 24, 24 n. 45, 301
Mannheim, Karl 16, 16 n. 16, 204, 204 n. 6, 302
Martindale, Don 117 n. 185, 257, 257 n. 5, 293
Marsh, Robert M. 208 n. 16, 302
Martens, Elmer A. 9 n. 35, 304
Marx, Karl 16–17, 16 n. 17, 21–22, 69, 302
Mason, Hayda 191 n. 50, 302
Mason, Steve 256 n. 4, 302
Matthews, Victor xi, 23 n. 38, 138 n. 60, 220 n. 55, 302
Maussion, Marie 129, 129 n. 17, 165, 165 n. 42, 168, 168 n. 58, 247 n. 45, 302
Mayblin, Bill 160 n. 24, 289
Mayes, A. D. H. 23–24, 23 nn. 38–39, 24 nn. 43–44, 302
Mendenhall, George E. 24, 24 n. 43, 302
Merton, Robert K. 151 n. 108, 193, 302
Michel, Diethelm 169 n. 63, 187 n. 38, 303
Miller, Douglas B. 3 n. 14, 7 n. 28, 158 n. 14, 170–73, 170 nn. 67–68, 171 nn. 69–70, 72–73, 172 nn. 74–75, 188 n. 40, 288, 303
Mills, C. Wright 20 n. 29, 118 n. 187, 293
Mitchell, Christine 235 n. 15, 303
Morgan, David 211 n. 23, 223 n. 59, 303
Mosala, Itumeleng J. 22 n. 34, 303
Moyise, Steve 244 n. 42, 303
Müller, Hans-Peter 1 n. 3, 6, 6 n. 23, 65–66, 65 nn. 31–32, 66 n. 33, 72, 132, 132 n. 29, 138–41, 138 nn. 61, 64, 140 nn. 66–67, 186 n. 38, 303
Murphy, Roland E. 9 n. 32, 187 n. 38, 267, 267 n. 32, 303

Nelson, Richard D. 227, 227 n. 68, 303
Nettl, Peter 153 n. 166, 303
Neusner, Jacob 303
Newsom, Carol A. 46, 46 n. 137, 60 n. 22, 78, 78 n. 78, 235 nn. 14–15, 260 n. 17, 303–4
Niditch, Susan 100 n. 98, 239 n. 29, 304
Nietzsche, Friedrich 56, 191–93, 191 n. 53, 192 n. 55, 304
Nisbet, Robert 142 n. 71, 304
Norem, Julie K. 232 nn. 4, 7–8, 233, 233 n. 9, 304
Nozick, Robert 191 n. 52, 304

Ogden, Graham 9 n. 32, 128 n. 13, 159 n. 16, 304
Økland, Jorunn 55 n. 1, 266 n. 30, 285, 304
Olbrechts-Tyteca, L. 148 n. 100, 173 n. 78, 305
Ollenburger, Ben C. 9 n. 35, 304
Oppenheim, A. Leo 114 n. 164, 304
Orihara, Hiroshi 203 n. 2, 304
Orrieux, Claude 99 n. 92, 107 n. 131, 108, 108 nn. 132–33, 136, 109, 109 n. 137, 267, 267 n. 35, 305
Overholt, Thomas W. 25, 25 n. 52, 305
Owens, J. Edward 262 n. 23, 305
Oyelade, E. O. 180 n. 13, 305

Pahk, Johan Yeong-Sik 149 n. 102, 305
Parsons, Talcott 117 n. 185, 151 n. 108, 152 n. 113, 153 n. 16, 179, 179 n. 8, 305
Patterson, James A. 232 n. 5, 305
Peck, Russell 43 n. 119, 305
Pedersen, Johannes 2, 2 n. 8, 29, 29 n. 64, 44 n. 126, 50, 50 n. 151, 305
Peltonen, Matti 211 n. 21, 305
Penchansky, David 60 n. 22, 305

Perdue, Leo G. 40, 40 n. 106, 42, 42 n. 112, 126, 126 n. 5, 171, 171 n. 71, 305, 316

Perelman, Chaïm 148 n. 100, 173 n. 78, 305

Perrin, Nicholas 142 n. 72, 226 n. 67, 306

Person, Raymond F. 113 n. 157, 153 n. 117, 306

Petersen, David L. 114 n. 166, 306

Pfeiffer, Robert H. 42 n. 114, 306

Phan, Peter C. 193 n. 58, 306

Pinker, Aron 127 n. 11, 128 n. 13, 130 n. 22, 165 n. 44, 306

Piovanelli, Pierluigi 209 n. 19, 306

Pippin, Tina 60 n. 22, 306

Pleins, J. David 137, 137 n. 54, 306

Podolinská, Tatiana 213 n. 30, 306

Polk, Timothy 9 n. 32, 159 n. 17, 306

Poulantzas, Nicos 151 n. 106, 306

Priest, John F. 8 n. 29, 9, 9 n. 34, 15, 15 nn. 10–11, 29, 29 n. 63, 306

Pritchard, James B. xiii, 306

Rad, Gerhand von 1, 1 n. 4, 6, 7 n. 25, 48, 48 n. 144, 125 n. 2, 306

Ranston, Harry 42 n. 114, 307

Ravasi, Gianfranco 187 n. 38, 307

Redditt, Paul L. 142 n. 73, 199 n. 75, 307

Reden, Sitta von 87 n. 8, 89 n. 22, 92 nn. 51–53, 57, 307

Reid, Charles J., Jr. 207 n. 14, 285

Rentería, Tamis Hoover 135, 135 n. 45, 307

Ringgren, H. xv, 286

Roberts, Adam 60 n. 22, 307

Rodd, Cyril S. 199 n. 73, 307

Rogerson, John W. 41 n. 111, 63–65, 63 n. 27, 64 nn. 28–30, 69, 307

Römer, Thomas 135–36, 135 nn. 42, 44, 136 n. 51, 307

Rose, Martin 2, 2 n. 7, 47, 47 n. 141, 307

Rosenberg, Stephen G. 99 n. 89, 307

Rostovtzeff, M. 93 n. 64, 94, 94 nn. 66, 68, 96 n. 72, 97, 103, 103 n. 111, 307

Rudman, Dominic 30 n. 68, 37 n. 93, 42, 42 n. 118, 190 n. 46, 271 n. 44, 307–8, 311

Runciman, W. G. 219 n. 54, 308

Sadri, Ahmad 151–52, 151 n. 107, 152 nn. 110–11, 113, 153 n. 114, 308

Sahni, Isher-Paul 208 n. 16, 308

Saldarini, Anthony J. 112, 112 n. 152, 143 n. 78, 308

Salters, Robert B. 4 n. 16, 268 n. 37, 308

Sandberg, Ruth N. 188 n. 43, 256, 256 n. 2, 268 n. 37, 269, 269 nn. 39–40, 270 n. 41, 274 n. 52, 308

Sanders, E. P. 255 n. 1, 274 n. 51, 308

Sanders, Jack T. 122 n. 215, 131 n. 28, 183 n. 30, 244 n. 41, 264, 264 n. 26, 270 n. 43, 308

Sandy, D. Brent 235 n. 14, 308

Sasson, Ann Showstack 67 n. 36, 308

Sawyer, John F. A. 166 n. 46, 308

Schäfer, Peter 89 n. 23, 90 n. 35, 91 nn. 39, 40, 42–43, 95 n. 70, 96–97, 96 n. 72, 109, 110 n. 141, 128, 129 n. 15, 308

Schafter, Amanda 206 n. 12, 308

Schams, Christine 113–14, 113 nn. 156–60, 114 n. 162, 308

Schiffman, Lawrence H. 267 nn. 33, 36, 308

Schluchter, Wolfgang 118 n. 187, 203 n. 2, 219 n. 53, 308–9

Schmid, Hans H.   6 n. 22, 29, 29 n. 67,
50, 50 n. 154, 51
nn. 155–56, 309
Schoors, Anton   40, 40 nn. 108–9, 41
n. 110, 49 n. 150, 164,
164 n. 39, 244, 244
n. 40, 247 n. 47, 251
n. 53, 309
Schraub, J. Jonathan   6 n. 24, 309
Schulte, Christoph   180 n. 15, 309
Schultz, Richard L.   241 n. 34, 309
Schwarz, Haley C.   207 n. 13, 309
Schwartz, Matthew J.   169, 169
n. 61, 309
Schwienhorst-Schönberger, L.   43 n. 121,
309
Scott, R.   xv, 93, 300
Scott, R. B. Y.   2 n. 9, 187 n. 38, 231
n. 3, 309
Scroggs, Robin.   13 n. 1, 309
Seesengood, Robert P.   244 n. 42,
298
Seibert, Eric. A.   134–35, 134 n. 41, 309
Seow, Choon-Leong   1, 1
n. 5, 3 n. 14, 16 n. 15,
30–31, 30 nn. 68–70,
38, 38 n. 98, 132, 132
n. 30, 142 n. 72, 150,
150 n. 104, 159 n. 16,
188 n. 40, 247, 247
n. 46, 310
Sheard, Cynthia M.   173 n. 78, 310
Shields, Martin A.   7, 7 n. 26, 10–11, 10
n. 37, 11 n. 38, 159
n. 16, 174, 174 n. 80,
273 n. 50, 310, 314
Shils, Edward   151 n. 108, 310
Shmueli, Efraim   118 n. 187, 310
Shuster, Martin   159 n. 17, 169, 169
n. 60, 170 n. 66, 310
Sica, Alan   205, 205 nn. 7–8, 206
nn. 9–11, 215–16,
215 nn. 39–40, 216
nn. 41–43, 221 n. 56,
310
Simkins, Ronald   22 n. 34, 72, 72 n. 58,
310

Simon, Maurice   310
Simpson, William Kelly   xv, 27 n. 56,
31 n. 76, 295
Sivertsev, Alexei M.   267 n. 36,
310
Skelton, David A.   183 n. 29, 310
Smart, Ninian   239, 239 n. 29, 310
Sneed, Mark   23 n. 37, 26 n. 53,
39 nn. 100–101, 60
n. 19, 73 n. 60, 125
nn. 1, 3, 132 n. 31, 137
n. 55, 148 n. 99, 181
n. 19, 186 nn. 36, 38,
239 n. 28, 245 n. 43,
260 n. 17, 272 n. 49,
310–11
Soares-Prabhu, George M.   118 n. 188,
311
Soden, Wolfram von   180 n. 12,
182 n. 20, 311
Sparks, Kenton L.   125 n. 3, 235 n. 14,
311
Stager, Lawrence E.   115 n. 168, 311
Steinberg, Naomi   22 n. 34, 137 n. 53,
311
Stenger, Mary Ann   193 n. 58, 311
Stern, David   265 n. 28, 311
Stern, Ephraim   121 n. 208, 312
Stern, Ian   97 n. 77, 298
Stern, Menahem   96 n. 72, 312
Stevenson, Lesley   235 n. 14, 290
Stowers, Stanley K.   226 n. 66, 312
Stratton, Beverly J.   61 n. 25, 312
Strong, Jeremy   235 n. 14, 290
Sugirtharajah, R. S.   67–68, 67 nn. 38–39,
312
Swedberg, Richard   21 n. 33, 38 n. 96, 118
n. 187, 144 n. 81, 145
nn. 83–84, 151 n. 108,
191 n. 51, 203 n. 1,
208 nn. 17–18, 209
n. 20, 211 n. 21, 312
Sweeney, Marvin A.   136, 136
n. 50, 312
Swidler, Ann.   179, 179 n. 11, 203
n. 1, 212 n. 25, 214–
15, 214 nn. 31–32, 215
nn. 35, 37, 312

Takahashi, Yuko 117, 117 n. 184, 119 n. 192, 312

Tal, Oren 97 n. 77, 98 n. 83, 100 nn. 94, 97, 300

Talbert, Charles H. 244 n. 42, 312

Talstra, Eep 142 n. 71, 312

Tamez, Elsa 68–69, 68 nn. 40–43, 312

Taylor, Walter F., Jr. 257 n. 7, 268 n. 36, 312

Tcherikover, Victor A. xiv, 31 n. 75, 89 nn. 17, 24–25, 90 n. 30, 91 n. 39, 93 n. 65, 94 n. 66, 95 n. 69, 96 n. 72, 98 n. 87, 99 n. 90, 101, 101 n. 101, 103 n. 112, 104, 104 nn. 113–14, 107–8, 107 nn. 126–27, 129, 109 n. 139, 120, 120 n. 202, 122 nn. 210–11, 267, 267 n. 34, 312–13

Thompson, Dorothy 91 n. 46, 92 nn. 53–55, 93 n. 59, 313

Tilley, Terrence W. 215, 215 n. 36, 313

Topazio, Virgil W. 191 n. 50, 313

Towner, Sibley 159 n. 17, 313

Trakakis, Nick 181 n. 17, 313

Turner, Bryan S. 17 n. 21, 56 n. 4, 117 n. 185, 178, 178 n. 5, 180 n. 12, 191–92, 191 n. 50, 192 nn. 54–56, 207 n. 14, 211 n. 22, 219 n. 53, 313

Turner, Eric G. 86 n. 5, 88 n. 15, 89 n. 17, 91 n. 41, 313

Turner, Stephen 20 n. 29, 313

Urbano, Cosimo 238, 238 n. 23, 314

Vajiragnena, Medagama 188 n. 42, 314

Vanderhooft, David 97 n. 77, 300

Van der Toorn, Karel 42, 42 n. 119, 46 n. 136, 114 n. 164, 234 n. 13, 313

Vander Zanden, James W. 70 n. 50, 314

Van Leeuwen, Raymond C. 4 n. 18, 18–19, 18 nn. 24–26, 33 n. 82, 51–52, 260, 260 nn. 18–20, 314

Vasileva, Lena 237 n. 20, 314

Vawter, Bruce 166 n. 45, 314

Visicato, Giuseppe 138 n. 58, 314

Voltaire 191 n. 50, 314

Walbank, F. W. 86 n. 4, 87 n. 8, 89 n. 18, 314

Walsh, Thomas 191 n. 50, 314

Walton, Christopher L. 211 n. 23, 314

Warrior, Robert Allen 67 n. 35, 314

Washington, Harold C. 273 n. 50, 314

Wazana, Nili 249 n. 50, 314

Weber, Max 17–18, 17 n. 22, 18 n. 23, 20–23, 21 n. 31, 23 n. 42, 34, 38, 38 n. 96, 51–52, 56, 65, 65 n. 32, 79, 106, 106 n. 125, 117–19, 117 nn. 183, 185–86, 119 nn. 191, 193, 126, 126 n. 7, 133–37, 133 nn. 32–35, 134 nn. 36–40, 141–42, 141 nn. 69–70, 142 n. 74, 144–45, 144 n. 81, 145 nn. 82, 84, 151–53, 151 n. 108, 152 nn. 109, 112, 166, 166 n. 49, 177–79, 178 n. 6, 179 nn. 9–10, 180 n. 13, 189–92, 190 n. 48, 191 n. 51, 194–95, 195 n. 65, 197 n. 69, 200, 203–5, 203 n. 1, 207, 208 n. 18, 209–10, 209 n. 20, 210 n. 21, 212, 212 n. 24, 213 n. 26, 214–15, 214

Weber, Max (*continued*)
　　nn. 33–34, 217–18,
　　217 nn. 45–47, 218
　　nn. 48–52, 219 n. 54,
　　222–23, 222 n. 58,
　　225, 225 nn. 62–63,
　　234 n. 12, 255
　　n. 1, 257–59, 257
　　nn. 5–7, 258 n. 9, 259
　　nn. 11–16, 264 n. 24,
　　265 n. 27, 267 n. 36,
　　275 n. 54, 280, 314–15
Weeks, Stuart　　4 n. 17, 143, 143 n. 77,
　　163, 163 n. 32, 315
Weinfeld, Moshe　　125 n. 3, 136 n. 51,
　　315
Weisman, Ze'ev　　128 n. 13, 130 n. 24,
　　315
Weißflog, Kay　　130, 130 nn. 22, 24,
　　315
Whitley, Charles F.　　140 n. 68, 315
Whybray, Roger N.　　9 n. 32, 34 n. 86, 49,
　　49 nn. 145–49, 78,
　　132, 132 n. 29, 315
Wiesehöfer, Josef　　85 n. 1, 315
Wikramagamage, Chandra　　180 n. 13,
　　316

Will, Édouard　　87 n. 9, 316
Williams, Raymond　　61 n. 24, 316
Williams, Ronald J.　　44, 44 n. 129, 316
Willis, Timothy M.　　25, 25 n. 49, 316
Wilson, John A.　　27 n. 56, 28–29, 28
　　n. 58, 29 n. 62, 32, 32
　　n. 79, 316
Wirth, Louis　　17 n. 18, 316
Wölfel, Eberhard　　14, 14 n. 8, 316
Woodside, D. Blake　　207 n. 13, 293
Wright, Benjamin G., III　　126 n. 5,
　　316
Wright, Erik Olin　　59 n. 16, 151 n. 106,
　　316

Yee, Gale　　22 n. 34, 60 n. 22, 72, 72 n. 58,
　　316
Yitzhak, Magen　　98 n. 82, 316–17

Zaret, David　　264 n. 24, 317
Zimmer, Tilmann　　3 n. 4, 165 n. 41, 168,
　　168 nn. 57, 59, 317
Zimmerli, Walther　　10 n. 36, 125 n. 2, 317
Zimmermann, Frank　　52, 52
　　nn. 158–59, 231 n. 2,
　　317
Zwerner, Jane Mary　　182 n. 21, 317

INDEX OF SUBJECTS

Absurdity, 63, 74, 76, *159–64*, 159 nn. 16–
  17, 163 n. 31, *168–71*, 170 n. 66,
  174, 186, 214, 225, 233, 238, 260
Administration/administrators, 37–38, 85
  n. 2, *88–91*, 90–91, 93, 95, 97, 111–
  15, 117, 119, 121, 128, 131, 136, 136
  n. 51, 138–40, 143, 145–46, 154,
  194–97, 207–8, 219, 243, 267
Alexander the Great, 56, 80, 85–86, 85
  nn. 1–2, 87 n. 8, 97, 123, 129
Alienation, 70–71, 73, 75
Aliens, 117
Anomie, 69–70, 73–76, 80, 193
Antiochus III, 113, 131
Apocalyptic literature, 36, 129 n. 20, 141,
  142 nn. 71–72, 199
Apocalypticism, 35–36, 39, 44, 71, 96, 96
  n. 72, 142, 196, 199–200, 200 n. 78,
  241, 241 n. 33
Aristocracy/aristocrats, 34, 38–39, 48,
  54–58, 62–63, 66, 68–69, 71, 73,
  75–76, 78, 93 n. 58, 105, *107–10*,
  107 n. 126, 109 n. 140, 112, 115,
  119, 123–24, 127, 129, 131–32,
  135–37, 139–41, 143, 153–54, 192,
  195–96, 218
Artisans, 120, 124, 138 n. 60
Asceticism, 3, 17 n. 22, 141, 210–11,
  217–18, 225–226, 226 nn. 64–65,
  256, 265, 265 n. 27, 266 n. 30, 273,
  276–77

Bedouin, 117
Bourgeoisie, 39, 53, 55–56, 65, 132, 138
  n. 64, 139, 141, 151, 257 n. 7
Bourgeoisie, petite, 77, 115, 267
Buddhism, 180 n. 13, 188 n. 42, 225

Bureaucracy/bureaucrats, 22, *208–10*, 216

Canonization, 4 n. 16, 54, 170, 255,
  266–77, 281
Capitalism, 17 n. 22, 64, 210–11, 219, 219
  n. 54, 232, 238, 281
Carpe diem ethic, 2–3, 3 n. 15, 9, 9 n. 32,
  28–29, 47, 53, 60, 66, 75–76, 143,
  155, 164, *167–68*, 172–73, 189, 194,
  197, 202, 224 n. 60, *224–28*, 229,
  237 n. 19, 242 n. 37, 243, 250 n. 52,
  251–53, 264–65, 275, 281
Christianity, 21, 52, 118 n. 187, 177,
  179–80, 182 n. 21, 188, 188 n. 43,
  192, 193 n. 58, 209 n. 19, 215–19,
  219 n. 54, 225–26, 257 n. 7, 264
  n. 24, 266, 266 n. 30, 267 n. 36, 270
  n. 41, 277, 281
Class guilt, 234, 247, 279
Class, lower, 31 n. 73, 35–37, 39–40,
  57–58, 61–63, 67, 71, 79, 96 n. 72,
  97, 106, *115–20*, 118 n. 188, 122–23,
  130, 132, 135, 137–40, 143, 145,
  147–48, 150–51, 154, 178, 191, 195,
  197, 218, 221, 223, 234, 243–44,
  247, 258, 267 n. 36
Class, middle, 38–39, 75, 77, *115*, 131–32,
  154, 257 n. 7, 267 n. 36
Class, retainer, 62, 111–12, 115, 124, 132,
  136–37, 143, 148, 153–54, 190, 223,
  267, 273, 276
Class, ruling, 33, 62–68, 71, 97, 105–7, 107
  n. 128, 110–12, 115, 120, 124, 130,
  135 n. 45, 137, 140, 148, 154
Class, upper, 21, 31 n. 73, 34, 34 n. 86,
  36–41, 59, 61–62, 93, 96 n. 72, 97,
  101, 104–6, 108, 110–12, 114–15,
  118–19, 122, 124, 126, 129, 131,

Class, upper (continued)
133, 135, 136 n. 51, 137–41, 143,
145–48, 150–51, 178, 191–93, 195,
224, 257–58, 267, 267 n. 36, 273,
276, 279–80
Cognitive dissonance, 18, 26, 162, 177,
197–202, 197 n. 71, 199 n. 73, 279
Colonialism, 20, 26, 31, 36–37, 41, 48–49,
58–59, 66–69, 90, 94–95, 98, 105–
6, 118, 128, 130, 133–34, 139–42,
154, 190, 192, 194–96, 200–201,
200 n. 78, 202, 218, 223–24, 232,
234, 248, 252, 267, 279
Commandment-keeping, 3, 40–41, 134,
217, 225–26, 226 n. 65, 256, 256
n. 4, 270–71, 275–76
Confucianism, 145, 145 n. 86, 195–96, 195
n. 64, 219, 219 n. 54, 259
Courtiers, 114

David, 114, 128, 128 n. 13
Death, 7–10, 8 n. 31, 28–29, 50, 66, 71–72,
74, 79–80, 142, 186, 198, 236–37,
237 nn. 19, 21, 238, 242, 242 n. 37,
243–44, 243 n. 38, 249, 262, 264,
266
Debt/debtors, 118–20, 93–94
Depression, 9, 33, 53–54, 65, 74–75 166,
173, 232–33, 236–40
Deus absconditus, 2, 53, 59–60, 164–68,
166 n. 45, 228–29, 253, 263, 274
n. 52, 276, 279, 281
Deuteronomists, 30, 34, 114, 119, 125 n. 3,
133–37, 135 n. 45, 136 n. 51, 137
nn. 53–54, 157, 181, 218, 257–58
Disenchantment/secularity, 205, 210–14,
211 n. 23, 228–29, 264, 276, 280–81
Divine benevolence/malevolence, 1–3, 2
n. 11, 5, 7, 49–50, 59, 149, 164–70,
165 n. 44, 169 n. 63, 175, 177, 183,
185, 187–90, 198 n. 43, 196–97,
215, 227–28, 246–48, 253, 258–59,
276, 279–80
Divine determinism, 3, 9, 165, 179,
189–90, 197, 241, 248, 258
Divine judgment, 47, 161, 161 n. 27,
159–64, 179, 184–90, 193, 196,
201–2, 246, 264, 272, 279

Divine justice/theodicy, 32, 34, 38, 76,
79–80, 126, 128, 131–34, 139, 142,
152, 154, 159–64, 161 n. 27, 166,
170, 175, 177–202, 180 nn. 12, 15,
181 nn. 16–17, 190 n. 49, 204 n. 4,
211 n. 23, 215, 227, 239, 246–47,
252, 255–56, 274, 279, 280
Divine omnipotence, 164–68, 177, 178
n. 4, 180, 185, 197
Divine sovereignty, 60, 65, 133, 164–68,
179, 185, 188–89, 202, 247, 259,
273, 275–76, 280
Divine transcendence, 165–68, 166 n. 46,
179, 188–89, 190, 211 n. 23, 258
Doctrine of retribution, 4–5, 4 n. 18, 14,
18–20, 34, 52, 62, 71, 181–83, 187,
187 n. 39, 194, 196, 200–203, 220,
222–24, 226, 228, 240, 242, 259,
260–61, 260 n. 18, 264, 272, 276
Collective retribution: 181 n. 18, 196
Dogmatism, 13–15, 18–20, 51–52, 224,
252, 260
Domination 21–22, 24–25, 64, 66–67,
106–7, 123, 131, 140–41, 191,
208–10, 209 n. 19, 224, 258

Elders, 22, 24–25, 209, 267, 279
Elijah, 135, 257
Elisha, 135
Evil, moral, 177, 181, 181 nn. 16–17, 245,
190, 193
Evil, natural, 177, 181, 181 n. 17, 188, 190
Existentialism, 159, 162, 168–70, 169
n. 60, 175, 266

Fatalism, 63, 179, 190, 238, 251
Film noir, 237–38

God-fearing, 15, 47, 49, 62, 173, 186–87,
201–2, 226, 242, 261–63, 270, 272,
274, 274 n. 52, 275
Governors, 102, 102 n. 109

Hasmoneans, 122
Hebel, 7, 7 nn. 27–28, 74, 81, 155–68, 155
n. 4, 157 n. 10, 158 nn. 11, 14, 159
nn. 16–17, 163 nn. 31, 35, 164 n. 35,
170 n. 66, 171–74, 235 n. 13, 246

Hegemony, 67–68, 87, 194, 279

Hellenization, 27, 31, *39–50*, 42 n. 118,
43 n. 119, 53, 62–63, 71, 73, 77–78,
81–82, 108–9, *120–24*, *131*, 226
n. 65, 256 n. 4, 267 n. 36, 274–75

Herders, 117

Heterodoxy/orthodoxy, 3–4, 6 n. 24, 10,
13–15, 17, 21, 27, 30, 42, 44, 49,
51, 55, 65, 73, 78, 81, 164, 167, 170,
178, 225, 234 n. 11, *255–59*, 264,
266–77, 270 n. 41, 273 n. 50, 281

Hinduism, 19, 118 n. 187, 145, 145 n. 85,
178, 188, 188 n. 42, 194

Horror films, 237, 237 nn. 20, 22, 238

Hubris, 81, 149, 166, 186, 217, 227, 259,
262, 262 n. 23, 264, 276, 280

Ideal type, 25–26

Intellectuals/intellectualism, 20, 41,
58–59, 66, 74–76, 114, 119, 133–34,
137–38, 141, 146, *148–54*, 150
n. 105, 151 nn. 106, 108, 153 n. 116,
178, 185, 190, 195–97, 201–2, 214,
218, 224, 227–28, 234, 248–49, 253,
256, 259, 274–75, 280–81

Irrationality/non-rationality, 19, 63,
166, 169, 173–74, 179, 197, *203–7*,
203 n. 1, 204 n. 4, 205 n. 7, 208
n. 16, 212–16, 216 n. 44, 221–22,
224–28, 225 n. 61, 228 n. 69,
229, 231, 253, 256, *260–64*, 276,
280–81

Islam, 177, 180 n. 15, 190, 193 n. 58, 209
n. 19, 211 n. 23, 281

Joseph, 128, 128 n. 13

Josephus, 95, 100, 100 n. 99, 102, 106, 256
n. 4

Josiah, 135, 181

Judaism, 177, 179–80, 180 n. 15, 182
n. 21, 183 n. 30, 184 n. 31, 192, 211
n. 23, 218, 219 n. 53, 225–26, 226
nn. 64–65, 255–56, 255 n. 1, 256
n. 4, 264–77, 265 n. 27, 267 n. 36,
270 nn. 41, 43, 281

Judges, 25, 102 n. 109, 120, 147, 207–8

Kings, 2, 22–23, 33, 44, 48, 58–59, 72,
75–76, 80, 86–88, 87 n. 8, 91–97,
99, 102, 108, 114, 116, 119, 127, 127
n. 11, 128–31, 128 n. 13, 134–36,
138–40, 140 n. 68, 143, 147, 181,
189, 199, 207–9, 218, 228, 241,
257–58, 266, 279

Labor, 72, *248–52*, 248 n. 48, 249 n. 50,
250 n. 52

Legitimacy, 23 n. 40, 38, 63, 67, 105, 191,
193–94, 202, 209, 214, 216, 218,
224, 226 n. 67, 228, 234 n. 12,
247–48, 253

Levites, 40, 105, 107 n. 126, 111, 114, 118,
124, 217, 219

Maccabeans, 122

Magic (versus religion), 20, 134, *212–14*,
217, 223, 227, 264, 276, 281

Masses, the, 40, 93 n. 58, 101, 105–6, 109
n. 140, 110–11, 123, 136, 143–45,
148, 154, 196–97, 196 n. 68, 202,
243, 267, 280

Materialism, 48, 82, 229, 249

Merchants, 77, 115, *120–21*, 124, 133, 139,
147, 150

Messiah, 134, 141, 142 n. 72, 199, 226
n. 67

Monarchies, 23, 37–38, 56, 67, 72, 76, 93,
119, *133–37*, 140, 209–10, 224, 251,
257–58

Montaigne, 56, 56 n. 3

Mysticism, 141, 184 n. 31, 225

Nobles, 65, 107, 115, 129, 139–40, 193,
208–9

Onias, 91, 109

Pariah people, 118, 118 n. 187, 134,
145, 192, 200, 218, 219 n. 54,
223, 255

Patricians, 23, 118, 118 n. 190, 133

Patron/client, 118 n. 190, 220

Paul, 118 n. 187, 227, 244, 244 n. 42,
266 n. 30, 274

Peasants, 23–24, 63, 97, 107 n. 126, *111–20*, 124, 132, 135, 136 n. 51, 248, 267

Pessimism
Function, 76, 231–34, 232 n. 6, 233 n. 10, 240 n. 32, *240–52*, 279
Literary, 44–45, 54, 58, 76, *234–40*, 234 n. 13
Nature of Qohelet's, 7–10
Rhetorical, *170–75*, 231, 232 n. 5, *239–52*

Pharisees, 21, 218, 226 n. 65, 255–56, 256 n. 4, 264–65, 267 n. 33, 273, 275

Plebs, 118–19, *133–37*, 195, 218, 257

Popular religion/official, 35, 52, 136 n. 52, 196 n. 68, 221

Power, 21, 36–38, 65, 75, 87, 93, 102–3, 105, 109, 114, 117, 119, 122 n. 211, 123–24, 128 n. 13, 129, 131, 133–34, 136, 138–41, 143, 145–49, 153–54, 178, 192, 209–10, 218, 220, 222, 244, 251

Prestige, 21, 74–75, 105, 111, 141, 144, 154, 195, 221, 243–44, 247, 249–51, 262

Priests, 23, 25, 36–37, 58, 87 n. 8, 93–95, 98, 102 n. 109, *102–7*, 109–12, 114, 115 n. 168, 116, 121, 123–24, 129–31, 136, 136 n. 51, 143, 154, 214, 217–19, 257, 265, 267, 273
High priests, 41, 91, 93, 95, 98–99, 102 n. 109, 103, 105–6, 109–10, 122–23, 131, 199

Proletariat, 120, *139–43*, 150

Prophets/prophecy, 21, 23–25, 37, 106, 114, 119, 134, 135 n. 45, 136–37, 136 n. 51, 141, 159, 199–201, 207, 209, 214, 217–19, 257, 259

"Protestant Work Ethic," 210–11, 210 n. 21, 218, 219 n. 54, 229

Ptolemy I, 86–88, 88 n. 16, 113, 121

Ptolemy II, 86, 88, 92, 97–100, 103, 119

Rabbis, 3, 4, 133, 225, 227, 255–56, *264–77*, 265 n. 28, 267 nn. 33, 36, 270 n. 41, 274 n. 52

Rationality/rationalistic, 5, 18, 64, 134, 149, 152, 161, 172, 179, 197, 201–4, 204 n. 4, 205 n. 7, 207, 208 n. 16, 210, 212–13, 215–16, 218–21, 224, 227–28, 228 n. 69, 231, 252, 256, 260–61, 263–65, 276, 280

Rationalization, 20, 22, 26, 38, 51, 83, 91, 134, 152, 154, 169, 179, 201, *203–29*, 203 nn. 1–2, 205 n. 7, 207 n. 13, 298 n. 16, 211 n. 23, 219 nn. 53–54, 231, 252, 259–61, 263, 276, 280–81

Relative deprivation, 36, 75, 142 n. 71

Rhetoric, 72–73, 76, 79–80, 148, *170–74*, 216, *231*, 239–52

Routinization of charisma, 23 n. 40, 106

Rulers, 27, 29, 86–87, 88 n. 16, 93, 107, 115, 129–30, 140, 143, 220, 267

Sadducees, 226 n. 65, 256 n. 4

Sages, 4, 18, 32, 34–36, 45, 59, 80, 113, 126, 130, 132, *145–50*, 220–21, 223–24, 228, 234 n. 11, 239, 241–42, 260–63, 267–69, 271, 276

Salvation religions, 133–34, 141–42, 153, *194–97*, 196 n. 67, 201, 218, 255, 259, 276, 280

Schools, 144, 144 n. 80, 147, 258 n. 8

Scribes, 5, 73, 75, 94, 110–15, 113 n. 157, 114 n. 164, 124, 125 n. 3, 130 n. 22, *132–37*, 135 n. 42, 136 n. 51, *143–50*, 150 n. 105, 153–54, 195–96, *218–24*, 228, 233–34, 239, 243, 247–48, 251–52, 257–58, 266–67, 267 n. 33, 273, 276, 279

Senate (Jewish), 94, 107 n. 128, 110, 120, 124

Sibs, 117–18

Skepticism
Function, 242
Literary, 35, 44–45
Nature of Qohelet's, 4–7

Slaves, 96–97, 108, 119–20, 124, 138–39, 145–46, 192

Solomon, 37, 72, 127, 133–34, 139, 141, 167–68, 223, 228, 266–69, 271–71, 276

Status group, *143–50*, 154, 220–23, 248, 252

Tax farmers, 90, 92–92, 95–97, 109–10, 123, 154
Taxation, 71, *89–98*, 101–3, 105, 109–13, 116, 119, 123, 248
Teachers, 146, 194, 267
Temples, 2, 86, 89, 90 n. 35, 91–92, 94, 96–99, 103–4, 110–13, 121, 124, 136, 138, 144
Theodicy, deferred, 183
  Dualistic, 179–80, 180 nn. 13, 15, 183 n. 30, 279
  Educative, 182, 182 nn. 20–22, 188 n. 42, 200
  Eschatological, 180, 183, 183 n. 29, 192, 194, 279
  Fortune, 38, 62, 181–82, 191, 191 n. 52, 202, 223, 223 n. 59
  Free will, *180–81*, 184, 189, 245
  Karma, 19, *178–79*, 194
  Predestination, *179*, 189–90, 210–11, 215, 264 n. 24, 274–75
  Suffering (misfortune), 134, 183, 192, 194, 202, 218

Tobiads, 65, 90, 95–96, 98–101, 100 n. 98, 101 n. 103, 105–10, 107 n. 131, 121, 124, 129
Tun-Ergehen-Zusammenhang, 4 n. 18, 71, 74, 193

Utopia/dystopia, 36, 65, 68, 69 n. 44, 142, 196, 199–200, 216, 280

Wealth, 21, 27, 37–38, 48, 123, 129, 131, 139, 141, 143, 146–47, 149, 154, 192, 244, 246, 249–51, 262
Wisdom, traditional, 6–7, 13, 18, 64–66, 73–74, 82, 149–50, 158–61, 164 n. 38, 165, 169–70, 173–75, 185–86, 193, 196, 228–29, 228 n. 69, 231, 241–43, 246, 248, 252, 255, 263–64, 276, 279–80
Worldview, 17, 20, 29, 61, *145–50*, 195–96, 214, 224, 235–36, 235 n. 15, 239, 239 n. 29, 251

Lightning Source UK Ltd.
Milton Keynes UK
UKHW04f1847260918
329589UK00001B/203/P